# INDUSTRY APPLAUSE FOR THIS BOOK:

"Cynthia Hunter has written a no-nonsense, telli-it-like-it-is guide for models and actors trying to find their way through the maze that is the entertainment industry. If you have the talent and drive, Ms. Hunter's book will be the road map to success."
-Marc Pariser, TV Agent for 17 years at William Morris and Creative Artists Agency.

"No matter where you start, no matter where you want to go in your career, this book is your guide. I have never seen anything as good as this."
-Michael Cutt, Actor - A two-time Clio Award Winner also known as Officer McGuire on SEVENTH HEAVEN, a Series Regular on NBC's CALIFORNIA DREAMS and also made famous the role of Dan Ford on Turner Broadcastings' SAFE AT HOME.

"If I had read Hollywood, Here I Come! before arriving, I would have done it the right way. An excellent guide for the industry."
-Shea Farrell, Actor - Associate Producer of ALLY McBEAL, and Series Regular on CAPITOL, HOTEL, THE LAW AND HARRY McGRAW and THE UNTOUCHABLES.

"I highly recommend this book to anyone who wants to have a career."
-Rain Pryor/Actress/Singer - Mrs. Farfingle Who from Whoville in THE GRINCH and HBO series RUDE AWAKENINGS .

"There is not a tougher industry to crack but those who come to Hollywood armed with the knowledge in this book will find their way and achieve their dreams."
-Rikk Galvan, Director of Production, Warner Brothers Online.

"Actors and models are going to have such an easy time starting a career with the help of this book."
-Marisa Coughlan, Actress - UNTAMED HEART, KILLING MRS. TINGLE and GOSSIP.

"I followed Cynthia's advice, land a part on a soap opera and got my union card!"
-Jay Diller, Actor - The Young and The Restless.

"Thorough, compelling, insightful; gives logical steps, and I found it enjoyable."
-Shadoe Stevens, Actor/Writer/Producer - Voice of HOLLYWOOD SQUARES, Series Regular on DAVE'S WORLD and WEIRD TV.

"I stayed up until sunup reading Hollywood, Here I Come! It's a how-to book that's funny, informative and entertaining. Don't leave home for Hollywood without it."
-Joe Murray, Writer/Columnist - Pulitzer Prize Winner, Nationally Syndicated Columnist for the New York Times News Service.

# Hollywood, Here I Come!

How to Launch a Great Acting or
Modeling Career Anywhere and
Land in Los Angeles

## Cynthia Hunter

published by
**YELLOW DEER PRESS**
Hollywood

# Hollywood, Here I Come!
## How to Launch a Great Acting or Modeling Career Anywhere and Land in Los Angeles

### By Cynthia Hunter

Published by:

Yellow Deer Press
P.O. Box 93335
Hollywood, CA  90093  U.S.A.

**Publisher's Cataloging-in-Publication**

Hunter, Cynthia 1959-
   Hollywood, here I come!:How to launch a great acting or modeling career anywhere and land in los angeles/Cynthia Hunter; –1st ed.
   p.     cm.
   Includes bibliographical references and index.
   ISBN 1-891971-08-5
 1. Acting–Vocational guidance–United States.   I. Title
   PN2055.H86 1998                  792.028'023'0973
   QB198-289                                 98-90182
                                             LIC

Book and cover design by Kristin Allen
Printed in the United States of America.

# WARNING-DISCLAIMER

This book is designed to provide information in regard to the subject matter covered. It is sold with the understanding that the publisher and author are not engaged in rendering legal, accounting or other professional services. If legal or other expert assistance is required, the services of a competent professional should be sought.

It is not the purpose of this manual to reprint all the information that is otherwise available to the author and/or publisher, but to complement, amplify and supplement other texts. You are urged to read all the available material, learn as much as possible about acting and tailor the information to your individual needs. For more information, see the main references throughout this book and other books at your local library or bookstore.

Acting is not a get-rich-quick scheme. Anyone who decides to begin a career in the performing arts must expect to invest a lot of time and effort. For many people, acting is a successful, rewarding outlet for their creative abilities and sometimes leads to a stable career.

Every effort has been made to make this manual as complete and as accurate as possible. However, there may be mistakes both typographical and in content. Therefore, this text should be used only as a general guide and not as the ultimate source of acting/performing arts information.

The purpose of this manual is to educate and entertain. The author and Yellow Deer Press shall have neither liability nor responsibility to any person or entity with respect to any loss or damage caused, or alleged to be caused, directly or indirectly by the information contained in this book.

If you do not wish to be bound by the above, you may return this book to the publisher, at the address below, for a full refund.

# CONTRIBUTING TO FUTURE UPDATES

I think of this as a living book. That means it changes and grows to keep up with a constantly evolving industry. Anyone can participate in the ongoing research. In your travels if you come across an agent, photographer, acting coach or anyone who provides a service to actors at a reasonable rate, please drop me a note. Most of the goods and services mentioned in the book were selected on the basis of level of quality and price. I received no compensation from any of these people. If anyone in Hollywood mistreats or attempts to "hustle" you, please write to me about that as well. Your stories may be included in the next update of this book. Log onto the website and send the information. The website is:

**www.hollywoodhereicome.com**

# ACKNOWLEDGEMENTS

I could never have taken on this enormous project alone, so I wish to thank my angels. To my siblings Mark, Jack, Jill, Karen and Wayne Dog for your encouraging phone calls and belief in my vision.  To Larry Moss who taught me to take charge of my future.

To my agents Denny, Pam, Tom and Ben at L.A. Talent and David Lipton at Artists Management for their support of my career without which this book would not be possible. To my friends Samantha, Jen, Les, Mazzy, Sage, The Tuesday Night Girls Group, Matthew and Michael for their love and support which gave me the courage to challenge myself.  To Dan Poynter for your enlightened guidance. To Steve Mayer  for all your great ideas and constant support.

To the actors who contributed their career tools to be displayed in this book:  Michael Cutt, M. Tiffany Reed, Kurt Bonzell,  Lauren Renihan, Cynthia Ettinger,  Neil Gold, Bob Sky, Sibel Ergener and Kevin Page.  To the photographers who helpfully released pictures of the actors in this book:   Melinda Kelley, Heather Dobson, Mark Attebarry, Chuck Sloan and Jerry Hinkle.

To my peers who reviewed chapters and lent their expertise:  Conrad Bachmann, Board of Governors and Dixon Dern, Chief Counsel, Academy of Television Arts and Sciences; Pamm Fair of American Federation of Television and Radio Artists; Lon Huber of AGVA;  and John Pavlick, Academy of Motion Picture Arts and Sciences.

To these professionals who jumped on the bandwagon and endorsed this project: Sean Kanin, Rain Pryor, Joe Murray, Marisa Coughlan, Marc Pariser, Deezer D., Shadoe Stevens, Beverly Sassoon,, Arthur Jay, Lauren Renihan, Shea Farrell, Michael Cutt, and Hudson Leick.

To all the people and organizations who generously contributed to this project: Pamm Fair, Assistant Executive Director and Carol Osborne of AFTRA for all your kindnesses; Grace Darby and Leo Cullum of The New Yorker magazine for the use of your hilarious cartoon; the Hollywood Chamber of Commerce for the use of the Hollywood sign; Robin Holabird, Editor and Erik Joseph of Locations magazine for the use of your informative article; to the lovely Katie Maratta for generously donating many of her cartoons called "Silent Pictures" for use as chapter covers; Lorraine Mead of Details magazine and veteran Hollywood reporter Nikki Finke for your insight; Linda Broderick of Thomas Brothers Maps; Judy Belshe for allowing me to reprint parts of her book It's a Freeway Out There and The Big Smooze to help us all understand child labor laws and protection of the young; Gillian Sharples of AFTRA-SAG Credit Union for her understanding of banking laws; William Hertz of Mann Theaters for your enthusiasm.

To all the actors who shared with me their most bitter defeats and experiences in the hopes it will protect future generations of actors. My overflowing gratitude and thanks from the bottom of my being. Bless you all.

HOLLYWOOD

To My Mom, a woman whose bravery and strength gave me the courage to reach for my dreams. I love you and miss you deeply.

**Lorraine A. Watson**
**1933 - 1997**
**Breast Cancer**

A heart that gives is a soul that's free.

# Contents

# Introduction

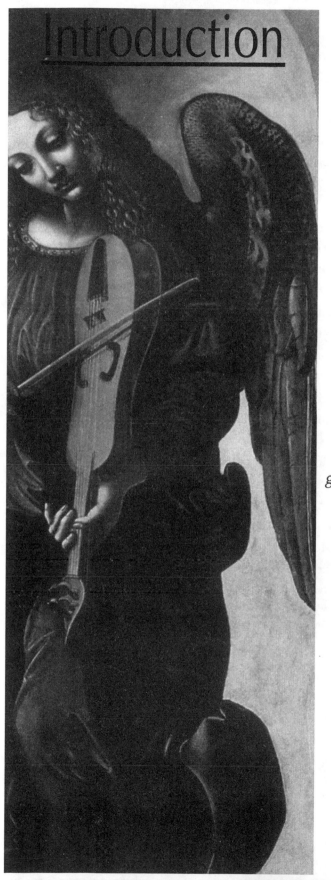

To laugh is to risk
appearing the fool,
To weep is to risk
appearing sentimental,
To reach out for another is to risk
involvement,
To expose feelings is to risk exposing
your true self,
To place your ideas, your dreams
before the crowd is to risk their loss.
To love is to risk not being loved in
return,
To live is to risk dying,
To hope is to risk despair,
To try is to risk failure,
But risks must be taken, because the
greatest hazard in life is to risk nothing,
The person who risks
nothing, does nothing, has
nothing, is nothing,
He may avoid suffering and sorrow,
but he simply cannot learn, feel,
change, grow, love....live,
Chained by his servitude's, he is a
slave; He has
forfeited freedom,
Only a person who
risks is free.

**—Unknown**

*"I do this because I must. I do this because it makes me feel more alive than anything else I do. I stand in the spotlight and everyone is waiting for me to speak. People will sit in dark theaters watching our work and waiting for us to help them to feel. Everyone wants the magic."*

**-Cynthia Hunter**

Sixteen years ago I moved to Los Angeles to begin my Acting career. I sold my car to get here and knew only one person when I arrived. In my suitcase I packed some clothes, a little money and a lot of hopes and dreams. The City of Angels was kind to me. Within three weeks I had an agent. Three weeks after that, I landed a Movie of the Week. I couldn't believe it! I had no working knowledge of my industry, yet the gates to the business had magically opened. I didn't know what to do next to keep the momentum going. I had this incredible sinking feeling of being in over my head. Professional actors seemed to know what they were doing, why didn't I? However, I had good fortune on my side.

I was willing to work very hard to make my dreams come true. I needed focus, direction and guidance. But actors can be a very close-lipped, superstitious lot. Some think that if you have the same information they have, you will take away their jobs. I new this just wasn't true. Now that CD Rom and other technologies are invading the market, not to mention hundreds of new cable networks, the opportunities today for actors are virtually limitless. I found that when everyone had the same information, determination, talent and luck would win out every time. The harder I worked the luckier I got.

Lots of kind, working actors taught me the ropes and now I will teach you. Each job you get must be maximized and parlayed into another job so you can keep the ball rolling. It never occurred to me to ask for a copy of my work. Thank goodness someone back home taped it. Now I had the beginnings of a demo reel. I had just been hired by a well-established casting director and I should have asked for help or introductions to other producers and directors so I could capitalize on this piece of work to secure more. You should also send out postcards announcing your work and dates with the time when it can be seen. Hollywood is a "me, too" town. No one wants to hire you first but everyone wants to hire you next.

I watched the movie with family and friends, never even telling my agent when it was airing so that he might watch, see my qualities and be better equipped to sell my skills. He represented many women who had appeared in *Playboy* magazine. I gave my agent the tape and after watching it he got very excited, referring to me from then on as his only female client who could act. My agent helped me to realize I need never compete with their bodies because I had talent. Since I had sold my car to get to Hollywood, I would take the bus early every morning to my agent's office and sit in the waiting room, available for auditions. I was always reading plays or books about the industry as I sat. He saw a sincere drive in me and consequently I was sent on every casting call I was remotely right for. After my second job I bought a car. It wasn't much to look at but it ran for three years before it died. I worked nights and weekends at a survival job so I would be available every day for casting calls.

Each year I acquired more experience and knowledge of this business which I applied to my career, and the effect was unbelievable: consistent success over and over again! I gained a reputation as an actress who knew her stuff, was easy to work with and possessed a genuine enthusiasm for the mystery that is show business. I figured out where everything was and how and when to use the expertise of others. Suddenly droves of newcomers were referred to me by family and friends. I consulted with each one, giving freely of my time, I found myself saying the same things over and over to each new person. Finally, I could not keep up with the demand.

And, so, the idea of this book was born! Now you will be touched by this valuable information. This book contains my story and anecdotes from my fellow actors. But, fundamentally, it is designed to guide you—every step of the way—over, under, around and through the pitfalls that you will invariably come up against on your way to a successful career in acting. By sharing all of the information and experience I have accumulated throughout my career and by shattering some of the myths, I hope to elevate the "savvy" of fledgling actors entering our profession, liberate veteran actors from a consciousness of scarcity, and give back to an industry that has given me so much. I delightfully share with you all of my insights, secrets and blessings for a fulfilling career.

When I embark on a road trip I typically go to AAA and get a map to see where I'm going and how I will get there. Think of this book and our time together as the treasure map to an incredible adventure awaiting you in Hollywood. It is based on my 16 years of experience doing 160 episodes of a soap opera, six Movies, 12 TV shows, 63 commercials, five cartoon series, and I've lost count of how many training films and modeling jobs.

Your adventure as an actor through the Hollywood system and beyond begins now—right where you are this very moment —in your home town. To begin, start thinking of your mind and your body as an instrument with which you "orchestrate" your craft. Begin thinking of your gifts as being manifested on all these levels.

Body—Exercise, feed, rest, play but always nurture your body. Know it. Listen for its nuances. Start developing your intuition or "gut"; you will need it to guide you when you get to Los Angeles.

Mind—The mind is always changing and thirsting for challenge. Feed and stimulate it. The mind is, likewise, often filling you with self-doubt and telling you why you "can't or shouldn't." Don't back away from negative thoughts. Be like a brave knight and venture forth into the darkest parts of the unknown forest of your own thoughts. Use these thoughts to know all of your different selves and apply them to your craft. Stretch, grow and strengthen your pool of life experience.

Talent—Look at your craft as both an art and a science. Constantly be developing your craft in one form or another. Get involved in acting classes, plays, dance, juggling, music, mine, language, studying the classics, painting, fencing, martial arts, voice class and sports. This is the Research and Development of your product. Mastery of any of these can bring attention to your resume and be listed as a "special skill".

Career—Get to know the body of work and names of people you admire. Who directs what styles? Who casts which types of film and TV? When you go to the movies or watch TV pay attention to the names of directors, producers, cinematographers. Who would you like to collaborate with? Many of these professionals live here and fortuitous opportunities happen every day.

Publications—Read the industry trade papers to see what the studios are up to and who is teaming up on which projects. Read actors' biographies to understand how they struggled, too, and achieved success. You are never alone.

Service— What can you offer to your community with your art? Get involved with performing organizations. Start sharing your gifts with the world.

Family—Gratitude. Express appreciation for the people who are your supporters— both your blood family and the strangers you'll bond with in Hollywood. These are the people who will sustain you along the way. Your accomplishments will not be made by your efforts alone; so, get used to keeping your ego out of the way.

Lastly, I would like to share a few insights that I have found to be true:

1. **If you think something will be difficult, it is.**
2. **There is always a quiet dissatisfaction with one's craft.**
3. **"It" is never enough.**
4. **There is never a perfect time to start.**
5. **You cannot seek fame; you can only attract it.**

Remember that little girl from Minnesota with a suitcase full of dreams? Now I make my living solely as an actress. Today I am living my dream and so can you! When you finish this book, I promise that it will save you time, money and give you an invaluable education. With those thoughts in mind . . . let's begin the adventure!

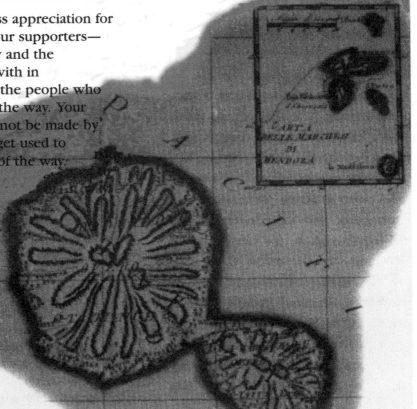

# Chapter 1

## On the Road To Oz

It's unbelievable! You're first acting job in a movie. Butterflies flutter in your stomach as you maneuver the car through the huge studio gates. The guard is directing you to a parking spot near Stage 7. When you see the red light on over the door indicating shooting is in progress your heart-beat quickens. Maybe you will get released early but you don't ever want this day to end.

Scanning the crew you locate the First Assistant Director and check in. She hands you a small script of your lines that fits in the palm of your hand called "*sides*" and says your dressing room is over here. It's so cool, a place of your very own that has a radio, couch, air conditioning a makeup up table with the groovy light bulbs and a bath-room, all the comforts of home. The best part is the name on the door. Granted it is hand-written and slipped into a slot but it means you have arrived. You have a busy schedule to keep and are ushered off to breakfast, hair and make-up.

The cook at the catering truck offers you a choice of breakfast burrito, sausage muffin or eggs. You sit outside on a sunny day enjoying your breakfast and realize how luck you are. The make-up people are waiting so off you dash.

A smock is thrown over your body as you slide into the chair. You watch as the make-up guy works with the dexterity of an artist. Picking up tips for auditions and photo shoots wondering why you can never do this at home. They put that very attractive goop on your hair and pass you off to wardrobe.

The clothes are so beautiful and you're very careful not to get any make-up on them. After trying on a couple of different outfits, poloroids are taken of each one and the director will decide which will work best for the scene. Then the hardest part of an actors'' day begins . . . the waiting.

All the morning fury of activity is over. If you're not shooting right away, there is no telling when you may work. Staying every poised to work is what exhausts most actors. You doze off to sleep in your dressing room. When you wake up in you're own bed at home and realize it was all a dream. It's a wonderful dream and I can assure you that if you're willing to work hard it's one that is attainable.

## A Couch Potato is Born

As an aspiring actor, you probably watch a lot of television and see a lot of movies. If you don't . . . start! But, this time, instead of watching TV programs, commercials, and movies as a viewer, look at the material through the eyes of an agent, producer, direc-tor, casting director or a studio executive. It will help you get a sense of what is currently appealing and competitive in terms of acting styles that draw the attention of industry pro-fessionals and, ultimately, the viewers. Then, you can start developing your own method of acting to increase the chances of your getting noticed. What TV shows and commercials are you right for? Make a list. You will use that list when we get to the chapter on landing an agent. Are there any local advertisers you could contact to pitch on hiring you for their next spot?

Read a million plays and go to the movies as much as possible. Start watching the credits and familiarize yourself with pro-ducers, directors, casting directors and local casting directors. Do your research on these people: rent videotapes and study their work. One day, you may find yourself standing across an audition room with one of these people. And, you'll already know their style and how to give them what they want.

## Finding Your Spotlight

Before you begin to seek work you must have a professional package that includes: picture, resume and demo reel for actors. For models your professional kit includes a com-posite or "*zed*" card, any copies of photo shoots, a modeling book or samples of pictures and a resume if you want to do commercials. Both types should have what I call the elevator speech to describe your type to prospective agents, managers and casting directors over the phone. I will teach you how to use this speech in this chapter and again in Chapter 6 - Getting and Keeping an Agent. What if you don't know any agents, photographers or coaches. Read on.

## All the Worlds a Stage

Are you studying with an acting or modeling coach and participating in theatrical productions? Get involved with local theater, even if you want to model Why? It gives you experience dealing with nerves and being in the public eye. A resume with lots of theater says a few things. You can count of me to be professional and I haven't been waiting for my big break, I have been creating it. In this environment you will hear about casting opportunities, modeling jobs and be able to easily find reputable coaches and photographers.

Start picking the brains of every actor and model you meet to find out who the good agents and photographers are in your area; or, alternately, call every talent agent franchised by local unions and get their recommendations. Does anyone's name keep coming up? If so, call and audit their class or if the case of photographers go review their books. Get the best acting or modeling coach you can afford but don't throw the money away. Do some homework and get recommendations from working actors, models agents or local casting directors.

Find out if your actor friends have an agent. If they do, ask them to introduce you or have them take your picture and resume into the office. Similarly, find out if your colleagues know any local casting directors they would be willing to introduce you to. If you cannot find a list of local agents, log onto our web site

at www.hollywoodhereicome.com under the products section you can purchase a list of talent and modeling agents for all the major cities in the US and modeling agents for Europe. In future chapters we go over how to pick a photographer or coach.

## Contacting Film Commissions

One of your career building phone calls should be to the film commission office near you. Cannot locate their office? Log onto our web site at www.hollywoodhereicome.com and for a very nominal fee we supply you with a list of film commissions or drama schools and universities, agents, photographers, photo reproduction companies, theater groups and adult and children's coaches. You look through our available lists and can get going on your professional career right away.

Does the commission have a hotline with local casting notices for film and television? If they do, visit the line each week and submit on any project you are remotely right for. If you are lucky enough to have an agent, be sure to include their contact information on your resume as well.

## Mastering the Elevator Speech

You need to be able to pitch yourself to agents, casting directors, local film schools and any local advertisers on television or radio. That is why I invented the elevator speech. Imagine you are in an elevator and the person next to you asks what you do for a living. How can you answer that question in a compelling manner with a fifteen second time limit. I don't just want you to say you are an actor or a model.

If their is an unusual hobby or skill you possess? Do you have an extraordinary physical characteristic? My elevator speech goes like this: I'm 5'9", have legs for days, snappy red hair and a sassy attitude to match. Do you get a visual on how I look in your mind? Have some clues how to cast me? That is what I want you to write for yourself. Get help, ask your friends to help. Try it out on strangers when you go anywhere that people are trying to get to know you.

Write a couple of different ones and see which one causes others to ask questions about you and your career. The fact that you are new to this career is a great selling tool. Everyone wants to discover the next star.

## Finding Local Jobs

Each movie and television show uses a main casting director and a local casting director. A main casting director works out of Los Angeles or New York and casts the major roles with well-known stars; the local Casting Director works locally and casts people to fill some of the smaller roles you'll be seeking.

These people are insanely busy so don't take up to much time. Just pitch them with your fifteen second elevator speech which includes your category (i.e., cop, reporter, waitress, etc.) and see if any parts for that type are available. If, after reviewing the information you just gathered you decide that one of the characters fits your description, submit your picture and resume for consideration to the casting director. If you happen to have an Agent, be sure to include their information.

When you are cast locally, ask the casting director who is the main casting director. That way, when you finally relocate to that city, you can contact that particular casting director and let him or her know that you were cast locally on such-and-such project, that you are new in town, and that you want to introduce yourself. Usually, they will be very open to meeting you because, in their eyes, you already have a track record and have worked with producers and directors whom you both know. These are invaluable contacts so use them to the maximum advantage.

If you don't have enough auditions to keep you busy then consider subscribing to the National Casting Notices available on our web site at www.hollywoodhereicome.com for $99 per year.

## Subscription to the Trades

Read the trades to keep up with what's going on in Hollywood. Any of them will send a subscription anywhere in the United States. Each week *The Hollywood Reporter* prints both the U.S. and International Film Production Charts. Twice a month, *The Reporter* prints up-to-date and comprehensive TV Productions Charts. Check out the Tuesday issue; this is especially fun because it contains all the production charts and box office grosses of currently released films. Additionally, the Tuesday issue publishes the International report where you can get an overview of the previous week's world entertainment news. Here is subscription info for all the trades.

You can have the *Hollywood Reporter, Daily Variety,* or *Backstage West* delivered to your home, no matter where you live. Each has casting notices or production reports telling you which companies are coming to your area to shoot on location. Here are the pricing structures for each publication and ordering information in the back of this book in the section called the Hollywood Little Black Book listed under Industry News-papers. All the goods and services I refer to will be listed there.

## Getting Ready to Launch

Now let's shift gears a bit and talk about some practical matters, like living expenses. Before you come to Los Angeles, start saving every any dime you can while you're at home. You will need lots of money because, I guarantee, that wherever your career takes you things will cost more than back home.

You're, also, going to need some very reliable transportation. Economy cars that are cheap to repair seem to work the best. Pick a car that can make the trip across country. Actors will be heading for Chicago, Dallas or Los Angeles. Models will head for New York, Miami or Chicago. For your first year in your new city you should keep your car insurance policy based with your hometown auto insurance company. The reason being that, if you change your mind about staying you'll wind up transferring your registration and then have to transfer it right back to your place of origin again. You can change everything over when you decide you're going to stay for good. It might even be a good idea to keep some money in reserve back in your home town. Money will be tight your first year in your new career and it is always reassuring to have a nest egg socked away for emergencies (car breaks down, lose your job, etc.).

Plan to give this career at least a year. It will take most of your first year to get settled in and get your career going. If you get an agent right away and book a job, consider yourself lucky. During your first five years you may work occasionally but most will not make enough money to make a living from industry-related jobs. I am not saying this to dishearten you. I want you to have realistic expectations and achievable goals. If you approach you career as something you will work at for the rest of your life, then time will be on your side and your patience, perseverance, and commitment will sustain you in a long career drive. Statistically, most Actors hit their target somewhere around the ten year mark in the business. So, don't panic if you don't work right away. It's normal.

## When to Make the Leap

How do you decide when it is time to leave your local market and step up to the big time in Los Angeles. Ask yourself the following questions and be rigorously honest with your answers:

1.  Do I book at least three out of every ten jobs that I audition for in my hometown?
2.  Am I financially prepared to sustain myself for at least one year in another city? Or do I have a great survival skill so I can easily get a job.
3.  Am I professionally prepared to make a career jump to another city?
4.  Am I emotionally and mentally prepared for another city?

If you say "No" to any of these questions, you might want to spend some more time in your hometown and continue working hard until your are authentically able to answer "Yes" to all of those questions. You need to be realistic. The competition in major markets is fierce and 80,000 members of the Screen Actors Guild and thousands of models are out of work on an average day. My advice: Wait until your confidence and booking ratio warrant a move.

If, on the other hand, you have honestly answered "Yes" to those four questions, you are probably ready to make your move.

## Learning New Tricks

Learn to sing, dance, juggle, do magic or any performing art. See if you can perform on any of your local TV shows. Get some tape on yourself if possible. It's always good to use your talent to be of service to your community, see if there are any televised charity events.

Study martial arts. It is a skill that can be used in movies and at the same time is a great way to improve your mental focus and physical agility. If you are not the physical type perfect a foreign language or polish your accents and dialects. This can bring you singular attention like Meryl Streep got in The French Lieutenants Woman or Sophie's Choice. In that same vein you could learn to play a musical instrument. You can use it in your acting repertoire or as a creative survival job. Become computer literate whether you can afford to buy a computer or not. It's a very sellable skill for a survival job. If you can afford to buy one, by all means do! That way you can build your mailing and contact lists on a label program for publicity. You can also typeset your own resumes and updates for significantly less money than having to pay a typesetter.

Also become proficient in as many sports and hobbies as you can. The more skilled you become the better your chances of landing a commercial or movie that requires that skill. Get as many parts in as many local theatrical plays as you possibly can. Find out from other actors and agents in your community which theaters are the most prestigious in town. Then, set your sights on getting a part in a production at those theaters. If you wind up getting a role in a play, be sure to add it to your resume with the name of the theater and the director.

Call the SAG Casting Hotline for information about upcoming auditions. Go on every audition you can. Don't get hooked into the outcome of those auditions; the more you audition, the more comfortable you become. Take a job as an Extra on a movie set in your area. You can use this experience to continue building your knowledge of film making and to make contacts. Go to the local colleges and see if student films are being made. Leave a picture and resume for casting consideration.

## Sparking Creative Fires

Read every famous person's biography that you can get your hands on. The library is filled with them. Study the stories on how now-famous people got their starts and overcame adversity. See if you can extract any ideas on breaking into the industry.

Watch the public access channel on your local cable network. Write down ideas for shows you might consider doing for yourself. Call the public access channel and inquire as to how to apply for your own public access show. Once you begin hosting or performing on a show of your own, buy a copy of your work for your demo reel.

Order the **CD Directory** on our web site and start learning the names of as many casting directors as you can. Stay abreast of the shows they cast. At the end of television shows and movies watch the credits. The names of the casting director along with the local casting directors are always there. Make a list of people you'd like to meet.

Make your own cue cards and practice *"coming off the page"* (grabbing the words quickly and looking up into the lens of a camera). Pretend you're talking to your best friend. Don't worry if, you appear a little awkward your first few times on camera. Many people think it looks easy and believe they can just wing it. Approach this just like you would a professional, paying job. What's important is that you are gaining experience, confidence and will eventually relax in front of the camera. That is one of the points the of this exercise: Being relaxed in front of a camera. This is a skill that is acquired through many, many hours of practice.

## The Eye of the Storm

Develop a spiritual base, be it religion, meditation, yoga or your choice. Start to develop a balance between work, recreation and spiritual pursuits. Start taking risks. I don't mean jumping off bridges. Try something that's a stretch for you, something that looks reachable but fills you with a kind of anxiety/excitement. Whether it's stand -up comedy, public speaking, or whatever pulls at your creative heartstrings, challenge yourself!

So far we have been tossing around ideas and finding ways to get work in your home town. Now we are ready to start developing all the different sides of your professional package so that you can move your dreams forward. It all starts with a magical thing called "image", Every great actor has one. Studios help you to cultivate it and newspapers use it to sell your next vehicle to the public. Turn the page and start imaging who you will become.

# Chapter 2
# Your Image

*Vision, like Love, takes no planning—for it just happens. It is directed by the Creator and made manifest by Creation. Take no care as to how you will live your Vision or how you will find your Love. For the Creator has planned all these things, and the way will become clear to your heart. You have been given a choice but if you listen to your Heart, there needs to be no choice. Your path is your Heart and all that you need to do is follow it. I have found that the grave mistakes that take place in Life are made when a person does not follow their Heart. When the heart is ignored, Life become complicated and distorted but when the heart is followed, we touch the Creator. Logic and reason are poor alternatives to a life full of Love and Vision.*

**Tom Brown, Jr.**
**— *The Quest***

Everyone in Modeling and Show business wants to discover the next big deal like Cindy Crawford or Al Pacino. Who are you? Are you a Leonardo DiCaprio type. Do people say that you remind them of someone famous? Are you a young anyone?

Right away I am going to give you the ability to outsmart the competition. It's something called "image." All of the top stars are known for one quality or another. Tom Hanks' quality is Joe Average Man and we can identify with him like we did with Jimmy Stewart. Tom is a very smart actor and would never attempt to play a sensual character better suited to someone like Antonio Banderas. Julia Roberts sells effervescent vulnerability better than anybody else. She brought that quality to her character in *PRETTY WOMAN* and it was a huge hit. When she tried to play heavy, dark dramatic roles like *MARY REILLY,* it went against her magical qualities and the movie flopped. She got back on top with *MY BEST FRIEND'S WEDDING,* doing what she does best. Image has to do with how people perceive you before you ever open your mouth. You are judged on look and what's going on in your eyes. That is why auditions are set from your picture. Casting directors and agents see the quality in your picture and when they meet with you they want to see if you can act.

You have to figure out how people perceive you and develop that into an image. Once you have determined your image, your hottest selling point, then you can attack the industry on a local level. When you have perfected this look, then you can bring it to Hollywood or another major market. As the saying goes: Sell the sizzle, not the steak. It's easier to get some career attention when people describe you as "intriguing" rather than "talented". "Talented" is one of the most overused words in L.A. and "intriguing" always peaks curiosity. First, some history of image development and then the fun begins.

Back in the early days of Hollywood, the studios created an image for their actors. It was based on how they were perceived by the public and not on their talents. Cary Grant was an elegant and smooth actor; so, he became a hero type, although he possessed extraordinary comedic ability. After his career was established, he was able to display it in the film *BRINGING UP BABY.* Vincent Price was perceived to be a dark villain and played those roles successfully most of his life. During an interview with Mr. Price at his home filled with precious art and fine wine, he would chuckle about his image because it had so little to do with who he really was: a gourmet cook, a kind and philanthropic man. He understood how important it was to separate ego from marketability. Vincent Price finally got to display more of his kind, benevolent side in *EDWARD SCISSORHANDS.* Goldie Hawn, the star, has spent most of her career playing a dizzy blonde. Goldie Hawn, the person, used her other talents of tough negotiation and business savvy to acquire ownership of *PRIVATE BENJAMIN* and other films for herself, making her one of the richest and most powerful women in Hollywood.

Before you get headshots (8" x 10" photos of your face), put out a mailing to casting directors or try to land an agent, you have to decide what it is as an image that you are selling. One of the most effective ways of identifying your right image is to find out how strangers perceive you. (I've designed a survey to help you to discover your perfect image. More about that in a moment.) Use Vincent Price as an example to contrast who he really was and who he was "perceived" as being so that you can experience for yourself how one's "image" may have very little to do with how one really thinks of oneself.

Your image is your most accessible marketing tool. Using it well can hasten your progress toward visibility, credibility and success as an actor. For years, I thought industry professionals perceived me as a tough, no nonsense actress. That was an image that seemed, to me, slightly on the dull side. But, that's who I thought I should project and that's the way I presented myself. It didn't take long before I realized I wasn't getting anywhere based on my own self-concept. So, I did some research on how others perceived me and I was both shocked and pleased to find the answers on my "survey" reflected my intelligent, spirited and fun personality as well as my sensuality. When I made the transformation in my presentation, I started getting results. But, don't believe me; listen to what an Academy Award-winning actress had to say about this very aspect.

## Famous Actors' Images

In her acceptance letter for the Lifetime Achievement Award from the Screen Actors Guild, Audrey Hepburn referred to herself: "[they] guided a totally unknown, insecure, inexperienced, skinny broad into a marketable commodity." These words came from an extraordinary actress whose success came from playing elegant women whose determination and spirit conquered any adversity; proof positive that we actors are not always the best judge of ourselves.

Arnold Schwarzenegger understands better than anyone the importance of marketability. If you saw his documentary, *PUMPING IRON,* it was a sweet and somewhat shy Arnold that was coming through. He did, however, state that he had a burning desire to be a movie star and was going to gear his whole life, after body building, toward that end and to do whatever it took to make stardom happen. For him, this meant changing his entire screen image. He realized that his instant sell lay in playing tough-guy action heroes. It catapulted him to the top. Once he became publicly certified and accepted as a movie star, he was free to try different character roles. But, until that point, all his heroes had sort of a mean and evil air about them. It wasn't until *TERMINATOR 2* that he broke free and became a tough guy fighting for good; a true hero. He even took some risks by trying his hand at comedy in *TWINS* and *KINDERGARTEN COP.* The point is: play your strongest suit first until you get established and accredited with the public. Then, try expanding your range and talents by taking the kind of risks that Arnold has.

As actors we try so hard not to get typecast. But, I say: At the beginning of your acting career, do one thing and do it so well that every time that "type" is needed, Hollywood can't think of asking anyone but you. Naturally everyone you'll compete against will have talent, but you'll have the edge. Then, as you move closer to the top, you'll have more choices to be anything you want to be.

## "The Survey Says . . ."

So, how do you discover the right image for you in order to get that edge? Well, now it's time for that survey I referred to earlier. The idea I am about to propose may be a little challenging—but hear me out. Here's what I want you to do. It's a little technique that I call "canvassing." Basically, when you canvas, you are giving yourself an opportunity to get a disinterested third party to evaluate the image you project based on their first impression of you. The image questionnaire provided at the end of this chapter will help you zero in on your natural sale. Therefore, your assignment, should you decide to accept it, is the following:

1. Make copies of the questionnaire. (Bring lots of pencils with you.)
2. Find a partner to canvas with you, so that when your partner approaches other people to ask for their participation, they will not be influenced by hearing your own voice.

3. Go to a public place where people are waiting and have time to kill.
(Ideal spots include college campuses, airports, malls, bus stations, etc.)

4. Have your partner ask someone if he or she would be willing to take a few minutes to fill out a questionnaire. (My favorite approach is: "Would you like to fill out a questionnaire? It's fun and it's free.")

5. Assuming you get a willing participant, have your partner explain that he or she will point out a person (you) to them and that, after observing that person (you) for a while, they will be asked to give their impressions by checking off their first impulses about this person on the questionnaire. Have your partner give the participant the questionnaire and a pencil. Then, have your partner point you out—and let the games begin! (If you don't have another actor to do this with, get a friend or relative to do it with you. It is critical that the person being observed not speak to these people in order to get a honest survey.)

6. Do this enough times to get a significant amount of surveys from which you can either make a fairly accurate assessment or, at least, get a good, strong sense of the image you project.

Don't worry about feeling embarrassed or uncomfortable while people stare at you and make their decisions. It is natural. Once, on one of my less confident days of surveying, I became so uneasy that I started tap dancing at Los Angeles International Airport just to ease my own tension! But, I didn't let my moods stop me. I even surveyed on days when I was feeling shy as well as confident. As I became more accustomed to the process, I started to experiment with many hair styles and clothing changes. In time, I felt I had experimented with a good cross section of looks and, still, people's responses generally stayed consistent. After I analyzed all the data I had collected, I made a determination to change my image from a dull, dependable, hard-working actress to an intelligent, high-spirited personality. And, wow, did I start getting responses from prospective agents and casting directors!

To help you analyze the results of your survey, I have broken the general personality types into four categories, which you will find on the questionnaire. Copy it and use it.

**Column I is categorized as The Ruler** (people who are regal or have an elegant quality)

**Column II is The Leader** (people who suggest a dynamic, powerful quality)

**Column III is The All-American** (people suggesting a wholesome, responsible quality)

**Column IV is The Rebel** (people who suggest a thrilling, dangerous quality).

Tally up your votes in each column and see where your strengths lie. It will help you to decide what types or parts you will be easily seen for. You can then gear the hair style and clothing attire in your headshots to reflect this image.

If you absolutely, positively refuse to try the survey, here's another way to discover your perfect image. I took an American Film Institute seminar that featured a class having to do with "essence." In fact, the name of the seminar was "Your Essence." The class was designed like this: an actor would stand in front of the group and the instructor would make statements about the actor. The group, in turn, would raise their hands whenever they believed that the statements about that Actor were true. When it was my turn, the class determined I was a non-religious, love-em-and-leave-em kind of gal, even though I am deeply spiritual and totally monogamous. I took this as a sign that I can play a wilder, more dangerous woman than myself. That truly excited me. I just figured: "I don't care what they're buying, I'm an actress. So, I will remind you again: the result may have no connection to who you really are as a person.

If you can't seem to get a lock on your image, **my web site** offers a consultation session that will clearly define your type. The consultation is specifically designed to define and build your image. Furthermore, we suggest hair styles, clothing and photo layout ideas to help groom you into making your new, professional image a reality. Included in the session we analyze any photos you have, redo or write an industry resume, design a sizzling elevator speech, pick TV shows and commercials you should target and teach you how to pitch agents. We're on the web at http://www.hollywoodhereicome.com

# Nudity and Your Image

There's a lot to say about nudity; but for now, I just want to focus on the aspect of nudity that has to do with your image. We'll cover the other aspects of nudity in Chapter 9 ("Auditions").

In the final analysis, choosing nudity as a means of bringing attention to your talent is a very personal decision. It can either work for you or against you. It's a crap shoot. The choices you make will not only shape your image but may, for better or worse, create a reputation that will stick with you throughout the life of your career. The fact that Jamie Lee Curtis, Sherilyn Fenn and Jennifer Jason Leigh all rose above the T & A "B" movies to achieve very successful film careers is not a demonstration for guaranteed stardom. In all likelihood, what propelled these women to stardom was having the good luck to choose nudity in movies whose stories and characters were exceptionally compelling. Similarly, Sharon Stone in **BASIC INSTINCT** and Annette Bening in **THE GRIFTERS** chose nudity for characters whose nudity was pertinent for the story. Soon after the release of each film, stardom shone on these talented actresses because these films, fortunately, were highly acclaimed

by the public. But, it could just as easily have gone the other way. If those movies had been made and released at another time, the audience response could have been either unresponsive or, worse, disapproving. Then consider where Sharon and Annette might be today in their careers!

I wish I had a recipe to offer you for making the right choice in every circumstance. But, I don't. What I can offer you are questions to guide you in deciding for yourself the right thing to do if and when an opportunity presents itself. So, ask yourself the following questions and be rigorously honest with yourself with your answers:

- In this particular film, is the nudity gratuitous or does it help to move the story along to create a dramatic/romantic relationship between the characters?
- If I choose to do the nude scene(s) and the movie is successful, what unspoken contract will I be making with my audience (i.e. what expectations will I be creating in my audience about my future work)?
- Will I be able to transcend these expectations and still be respected?
- Will I lose credibility as an actress if I do a nude scene in this particular film?
- Am I willing to incur the disapproval of my friends and family by doing a nude scene in this particular film?
- Can I look at myself in the mirror every day and authentically know—not pretend to know—that I made the right choice?

# Characteristics and Your Image

Now let's talk about mannerisms. Mannerisms, whether they be dialects or body gestures, can either enhance or detract from your image. For example, let's say you are—in reality—an elegant looking person born and raised in Tennessee. Perfect! Because the part you're auditioning for calls for an elegant-looking person, just like you; but, the minute you speak, your natural rural patterns emerge. This puts your real-life personality in direct conflict with your projected screen image. Now, I am not necessarily advocating speech/diction class for everyone. Tommy Lee Jones has had a fine career and not once has he had to change that southern drawl of his; he uses it successfully to enhance the characters he portrays. The point I am trying to make is that, just like nudity considerations, know your limitations. Be honest about what you're willing or not willing to do for your career and the consequences of your choices.

The same point holds true for your sexual orientation. Natural effeminate mannerisms for men and masculine traits for women can be very limiting to the types of roles you may be considered able to do. Naturally, there are exceptions. It is a well-known fact that Harvey Fierstein is gay; he doesn't hide it. He has played straight and gay roles because of his ability to add or lose his mannerisms and affectations.

So, unless you are absolutely convinced that you can completely hide some subtle, indelible mannerism that you were born with by attempting a role you're just not capable of executing, don't do it. You'll only wind up looking ridiculous. Don't pretend to be something you're not, especially if it costs you your professional credibility and your emotional well-being. Be honest with yourself about your mannerisms. But, if, in your opinion, it's at least worth a try, get some coaching to determine whether or not you can effectively and credibly broaden your range.

Incidentally, regarding the disclosure of your sexual orientation to anyone in the industry, this is yet another personal decision you will have to make. It is a private issue that need never be made public. Just be aware that, even though Hollywood proclaims tolerance and waves liberal banners to the world, your sexual orientation could negatively bias some professional career handlers (producers, agents, personal managers, etc.) against submitting you for certain roles. Your decision to share this kind of personal information with anyone should be based on the sense of trust, discretion and alliance you receive from another person.

Your image is not just about how you look; it is, also, about how you take care of yourself. It's no coincidence that gyms, personal trainers, tanning, nail and hair salons are so popular in Los Angeles. You never know on any given day when you might be called for a last-minute audition. So, for an actor, taking care of yourself must be a way of life. Given that most actors are more than willing to do this, I would strongly encourage you to follow suit in order to keep up with the competition.

## The Gym

They're everywhere so pick one close to home or work. Also, shop around to get a deal. Yearly rates generally run less than monthly gym memberships.

**Bally's Total Fitness** has bought out most of the health club chains in Los Angeles, including: Nautilus Plus, Holiday Health Spas and Sports Connection. For a first-year fee of $149 and a yearly renewal of $99, you are entitled to a Premiere Membership. This gets you into any of the health clubs that Bally's owns anywhere in the country. Most of them are open 24 hours a day.

If Bally's doesn't interest you, get a copy of *The Working Actors Guide off* the web site which has a comprehensive list of clubs all over town, in my phone directory in the back of the book I have including three popular exercise studios frequented by industry professionals. It is easy to make friends at health clubs with people in show business at all different levels. Since this is a relationship business the gym is a great place to start in any city to build new friendships that can translate into working together in the future.

# Personal Trainers

If you can afford it, get a personal trainer to get you started. And, if you can find a reliable trainer who also has other industry clients. That way you can chat about the business while you're sweating. Sometimes it can even turn into a networking opportunity. Almost everyone in show business works out because it is such a body conscious industry. I don't like the rules, I just play by them. Hopefully as baby boomers mature they will not only put people in productions that are of an average weight but also will allow people to naturally age and not constantly pursue the fountain of youth. My recommendations: Craig and Chris Price are from Texas with sweet southern drawls and the gentility to match. But don't be fooled they'll put your body through an amazing workout. There Mom, Buffy who is one of the sweetest women on the planet, runs their business and books appointments. She also makes the most delicious health food cookies in LA. These cookies can help you with weight loss and getting the required amount of fiber that a body needs to function properly. They are in the phone directory in the back of this book.

# Nutrition

We actors are always watching our weight, especially since the camera adds about ten pounds to us. At the risk of sounding like your mother, I would recommend the following conscientious, self-caring measures: Get a good vitamin routine so you don't get run-down. **Great Earth Vitamins** has a well-balanced vitamin program in one cellophane packet per day. They have six locations which are all listed in our phone directory.

Read the fat grams on all foods you buy. Three or less is good. Fat-free is best. Most importantly, if you drink four quarts of water a day your body will age more slowly than average. Another way to slow aging is by taking anti-oxidants. These enzymes coat the free radicals in the body, slowing the aging process and preventing cancers. During cold and flu season you can take Ecchinacea and Goldenseal, available in liquid form, and Co-enzyme CoQ10. Both boost your immune system. The cheapest way to buy CoQ10 is under the Trader Joe house brand at their stores all over town. For the location nearest you look in our phone book under Groceries - Low Cost. For a complete list of health foods look in *The Working Actors Guide* — "Health Food Stores" section.

# Hair

Always be clean and well groomed for auditions, interviews, appointments, etc. I found a great shampoo called Biolage by Matrix and a conditioner that makes your hair shine. Look for Original Crema Hair Treatment by Terax. Both are available at any beauty supply. Make sure your hair has a shape and style that fits with your image. Facial hair should be trimmed and neat too. Whatever it takes, even if you're nearly broke don't neglect this area! Fantastic Sams and Super Cuts offer deals at $10. I personally recommend any of the salons listed in our phone directory.

# Nails

Clipped and clean is the key here. No nail biting or bleeding cuticles that we nervous types are famous for. Gals, chipped nails are okay when your hangin' in the hood, but not on auditions. Salons here in Los Angeles offer manicure and pedicure rates that are the best in the country and offer a manicure and pedicure combination for $14. Beauty training schools do it even cheaper.

# Aging

Actors tend to be obsessed with halting the aging process. More so for women than for men. Here's something to help:

1. Olive oil and bath beads in a tub help to rehydrate the skin and seal in moisture. I have used it for years and my skin, even though I love the Southern California beaches, is holding up well.

2. To remove wrinkles from hands, dip them in a tray of melted paraffin wax from the grocery store and water. Wrap them in plastic wrap and small heated towels. Sleep with them covered. In the morning, unwrap the towels, peel off the wax with the plastic together and you will be amazed. Another trick is to wash hands in warm water. Cover with generous amounts of hand cream and cover with thin winter gloves. Remove in the morning and the wrinkles have softened or disappeared.

3. Use Oatmeal Skin Scrubs with a Loofah to give skin a healthy glow.

4. Use a steam room—not a sauna— which tend to dry out your skin.

5. Drink plenty of water. Tobacco and alcohol age skin terribly, so watch it!

6. Finally, here is an ancient anti-aging bath soak I recommend: In a one foot square of muslin or cheesecloth, place: 1/4 cup thyme, 1/4 cup mint, 1/4 cup rosemary, 1/4 cup lavender, 1/4 cup camfrey root, 1/4 cup house leek. Toss it in the tub, let it steep and just add your body.

## Permanent Solutions

It used to be when you wanted to alter your features or wrinkles, it would involve an endless series of collagen injections at $350 to $500 a pop. The collagen would be gone in three to six months. Now there's a new product that is permanent. Imagine, no more laugh lines that aren't so funny. It is called PERMA and is made of cow collagen. Its unique make-up encourages your own collagen production and provides an infra-structure for your own collagen to adhere to. This product is all the rage in Europe and is now being clinically tested in America for FDA approval. One doctor in Los Angeles administers more of this permanent collagen than any other and was featured on our local NBC network news. His name is **Dr. Douglas Hamilton.** He has two offices for your convenience.

Want to poof out your lips to make them pout? That can be done with collagen as well. I would try the type of collagen that is not permanent to begin with just o see how it will look and if you like it. Then, after you have achieved a fullness that meets your expectations, show your doctor right away so it can be matched with permanent collagen. That way you get the look you want and avoid having to redo lips over and over again.

It is the common thought in many schools of plastic surgery that our face does not sag as previously thought rather, our bones and teeth recede and that causes the skin to slacken as it isn't being held out as far as when we were young. I am told by Dr. Hamilton that future plastic surgery could include molds made from dental records when we are in our late teens or early twenties and artificial implants for your face will be constructed and inserted.

So that takes care of the bigger lines but what about the smaller ones around the eyes, between the brows and across the forehead? Well, you can use a process known as Botox to relax smaller lines in your face. Botox works like this. The doctor injects the drug, which is in fact a poison, into the nerves of your face. The effect freezes or neutralizes the nerve so that even if your brain sends a signal to your forehead to squint in the sun, your brows do not move. Very cool, huh? You need to take care in choosing a doctor who has done this process many times as it temporarily freezes your face and it does not wear off for about three to six months eventually becoming permanent over time. Enter Dr. David Kim who, despite his young age, is an artist when it comes to injecting the face with botox.

As you can see from this chapter, image is critical to building your career. Use the gym to keep your body toned up and physically fit. Eat the right foods and supplement your diet with vitamins and minerals. Keep your nails and hair well groomed. Don't obsess about age but do what you can to maintain a healthy look, since that's what attracts Hollywood's film makers.

All of these things, taken separately, may seem trivial and irrelevant. Taken altogether, however, they make for a powerful combination in creating the image you intend to present to the world. And that's why you should not shoot your photos until you have a clear idea of the image you are selling. Otherwise, you will be wasting your money. The clearer that your image is to your agent, the easier it is for him or her to sell your talents. Paying attention to and caring for your physical appearance can easily make the difference and get you noticed because you sparkle and shine. It's very alluring to feel really good about yourself.

## IMAGE QUESTIONNAIRE

**How old do you think this person is?** _____

**CIRCLE YOUR FIRST IMPRESSIONS OF THIS PERSON.**

| COLUMN I | COLUMN II | COLUMN III | COLUMN IV |
|---|---|---|---|
| contemplative | fearless | finicky | clever |
| admirable | dynamic | enthusiastic | affectionate |
| concerned | exact | inquisitive | spirited |
| generous | powerful | willing | direct |
| refined | unyielding | hardworking | passionate |
| noble | secure | loyal | quick |
| formal | hopeful | dependable | spontaneous |
| graceful | effective | respectful | heartfelt |
| ethical | antsy | committed | easy going |
| superior | determined | generous | comical |
| humane | practical | gregarious | adventurous |
| understanding | firm | modest | amorous |
| aristocratic | inflexible | decent | sexy |
| wise | busy | amusing | charmed |
| gentle | confident | compassionate | wiry |
| calm | reasonable | affectionate | secretive |
| elegant | demanding | truthful | flirtatious |
| attractive | precise | idealistic | sensual |
| bright | fair | frisky | capricious |
| classic | direct | comical | gentle |
| regal | serious | committed | in your face |
| stuffy | concerned | stubborn | devious |
| obstinate | fierce | clumsy | foolhardy |
| snobby | driven | edgy | cavalier |
| arrogant | foolish | self-conscious | resistant |
| grandiose | impatient | confused | defiant |
| curt | controlling | tense | wary |

## THIS PERSON WOULD MAKE A GOOD:

| | | | |
|---|---|---|---|
| Judge | Executive | Cop | Criminal |
| Doctor | Athlete | Secretary | Photographer |
| Charity person | Attorney | Political aide | Stripper |
| Diplomat | Scientist | Teacher | Hairdresser |
| Mistress | Airline pilot | Plumber | Terrorist |
| Stewardess | Accountant | Nurse | Reporter |
| Model | Martial artist | Soldier | Rock star |

# Chapter 3
## The Hustle

*"A wise person is cautious and avoids danger, a fool plunges ahead with great confidence."*

**—Proverb**

There is an entire business that exists to feed off of an actor's frustrations and paranoia about his or her career. There are people who will try to separate you from your money, your clothes and your soul. In this chapter I will show you how to recognize many of the well-known scams that are run against actors. Then, I'll teach you how to check someone out so that you can separate the Samaritans from the charlatans and side step the weasels.

Legitimate agents and managers are swamped with casting notices daily. For these professionals, there is no time limit on opportunities available for their clients . . . and more come each day. Con artists, on the other hand, use time as a way to pressure you into handing over hard-earned money for pictures, classes or career counseling. They goad you into believing that you are on the brink of a job or big career break if you can just act quickly. This is a technique used by con artists to take your money before you have time to analyze the situation and come to your senses. They prey on your desire to have immediate results. Beware of anyone who guarantees you success by enticing you with the "no previous experience necessary" come-on. The only thing that will guarantee the possibility of your success is working with reputable, licensed Agents and establishing your own talents over a long period of time.

## How It All Works Want Ads

Unfortunately, one of the first places novice actors and models look for work is in the want ads of their city newspapers and Yellow Page Phone Directories. This is the last place an actor will find work! Most are come-ons of some sort. During the research for this book I called an agency that had placed a "Modeling—no experience, no fee -come-on in the want ads. They told me that I could showcase my modeling abilities at a local night club (not a place where industry people look for talent). If I did well, they told me, I would be "featured" on their cable TV show. It turned out to be public access, available to anyone, free of charge, who wants to put together a show. Of course, *"there would be a fee involved to be on the show."* What I eventually discovered was that the "free" showcase was designed to hook me, preying on my eagerness for instant recognition so that, ultimately, they could collect a fee for their TV show. Oh, that so called TV show turned out to be a public access show they produced for free at the local cable company. Everything they promised is very real but modeling agents don't look for new talent on public access cable TV shows.

Modeling agents who are not franchised receive free listing in well-respected industry publications such as **Ross Reports** (available at news stands) and are flooded with submissions, so they have no need to advertise. The same holds true for both non-franchised talent agents and casting directors alike who receive free listings in valid industry publications.

## "I'll Get You Work"

Pay attention to ads in local trade newspapers offering to get you an agent. It is against the law for any agent franchised by a union to advertise for talent. In fact, there are so many qualified actors seeking representation (over half of the Screen Actors Guild membership is looking for representation at any one time) that agents don't have to resort to advertising. Nevertheless, there is widespread abuse of the want ads listed under "Modeling Agency" and "Talent Management."

Here's how it might happen: You call and speak to the person whose ad promises to get you work. The first thing you have to do, is come to their office for group orientation.

So, you go. At the office you are interviewed. Eventually, the conversation turns to business. It's usually there, at this office, that you'll be asked to pay "a small fee to get the ball rolling." Naturally, the office gives a legitimate appearance, but the fact is that they are renting the office just like everyone else and it's your money that pays the rent.

Weeks may go by with not a single call from your *"agent or manager."* When you query as to why you haven't been on an audition, the *"agent"* will have a list of reasonable sounding excuses. You'll hear excuses like: "Gee! It's such a slow time in the industry. Not too many projects going into production right now." Or, "Y'know, at second glance, I don't think your pictures really are quite good enough for me to sell you." They can then pass you off to a photographer and get more kickback money. Also they may then, suggest that you take their class on acting. It is illegal for a SAG-franchised agent to also teach for profit. Eventually you'll either leave in despair or be dropped as a client.

In the real world of show business an agent signs a client because they believe in and the client's ability to secure jobs. They are excited about submitting the client's pictures. If you have "bought" a relationship with an agent, I do not believe he or she will have this same passion about you. If this has already happened to you, call the editor of the publication in which you saw the ad and explain what happened or contact your local police department bunco division.

Most importantly, if the agent is franchised by a Guild, call that union and file a complaint. It may be tough for a Guild to prove the agent ever received any of your money, especially if the agent received it in cash as a kickback. If enough complaints pile up on any franchised agency, the Guild will investigate.

Unfortunately, there are some unethical agents who are franchised by SAG. In one case, a licensed agent working in Los Angeles asked prospective male clients to unbutton their pants so that he could check for tan lines. If an agent breaks the rules of proper conduct, you can turn that individual in whether you are a guild member or not. Recently, eleven actresses came forward to the Burbank Police about an agent They reported that he coerced each one of them into sexual improv's as part of their audition for his agency. During the reading, he would attack them, holding them down while he kissed and fondled them. Because of a few courageous women, he is now doing hard time in the big house.

If enough people speak up, these unsavory characters will get their licenses revoked and prosecuted for their actions. Actors and models often fear repercussions if they speak up. But, remember . . . these so-called agents are nobodies and you don't want them for representation, no matter what they say they can do for you.—or, worse, what they may wind up doing to you. So, don't be afraid to speak up. You won't be the first.

## "Break Into Commercials or Modeling?"

These invitations are issued by lots of companies all across the country; some valid, some not. Most are offered by teaching institutions not agents. Because, as we know, agents can't advertise. Here is how some modeling or acting schools feed the pipe dreams of young men and women: You'll hear about invitations to attend a special audition advertised on local radio stations or in national magazines. To induce you further, a promise is made that a representative of top agents, producers or fashion magazines will be available to screen for new talent. Most everyone screened is accepted into the school. Then, of course, they recommend classes to groom you for stardom. And what do you get? Expensive classes and substandard photographs.

I don't know about your hometown, but in Los Angeles none of the top acting coaches or photographers work in schools. They work for themselves because their services are constantly in demand. Oh, and the representative? Well, the fact of the matter is that representatives can be anybody and may have been paid for their appearance. One school in Northern California advertised that they were "casting" for parts in a film. Over 1,000 people showed up and 65% of them were signed up for—you guessed it—classes. There was so much money involved that the modeling school gave away a car to their top sales consultant. The movie they were supposedly casting shot for only one day. Then the school announced that the production company ran out of money. Angry parents complained to the radio station that ran the advertisement. It fell on deaf ears since the owner of the school and the radio station were one in the same.

One school in Los Angeles makes so much money signing people up for classes that they can pay for their advertisements in well-known national magazines. Another school advertises "talent searches" on the radio every couple of weeks, claiming that they can help you break into movies and TV. They pay for these ads and their salaries from the classes and photo packages they sell. Based on one turn-out I attended during my research, I would have to say that the owner of that school must be driving around in a Rolls Royce by now.

Most training facilities for models are run by honest people with your best interests at heart. Modeling and acting schools are just that

. . . tuition-based schools. They are in business to give you a good foundation of the skills necessary for modeling and the confidence for you to go forth in the world to make your own dreams come true. Be wary of anyone promising fame and fortune with little or no effort on your part except to write them a check.

## Protecting Your Children

Currently, the primary target of many of these talent school searches is children. Parents who believe in their child's abilities have a hard time saying "no." If you really want to help your children break into show business, read Chapter 20 for Child Actors and proceed with caution.

When legitimate advertising clients are looking for models, their first call is to a reputable modeling agency. That should be your first call as well. Reputable modeling agencies hold open calls once a week, available to anyone interested in a modeling career. You don't even need to bring professional photographs to these calls; a few snapshots of yourself will do. These professionals will give you an honest opinion as to the likelihood of success.

And . . . there is never a fee involved at open calls. If you are signed as a client at a modeling agency and they determine some training is necessary, such as how to walk a runway, it is provided for you at the agencys expense. The only time you pay a fee is when your modeling agent books a job for you. They generally get 10-15% of your fee and will bill the client on your behalf, collect the money and cut you a check. If you have any questions, doubts, or just want information about a modeling career, go to an open call and ask them. Don't ask someone who's selling classes.

## "I'll Put You On Television"

This group does exactly what they promise. There are ads in acting publications

claiming to get you on TV. Now here is where you have to stop fantasizing about your future. When I think of being on television, it is on a prime-time network show. Many groups in Los Angeles can guarantee to get you on their cable TV shows but I have already told you that busy, successful industry directors and producers do not channel surf the public access shows, looking for talent.

You may also be offered appearances in low-budget films for foreign distribution. All of this at a cost of $30-50 per week to you. You may or may not be auditioned before becoming part of a talent pool or their repertory company. It's your money each week that pays for their expensive ad to lure in more desperate actors. If you want to do something constructive, get involved with any of the well-known theater companies listed in this book and land a play. That way, industry professionals may actually get to see your work. Or get your own public access show and use the tape to try an land a great agent.

## "We Will Put Your Headshot in Our Magazine Which is Delivered All Over Town"

This is a declaration made by a number of publications that do exactly what is promised—to get your picture published in their magazine and delivered to the offices of thousands of industry professionals. Unfortunately, publications like these are found on the coffee tables in the waiting rooms of these offices—not in front of the faces of industry professionals.

Generally, these publications are considered to be an industry joke. Most people in the entertainment industry know that inexperienced actors and models will pay large sums of money to be in a magazine that guarantees recognition and exposure.

An actor whom I will call John, described his experience: "I was asked to read some commercial copy so that they could 'judge' my talent before agreeing to feature me. After the read, the woman I read for assured me that my use of props proved to her that I was genuinely talented. I couldn't wait to sign up! I was passed along to another person who would help me decide what size ad would be appropriate for the magazine. I got so pumped up, I switched from a quarter page to a full page ad at a cost of $5,000."

It has been several years since he made that costly mistake. John never even received one call from the magazine ad. In retrospect, they made a green actor believe that he would be discovered and, in the process, happily took his money. Now John wishes he had the money back to spend on car, acting classes and the best headshots possible.

## "Do Your Own Radio Show"

The advertisement runs something like this: "No experience necessary and free training to host weekly radio shows." However, when you attend the introductory orientation, you discover that you are expected to pay $9 to $50 per hour to put your show on their station, with the eventual promise that if you're good you'll be paid up to $100 per hour for your talented voice. When I posed among the masses at this call, I saw no one  turned away that day. Some of the people I spoke with had no previous experience, we're unemployed and looking for any job, or extremely shy and barely audible. They were all accepted provided they had the necessary hourly fee. If you really want to learn to be an on-air personality, there are plenty of college radio stations or small-town stations within driving distance of large metropolitan cities where you can work up to on-air personality. If you work at the station answering phones or pulling music and aspire to be on the air you will most likely start you off doing radio commercials,I took some voice-over classes and landed an on-air, weekend "Entertainment Reporter" job at Power 106 FM, a top-rated station in Los Angeles.The job was advertised in **Backstage West**, a known industry publication. I submitted a tape I made at a friend's recording studio and was interviewed no less than three times by station personnel before landing the gig. People off the street don't just end up with a radio show. It takes talent, training and the right opportunity.

## Photo Scams

Any person or agency that advertises in the Help Wanted section of a newspaper or posts signs in public places promising lots of money and immediate, available work is usually a photo scam artist. Photo scams are often set up either by unlicensed agents or disreputable "managers" who are not required to be franchised by the Guild. The police and the **Department of Consumer Affairs** consider these people who advertise for jobs an employment agency, not a talent agency. And as such it is against the law for an employment agency to have any incidental service, such as a photographer and a studio on the premises and to require payment for this incidental service.That's the law!

Anyone who has lured you in with the promise of immediate work , even as an Extra and then asks you to pre-pay for certain services (e.g., pictures that they will provide you with) to obtain that work is breaking the law and committing a felony.

Time is of the essence to all photo scammers.They know that they may have to close their doors and move to another location at a moment's notice. So, they pressure you into

making an immediate decision to get your photos done right away; otherwise, they tell you, you will miss the perfect opportunity for a film or television project currently being cast. What's more, the project will only be available for the next few days. Naturally, they've heard this "from reliable sources.".

As a novice you think. "This could be my big break! I better get my pictures done now or I'll lose this opportunity!" Eagerly, you run off to the ATM machine and quickly return to them with a pile of your hard-earned dollars. Once they have your money in hand, they perform a rush photo shoot for this "special job" that will supposedly launch your career.The next day, you return to get your professional 8 x 10 photos. Instead, you get a proof sheet with little tiny pictures and maybe a blow-up of one or two shots. You're disappointed. But, at least, you have one or two photos you can take to whomever is casting this special project.

Oh, really? To walk out the door with your 8 x 10's in hand, you have to pay these scam artists more money even though you were led to believe that it was included with the initial fee. By this time, you're short on money and time; so, you just go ahead and give them more money out of frustration and desperation.After all, you don't want to miss that big opportunity waiting for you. Finally, you get the 8 x 10's you've waited for; and guess what, they are substandard and unuseable in the industry. And, of course, that career-making opportunity they spoke of when you gave them the first stack of money? Gosh! I guess the parts already been cast.

There are some headshot photographers in Los Angeles who will ask you if you would like to be "featured" with a giant photograph in the front window of their studio. The cost can be up to $300 per month but they will assure you that many industry professionals pass by their location daily. This is not a scam but it is a foolish use of your money. In my opinion, it doesn't call attention to you; rather, it calls attention to their headshot business.

Many photo scams are set up by agents who insist you use a certain photographer. This way, the agent gets a kickback from the photographer. By contrast, legitimate agents have photographers they *prefer* to use because of the consistently good photos they produce. An honest agent will let you make the selection so that you can meet and find a photographer you are comfortable with. Good agents can give you a list of several good photographers to contact.

# Professional Managers

Sometimes there are dishonest "professional managers" who advertise in newspapers and industry trade publications. When you meet with one, he or she guarantees to have you submitted frequently to casting directors and promises to let you know to whom you've been submitted. It's a bogus promise. Any management company can purchase casting notices for a fee and submit photos of their clients; but, that does not mean the casting directors will even open the envelope. Casting directors generally won't open a management company envelope unless they are very familiar with the managers and their clients.

Here's another example, a little extreme perhaps but accurate in its intent: A guy who says he is a manager places an ad in an acting newspaper for a project currently being cast. He calls women who do not have agency representation who have submitted their picture for casting and wants to set up an audition with them over the phone. He only approaches girls without agents to see through the scam and protect them. To help convince her of his credibility, the manager tells her that, when she shows up for the audition, she is going to meet the star of the movie. Don't say anything if you recognize him as s former series regular on a 70's hit TV series. Using pseudo fame for bait.

Now this actor, he will tell her, has a sequence in his film that requires him to do a love scene .but . . . he's never done one before. He further confides in her that the actor is really nervous about it and asks her if she can help him rehearse. That way the manager will also get a full report from the TV star of her range of talent. For doing the manager this favor he will, of course, get you a small part in the film, too. Of course.

The girl arrives at an apartment building, not an office and walks into a unit with girlie pictures all over the walls. If she had earlier done her homework and checked this guy out, she would have discovered that the manager who is coercing her into the love scene and the guy from the hit TV series are the same person. The only acting is on the part of the so-called manager.

Here is how a manager really starts out in business. Let's say an agent decides to leave an agency to become a personal manager, which is how it usually happens. He or she takes a handful of top income-producing clients to start the new business. No legitimate personal manager ever looks for new clients by placing an ad or casting notice in any publication.

I have heard from the students in my seminars of managers and some disreputable agents asking clients to contribute $20-200 per month to help with start-up costs of their business such as telephone, casting notices and delivery service. Do not fall for this. You do not need to finance anyone else's growth and education in the entertainment business. If this is offered to you, decline. Report agents to all the Guilds and managers to the Conference of Personal Managers in my phone list.

## Casting Services and Party Networking Groups

Guess what? There is no such thing as a casting service. These are buzz words which, to you, should mean red alert. The people who run ads to lure you in for their "casting services" will show you letters from actors and directors as testimonials to their greatness and to give themselves credibility. In fact, these letters were probably generated on their own computer. You can tell the moment you are being baited because they try to impress you with all the feature films they are "currently working on."

They'll talk about feature films rather than TV shows because they know that anyone can check out a TV show easily enough by calling the network or casting director to verify the personnel roster. When they feel they have you hooked, they begin to reel you in. And, so, comes the request for a large sum of money so that they can place you in their "active" file. The worst of these promotional groups promises to have your picture hand-delivered to all the producers and directors in town who are currently in production. There was some scandal several years ago where it was revealed that one particular company never sent any pictures out but, instead, would stack them in a corner of the office.

Another empty-promise event is the *"industry mixers,"* a visit from a producer, director, or casting director to a gathering of eager actors. Often, these mixers include a preliminary briefing session so the actors will know who the visiting guest is and which project the guest is presently working on. I once saw the name of a TV producer with whom I am familiar on one company's promotional material and asked him why he would lend his name to such a seedy operation. His answer was this: "I go there to find actors who will intern in my office for free and I go there to pick up women." All of this

at a cost of $300 plus a month to you.

Or, here's another bogus bunch: networking groups that will offer to put your picture and resume on **CD Rom.** Every few years the CD Rom approach to casting pops up in Los Angeles—but has never caught on because casting directors do not want to pay for this service when stacks of pictures are delivered daily to their offices.

## Seminars

*"How-to-Get-Ahead-In-The-Business"* seminars are found all over Los Angeles. Some even take their show on the road. Be aware of seminar instructors or consultants who advertise in acting publications; some are cleverly disguised, unsuccessful actors trying to eke out a living. Some seminars are offered in overcoming fears and removing blocks. They are more like therapy. One organization in particular holds its "seminars" at a glitzy sounding center. It sounds good but is tied to a religious organization and comes with a heavy dose of their belief system.

When inquiring about any seminar, ask for an itinerary to make sure you will get the information you want. Don't be afraid to ask for credits and credentials of the seminar leaders. I only take advice from people who are successful at what they are teaching.

## Rich People, Escorts and Hooking

Attractive actors and actresses get approached everyday in Hollywood by individuals offering to introduce an aspiring performer like yourself to wealthy and influential people. An unsavory character like this may offer you a simple job to escort a rich person to the "right" Hollywood parties under the guise that: "If you're nice, this person will help your career." When the wealthy person meets you, he or she will be enchanted with you and will promise to help you with your career. He or she may even go so far as to seduce you with expensive cars, apartments, condos, and a monthly allowance. In reality, rich people have their own agenda and have no vested interest in helping you succeed. In fact, some are so self-serving, they will tell you exactly what you want to hear just to keep you around to service their own needs—not yours. Months and years pass and your career goes nowhere. By the time you realize it, your "package" is shot and used up. Of course, it's been a set-up from the get-go.

If you consider becoming a stripper or a hooker and think no one will be the wiser, think again. When you meet industry people, and I assure you, it will happen, they will not want to be publicly associated with you. In their eyes, you are never considered a serious actor or actress .

Veteran Hollywood writer Nikki Finke in an article from the October 1993 issue of **Details** magazine, outlined how Heidi Fleiss found her prospective call girls. "Heidi used a photographer friend to spot potential call girls. Because actors and models can be so desperate, the Los Angeles market provided her with an endless supply of MAW's—Models, Actresses, Whatever." It may look like easy money at the time, but it is a rough road to go.

## 900 Casting Lines

Telephone casting information is generally ultra-low-budget or no-pay jobs. If you wind up calling these 900 numbers yourself, you'll be kept on the line for long instructions or lead-in messages. If you stay on the line long enough, you'll eventually hear a pre- recorded tape of casting information spoken very, very slowly "so you can write it down." Some of these numbers will charge a long distance fee, plus a fee per minute. In my opinion, they are expensive and worthless.

## "I'll Put You in My Movie"

I've saved the best and most overused line in Hollywood for last. There are many men and women wandering the streets of L.A. claiming to be producers and directors with projects to cast. All it takes to be one of these so-called producers or directors is a business card and a voice mailbox, which anyone can get for $6 a month. They may approach you anywhere or place bogus casting notices in papers. Most will tell you all about their project and convince you how right you might be for a part. Listen carefully to their pitch; they are different from legitimate producers or directors in two critical ways: (1) Wanna-be producers or directors will give you way too much information. It's as though they are trying to sell you on the idea rather than selling it to a potential investor or a studio. and, (2) A less than well-intentioned producer won't want to deal with your agent.

Busy industry professionals don't have time to chat long about a project unless you're investing in their film. Later in this chapter under Be Your Own Detective I will show you how you can determine the legitimacy and intentions of any person donning a professional title in the entertainment industry. In the meantime ask anyone who approaches you these questions to collect information.

**1. What is the budget for the film?**
Two million dollars or less is considered low-budget. A budget of $100,000 or less is a guerrilla shoot, made specifically for video. Generally, these kinds of pictures provide poor working conditions and less than industry-standard demo tape clips for actors. If you just want the experience, only work with people you already know and trust.

## 2. Who are the stars committed and contracted to the project?

If you've never heard of them, unless you are familiar with a producer's or director's name and work, don't be afraid to ask what they've done. If you haven't ever heard of the "star," look him or her up in the *Academy Players Directory* on the fourth floor of the Motion Picture Academy of Arts and Sciences and find out who the "star's" agent is. Call the agent and find out if in fact that star is indeed contracted or attached to the project.

## 3. What other projects have you produced?

See if you recognize any of the credits. Go to the video store and rent their movies to check out their style and quality.

## 4. Who is the casting director on the project?

Remember the name to look up in your *CD Directory,* for sale on our web site to see what other types of projects they have cast.

## 5. Will it be done with a major studio or an independent?

A small production company working under the banner of a major studio or a well-known independent production company, like Artisan (Blair Witch) afford the best credibility. Press for the name of a company. Call the main switchboard on the studio lot or at the independent to get the direct phone number of the production office to verify it's existence and ask if that person works there and their title.

## 6. When is your start date?

Casting is generally done a month or two before the start date.

## 7. Is your money in place?

The answer to this last question is the most difficult area to verify. If the money isn't in place, the entire project is, at that point, just a hope or fantasy. Other than checking with the film maker's bank to see if there are funds in some kind of production or escrow account, which the bank may or may not tell you, the only thing you have left to substantiate a money-in-place claim is . . . your intuition. So, watch their eyes closely, see if they balk with their answers, and listen for your own inner alarm bells as faint as they may be.

There are a lot of people attending cocktail parties who say they are producers in the hopes of getting lucky for the evening. The real ones will stand up to any scrutiny.

Some schemers will try to lure you in with promises of a part in a film. Sound familiar? Be on the lookout for "producers" with impressive monologues; like, those who sometimes drop the name of a star whom they claim to know very well or those who start hanging out with you and tell you how much talent and big-star potential you have.

Somewhere down the line, they may hit you up for money so that they can fly themselves somewhere to "arrange the rest of the financing." And do I even have to elaborate about the extent to which some of these phonies will go to flatter you as a build-up to press you for sexual favors? Complying with their wishes is a one-way ticket to nowhere.

An example of such shady practices: A charlatan producer (usually as desperate to get work as you are) will call a small talent agency looking for a girl whose photo he's seen in the very reputable industry directory. He says he wants her to come in to do a screen test for the lead in a huge film. He promises contracts to

follow and works out a screen test deal with the small agent.

Naturally, he would like her to come to the office and meet the executive producer first. The appointment is set late in the day. Upon arrival she is given a script and a tour of the offices. But . . . the executive producer never shows. Then, the phone rings; and the actress and the producer have to go meet the exec for dinner. At dinner, while waiting for this mystery man to appear, the producer woos the girl with flowers, an expensive meal and lots of liquor. The executive producer still never shows. (Who would have guessed?) Finally, the payoff: he explains to the girl that his own claim to fame is that he is a sought-after lover and produces magazine articles to prove it. Ladies all over the world want him, but he wants you. Sound far-fetched? Two very upset and scared actresses called me with the same story or I wouldn't have believed it either.

## Be Your Own Detective

Actors, all too often, are afraid to ask questions for fear of becoming a threat or a nuisance to people who are in a position to forward their career. Reputable producers, directors, agents, casting directors, personal managers, etc., will willingly and easily be able to answer any questions you have about their credentials. So, if you're in doubt about someone's credibility, take that person's card, be friendly and start checking him or her out.

## Checking People Out

At the end of the previous section, you were given a few questions to ask when checking out a producer, director or a specific project. This section gives you organizational and publication resources to do just that.

If you want to check out a director, look up the **Directors Guild of America (DGA)**, in our phone book in the back. Each year, the DGA publishes a list of its membership at a cost of $15.00 per copy. This list includes the name of a member director, that director's agent or a contact address and a list of the director's credits. So, if a director with whom you are unfamiliar approaches you for work, use the DGA membership list to see what other films he or she might have directed.

If you are approached by a first-time director to appear in a low budget film, checking the person out will be difficult because no information about that director will be listed anywhere. In that the case, do some research. Locate a title to a film that director may have associations, possibly co-producing. If you find one, rent it. When you watch the film, analyze the production quality, lighting, directing and writing to decide if having a piece of tape of your work with that director would be of benefit to you. If you are brand new to the business, you might want to consider doing that director's project just for the experience; but, expect to be paid little or nothing, to use your own clothes, to do your own make up and, generally, to work under poor conditions with extremely long hours.

## Research Resources

Great sources for researching people, places and things in the entertainment industry is the internet and in NY or LA **Samuel French Bookstores.** Many of the books there can assist you in finding the credits you are looking for You can probably browse through a display copy on the shelf to run down anyone's credits.

One of the most comprehensive lists of entertainment industry professionals is The *Hollywood Creative Directory.* They have about nine separate directories depending on the area of interest. The *Hollywood Creative Directory* has over 6,000 names of studio, network and production company executives. Most of the lists run about $50. *The Hollywood Creative Directory* can also be be found in our phone book.

*Hollywood Creative Directory* can also be be found in our phone book.

Another company, **Hollyware Film Credits,** puts out a *Directors Reference Guide.* Still another is *Michael Singer's Film Directors, A Complete Guide*. He also publishes listings for producers, casting directors, writers and TV directors. Both the Director's Reference Guide and Michael Singer's Film Director's, A Complete Guide give a full range of credits on every reputable film. Both are also available at **Samuel French Bookstores.**

## Checking Out Casting Directors

If you need to check out a casting director, contact **The Casting Society of America (CSA).** CSA publishes a list of credits of their membership each year. Not all casting directors are member of **CSA**; but if they are, it is your guarantee of a person with a high level of commitment to his or her work. There is also the *CD Directory* which details most of the active casting directors and their office addresses is in our phone book in the back.

There are things you can do on your own to supplement the organizational and publication support you use: (1) to check out a casting director, call the production company they claim to be hired by and find out if, in fact, they are casting the project they claim to be working on; (2) contact an agent (yours, if you have one; a friend's if you don't) to see if they are familiar with the person you're checking on; (3) talk to everyone you can think of, including the people who introduced you to the person you're checking up on; (4) call your acting coach; or, talk to other actors who read *Variety* and *The Hollywood Reporter* everyday to determine if anyone knows anything about the person you are checking out. However you go about it, just remember, knowledge is power.

## It Can Happen Anywhere

Most approaches come in ordinary places—restaurants, walking down the street, cocktail parties, etc.—by men and women trying desperately to find quick and easy sex. Novice actors are easy prey. And gentlemen, not all of the perpetrators are men, some women and gay men pull these antics too.

Now, this is not to say that there aren't plenty of well-known producers and directors who won't try to get in your pants. There are some actors and actresses who do, and it can get very uncomfortable. You have to ask yourself: Would I go out with this person even if they didn't make movies? Many actors have slept their way to the top, but not without a very heavy emotional price.

## Fighting Back

If someone does manage to scam you, the most important thing you can do is fight back! There are some good folks who are ready, willing and able to help listed in the back of the book under Help I've Been Scammed. In the Appendix, you will find a copy of an article entitled "Glam Scam—What's Wrong With This Picture?" originally published in *Locations Magazine*—**Expo '94 Issue,** written by Erik Joseph, the Assistant Director of the **Nevada Film Office.** It covers several kinds of scams currently being perpetrated on models and actors across the country and is well worth reading.

# Chapter 4

# Say "Cheese" Please

*Our deepest fear is not that we are inadequate.*
*Our deepest fear is that we are powerful beyond measure.*
*It is our light, not our darkness, that most frightens us.*
*We ask ourselves, who am I to be brilliant, gorgeous,*
*talented and fabulous?*
*Actually, who are you not to be?*
*You are a child of God.*
*Your playing small doesn't serve the world.*
*There's nothing enlightened about shrinking so that*
*other people won't feel insecure around you.*
*We were born to make manifest the glory of God that is*
*within us.*
*It's not just in some of us; it's in everyone.*
*And as we let our own light shine, we unconsciously*
*give other people permission to do the same.*
*As we are liberated from our own fear,*
*our presence automatically liberates others.*

**Nelson Mandela**
**—1994 Inaugural Speech**

Once you've decided upon an image, the next step is taking that image and getting it in front of the faces of people who have a strong interest in doing something with it. The most powerful way of gaining the attention of agents, casting directors, producers and/or directors is with photographs.

In this chapter, I will show you the three types of photo formats that are customarily used in the entertainment industry. By using the criteria I've established, you'll learn how to identify the kind of high-quality photographs required by industry standards. Once you can distinguish good photos from bad, you'll be able to select the right professional photographer to shoot your pictures. Also, I'll coach you through a photo session and offer you some suggestions on how you might want to have your photos processed. Also you will have to check out prospective photographers using the tips from Chapter 3.

## The Photograph

One of the most important instruments you'll need in order to command the attention of key industry professionals is your headshot. *"Headshot"* is an industry term used to designate an 8" x 10" photograph for theatrical and television purposes. A headshot can be either a photo of the head and face thus, the name "headshot" or it can be a photo depicting three-quarters of the whole body.

## Different Styles of Photographs

If an actor or model is seeking work in commercials, submitting a headshot to agents and casting directors is now the standard practice. The trend used to be to submit a *"composite."* A composite is an 8" x 10" photograph made up of smaller shots depicting different "looks" or images. Both headshots and composites are routinely printed in black and white.

The third kind of photo format is a variation of the composite. It's called a *"model Zed card."* What distinguishes a model Zed card from a regular headshot or a composite is that Zed cards measure 8 1/2" x 5 1/2" inches and are printed on two. Busy working models may have four or six sided ones on a folded card. The photo on the front of the card is a headshot, usually in color. The back includes an array of photos that illustrates an model's different "looks," such as: casual, beach, family or relationship shots, athletic or fun energy shots and classy, elegant shots including a three-quarter length body shot.

## What's Hip and Happening

Ask a hundred people and you'll get a hundred different opinions about what works in a headshot. The latest trend in Hollywood for theatrical headshots is: the moodier the better. Your face should tell a story. You can work with a budding family photographer to see what clothes work to present your "image." But, better to wait until you get to a major market to get your photos done. The professionals here know the market better than cousin Billy "the photographer" back home. And, don't even think about having your friends take your picture. You'll be laughed right out of casting offices.

If you want to get a good idea of what casting directors look for in a good headshot, in LA go to the **Academy of Motion Picture Arts and Sciences** and page through current issues of ***The Academy Players Directory***. In New York, Chicago and Miami you can go to the Agency Division of both Screen Actors Guild or AFTRA to look through their copies of these directories.

Look at your competition's' headshots and notice how they have polished and projected their chosen image. Observe which photos draw your attention and why. You can use your research for ideas of poses to try with your photographer when you shoot your own headshot. Check out photos in any fashion magazine to get ideas for photo layouts for you to recreate with your photographer?

At the end of this chapter there are samples of headshots, composites and Zed Cards used by working actors. For example, you will see how commercial shots have an upbeat quality that differs from theatrical shots. Look at the hometown headshot that actress Lauren Renihan was generous enough to share with us. Notice the contrasting image of a stunning, easy-going confidence created by a seasoned industry professional after she arrived in Los Angeles. See the difference? I want to express my gratitude to Lauren. This lovely lady put aside any embarrassment so that you, the reader could learn from her photographic experience.

## Finding the Right Photographer

Your headshot is your calling card. The entire decision that a casting director, producer or director makes to call you in for an audition rides on the quality of your photographs; so, spend some money and choose your photographer carefully.

According to photographer Robert Kim, some of the key questions you should ask a professional photographer whom you are considering to shoot your photos are:

• Cost of shooting fees. Some may require a deposit to hold your appointment.
- How many rolls will be shot and how many 8 X 10's are included?
- How much do additional prints cost and can you keep the negatives?
- How much time will the photographer give you to take pictures?

•Will makeup and hair be included in the cost?

The most important aspect of deciding on the right professional photographer to shoot your photos is your relationship with the one you finally choose. Ideally, what you should experience around them is a sense of mutual trust and a natural, easy, comfortable feeling between the two of you? Who makes you feel relaxed when you interviewed them?

## What You See, Is What You Get

Equally important is a photographer's professional skills. Meet with several photographers and go through their portfolios of headshots. Don't be unduly impressed by pictures of beautiful models and famous actors. Every photographer has shot at least one famous person. As you're examining each portfolio, look to see if the pictures are interesting to you. Ask yourself the same questions an agent or casting director would ask themselves:

- Would I want to meet the person in this photo?
- Does the photo bring out an interesting quality of the person being shot?
- Do the eyes "pop"? That is, are they full of life and sparkle? Do they evoke a mood?
- Are the photographer's pictures of men, women and people of color all equally dynamic?
- Is the photograph in focus?

## Where to Find Photographers

Call all the agents in your city and ask for a referral list of photographers. Ask other actors and models. Check out photography classes at Universities and Art Schools if you are a modeling trying to build an affordable portfolio. Art photographers cannot be used by actors though. Lastly, check out our web site for a recent list of professionals in most major cities. Actors and models in LA can use the list of my personal photographers in the back of this book.

To secure the vast array of photos needed to build your Zed card, go to the top modeling agents in any city and ask them for a list of *"test photographers."* Those are photographers who are building their portfolio. If you think you might want to use a test photographer, you can usually barter your modeling fees in exchange for their photographers' fees.

## Photo Shoot Do's and Don'ts

Dress for your image. Sell your abilities. Have a relaxed expression unless you're a comedic type or are taking commercial shots. Show your personality. Say something with the photo. Please yourself. The photo must look just like you when you walk in for the audition. If you have make up or a hair style in the picture that you won't be able to reproduce for the audition—don't do it! Nothing upsets casting people more than photos that don't look like you.

Don't wear wild jewelry or hats. Don't wear glasses—unless you wear them all the time in life. No busy prints or wild stripes in clothing. Keep your hands away from your face. Not too much makeup or cleavage. No two-day stubble shots for men unless you are trying to create a character. Don't stay up late or drink the night before a shoot Look your well-rested best.

## Wardrobe Tips

The most important thing to remember about wardrobe is that you should be comfortable. For a casual look, both men and women should consider cotton shirts, denim or plaid, textured sweaters, jeans and catsuits. When creating the business look men should wear suits, jackets, vests, and power ties. For women, wear elegant but simple dresses. Also,

blouses that are silk or lacy and bring some lingerie teddies and camisoles; they make great tops. Referring back to the different types in the image chapter here are hints.

Rulers should think Armani for an upscale look and the horsey polo wear reflected by Ralph Lauren for the casual look. For the Leader, think Brooks Brothers for men and Ann Taylor for women. If you are an All-American for your upscale look, think Calvin Klein and casual lifestyle reflected by The Gap. For the Rebel, consider shopping at trendy boutiques to get that upscale look and thrift stores for a more down scale version of yourself.

## Make Up

If your photo shoot does not include the services of a make up artist/hair stylist, I insist you book one yourself. Most photographers have one they

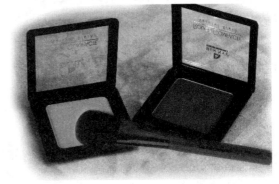

like working with, but if not, there are a few very talented stylists I have used over the years listed in the phone directory. Don't blow your photo session by scrimping on money and not hiring a professional. Street make up is not enough.

If you can't afford to hire a make up artist and plan to do your own make up, the people at **MAC Cosmetics** offer an industry discount of 30%. If you want a make up lesson, they offer a package deal: $90 gets you 90 minutes of lessons from a professional make-up artist, a video to take home with you, and a tube of mascara. So, there's no excuse to look like a Plain Jane at those photo sessions. Bring your SAG card and driver's license to set up the account. **MAC** has a wonderful line of make-up and a staff of professional artists to show you how to use it.

Beauty supply stores will often offer you a 10f% for make up and hair care products if you explain you are a model or actor.

## Beauty Tips

If you have a pimple the night before a shoot, don't try to pop it; that will just irritate the skin. Put toothpaste on it overnight and that will shrink the blemish. Conceal with **Joe Blasco Red Neutralizer Makeup** available at the **Joe Blasco Make-Up Center**. They offer discounts to actors. If your face is puffy, apply ice before make-up. If you have fatigue lines or wrinkles that you don't normally have, apply Preparation H Suppository Cream to your face. It smells bad but it works. What also works on puffy eyes is applying ice packs or using Mary Kay Instant Action Eye Cream, which shrinks swelling immediately. Don't cover up any natural wrinkles. Casting people love our character lines these days. Women should use a professional makeup artist. Men, on the other hand, need not worry about putting on make-up.

## Borders On Photos

The time to decide which borders are right for your picture is when they are processing your original 8 x 10 print. Discuss this with your photographer and let them know what you want. If someone suggests that you print your photo *"borderless,"* that means the picture takes up the full space of the paper with no white borders around the edges. If you use borders, get a nice, clean square for theatrical shots. Select either a clean square or the recently popular sloppy borders for commercial shots. *"Sloppy borders"* look uneven, as though they were painted on with a paint brush.

## How Many to Print

Before you print your pictures in 8x10 size, have the photographer print up photos you think you will like in a 4x6 size. This will help you to decide and save lots of money.

Your first set of photos will be used to try and land an agent, print only a short run of about 25-50 photos. The reason for this is that, if you find an Agent interested in representing you, he or she may select a different photo than the one that you chose; then, you will be stuck with an expensive pile of expensive photographs you can't use.

Once you and the agent have agreed on the right headshot, you can mass-produce them on photo paper or lithography. There's a lot more to know about printing your photograph, and we'll go into further detail about that in the next chapter on the rest of the publicity package

## Retouching and Airbrushing

Currently, retouched photos is a sticky subject with L.A. casting directors and agents alike. They want to see all your characters lines also called wrinkles and skin quality. The "real" look is currently vogue. So, there's what you can retouch. Flyaway hair in your eyes, sloppy eyeliner, red eyes, zits. Retouchers can also whiten eyes and add more shadowing or eye lashes. Hopefully, you picked a good photographer and make up artist so there won't be much work. If your skin has "pock marks" from acne, don't airbrush them away. See a dermatologist before shooting pictures; they have a new technique to eliminate them.

## Dress Rehearsal & Prep

Try all your photo clothes on prior to the shoot. Make sure everything fits and is comfortable. Dry clean and press everything. Put shoes and matching stockings in a travel bag. Take off most all your jewelry and don't wear a watch.

Now for your emotional preparation. I want you to get a Thesaurus. It is a dictionary that has words that all mean the same thing. Think about what your selling with your image. Is it honesty, leadership, aloofness, danger? Start looking up words and make of list of verbs. Verbs are action words. Put the best ones on 3"x5" cards. It is impossible to take a boring shot when you are looking though the lens and trying to effect change in the photographer. Make them feel you speaking to them with your eyes.

I don't know how to act sexy but I do know how to be seductive, flirtatious and provocative. It's difficult to play tough or but you can be assertive, rowdy, inflexible or stubborn. You get the picture, or rather the dictionary. It's all in your asserting the words.

## The Day Of

Expect to be a little bit nervous even if you are a seasoned veteran. It's normal. I realize it is just my body giving me adrenaline to help me make something magical. Decide on a order for the shoot. I usually go with casual to dressed up and put on the first outfit.

Bring some of your favorite music. Put it on, place your 3x5's on the ground and go. Breat and trust the univese to help you with the magic. You'll be both amazed and pleased!

## A Word of Caution

Now what I'm about to tell you is very important; so, pay close attention. Watch out for any talent agents who insist on using their photographer. If an agent won't consider other photographers, it is highly probable that this agent is getting a percentage of your fees in kickbacks. Also, be wary of any photographer associated with an acting school because they are frequently offered as a package deal with classes and are generally considered sub-standard in the industry.

These are extremely unethical and unprofessional practices. So, if you run into any scenarios like the ones I've just described, there's only one thing you really have to do...**RUN THE OTHER WAY!**

## Cheap and Sorry

There are many photographers who advertise in **Backstage West** and claim that they can deliver your ideal photographs for as little as $35. Lots of actors have used them with disappointing results. One such actor reported to me: "I thought I could get away with getting my headshots done as cheaply as possible. The ads sounded good. So, I tried it. I threw my money away and got what I paid for." That's why spending the extra money with a respected and well-known professional is work the effort. Photos from a reputable photographer will last about two years. One of the best resources for photographers is your fellow actors who have great photo experiences and can tell you something like: "Since I got these new photos, I'm going out on interviews all the time." If you have an agent ask to see the photo of the people in their talent pool who book the most jobs. Then go see them.

Jennifer Hipp

Jennifer Hipp's photo is marqueed using a "lots of white" layout.
Photo by Melinda Kelley (818) 353-8008

**Randy Close**

A moody, hip headshot currently very popular in Hollywood.
Photo by Mark Atteberry, Idyllic Photography (310) 226-7110

Lauren's home-town headshot and the professional photo that replaced it in Los Angeles.

Photo by Theo and Juliet Zeif-Fridluis—(323) 896-9693

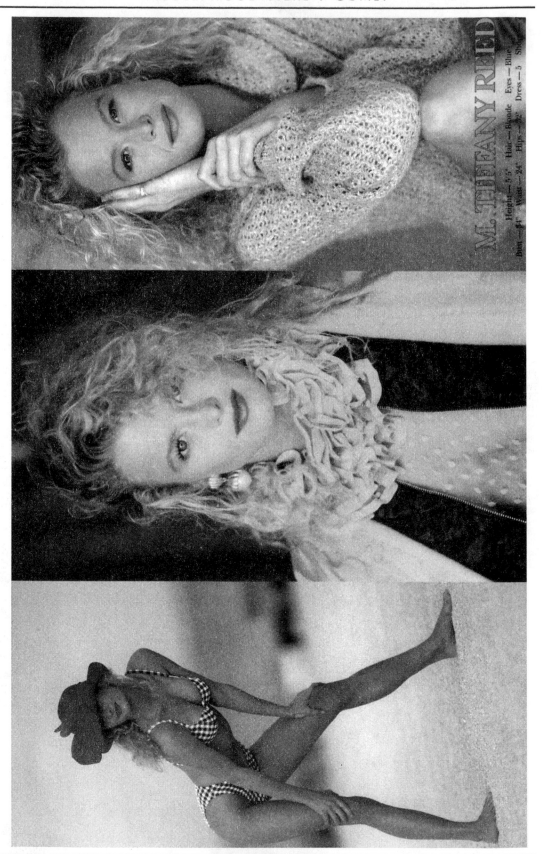

A Zed card: 8 1/2" x 16" folded in thirds. Photo: Jerry Hinkle—(305) 595-4905

M. TIFFANY RED

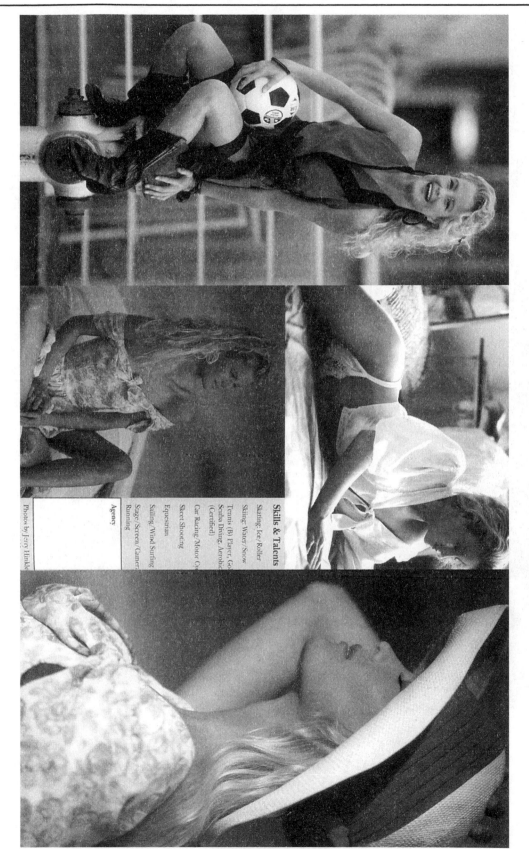

Skills & Talents

Skating: Ice/Roller

Skiing: Water/Snow

Tennis (B Player); Go

Scuba Diving; Aerobic

(Certified)

Car Racing/Motor Cy

Skeet Shooting

Equestrian

Sailing/Wind Surfing

Stage/Screen/Camera

Running

Agency

Photos by Jerry Hinkle

The inside of the Zed card from the previous page. It is printed in black and white.

**Michael Cutt - Two time Clio Award
Winner for TV Commercials**

Another hip layout is to put a photo on it's side like this.
Photo by Heather Dobson (213) 444-0116

# Chapter 5

# The Rest of the Package

O K. Get ready. We're heading into the final stretch here with your photos. In this chapter, I'll discuss the two ways in which you can print your photograph. Then, I'll show you how to package your photo with your resume and get ready to take it . . . on the road and out into the world. If you take my advice you will have a more professional look than most of your competition. Stick with me, and I'll make your journey a whole lot easier.

## Photos verses Lithos

What distinguishes a photograph from a lithograph is the method of reproducing the final print. A photograph is printed from a negative while a lithograph is printed from a plate. It used to be that theatrical shots were only reproduced in limited quantities using a costly photographic printing procedure. Commercial shots were done in larger quantities using the lesser expensive lithograph process. Now both are equally accepted by agencies and casting people as long as the pictures are sharp, clear and non-grainy. Zed cards, however, are always reproduced using the litho process. Photographs are a little bit more costly than lithos but you get a truer print of the original negative with a photo.

## Photos

Once your photograph is processed, you will be charged for both the 8 x 10 negative and a "name strip." A name strip is your name set in type and made up in negative form. Pick a type style that fits your image but is also very readable. Always have your name on your picture in case it gets separated from your resume. It happens a lot. Keep your photo negative and name strip if a safe place because you will need to reuse them when ordering more photos. Name strips can be transferred from negative to negative; this way you avoid paying $10.00 or so to get a new one each time. Pictures take time, usually about a week. So, order them well in advance to avoid rush fees.

When you get your first set of headshots and want to send it out to find an agent, start out with a small mailing. This is a great way to test the waters and see what the response is to your pictures. After you first sign on with a talent agency, they'll probably distribute your photo and, subsequently, deplete your supply pretty quickly. Once you acquire an agent, he or she will pick a new photo from your proof sheet or use the one you selected. Then you can order larger quantities and reduce your cost per copy.

When it's time to print more of your pictures, you might consider lithos—but ask the agency how they feel about it first. A good agent should be savvy about the quality of photos you will need to attract the attention of casting directors. One agent I signed with insisted that I use a particular photo reprinting house which, I later discovered, produced poor quality results. Not only did that printing house generate poor quality workmanship, but the printer charged extra for everything. It wasn't a case of kickbacks so much as that particular agent, who was new to the business, just didn't know any better. Remember, some new agents in the business may not know any more than you about this area.

Most good companies offer short runs on photos so that you can test your headshot to see if it's going to be effective or long runs of 100 or more if you find it works. My favorite picks are up on the web site and in the phone directory.

## Lithography

"Lithography" is a printing—not a photographic—process. Lithos are substantially cheaper and are printed on heavier paper than are photographs. Prices for lithos include your negative, which the printers keep on file with your name strip.

Commercial agents and casting directors have always used this cheaper process. Some theatrical agents like them and some don't. Check before printing. You can get anything from 100-500 photos using this process. I suggest you get a short run of 25 photos not lithos with your commercial headshot to find an agent. Once you sign with an agent, you can both decide on a permanent photo to run off in larger quantities by using the cheaper lithography process for 8 x 10's. Lithographs take anywhere from a week to 14 days to get printed; so, plan ahead. A comprehensive list of lithographers with two that ship anywhere in the world are listed in the back of the book.

## Packaging Your Photo

Having completed the photo process and printed your photo, you're now ready to package it. Packaging your photo means nothing more than attaching a resume and preparing the completed package with a letter of introduction for a mailing to solicit agents, casting directors, etc.

You letter of introduction can be a piece of good paper cut in thirds down the page and turned longways so it will not cover up your headshot. In the letter you will reintegrate your elevator speech. Remind them again who you are and how they can sell you. So, now, let's take a look at the resume and I'll show you how to tailor one that rocks the house without lying.

## Resumes

In the beginning of your career, no one will expect you to have an extensive resume. The best thing you can do for yourself is to begin building a resume while you're still living in your hometown.

Before leaving home, accumulate as many credits as you can from as many different venues. Perform in as many local theater or fashion productions as you can, whether they be in school, public theater or charity events. Or, try getting hired on one of your area's local TV shows, perform in a commercial spot or do a print ad for one of your area's local merchants. Getting a job like this would be a great advantage, even if it's only a one time deal for no pay. These credits will still help to build your resume. It is about building a body of work over a long period of time

Here is another other idea for gathering credits in your home town. Every local cable station has a public access channel. By law, anyone with an idea for a show can apply and be given access to use the public airwaves. With the exception of pornography, the content of a show can range anywhere along the creative spectrum: from cooking, doing scenes from plays, talk show formats or anything your imagination can come up with.

Two of my friends played a couple of burnt out surfer dude's who did movie reviews a la Siskel and Ebert. They called their show *"SURF DUDE'S AT THE MOVIES."* To pay their expenses, they got the local **AMC Movie Theater** to sponsor them. AMC gave them free movie passes to watch the movies and review them. Their cable show was hilarious and had quite a following. If you're interested in doing a public access cable show so that you can add a credit to your resume check out our web site at www.hollywood-hereicome.com and order the book called *How to Star in Your Own TV Show for $50 or Less.* Then call your local public access station for details on producing your own show. Or, alternately, find out if anyone else is producing a public access show on which you can perform. In Chapter 7 I will go into further detail with ideas on how to build film and television credits while you're still living in your home town.

## Drafting Your Resume

The intention of this section is to give you every opportunity to have the best, most truthful resume possible. So, be forewarned: If you lie on your resume, you're treading on dangerous ground. For example, a casting director could call you in and see that you've mentioned a film or TV show which they might have previously cast. If they discover that you've lied to them, not only will you have to endure a very nerve-wracking, accusatory interview but you could get black-listed by that office. To make matter worse, they may call your agent and you could lose your representation as well.

With that in mind, let's start drafting your resume. Let's assume you already have some credits under your belt. Resumes are laid out in a specific order. At the top of the page, your name should be centered—in big letters. Upper and lower case, rather than all upper case is more readable.

Directly under that list any union you have joined and are current with the dues. Under your union affiliations and to the left-hand side of the page is where you list height, weight, eyes and hair color.

To the right hand-side of the page is where your agent's logo with phone number appear. If you have no representation and are doing your first mailing, this is where your service phone number appears. **Never** list your address or home number . . . never, never, never! These resumes are regularly discarded in the trash and can be picked up by anyone; so, spend the $6 per month and get a voice mailbox to route calls to until you land an agent to protect you.

Next, make three columns. These columns are for information pertaining to each of the different categories or formats in which you have worked. So, for your first category, print the word "Film." Place the title of the film in the first column. As you start listing your film work, I recommend that you name your most well-known film at the top, not the most recent work you have done. Across from the title, in the second column, put the size of the role (i.e., Starring, Co-Starring, Featured, etc.). Finally, place the name of the studio or production company followed by a slash and the director's name in the third column. Never list your character's' name, it will peg you as an amateur. Don't forget student films.

The next category below Film is "Television." When you first begin to build a resume, you may want to combine these two categories—especially if you have only a few credits. In the first column, put the name of the TV show and designate whether it's a Pilot, a MOW (Movie of the Week), or a Mini-Series. For regular weekly episodics you don't have to list anything but the name of the show. In the middle column list whether your role was either a Lead, a Series Regular, Recurring, Guest Starring, or a Supporting role. "Series Regular" can be used if you were on a series in which you had a weekly role or even if it was on a pilot which was canceled after one show. Recurring means you're not on the show every week but your character comes back from time to time. "Guest Starring" covers roles that are featured for one week on an existing series. "Supporting" is a word I use to indicate roles in which an actor has five lines or less. Supporting roles are, also, known in industry slang as "5 and unders." Frequently used on soaps, "5 and unders" carry the onus of being only slightly better than an Extra. My word gives the actor some dignity because any actor working today rarely does a scene alone; therefore, he or she is supporting all of his fellow actors' work. The latest trend has been to leave the words "guest starring" and "supporting" off the resume and only label the shows in which you were a Series Regular or Recurring Actor. All the shows you appeared on, in whatever capacity, are listed.

The category following Film and Television is "Commercials." Beginning actors with scant credits may need to use a Commercial category in order to fill up the space on the resume. Never itemize your commercials, whether you have them to list or not. Simply print "List available upon request" under this category. This is done for two reasons: First, because your general resume will also be used as your commercial resume. You won't want a prospective advertising client to discount you because you might have done a commercial years ago with the advertising client's competitor. If Lexus, for example, wants to hire you but sees Ford Motor Company listed on your resume, they will think it might be currently airing and will not hire you because it presents a conflict to their ad.

Secondly, listing all your commercial credits makes you look like a novice. Advertising agencies are always looking for a new fresh face. You first-timers, try to do some local commercials in your home town, even if it is for a friend and you are paid little or no money for the job.

The next category under Commercials is a special category for beauty queens, stand-up comics, MC's, magicians, disc jockeys or other professional performers. The category title will vary according to what you do. In this case, list the personal appearance, comedy club, radio station, charity event, etc., in the first column. Leave the second column blank Then, place the city in which you performed in the third column.

"Theater" or "Theatre" whichever way you like to spell it is next. List the name of the play in the first column, the character you played or the size of the role in the second column followed by the name of the theater followed by a slash and the director's name in the third column. If your performance was done in school: every school theater has a name so list it like that as Robert Fulton Theater instead of Marion Middle School Christmas Play. If you happen to have performed in a New York theater, refer to each one in your resume as either Broadway or Off Broadway. Everything else is Off-Off Broadway. Los Angeles still loves and respects a strong theater background; so, I can't stress enough doing as many plays as possible.

Next is the "Training" category. Many casting directors pay special attention to this area to see who you study with and if you are currently studying some form of your craft. This can include: runway modeling, fashion print, cold-reading, scene study, voice, movement, dance, stage combat, improvisation or stand-up comedy. List the type of class and the name of the teacher. Follow this with the city you studied in. Also list any degrees involving theater or cinema from a college.

The last category is "Affiliations and Awards." This is optional. If you received a nomination for a local TV award, a drama award, or if you belong to an industry related organization (e.g., **Women in Film**), you can list it here as a conversation piece. If you were voted Miss Congeniality or participated in a beauty pageant, that can go here as well. However, if you received awards in a charm or modeling school, it's best to leave them off. That smacks of amateurism.

Finally, list your "Special Skills" across the bottom of your resume. Here you list: any foreign languages and dialects you can speak fluently; a musical instrument, if you play very well; your hobbies; and all sports with a skill level high enough to perform in a commercial, film or on television. If you lie about this category and are hired for a job and cannot perform the sport or whatever, you will be dropped by your agent and blackballed by that casting director, production company and sponsor. Just concentrate on things you do well. You can expand this list as you acquire more skills.

## Typesetting Your Resume

Now that we've covered the content of your resume, let's lay it out. It's preferable to layout your resume yourself on a home computer using a graphic design program. That way you can try many different styles and save lots of money. Professional typesetters charge $5-$20 to layout your resume the first time and print one copy. Your resume will be kept on file and each time it is updated the cost is approximately $5-$10. If you need a good one check the phone book in the back.

## Paper

Next,  go to a paper company and pick up a ream of good paper. Marble, parchment or light-colored paper is great, costing about $10-$15 a ream. Never print your resume on red, green, dark brown or deep blue paper because it is difficult to read. Next, get a piece of heavy, white paper to use in the initial layout of your resume. Using the top and left-hand margin, position the paste-up of your resume on the heavy paper; this way, you only have to cut the resume along the right side and the bottom so that it winds up measuring 8" x 10."

Take your paste-up to anyone one of the **Staples Office Supply Stores or Office Depot** anywhere in the U.S. and get 100 prints copied on your paper at a cost of $3. They also have a great selection of nice paper for your resume. Other paper stores in LA are in the phone directory.

## Xeroxing Your Resumes

Now you need to cut your resume down to 8" x 10". Either buy a paper cutter for about $30 at **Staples or Office Depot** or get the copy store to cut them. The cost is $1-$2 per cut. See? That paper cutter will pay for itself in no time. Now you're not just an actor or model, but a creative graphic artist as well!

Of course, if you have a computer, all this typesetting business is unnecessary. So, if your computer has a choice of fonts and you feel that you can do a competent job, go ahead and lay your resume out yourself. Just make sure that the font is easy to read. And make sure you use a good quality paper. Although you will still need a paper cutter to cut your 8 1/2" x 11" paper down to the standard 8" x 10" size, make sure that you set the proper margins on your computer so that your text fits well within the newly cut 8" x 10" paper. Then, print out as many copies as you need from your computer. Or, just print out one copy and go to the nearest copy store to get as many copies made as you need on the appropriate paper.

## Putting It All Together

It bears mentioning that both the resume and the photo should be attached to each other—facing out. To attach the back of your resume to the back of your picture, you can use one of two techniques: either (1) staple it or, (2) for a more polished look, use **Scotch Photo Mount Spray Adhesive** or **Elmer's Glue Stick** to glue it on. Now your package is ready to rock & roll. Submit away to prospective agents and casting directors with the confide of a seasoned veteran.

## A Pictures Worth 1,000 Words

Here are some examples of resumes—from beginning actors to seasoned veterans—that demonstrate some of the styles and approaches you can use to be as simple or creative as you want with your layout.

All right, everybody, fasten your seat belts. It's going to be a wild ride. It's time to go out into the real world. To make your ride easier and safer, I'm going to first give you a road map that will tag all the potholes and road hazards in your way. The next chapter will detail all the kinds of scams you will run into from people who have an agenda other than an authentic desire to see you succeed. Nervous? Don't be. I'll teach to how to recognize charlatans. You'll get to where you're going . . . and stay out of harms way. Besides, what is life if not an adventure?

*THIS EXAMPLE SHOWS GOOD USE OF SPACE ON A NEW ACTRESSeS RESUME:*

# Lauren Renihan                    **AFTRA**

Height: 5'5 1/2"                         (818) 506-0875
Weight: 125
Hair: Amazing Auburn
Eyes: Cobalt Blue

## FILM/TELEVISION

| | | |
|---|---|---|
| School Specials | Host | WHLO. Boston |
| | | Jay Greenberg, Director |
| The Mosaic Project | Supporting | Caroli Pictures |
| | | Jon Sjogren, Director |
| The Bastard | Supporting | TO BE Productions |
| | | Thomas Bolger, Director |

## THEATER

| | | |
|---|---|---|
| Absurd Person Singular | Lead | Atwood Theater |
| | | Peter Klaus, Director |
| My Cup Runneth Over | Lead | Brimmer Street Theater |
| | | Rebecca Messer, Director |
| Hurly Burly | Supporting | Blackman Theater |
| | | Bruce Hoffmann, Director |
| Geography of a Horse Dreamer | Co-Lead | Foothills Theater |
| | | Colleen O'Laughlin, Director |

## COMMERCIALS       List Available upon request

## TRAINING

| | | |
|---|---|---|
| Scene Study | Cameron Thor | *Currently studying |
| Improvisation | Avery Schreiber | |
| Voice | Laura Hart | *Currently studying |
| Commercial Workshop | Stuart Robinson | |

## SPECIAL SKILLS/INTERESTS:

DIALECTS: Southern, British Cockney and Australian.
LANGUAGES: Conversational Spainish, Fluent in Italian
Singing - Second Alto, Musical Instruments: Piano, Violin,

Tennis, Ice Skating, Photography, Painting, Sewing

**NOTICE THE NICE USE OF LARGER TYPE TO FILL THE PAGE.**

# Al Sapienza
## SAG/AFTRA/AEA/ARM

**Theatrical:**
**THE IRV SCHECHTER COMPANY**
9300 Wilshire Boulevard, Suite 410
Beverly Hills, CA 90212
(310) 278-8070/FAX (310) 278-6058

**Management:**
**JEFF WALD**
Entertainment Inc.
Scott Hart
(310) 442-3517

## FILMS

| | | PRODUCER/DIRECTOR |
|---|---|---|
| PRETTY WOMAN | | Touchstone/Garry Marshall |
| FRANKIE & JOHNNY | | Paramount/Garry Marshall |
| STRANGERS | Starring | Propaganda/David Lynch |
| CIA II: TARGET ALEXA | | PMEnt./Lorenzo Lamas |
| FINE THINGS (MOW) | | NBC/Tom Moore |
| HER SECRET LIFE (MOW) | | NBC/Buzz Kulik |
| THE FOURTH MAN (MOW) | | CBS/Joanna Lee |

## TELEVISION

| | | |
|---|---|---|
| E.R. | Recurring | NBC/Peter Bonerz |
| REASONABLE DOUBTS | Recurring | Lorimar/Robert Singer |
| MAN ABOUT TOWN | Pilot | MTM/David Steinberg |
| MATLOCK | | Viacom/Richard Lang |
| RENEGADE | | Cannell-Segall/Jim Bagdonas |
| FALCON CREST (2 Episodes) | | Lorimar/Reza Badiyi |
| CAGNEY & LACEY (2 Episodes) | | Orion/Sharron Miller |
| WHO'S THE BOSS | | Columbia/Tony Singletary |
| JAKE & THE FATMAN | | Viacom/Richard Lang |
| KNOTS LANDING | | Lorimar/Timna Ranon |
| HUNTER | | Cannell/Randy Roberts |
| FROM THE DEAD OF NIGHT (Mini-Series) | | Phoenix Ent/Paul Wendkos |

## THEATRE — Broadway

| | | |
|---|---|---|
| BEATLEMANIA | Ringo Starr | Winter Garden |

### — Los Angeles

| | |
|---|---|
| DRACULA TYRANNUS | Tiffany/Jules Aaron |
| MISCONDUCT ALLOWED | Tiffany/Minda Burr |
| IDA | Tiffany/Jules Aaron |
| LADIES ROOM | Tiffany/Kim Friedman |
| ARE YOU NOW OR HAVE YOU EVER BEEN (Dramalogue Award) | Back Alley/Allan Miller |
| THE GREEKS | Back Alley/John Schuck |
| BRONTOSAURUS BLUES | Victory/Mike Schlitt |
| IRON CITY (Dramalogue Award) | Alliance/Richard Holden |
| 27 WAGONS FULL OF COTTON | Alliance/John Randel |

**SPECIAL ABILITIES**—Singer, Drums, Guitar, Private Pilot, Motorcycling, Horse-back Riding, Tennis, Baseball, Football, Snow & Water Skiing, Scuba Diving, All Sports, Athletic Build **TAPE AVAILABLE**

# Chapter 6

# Getting and Keeping an Agent

### Attitude

*The longer I live, the more I realize the impact of attitude on life. Attitude, to me, is more important than facts. It is more important than the past, than education, than money, than circumstances, than failures, than successes, than what other people think or say or do. It is more important than appearance, giftedness, or skill. It will make or break a company... a church...a home. The remarkable thing is we have a choice every day regarding the attitude we will embrace for that day. We cannot change our past... we cannot change the fact that people will act in a certain way. We cannot change the inevitable. The only thing we can do is play on the one string we have, and that is our attitude... I am convinced that life is 10% what happens to me and 90% how I react to it. And so it is with you... we are in charge of our Attitudes.*

**Charles Swindoll**

I know you'll want to get an agent right away but there are some critical facts to keep in mind. At any given time, approximately half of all Screen Actors Guild members are without representation. That means that 45,000 guild members are looking for an agent. I say this not to discourage you but, rather, to make you aware that the multitude of actors seeking legitimate representation outnumbers the supply of qualified agents. As we discussed in "The Hustle", less than legitimate "agents" or "agencies" are eager to exploit this demand. If you see that an agency is "advertising" in newspapers for clients, know that it is highly unlikely that they are on the level because an agency that is franchised by the Guild is forbidden to advertise. Don't fall prey to this common front for representation; they're probably photo and acting class scams.

So, how do you find a legitimate agent? First, lets look at what an agent is, what they do and how you can best find one to represent your career.

## A Day in the Life of an Agent

A good agent looks for new talent he or she believes can be nurtured into a successful and long-lasting career as a star or, a busy character actor who sometimes work more or top model . Most importantly, a good agent will work hard at setting up as many interviews and auditions as possible for the sole purpose of getting the actor or model employed. Hopefully, an agent's efforts will result in a budding, gratifying, and successful career. Once an person has been employed, it is an agent's job to negotiate the contract in a way that best satisfies and responds to the needs of their client.

A typical day for most agents start very early in the morning, usually beginning the day by reading *"the trades"* (industry newspapers) in order to stay abreast of the most recent changes in the industry. More pointedly, agents will read the trades in order to scan the casting landscape in search of casting opportunities for their clients. Next, agents will have **Breakdown Services** deliver that day's casting notices to either their home or office.

After earmarking specific projects, they begin compiling a list of actors whom they represent to be submitted for each appropriate role. Pictures and resumes are pulled, cover sheets typed and packets put together for messenger or personal delivery to casting directors, studio executives, or producers. Occasionally, an influential agent might deliver the submissions personally in order to pitch his or her best clients; in which case much of their morning is spent waiting in a lot of outer offices to be seen for three minutes. Smaller, less influential agents who attempt the same tactic as the more seasoned agent are usually asked to just leave packages.

Some agents use the morning to cultivate new relationships with casting directors, producers, directors, and studio executives. By late morning, an agent might grab some take-out lunch and come back to the office to go over any last-minute casting notices that might have come over the fax.

The afternoon is spent taking and making calls to secure appointments for clients. Late afternoon and early evening is used to contact actors with appointments and to make sure the clients get the right material called *"sides"* (several important scenes pulled out of the entire script to be used for auditions) or a full script. Afternoons are also the time when they see new clients.

An Agent generally stays in the office until seven or eight in the evenings. If an actor or model has not called back to confirm his or her auditions for the next day, an agent is forced to take home the burden of worrying whether or not the client will show up for the scheduled appointment. Their evenings are spent attending plays, fashion shows or showcases to search for new talent, reading scripts, watching tapes or television shows and trying to reach clients who have not confirmed appointments. Not calling to confirm, or being unreachable is the quickest way to lose an agent. They work very hard to get you an appointment—don't let them down.

I hope, from this overview of a day in the life of agents, you can see how busy they are; so, don't be hurt if no one rushes to the door to take your hand-delivered picture and resume. Late afternoons—from 4:30 to 6:00—is usually the best time for you to do your follow-up phone call to a mailing.

# Finding an Agent

Show business and the fashion business, like any other industry, have busy seasons, so time your approaches or appointments with agents to coincide with a slow period, or downtime, when an agent will have time to meet with you.

Here is a general breakdown of a typical year in the life of the fashion world and motion picture/television industry:

### Mid-January to May
Pilot season of new shows followed by a heavy work period in episodic television shows.

### May to August
Hiatus, the time when most TV shows are on vacation and reruns are being shown. The bulk of low-budget features are done during this time to take advantage of TV stars on vacation. This is also the time when an agent is most likely to meet with you.

Models are busy showing the new fall line in New York, Paris and Milan.

### September
Fall pilots and more episodic work. Another busy time.

### October to December
The busiest commercial time of the year. If corporations haven't spent their advertising budget yet, they do so now, before the year ends and the budget money is lost.

Models are showing the spring line in New York, Paris and Milan. Editorial and catalogue work goes on all year round.

### December 15 to January 1
During this holiday season, very little shooting happens, and if an agent is in town, she or he may agree to meet you now. However, you stand a better chance if you arrive in spring and get set up to meet the agents in the slower summer months.

There are several ways to get your foot in the door:

(1) If you're taking acting or modeling classes, ask your coach to recommend agencies;

(2) Ask any industry friends if they would carry your pictures in to their agents' office or if they will call them on your behalf. If not, ask your friends if you can use their names in your letter to their agent;

(3) Many of the showcases recommended in the chapter Classes and Jobs, Jobs, Everywhere" have a special agents' evening. Here you can meet and work in front of prospective agents.

(4) **SAG** offers an opportunity for actors to meet agents every year when they run the **SAG Annual Agents Showcase.**

(5) If you're in a play, have your fellow actors invite their agents and are willing to introduce you.

(6) Do charity fashion work and smooze any agents or industry people for introductions to their contacts.

(7) Also, you can send out cold mailings

of your picture and resume which, in the search for a commercial or commercial print agent, can be quite successful. Persistence is the key here; agents do not typically respond until the fourth or fifth contact to the office.

(7) Ask your local film commission for a list of any casting directors, directors, producers and agents from your state, who now live in Los Angeles.

(8) Ask industry contacts for a referral.

Let me offer one final option to finding an agent, as valid as the ones I've already mentioned. We offer a career counseling service where you can meet with me by phone or in person. Currently we enjoy a 85% success ratio for placing actors and models with agents. The process begins with a 90 minute interview in which I gather information about you in order to determine the best way to uniquely market you to the right agents. Then I tune up your resume, write you a compelling elevator speech and teach your savvy marketing ideas to make you irresistible to agents. We pick a selective target list and then focus all your passion and power toward some well chosen goals and turn you lose on an unsuspecting industry. Since I have packed your head full of new ideas about how you view success and failure, you don't take no for an answer. The results are consistently magical. Log on the web site www.hollywoodhereicome.com or call us at (800) 4DREAMS for a time slot.

No matter what, you cannot stop the search or give up hope until you've landed an agent. Jeffrey Katzenberg, former executive at Disney and currently one of the partners at DreamWorks, SKG said: "If they throw you out the door, climb in a window. If they throw you out the window, get in through the basement . . . but find a way in!" Learn from the best.

## Mailings

When putting together your mailings, include a cover letter, a picture and a resume with a phone number where you can be reached. You should never use a pager; instead, use a voice mailbox so a message can be left. When writing your cover letter, try to think of one thing (e.g., the fact that you're a brand new face in town, a great play review, an outrageous hobby or talent such as juggling chain saws) that will grab an agent's attention and get you a meeting. If you are acquainted with anyone in the industry, ask for referrals or for permission to use those names in your letter. If you've worked on any films in your home state, be sure to mention that as well but . . . keep it brief. As a newcomer the most important thing you are selling is the fact that you are new. Agents love to have a crack at handling new faces

Commercial and Modeling Agents take clients based on a "look"; so, if you have a strong picture, you'll probably get an appointment if they are looking for your type. Later in this book, we will discuss how to put together a good actors demo tape to give to prospective agents. Models should have a strong portfolio with a variety of layouts.

There is a great book available to assist you in your research to find a good agent. It lists all the franchised agents in L.A. The book is called *TheAgencies, What An Actors Needs*. It lists each agency, the address and phone number. Also each particular agent and his or her respective division (e.g., television, theatrical, commercials, etc.) along with a short description of the size of the agency and the types of actors and models on the client list. This way you can target your mailing to a particular agent.

We offer many other tools on our web site to aid in your agency search including:

**The Right Agent** - L.A.
**Agency Labels** - L.A.
**Casting Directors Labels** - L.A.
**Personal Managers Book** - L.A.
**Agency Lists** for most major cities,
**New York Black Book** - NY
(agents, photographers, & coaches )
**The World Agency List** - Europe
**Private Consult with the Author**
www. hollywoodhereicome.com

If, instead of mailing your package to an agency, you decide to hand deliver your picture to the agencys' receptionist, be prepared to have only about 15 seconds to make an impression. Rehearse your 15-second elevator speech beforehand. Don't overstay your welcome but be aware that these receptionists, although busy, can speak to the agents about you. If you're not an outgoing people person, this way is not for you. You might prefer to send pictures and follow up later with a phone call or have a friend bring you in. There are many types of agencies that may represent you: theatrical, commercial, modeling, voice-over, print, industrial, dance, comedy, variety and specialty acts and literary. So, let's take a look at the different types of agents, what each of them does and what you should know before signing with one.

# Interviewing a Theatrical Agent

A theatrical agent represents and submits clients for theatrical motion pictures and television shows. A theatrical agent also represents clients for **Equity theater.** When you meet with a theatrical agent for the first time, do not overdress. Instead of thinking your professional they think you are just scared.

Here are some important questions you should ask a theatrical agent so that you can determine for yourself whether or not you would be signing with the right agent:

1. How many clients do you have?
   (A client list is available any business day at SAG, if you are a member.)

2. How many other actors do you have in my category?
3. How do you see me and how will you sell me?
4. What is your game plan?
5. Which casting directors do you know well enough to set up general interviews with?
6. Will you personally handle me or will I meet the other agents as well?
7. What would be your intended goal with regard to my career?

In addition to asking the agent those questions, be observant. One-person offices are fine as long as the agent doesn't have too many clients. Ask yourself: Are they organized and seem to have control? How do they handle themselves? Is the phone ringing for bookings? If they negotiate or take phone calls while you're there, go ahead and eavesdrop. If you over hear them say something to a client like: "Call me back every few months to remind me who you are"—find another agent. They should be thinking of their clients every day and know them well.

And, incidentally, if the agent mentions listing you in an agency directory and asks you to pay for this listing, don't fall for it. Such directories are never used in the industry; this is just a ploy to get your money to pay the agents rent.

When meeting with a theatrical agents for the first time, you should walk in prepared. (1) Make a list of television shows that you think you are right for; (2) Prepare a list of industry members you have met with and people who have seen your work, including casting directors, directors and producers; (3) Have a demo tape. If you don't have a demo tape, **do not** go out and make one just for this occasion; a quickly made demo always ends up looking cheesy. If you have actual jobs that can be edited into a tape, that's a different story. We will cover that in Chapter 14 ("Building a Demo Tapes"); (4) Be ready to perform a scene or to try a "cold read."

Pick a scene that shows off your talents,

both in comedy and in drama. Keep it short, about five minutes or less. Try not to pick a scene that is too recognizable or is often done from a play or a film. Rehearse your audition scene with your coach before arriving at the talent agency. Two important pieces of advice when doing a scene: (1) Never bring a weapon into the office, and (2) don't touch the agent or use his or her possessions as props. Agents are territorial about their stuff and your actions could shift the focus away from your scene.

If signed ask them for their logo so you can provide the agency with a stack of 8 x 10's and resumes. If they aren't crazy about your 8 x 10's, bring in your proof sheets from the photo shoot and let them pick one. Make sure your resume and picture fit neatly together; if you have a resume that hangs over the side of the picture, it might get torn off and look very unprofessional. Every time you acquire a new credit, go in and replace resumes with updated ones.

If you and the agent decide to work together, you may, initially, enter into a professional contract on a trial basis, either by a written contract or by an oral agreement. If, after this trial period, you are satisfied with each other, you will be signing your first contract. If you go under contract, you may be asked to sign one for both **SAG** and **A.F.T.R.A.** Under these Guild's regulations, the first contract can only be for one year with a 10% commission for the agent 15% for print. The contract can be renewed for one to three years.

There is a copy of the **A.F.T.R.A. Agency Contract** in the Appendix of this book to guide you. Read it over and ask your new agent or the Guild any questions before signing with them.

## Signing With an Agent

So, let's say you've met with an agent whom you like, you've checked this person out to your satisfaction, and you've been offered a one-year contract to sign. Here are some basic rules that you should be aware of:

According to the SAG contract, agents must pay you within three days of receiving your check, if you work locally and within seven days if you work on location. Agents receive 10% commission on daily and weekly rates, overtime, wardrobe fittings, the first three network prime time reruns, cable, video and features sold to television. Agents are not entitled to commissions on: syndicated residuals, Fox reruns, foreign runs, meal penalties, mileage and per diem.

And here are some good tips: Never pay an agent until he or she gets you work. Your agent may ask you to sign papers to give the authority to deposit the check from your earnings into his or her client' trust account and dispense your moneys out of that. Your other option is to send them a copy of your paycheck along with a personal check in the amount of their 10% commission. That's up to you. But before signing anything, read all contracts and papers carefully and get copies of everything you sign. If you do not understand something . . . ask, ask, ask. If necessary, get a lawyer to read it. When you've had all your questions answered sign your contract and get ready to take your career closer to your ultimate goal.

## After the Signing

Once you get acclimated to your new association, there are some practices I consider to be important in order to maintain a good, working relationship with your agent: From time to time, I recommend dropping by the office in the afternoons to see if your agent is running out of your pictures. **Never** call or drop by in the mornings, unless the agent specifically asks you to or unless you need to confirm an audition. As I mentioned earlier, agents, generally, are very busy during that time. Calling your agent between 4:00 and 6:00 PM is best, if you have any questions.

**Always** call whenever you leave town and *"book out"* (a term meaning that you are unavailable for auditions, either because of a vacation or a job) with your agent. Leave an out-of-town phone number, in case something important comes up. Inevitably, whenever I leave town, I always seem to get booked for a job and have to come back. It's the actor's curse that's a plus.

Your agent can be useful in a variety of ways that you may not have even thought of. For example, after you have given your agent a list of industry contacts, your agent will watch the casting notices and will use your list to help secure work for you. Or, another occasion might arise where you have given a bad reading on an audition; in that case, your agent can make a call and smooth things over.

And, here's still another scenario where an agent can be valuable: let's say you meet a producer or a director at some social event and this person wants you in his or her film. Furthermore, this "professional" calls you at home to discuss money or your billing. This is the perfect situation for you to use your agent as a buffer. Let this person graciously know that your agent negotiates all money deals and ask if you can you have the agent call them? If they say no, move on! Either there is no movie or this person is just a character who wants to take advantage of you.

Which brings up a related point: check with your agent before accepting any work, especially theater during peak casting periods. An agent wants his or her clients to have very few conflicts with scheduling.

## Leaving an Agent

Occasionally, clients leave agents for various and sundry reasons. Usually, the cause is dissatisfaction with the current agent's performance; **Never** leave an agent until you have found a new one who you are sure will work harder for you than the last one. If you do leave, however, and are in the union, a letter must be sent or delivered to the agent with a copy going to The **Agency Department** of the **Screen Actors Guild** or to **A.F.T.R.A.**, depending on which guild agency contracts you signed upon meeting your agent. With **SAG**, you cannot leave your agent

until five months after the signing of a union contract, however, if you have not worked 20 days in five months, there is an escape clause in the **SAG** guidelines that allows you to leave. In your letter, you must include the words "as per **Paragraph Six** of the **SAG Contract.**" For **A.F.T.R.A.**, you only need to wait 91 days, to write your letter when you want out of your contract. You still must include a reference to "**Paragraph Six** of the **A.F.T.R.A.** Contract" When you leave, express gratitude and show respect to the agent for having brought you to the point you're at now. You never know if you'll ever have to go back with that agency.

## Commercial Agents

A commercial agent submits clients for TV commercials, music videos and, occasionally, industrial training films. The good news is that commercial agents are the easiest kind of agent to land.

Commercial agents understand that this particular area of the entertainment industry is a numbers game; consequently, they will sign many actors and models to their agency of the same type and look. Don't let this shake you. When a call goes out for a certain type, the agent will get as many appointments as needed to cover all of their clients in that groove. Many commercial agencies have between 200 to 400 clients, depending on how many agents are in the agency. Commercial agents customarily look to sign up actors and models who are both versatile in talent and amicable in personality. Additionally, most commercial agents, also love to find new people for the industry, which makes this a great opportunity for newcomers .

## The Right Commercial Agent

Before you interview with a commercial agent, watch a lot of TV. Pay attention to how actors and models "sell" certain products. Observe which clients prefer *"soft sell"* and which are zany or over the top. That way, when advertisers or casting directors ask you to read some commercial copy for your audition, you'll have an idea on how to do it.

Commercial agents will almost always ask you to read, unless you have extensive credits and a demo reel. Make a list of all the commercials you have done, even if they were local ones in your hometown. List the advertising agency and the director as well. A commercial agency may have a relationship with that ad agency and, therefore, will keep an eye out for future commercials, also known as *"spots"* that you might be right for. In addition to your credits, provide your prospective commercial agent with a list of your industry contacts. Ask prospective agents this:

1. What looks are most sellable for me?
2. If I change my hair or get a certain kind of photo, will that help you sell me in other areas as well?
3. Will you handle me personally, or should I meet the other Agents?
4. How many clients do you have?
5. How many are in my category?
6. How many national TV spots did you clients book this year?

Getting this kind of information will give you an idea how busy a specific commercial agent can get. My commercial agents handle about 300 clients and booked 109 nationals commercials last year. The point is: the busier the better. But, if you can only find one commercial agent who wants you, go with that person. A less busy agent is better than no agent.

The "looks" that are most sellable in commercials are: the average person on the street, interesting character faces, blue- collar workers (like construction workers and plumbers), moms and dads, grandmas and grandpas, business people, specialty talents (dancers, singers, jugglers, etc.) and athletes or models for beauty and image ads..

With regard to athletics, a commercial agent will have you fill out a form so that you can list your skill level in a variety of sports. Be honest. If you tell agents that you can ride a horse but you really can't and they send you on a call, you will have wasted their time and compromised their reputation since they could have filled the audition slot with another qualified actor.

## Signing With a Commercial Agent

As with theatrical agents, if you're put under contract, you may have to sign both **A.F.T.R.A.** and **SAG** contracts for one year with three-year renewals. **A.F.T.R.A.** covers all commercials shot on tape and **SAG** covers all commercials shot on film. After you've signed, provide your agency with a stack of photos and resumes with the agencys' logo on them. Always be ready at a moment's notice for *"rush calls"*; so, keep a pager pr cell phone handy. And, always have pictures and resumes in your car. Be well groomed on a daily basis; you never know what might happen at the last minute.

## Modeling Agents

How did Kim Bassinger, Andie McDowell, Tom Selleck and Cybil Shepherd all get their start? You guessed it—modeling. For Cindy Crawford, Naomi Campbell and Claudia Schiffer it has been a great ride. A modeling agent books high fashion, runway, catalogue, swimsuit, lingerie, shoes, petite, oversized and body part models.

Often, modeling agencies have open calls. During an open call, you will get free career advice from experienced professionals. If you have any doubt about your having what it takes to work in this market, show up at an agencys' open call and ask questions of any of the professionals available. It costs nothing. And bring photos. They do not have to be professional. If you have no professional photos, bring in snapshots that capture your image. Here's some types of modeling agents.

## High Fashion Models

Currently, here are the characteristics that most modeling agents look for in a prospective client for high fashion modeling: Women high fashion models are 13-18 years old when starting out, 5'9" or taller and rail thin. Men should be 16-21 years old and 6' or taller. Petites are 5'6" or smaller and oversized models are size 14 and up.

Modeling schools are not agencies and you don't have to ever attend one to be a top model. However, all the top modeling agencies are franchised by SAG and abide by their rules. This is important to know because there is no specific guild or contract to protect models or the modeling industry from someone trying to run a scam for photos or "model training," etc.

## Runway Models

Runway models are trained by the talent agency that signs them to a representation contract. Women are also rail thin. You must be a perfect fit for a standard clothing size, whether male or female. Both sexes should move well and not be self-conscious.

## Body Part Models & Photo Tests

Body parts models are distinguished from runway models and high fashion models by the fact that they have great ears, legs, necks, backs, or hands but not necessarily all of these features at the same time. A body parts model's ZED card contains close-ups of his or her best features.

Whichever category you will be considered for, you will need photographs. If you

have no photos or need additional photos for the agent to make a proper decision, he or she will give you a list of *"test photographers"* These are photographers who will shoot test shots for your portfolio as well as for their own. The cost is generally just for film and processing, usually not more than $20/roll.

You will use these test photos along with others to compile a ZED card. A sample of one card is included in the chapter "Say Cheese, Please!". The ZED card can either be in color or in black and white, with the latter being the most popular. For fashion modeling, the front cover of a ZED card is usually a color headshot. The card back has various fashion layouts.

To get a sense of whether or not you might be successful as a model, ask a modeling agent the following questions:

1. Do I have a high fashion look?
2. Could I be considered for runway?
3. Would you be interested in having me test with some photographers?
4. Do you have any layout ideas off the top of your head for my test shoot?

5. Am I right for your new faces division?
6. Would you like to representing me?
7. If not, can I lose some weight and come back in the future?

If one agent says no, don't stop there, unless it's a height or weight problem. I was turned down by one agent only to be signed with another two weeks later. "No" could mean anything, such as: "Come back when you lose weight" or a hundred different other explanations. So ask but don't take it personally. If you are rejected maybe they are trying to help you become more marketable. The agent is just responding to his or her own self-designed requirements. Or maybe just looking for whatever happens to be currently fashionable at that particular moment in time. Never answer ads in newspapers for modeling agencies. If you're serious about modeling, you should read "Glam Scams" by Eric Joseph in the Appendix before beginning. Log on our web site to request a list of agents in your area, NY or LA.

## Commercial Print Agents

Commercial print agencies are very different from modeling agencies. Commercial print agents find jobs for their clients in the print media: magazines, newspapers and brochures. Think of photos of the family or couple on a cruise ship. The people on a date, at a sporting event or using any products.

Commercial print model's work involves paid advertisements from large corporations. They may be used for print and electronic media. Commercial print agents seek similar types as commercial agents.

## Finding the Right Print Agent

To find a commercial print agent, either mail in your commercial headshot and follow up with a phone call or drop your package off at the agency with whom you are seeking representation. If you have a specialty shot of a business person, plumber, etc., be sure to include that in your package as well. Models

can include their ZED card.

Once you get an interview with an agent, you should ask that agent the same questions as you would a commercial agent with the exception of how many national spots they had that year. When you interview, you don't have to dress to fit your type; they have good imaginations. There is never any reading of copy; the agent just wants to know how easy you are to get along with and how enthusiastic and relaxed you are.

If you have a pager or cell phone, let the agent know you are available for last-minute calls. Should you get signed with a commercial print agency, you will have to provide them with a stack of pictures and resumes with their logo on it.

Many commercial print agents never sign contracts since there really isn't one that covers modeling. I have been with my commercial print agent for three years, have worked a lot, and have never signed any contracts.

## Voice-Over Agents

Voice-over agents handle all the people whose voices you **hear** on radio, television and in the cartoons. A few years ago, this area was ignored by most actors who didn't understand how lucrative using your voice rather than your image could be. Now the market is saturated with celebrities with identifiable voices who receive multi-million-dollar fees by lending voices to a product. Examples include Gene Hackman for United Airlines and Martin Sheen for Honda.

So, as you can probably tell, the competition to get a voice-over agent and voice-over work is fierce. Nonetheless, you can start building your audio demo tape at any stage in your career, regardless of whether you are still living in your hometown or have moved to a larger major market.

To begin assembling a packet for an agent, get a copy of an audio reel-to-reel tape of all the voice-over work you have ever done. If you can't get a hold of a reel-to-reel to use for your demo, get a cassette copy instead. We will go over how to build a voice reel in Chapter 14, "Building a Demo Tape". In your packet to these voice-over agents, include: a demo reel, a picture, and a normal industry resume of your theatrical, TV, stage, and commercial credits. In addition to these items, include a separate resume of any voice work you might have done. In this resume, include: the names of all clients; a note to designate whether the jobs were for a national, regional or local spot; and, the advertising agency handling it. Also, if you have any narration credits, include them in this separate resume along with the client's name and advertising agency.

## Industrial Agents

"Industrials" are corporate training films and "how-to" videos used to teach employees and customers about new products and improved ways of implementing corporate policies. They are a great marketing and management tool for companies. Some agents handle clients for live presentations at trade shows as well. One of the best examples of these live presentations are the spokespeople describing the cars at the auto show.

There are many opportunities in this market for actors who don't mind driving out of the area. In LA most agents are located in Orange County and San Diego. This type of work offers the opportunity to make a fairly steady income. Some of the casting notices go out to all the agents in town, even though few agents are actually interested in pursuing them since it is a bread and butter product, not as glamorous as movies or TV.

If you are a spokesperson type, there are a few skills you will need to acquire before submitting your picture to an agency for representation: You must be adept at reading a *"teleprompter"* or using the *"earprompter."* A teleprompter is a machine that is placed in front of the lens of a camera on which your dialogue is projected. The lines of dialogue scroll up so that you can read each line as it appears right in front of the lens. You may want to rent a teleprompter to practice but

it's highly impractical because the rental is about $500 a day. But, if you team up with another actor and make cue cards with lots of dialogue on them, you can simulate the

scrolling function of a teleprompter by raising the cue cards. Use this rehearsal to train yourself to overcome the natural tendency to move your eyes from side to side. That way, when you're asked if you can use a teleprompter, you can comfortably say yes.

Another skill is using an earprompter. "The ear," as it is commonly known, is a small tape recorder on which the entire script is recorded. The tape recorder is connected to a radio transmitter loop which is worn around your neck under your clothes. The speed of the tape is controlled by a hand or foot activator. The radio signal is then transmitted to an invisible ear piece much like a hearing aid, which is hidden in your ear. By depressing the activator, you can also either back up the tape or make it go forward. Mastering the earprompter is a skill in itself because, to do this well, you have to learn how to speak one line of dialogue while listening to another.

Brian Collins is one of the industry's premier instructors on earprompter training. Brian offers a wonderful seven-hour course for only $200, limited to three to six actors per class. Not only does he provide all the equipment you'll need but, if you're interested in obtaining an earprompter system for your own personal use, he can he tell you where to purchase one at a cost of anywhere from $348 to $1,000. Brian has also been one of my greatest resources for finding ways to promote myself in this industry because he is a top working spokesman in this field and has a savvy advertising

campaign. Sign up for his class or products by dialing (800) SPOKESMAN.

# Finding an Industrial Agent

To get an interview with an industrial agent, send a brief letter explaining your interest in doing industrials, your willingness to drive and your skills in the use of teleprompter or earprompter. Enclose a picture, a resume, any specialty photos and a demo tape, if you have one. On your agency interview you may be asked to read copy; dress sharply for this meeting so they don't have to try and guess what you might look like as a spokesperson.

# Signing With an Industrial Agent

Most scripts are broken up into two categories: (1) "Spokespeople," who tie the scripts together, and (2) "actors," who perform vignettes by playing whichever type of person the script calls for, just like in the movies. Because a lot of industrials are shot non-union meaning that, with the possible exception of the actors, neither the crew nor the production staff is affiliated with a union, agents can take any percentage they negotiated with you. So be tough! Don't give up more than 15% but try for 10%. of your earned salary .Try to get agents to negotiate their fee on top of yours. If, on the other hand, the industrial project is a union shoot, the commission is always 10%, no matter what kind of role you perform.

You will be expected to negotiating non-union commissions with the agent during the initial meeting after you've decided to work together. If the agent doesn't bring it up,

you should. After an industrial agent has taken you on as a client, there are usually no contracts, just a verbal agreement. As with all other kinds of agents, you must provide your industrial agent with pictures, resumes with the agencys' logo and several demo tapes, if you have them, for the agent to send out in lieu of an audition.

# Specialty Agents

These very specialized agents handle sports figures, stand up comics, cabaret acts, dancers, circus people, MC's, soap opera talent, talk show hosts, radio personalities, the physically challenged and novelty acts. If you possess one of these talents, you should have a photo that reflects it. Package your photo along with a resume of any acting work, as well as any credits in your specialty area. Mail it or deliver it to one of the specialty agents in town. You might want to include in your package some press clippings or good reviews of your act from newspapers or magazines.

# Finding a Specialty Agent

In LA we have specialty agents listed in the front of the book **The Right Agent** available on the web site. Once you get an interview, you'll want to ask the specialty agent how many clients with your talent the agency has signed and how many gigs per month do they book for your area of specialty. This ought to give you a pretty good idea of whether the office is busy enough for you. Also, ask if they have any ideas on how to expand your income base. One circus performer I know purchased his trapeze rigging so that he could travel and put on a show at corporate conventions. Now that is very creative. Think of how you can go into previously untapped markets.

## One Final Note

One final note about agents. You can only be contractually signed with one agent in each category. However, you can work with as many agents—on a verbal agreement—as you wish. Since you will have many resumes with different logos for each category represented, I suggest you make a master resume. As you acquire each new agent, print up a copy of the master, put the agency logo on it and make copies from that version. All the kinds of agencies listed in this chapter can be found in a book called *The Right Agent.* This book is available at our web site.

http://www.hollywoodhereicome.com

On a personal note, don't waste your agent's time by complaining about your private life. It puts agents off and they may think you're too emotionally unstable to go on auditions. Instead, seek out help and see a shrink.

## What Does a Manager Do?

Personal managers are not agents. They are not bound by any code of ethics or franchise rules from SAG nor are they required to put up a bond to guard your money. By the same token, they are not technically permitted to negotiate salaries for their clients; only a SAG-franchised agent can do that. Therefore, anyone can be a manager—anyone with no particular qualification but a business card and a phone.

So, what's the value for an actor in having a manager? What does a manager do that an agent doesn't? A manager is most useful to an actor who works regularly as opposed to a newcomer who is still in the process of cutting his or her teeth. For a regularly working actor, a good manager coordinates auditions and shooting schedules, reads scripts for possible roles, introduces the actor to industry professionals including agents, creates an image and direction for

the actor's career and enters into contracts on behalf of the actor. Additionally, a manager finds other people to assist the actor's career such as publicists, business managers, shrinks and powerful agents when it's time to move up.

## Management Contracts

So, what does a manager get for all this effort? Customarily, a manager's cut starts at 15% and can go as high as an actor agrees to. What's more, a manager gets that agreed-upon percentage for every and any kind of acting or modeling job the client does, even if the manager wasn't remotely responsible for getting the client a particular job.

Management contracts are binding, legal and hard to get out of. So, it is imperative that you check out prospective managers more thoroughly then anyone else in the entertainment industry who will be assisting you with your career. If you sign a contract with a manager who spots your potential but does nothing for your career, you're still bound by contract to pay the manager his or her percentage, which could add up to big bucks when you hit it big. Before I knew how to check out managers, I foolishly signed with one such opportunist. It took me several months of negotiating to be released from my contract.

## Checking Out Managers

There are a handful of really good, hardworking managers in this town. An effective manager will only carry no more than ten clients; this way, they can give specialized attention to each client as it is needed.

Here is the best way to determine if the manager you are considering is a hard working professional dedicated to the advancement of his or her clients: Ask for a list of clients whom the manager represents. Better yet, see if you can get the name of the actor's agents from the manager. Call these agents and explain to them that you are considering management from so and so. How are they to work with? Ask the agent to pass your phone number along to the actor so that you can get some direct feedback with someone who has had experience with the manager in question. Next, check with **The Conference of Personal Managers** in our phone book to see if the manager is a member in good standing of that organization. They also publish a list of their membership, in case you need a place to start looking for a manager. Last, order a copy of *Personal Managers* from our web site. This great resource has addresses, names of managers and an outline of what they are about and the types of clients they handel..

# Working With a Manager

If, after collecting all this information, you decide to go with a particular manager, make sure that he or she has a good working relationship with several agents to whom the manager can introduce you to as a prospective client. If a particular manager can't help you get an agent, you may want to pass. If you are still not sure that you're with the right manager, see if you can negotiate a six-month trial contract to see if you work well together.

Here are some sure bet tips that you are definitely with the wrong person: If a manager ever asks you for a monthly fee to cover postage, phone bills or a marketing fee, usually $25 to $200, **run for the door.** Managers are supposed to build their business on their own dime and the fees they collect from getting clients work. Also, be on the alert for manager scams that are disguised under career advice. Here's how that works: A "manager" will refer you to a photographer for pictures, and an acting and voice coach that the manager chooses and all of whom gives the manager kickbacks. You can test managers to see if they are getting kickbacks by saying you'd rather check out the voice, photographers and acting coaches mentioned in this book. It doesn't necessarily have to be true . . . you're testing them. If they say it's fine for you to do your own research, then they are probably on the level and really have your best interests at heart. If they suddenly turn on you and chastise you or say that you are to difficult to work with, you are probably being

set up to be scammed. I know you need all the help you can get to succeed in your career and managers, after all, are great salesman; but, don't let yourself be sweet talked, go ahead and check them out.

# Academy Players Directory

The *Academy Players Directory* is a group of books published by **The Academy of Motion Picture Arts and Sciences** (Oscars) that contain the photographs of actors, with a brief list of credits and a list of agency and manager contacts. The directory is updated three times a year. To qualify for a listing, you must be a member of a guild or be represented by a franchised agency.

The *Directory* is broken down into separate volumes, each with a different classification to enable an actor to best market him or herself. These books are used daily by casting directors, directors and producers who pay a fee to receive them.

Some of the ways in which The *Directory* is used are as follows: If your agent is pitching you to a producer for a project that is currently being cast but doesn't have enough time to get your picture to the production company, the producer will look you up in the *Academy Players Directory.* Or, if producers and directors are searching for a certain look for their project, they will browse though the *Directory.* Of course, there are some less than honorable "professionals" who use the *Directory* for ulterior motives, such as paging through each volume looking for women and men to date. That's why you should never list your home telephone number in the *Directory.* All phone numbers listed under your headshot should go directly to your agent or manager.

As you can probably tell by now, the *Academy Players Directory* listings are invaluable to actors for more reasons than just displaying a nice picture. So, I strongly urge you to make use of the *Directory.* Here are some important facts about the *Directory* and some of the additional benefits that you can derive from it: It is updated every four months, which is a great advantage for actors who change their appearance or their agencies with some frequency. The directories are also circulated in major markets such as Los Angeles, Chicago, New York and Florida.

Your photo is also included on their CD-Rom and web site for no additional charge. **Your agent may not remind you of the deadline, so post it somewhere in your calendar or apartment.** Submissions and changes are accepted before the deadline and can be made by mail. You can select a photo that you and your agent have agreed upon. But, if you choose to submit a photograph and the head in the photograph is too small for the book, they will let you know. Your picture is kept on file for three months after publication and can be retrieved if you want to save it; otherwise it is thrown away. The cost for publishing your listing is $80 per year, or $30 per issue, and will not be automatically renewed if you pay the yearly fee. In my opinion, it is the best use of your money.

Call the *Academy Players Directory* and have them send you an application  E-mail can be directed to: players@oscar.org or visit the web site at: http://www.oscars.org At the *Players Directory* office, past issues of the *Directory* are for sale.  Not only are they fun to look through but you can get some great ideas for your own headshot. In addition to past issues of the *Directory,* the office also offers free copies of the *Directory Reference Supplement* which lists talent agents, literary agents, members of the Casting Society of America, and radio and television references.   For more on using this reference guide, see Chapter 18 "The Future".

# Answering Service Savvy

If someone you either don't know gets a hold of your service number to ask for a meeting or an interview, return the phone call, ask for his or her number and assure that person that your agent or manager will be calling to discuss the request. Call your agent as soon as

you can to alert them of the call that came through on your service.  Most importantly, have your agent check this person out.

If you do not have representation, use the questions in Chapter 3 "The Hustle" to help yourself authenticate the person who contacted you as well as the project he or she is are proposing. If, after doing your research, you feel that a further conversation or meeting is warranted, make sure to bring someone with you who for protection as you don't know anything about the intentions of the person who contacted you. Then, when you are convinced that the person and the project are legit and that a bona fide offer is being made to you, get representation. Ask a friend who has an agent or ask your coach for a referral to an agent who can negotiate the deal on your behalf.

# Audition Guidelines

So, if you wind up going to an interview or audition without representation, follow these guidelines:

1. Don't go to an audition or interview alone.  Safety in numbers works.
2. Don't go to a hotel or apartment.
3. Don't go at night. Whether you know it or not, that's a date.
4. Don't audition for any overtly sexual scenes without a chaperon.
5. Don't ever take off your clothes. If the role calls for nudity, you should only be seen in a swimsuit at an interview or audition. If the producer or director

isn't satisfied with that and insists on seeing you nude, only remove your clothing in the presence of a chaperon of the same sex. Insist that the chaperon stay in the room the entire time until you are fully reclothed. But, most of all, you have to be responsible for making the choice to disrobe. No one else can "make" you do this.

6. Take care of yourself first and address their needs second.

Finally, let me leave you with a final word that underscores this chapter and, in fact, the entire thrust of this book. In the final analysis, you are the one accountable for your own career; you are the one responsible for making choices about with whom you will associate, which roles you will choose or turn down, who you will trust, what you will and won't do to further your career, and what you choose to know and what you choose to pretend to know. Because you are paying your agent only 10% of your earnings and you keep 90%, you should be doing at least 90% of the work to further your own career.

Nurture your relationship with your agent. Even though you are paying them 10% for an established reputation, industry contacts and negotiating skills, acknowledge the efforts that your agent makes on your behalf. From time to time, shower your agent with inexpensive gifts (i.e.flowers or cookies). Whenever you drop in to see your agent, go in looking like a million dollars. Most actors don't usually do this; so, you will stand out as someone your agent is proud of and grateful to have as a client. Keep your agent informed of all the other areas of your career. If you book a job with one type of agent, tell all the agents who represent you; it fires them up and reaffirms to them that they have made a wise selection with you as a client.

Always be aware that you are building a

career to last decades. Pick the most powerful agent you can get. Stay busy. Always keep building your credits for your resume in the areas of film, television and theater. Know when to take the next step up on the ladder to a more powerful agency.

When you get to the top, be on the lookout for good material. Stay humble. If you are offered a really great part for less money than you've previously been earning, take it. It is this kind of thinking that landed Nicholas Cage in a movie called *LEAVING LAS VEGAS.* He took the role for far less than he usually is paid. This well written role that he played so well garnered him an Academy Award.

# Chapter 7
# Acting Classes and Jobs, Jobs Everywhere

*Nothing in the world can take the place of persistence.*
*Talent will not;*
*nothing is more common than unsuccessful men*
*with talent.*
*Genius will not;*
*unrewarded genius is almost a proverb.*
*Education will not;*
*the world if full of educated derelicts.*
*Persistence and Determination alone are omnipotent.*
*The slogan "Press On" has solved,*
*and will solve, the problems of the human race.*

**Calvin Coolidge**

What do Al Pacino, Jessica Lange, Dustin Hoffman and Kevin Costner all have in common? They all continue to study with an acting coach even though they are well-established and successful stars. In your beginning acting years in Los Angeles and certainly throughout your entire acting career, it will be essential to continually hone and refine your craft. And lest you think that a steady acting study program is a commentary on your abilities as an actor . . . think again.

Acting is an attitude that requires your commitment to excellence. You can think of this lifelong commitment in one of two ways: Either you are practicing to be a master actor and model, in which case your inner experience will be one of dissatisfaction, inadequacy, and struggle regarding your work. Or, you can look at yourself as already being a master actor and model who practices his or her craft reverently on the way to higher and expanded levels of talent. Personally, I have learned that choosing the latter leaves me with the experience of already being empowered, prepared, satisfied, and competent. There's nowhere to get to because I'm already there. So, all that's left for me to do is to stay prepared for imminent opportunities and keep getting better at my craft each day.. That's why I continue to attend classes and will do so for the rest of my career, no matter how successful I become.

In the first part of this chapter, we will take a look at the criteria you should use when considering the right class and the right coach. The rest of the chapter will show you where and how best to find opportunities even if you don't yet have an agent.

## The Right Stuff

Naturally, the most important thing to look for in an coach is finding someone who recognizes your talent, who is willing to nurture your gift, and who will demand in a loving way that you to be the best you can be. Similarly, there are standards you should set for yourself in deciding which classes will move you toward your career goals.

Here are some questions to ask yourself and the coach when seeking a good acting :

1.  **When does class meet?**
    Look for schedule conflicts with your survival job.
2.  **Can I sit in on other classes that you teach on other nights for free?**
    You can learn almost as much by watching others as you can by participating.
3.  **How many students in each class?**
    This will give you an idea of how much personal attention you will receive.
4.  **How often can I get up to work?**
5.  **In the case of acting who picks the partners and assigns the scenes?**
    Finding your own scene and partner can take up a lot of extra time. If you can, find an acting coach who takes the initiative to make those assignments.
6.  **Is there an orientation class I am required to take before advancing?**
    Some coaches put you with an assistant for brief or long periods of time before you are permitted to move up to a higher class and work with the renowned acting coach in whose class you enrolled.
7.  **What is the average length of stay in the class before moving up?**
    Make sure you won't be with the assistant for years.
8.  **What does class cost per month?**
9.  **Can I audit the class before I decide to enroll?**
    Some top coaches in town will not let you audit a class because they feel it is invasive to the students currently studying. Others allow audits. Check their reputations before signing up.
10. **How long is the waiting period to join class?**

No matter how prominent an acting coach and his or her classes, if there is too long a waiting period, either busy yourself elsewhere while you're waiting or continue looking for another.

To assist you in your search, I am going to giving you a list of well-known acting coaches for LA in my phone directory. Most of these top professionals do not advertise in any acting newspapers because word of mouth referrals keep their classes filled.

Don't feel that you have to stay in a particular class just because you are with a top coach. In fact, you may want to switch coaches every couple of years or so. This is a common practice among actors and models, which provides some stimulating benefits. Changing classes and coaches from time to time gives you a fresh start, offers a new perspective, and brings additional validation to your talents.

A word of caution: If you find a casting director who also teaches acting classes, be aware of the possibility that, although he or she may know what sells, that casting director may not know how to get you a role or a part in a project. Run the other way if an "acting coach" runs a class out of a showcasing facility. "Professional coaches" who operate this way usually have a more senior agenda other than a commitment to an actor's interests since the showcase owners get a huge chunk of your money.

Shy away from "Academies" and acting schools that have chains, are named after famous people or offer a large curriculum. In Hollywood, only an individual coach is hot—not an entire school. Stay away from schools bearing the name of the founder, especially if that person is dead or no longer teaching. When the namesake goes, the magic goes too. One effective way of finding a legitimate, reputable, and competent acting class or coach is by asking other working actors and models who you know. We are building a list of good coaches worldwide on our web site.

# Finding Plays for Acting Class

Once you've found the right acting class and begin studying with a coach, you'll have to read and do scenes from lots of plays. Almost all plays can be found at **Samuel French Theatre Bookstores** in New York and L.A., or by mail order at a cost of $7.00 a pop. But, before you run out and start blazing through your checkbook, check you local libraries and used bookstores. All the libraries have a play section and author compilations.

For more plays try used bookstores. where you can get plays at a fraction of the cost for a new one.

# Additional Entertainment Classes

If, for one reason or another, you are neither able to make a long-term commitment to a professional acting class nor able to afford the cost of one, there are other alternatives to assist you in shaping your acting career. Although attending a professional class with a reputable acting coach is the optimum way to cultivate your talent, the following alternative "classes" provide useful data. These classes can be in addition to your on-going training.

Take a look at the list of classes offered by alternative learning centers such as universities, community colleges and adult learning centers. These centers advertise upcoming classes in magazines usually available at display boxes and coffee shops all over major cities. They often have national speakers with vast experience as teachers. But be aware of the distinction between the kind of experience you would receive in a long-term, professional class and the kind of knowledge you would acquire in a short-term, alternative seminars. In L.A. the centers are called **The Learning Annex** and they are great networking opportunities because you can often get to meet producers and directors you could never get to any other way.

Jason Alexander from Seinfeld has a hilarious class on an actor's perspective of the biz; producer/director Tony Adams of the *PINK PANTHER* movies gives instruction on pitching and making movies.

Recently, one power-packed seminar included: Sara Duvall, Exec. Prod. of **FRIED GREEN TOMATOES;** Carl Mazzocone, Prod. of **BOXING HELENA;** Nancy Meyers, Writer/Prod. of **PRIVATE BENJAMIN** and **BABY BOOM;** and two major talent agents. This seminar provided a unique opportunity for an actor to connect one-on-one with all of these established professionals while, simultaneously, learning the fundamentals of independent film making—all in the same evening for the low price of $39.

## Jobs, Jobs Everywhere

After you've been in acting classes for awhile, you'll eventually want to take your training and test it out in the real world. After all, that's what you've gotten into the business for, isn't it? There are acting opportunities galore in every big city if you know where to work.

One of the residual aspects about exercising your talents is the process of accumulating credits. Credits will become invaluable to you as a way of providing evidence and credibility to other industry professionals that you are a competently trained professional. So, let's take a closer look at where to find acting opportunities and how to build this portfolio of credits for yourself. especially if you don't already have an Agent.

## Where to Look for Work

Although **The Hollywood Reporter Daily Variety** are the most widely read trade magazines among all entertainment industry professionals, there was two excellent publications designed specifically for models and actors—**The Ross Reports** and **Backstage(NY) and Backstage West(LA).** Because these publications are most widely used for casting information within the acting and modeling community, I am going to refer to them in this chapter to help you familiarize yourself with the way they list their casting information. This way, you'll know what and how to look for casting opportunities.

### Backstage and Backstage West.

Owned by **Billboard** magazine, this publication is well-staffed with informed personnel. Most importantly to you it is packed with informative articles that are pertinent to new arrivals.

Central to this magazine's format are the indepth character descriptions in their casting notices. Just take a look at the spectrum of listings that are provided to readers looking for work:

SAG Films
Non-union & Union Films
Television
Commercials
Equity Stage
Equity and 99-Seat Waiver Theater
Stage
Staged Readings
Cruise and Casino Jobs
Theme Parks and Tours
Ensemble Groups
Variety
Improv Clubs

Grad Student Films
Student Films
Stage Tech
Film and Video Tech
Writers
Variety Acts
Cabaret Clubs
Comedy Clubs
Dance
Music
Music Videos
Teaching Positions
East Coast Interviews
East Coast Tech Jobs

In addition to this comprehensive listing of casting opportunities, **Backstage and Backstage West** also publishes great industry-related articles, interviews and reviews.

**Backstage/Backstage West** is also available by subscription ($75/year) and at the newsstand ($1.85/issue). What I personally like about this publication is that the magazine's advertising department carefully monitors its casting call placements in order to prohibit paid ads from being published by any of the known scam artists. This is a well put together newspaper and I recommend it highly. **Backstage and Backstage West** will mail their publication first-class anywhere in the country for $199 per year. To order a subscription call: (800) 458-7541. If you're in Los Angeles the paper is available at most news stands and area 7-11 Convenience Stores.

### Submitting Pictures and Resumes

Typical of most formatted magazines are the featured columns which highlight various topics for a reader's interest. Throughout the next few pages, I'll isolate some of those columns so that you can see how each category of opportunities lays out its casting notices for your consideration. Here is how to submit yourself for a role in each respective category.

All submissions should include a picture and resume. Place a Post-It note with the name of the character you are interested in playing right on the picture. A small, personal note is optional, but keep it to one or two lines regarding previous experience that might be pertinent to the character. If you don't yet have an agent, write the note as though you have one. Make up a name and ask them to contact your client (you) directly and list your contact number. If you already have an agent, make sure you obtain permission from them first before using their name on your submission letters. Here is an example of an actor posing as his or her own agent and writing a letter:

Dear Sylvia: (Your name) has just returned to town after finishing work on a feature and is anxious to begin another. (He/She) is a strong (actor/actress/model) and would be an asset to any production. You may contact (him/her) service directly for an audition. Mimi and Laurie, ABC Agency.

Finally, put the contents in a plain manila envelope and only seal it with the metal tabs to make it easy to open. Print or type the production company's address on the envelope. Do not include a return home address; use a P.O. Box or no return address at all. In the lower left-hand corner of the envelope, print the name of the project along with the name of the character you wish to play.

### Features & Television

An ad in these columns will begin with the name of the production company and include both the start date and the length of principal photography, if it is known. Next is a breakdown of the roles by character name, including the age and a brief description of the character qualities. Last is the mailing address to which you can submit your picture and resume. Although the column named

"Feature Films and Television in Development" is not always as complete as the one in *Variety* and *The Hollywood Reporter* you can, sometimes, pick up other pertinent information not always listed in the trades.

## Non-Union Films

Casting notices under this column are plentiful. And for good reason. The reality of non-union work is this: if a non-union production company could afford to "go union," they would so that they could access the best and most recognizable working actors. But, they can't. So, non-union film makers are forced to rough it with whatever resources are available. Usually, the hours are long, the working conditions are tough and, at the end of the shoot, a piece of tape of your work may or may not be usable for your demo reel.

But, at least, you'll have some acting experience under your belt and another credit for your portfolio. If for no other reason, you should do it for the experience of being on a set and for the love of your craft. And, because there are no union jurisdictional prohibitions on a non-union film, you can learn everything you want to about writing, directing, producing, and the technical crafts.

## Equity and 99-Seat Waiver Theater

The first piece of information in this column is the title of the play followed by the names of the writer, producer, director and choreographer. Following that are the dates indicating how long the play is intended to run and, then, the name of the theater. After that is a list of any singing and/or dancing skills an actor is required to perform. Finally, there is, an address with a date and time on which open calls will be held. Usually, this column will mention that all roles are "open" — instead of giving a character breakdown.

So, you'll have to either know or read the play before your audition time in order to get the gist of the characters involved. Please note: Because the casting notices for equity plays are done under the jurisdiction of union guidelines, you cannot read for the plays unless you are a member of Equity or have an eligibility card through your SAG credits. Anyone, however, can go to the open calls for and perform in an Equity waiver play which these listing usually cover. Guidelines for joining Equity are covered in Chapter 12.

## Non-Union Theater

Columns in *Backstage West* that list non-union theater casting notices are given in the same way as union theater casting notices. The difference is that non-union theaters offer little or no money to actors. Still, you should take an opportunity to perform in a non-union play if only for the sake of practicing your craft and gaining another credit. Don't, however, expect your work to get a lot of attention. It could happen; but, it's rare for industry professionals to take the time to see a non-union production in a theater.

## TV/Video, Music Video and Commercials

Some think this column is at the low end of the totem pole; but, I once responded to an ad in this section and became a entertainment reporter for a top FM radio station in L.A., doing "live" remotes on Friday and Saturday nights. The pay was minimal, but the job was a blast, the tapes I made from the broadcasts were priceless, and I got to meet all kinds of people to help me in my career.

## Singers and Comics

This column offers a weekly listing of open mike opportunities. Anyone can sign up for an open mike slot and perform.

## "Screen Scene"

Although this weekly column doesn't provide casting notices, it does help you to keep up with who's starring in which projects. Columnist Tom Provenzano is well informed and reading his column will afford you an opportunity to talk intelligently with casting directors and producers about their current projects.

### Free-Standing Ads

This actually isn't a column per se. These ads for feature film, television, modeling and commercial casting appear throughout the papers. The production company that paid for these ads has already shown its colors by spending a lot of money to find the most talented people for the roles.

## Create Other Opportunities

### Breakdowns on the Net

Normally it is impossible for actors to have access to the casting notices put out by **Breakdown Services**. Information on certain kinds of projects especially Equity waiver theater, non-pay student films, non-union films and open casting calls were only available through agents. Since there is very little money in these types of projects, agents were not passing information along to their clients. Gary Marsh, owner of **Breakdown Services** is now offering this information to anyone by accessing the internet. These casting notices are on the web at www.breakdownservices.com under the section entitled "Actor Access." This information is free to any actor with a computer and internet access.

### Low-Budget Filmmakers

To aid you in the search to identify low-budget film companies, I have compiled a list of some of the most active production houses in Los Angeles. Call the production company and find out if they have an in-house casting director or, alternately, the name of the person in charge of their casting files. If they don't have a casting person, ask which director is currently in pre-production. Then, send your picture and resume to him or her in care of the production house.    Recently, I gave this list to a writer friend of mine who already had a low-budget, successful film to his credit. Since giving him this list he has cut a deal with one of the companies on this list and is making his second film. Ask your local film commission for a list of area film makers so you can follow this same procedure to submit for projects in your own area. My list is in the back phone book.

## Student Films

For the beginner, I cannot recommend film school projects enough. They are, often, so well made that they rise to a prestigious enough level to be entered in film festivals and screened for the motion picture industry all around the world. The only real drawback for an actor doing a student films is that you often have to be patient with first-time directors, producers and writers until they figure out how to make their vision happen. The upside is that you could be on the crackling edge of something great and . . . you get another credit.

Although you'll occasionally find casting notices for student films in *Backstage West,* the best place to find them is in the **Breakdown Services** internet access at www.breakdownservices.com under "Actor Access" or from your agent, if you have one. If you find a role that you think you'd be good for, submit yourself. Even though an actor rarely receives pay for these projects, you will be treated with respect and, if requested, can obtain a copy of your work for your demo reel after the film is in the can.

I did a small role in a 20-minute short entitled ***ENEMIES—A LOVE STORY*** at the

American Film Institute (AFI) a full four years before it was made into a feature-length film. It was shopped all over town—with me in it! In another student film, a director acquaintance of mine, Jonathan Heap, was nominated for an **Academy Award** for his UCLA film school graduate project. In still another instance, Paul Sarnoff, a very gifted actor, was in a student film that was nominated for an **Academy Award.** When they rolled the clip on the awards show, there he was for all the industry to see. You couldn't buy publicity like that. So, can a credit from a student film start an acting career? Yes, yes, yes!!

Because the motion picture industry has become such a dominant phenomenon throughout the world, film schools have popped up all over the place. Before leaving your hometown, check with your local university to see if it has a film program in which you can participate and receive a credit as an actor, to build up your resume.

In the phone book are the three major film schools in Los Angeles. Either before leaving your hometown or once you've arrived here, go to the film schools and find out how they cast their projects and if their are any ones upcoming. Could you could read for something?

# Showcasing

Not too many years ago, it was part of every casting director's job to go out and see plays to discover new talent—whenever they could find the time. Industrious actors got sick of waiting to be discovered on some rare occasion when a casting director just happened to be in the audience one night. So, some actors started putting together an evening of scenes—called a *"showcase"*— specifically designed for a casting director to see the work of about 20 actors in an 80 to 90 minute period. This is, basically, how the first crop of showcases evolved: A group of actors had broken into teams, each team responsible for contacting and inviting agents, casting directors, managers, producers, and directors to attend an assortment of scenes. Although it was difficult in the beginning to get any serious attention from an industry professional, the effort eventually paid off. Now, Hollywood is teeming with showcases, offering complimentary tickets to the industry and a food-and-wine catered event. I personally produced two showcases at the **Tiffany Theater** on *"dark nights"* (nights not scheduled for a public performance) using the existing set. It showcased 21 actors in 80 minutes. We distributed a flyer through **Breakdown Services** and took out a quarter page ad in *Variety*. The house was full for the first two evenings and standing room only for the following week. The entire operation cost each actor $275 to pay for expenses and took two months to pull together.

In time, due to the success of this venue, a new breed of showcasing has sprung up all over town. The drill goes like this: A company of Actors is created for profit. Casting directors are contacted by the company and offered $100 to $300 to come in for an evening and screen new talent, something that casting directors used to doing for free. Flyers are sent to actors with the names and dates of the industry professional who will attend. If an actor wants to participate in the showcase, the Actor pays $20 to $30 to the for-profit company in order to meet these casting directors. Here is a list of for-profit showcases in town:

It bears mentioning that ethical issues have been raised over for-profit showcasing. Some casting directors refuse to participate in this charge-to-be-seen arena; but their assistants, usually overworked and underpaid, willingly come. Some casting directors, however, even use this particular venue as a way to supplement their income during slow periods. But, most importantly for you, there are other dedicated casting directors out there authentically looking for talent. Showcases aren't going away, so with a little homework, you can make them work for you.

## Union-Sponsored Showcases

The **Screen Actors Guild** and **A.F.T.R.A.** do not sanction pay showcases; instead, they offer free showcases each month in association with the Casting Society of America. To participate in these showcases, actors must be a member of the union hosting the event and be current with their dues. Your prepared scene can be no longer than three minutes. For union showcase phone numbers, check the listing in the back. Whichever path you take—for-profit or not-for-profit—showcasing is a great way to introduce yourself to the industry, but be very sure you're ready to perform publicly! Ask your acting coach for his or her feedback about your readiness to showcase. If you're not ready and do a bad job, the casting person observing your work will forget about you in about two years. Or worse, if you go to an audition in which that casting director presides, he or she might easily write you off or simply discount your audition altogether. That's why preparation and ongoing training are of utmost importance to developing your acting career over the long term.

So, when you feel ready, call all of the showcases from the list in the phone section in your budget range and go audit a class. If you like the way a particular showcase is run, get yourself on their mailing list. Once you've decided on the showcase group you'd like to join, there is some homework you'll need to do: Before you sign up for any showcases, find out which casting director will be attending your showcase and which project that casting person may currently be casting. If the attending casting person has no current project or has just finished one, then you may want to wait for a showcase that will be more helpful to your career.

Although getting favorable attention from any reputable casting director is worth the price of admission, I recommend that you focus on casting directors who work on episodic television because they have to find actors each week for their shows. If you know that you're going to be showcasing for one of these episodic television casting directors, watch the show they cast and get a feel for the style—(e.g.) sitcom or drama. Ask yourself questions such as: do the characters on the show seem like real people, character actors or the glamorous types? How many guest stars appeared that week? How many were unknowns? Most importantly, does your "type" fit into their format. Doing this kind of homework and inquiry will economize your money, time, and talent.

One last thing to remember about showcases: don't let your feelings be hurt if most of your showcasing performance are met with either rejection or disinterest. It's just one person's opinion. And, opinions are like noses . . . everyone has one. Keep moving, keep growing. Remember: There are, at least, ten casting directors out there looking just for you at any point in time. Your job throughout your career is to find them.

## Theater in Hollywood

A good role in a play at a respected and well-attended theater is the best showcase of your talent. Try to get in to a play with a director or an actor who has a well-known name. A well-known "name" in the production will draw key industry people as well as attract the attention of important reviewers. What you can realistically hope for is a great critical review of your performance and, perhaps, a **DramaLogue Award.** You can use these critics' reviews of your work in a publicity packet to lure casting directors and agents to come see your work.

Offer industry comps (free tickets). Work out a deal with the producers for free tickets or to pay only for tickets actually used. Many people will reserve tickets and never show up. Your guests will usually bring a colleague in the industry, rarely a date. If you send out a flyer in **Breakdown Services,** follow up with a phone call.

Industry professionals and casting directors get about 50 invitations per week to shows, so find something special to promote about your play. Offer a ticket to the assistant. Since these vital support people are often overlooked for screenings, plays, etc., they might be more than willing to accept your invitation.and they have influence with their bosses. Get other cast members to call. If many calls come in, the buzz creates the image of a hit show. See Chapter 13 "Publicity and The Trades" for examples and guidance in creating a *Playbill* biography.

Get a copy of ***Backstage West's*** legitimate theater list in December. Most industry people will not go far to see a show. **Theater Row,** located on Santa Monica Boulevard between Vine and Highland is good. Theaters in Burbank near the studios will work, and the **Odyssey Theater Complex** in West L.A. is popular. Just make sure the theater you pick to perform in is air-conditioned.

Another way to work in a play is to join a theater group. Well-respected companies have heavily attended performances. Most require an audition, dues and cast only from within the group. Some of the most respected groups are listed in our phone book.

## Extra Work

Working as an Extra is a great way to get hands-on knowledge of how a movie or TV set is run. Work is available for both union and non-union Extras on every major production in Los Angeles. On union shows and films, preference is given to union Extras first. On television shows, the union Extras get the first 15 spots; in feature films and commercials, the union quota is the first 30. So, you can see that in crowd scenes, there is an opportunity to work right away if you are not yet in the union; however, you have to find a reputable casting service to represent you. I recommend, before attempting any Extra work, that you read Cullen Chambers' ***Back To One.*** It is a complete guide to Extra work, including a rating (from one to four stars) of all of the casting services and calling services. It will give you an in depth account of doing Extra work. He also covers Extra Work opportunities all across the country. ***Back To One*** can also be ordered on our website.

## Non-Union Extra Work

If you work on a shoot as a non-union Extra, there is little obligation— legally—on the part of a production company to treat you fairly. There isn't a non-union Extra contract that outlines and insures proper treatment, except for the **labor laws** of the State of California. Currently, the going rate for non-union Extras is $40 for eight hours of work. Ask the casting service if there is any provision made for overtime past eight hours; hopefully, they will have worked out a deal. So, even though there is no contractual agreement for non-union actors as there is for union affiliated actors, the production company will feed you. However, your meal may turn out to be a box lunch (cold sandwich), so bring a snack.

## Union Extras

In contrast, union Extras are working under a specifically negotiated union con-

tract. Union Extras are paid $65 per eight hours. Every six hours they must receive a meal, unless the camera is rolling at the end of the sixth hour. Legally Extras can be fed after the director calls "Cut!" on that sixth-hour take without the imposition of a *"meal penalty"* (additional monies paid if a working cast or crew member has not been fed after the allotted six hours). The amount of money paid for meal penalty and all other rates are available by calling **Screen Actors Guild.**

Additionally, the following items are added to the base rate of $65: Body make up (other than face); facial applications (beards, moles, special effects); and, wigs. The following items are not added to the base rate: Car allowance; handling of animals; skateboards or other character items; and, wardrobe.

In our phone book is list of casting houses that offer their services under the **Screen Actors Guild Extras Agreement.** These companies may charge a fee, which should not be more than $20. Call for open interview times. If you are in the union and wish to do Extra work, let these casting services know right away your availability.

## Extra Work Professional Conduct

Let's go over some of the common problems that you, working as an Extra, can run into on the set— whether you're union or non-union. Believe it or not, 5%-10% of all Extras booked do not show up for the job. This will black ball you with your casting service faster than anything. This is where having a pager becomes invaluable. You should let your casting service know that you have a pager and that you will be available for any emergency last-minute bookings or for replacing people who do not show up.

When you arrive on the set, **you must check in with the Extra Coordinator or the Second Assistant Director** at or before your call time. If you are given the wrong call time by your calling service or casting service, you are the one who will get blamed, so double check all call times. If you leave the set, for any reason, let the person in charge know where to find you.

The second most prevalent problem is stolen *"work vouchers."* When you check in, you will be issued a voucher that must be filled out and turned in at the end of the day in order to receive your wages. If you lose it, you will not be paid. Fill it out right away and put it in a safe place. Theft on the set is not limited to vouchers. Never bring expensive watches, cameras or large sums of cash. It is almost a guarantee they will be stolen. Also if you don't ask your service about the proper attire for that day's shoot, you may show up wearing the wrong clothes or hair style and, thus, will not be able to work. It is okay to bring changes of clothes with you.

## Extra Work—What To Expect

Before the job and throughout the work day, be clear about what's expected of you. Actors have a tendency to believe that they are the most important people on the shoot, which, in some respects is true; however, when doing Extra work, your impulse for self-importance should be tempered with a dose of reality. Complaining about your hair, the food or having to stay on the set longer than you were told is irrelevant to the task at hand. You have to go to the job expecting to work overtime or to make last-minute changes that are asked of you. If you're not willing to adapt, then don't take the job.

If, at the end of the day, the production company decides to use your services the next day, that is what is referred to as a *"recall."* They may not notify you about a recall until the end of the day. If previously hadn't been booked for the extra days when you were first assigned the job, you always have the option to come back or not. If you are recalled because you have been established as a recognizable face that needs to be matched in subsequent shots but are unable to be there, you have a conflict. If that happens, respectfully let them know that you did not anticipate this situation, that it poses a conflict for you and request that you both

work something out. If they notify you ahead of time about a possible recall and you are not honest, hoping they'll shoot around your schedule, guess what? You get black balled.

## Extras—Getting Help

If you think a production company has violated your rights and you are a member of **SAG**, contact the union and they will review, investigate and, if appropriate, enforce your complaint. Here is an example of how the union can resolve a problem for its members: A female Extra was hired to *"photo double"* (a person who physically resembles a "star") an actress. Her casting service told her on Thursday—one day before she was supposed to start—that she was booked for the following Friday, Monday, Tuesday and Wednesday evenings. At that point, they also told her what the specifics of her work would entail; so, she had her hair dyed and prepared for four evenings of night shooting.

During her second night on the set, the producers told her that she would have to walk under a shower of sparks for their next shot. Since this relatively hazardous piece of action was never discussed prior to or at the time of her booking, the woman rightfully asked for *"stunt pay"* moments before the shot was to occur. It was denied and she was fired. Furthermore, the producers also decided not to pay her for the remaining evenings for which she had been booked. She called SAG immediately. The result: To avoid a heavy fine from SAG, the Producers ended up paying her for all four originally booked evenings, not just the two evenings she worked.

In Chapters 11 (" The Screen Actors Guild") and 12 (".A.F.T.R.A., Equity and A.G.V.A."), we'll look deeper into the province of unions. For now, if you are serious about learning more of the rules that govern union and non-union Extras, ask your fellow actors if they know of any professional organizations for Extras. The more you know about every aspect of your business, the better off you are.

# Public Access

Still another avenue for receiving a credit in your portfolio is through public access television. Each cable station in every town, including Hollywood, is required by law to make a certain number of program hours available to the public. These shows are called public access programming. They are written, directed and performed by anyone who signs up and pays a tape fee of about $50.

If you have a clever idea for a show and

it catches on with viewers, the program director will find a regular time slot on the access channel for you. I cut my talk-show teeth on public access and practiced my craft on live-to-tape TV. They won't stop the tape if you make a mistake and there is no editing in this format. It's wild and woolly and I recommend it for all actors.

You could do plays, scenes, talk shows, cooking shows, variety shows or any topic you are knowledgeable about. Since you only have an hour to build the set, tape the show, and strike the set, you'll need to prepare and rehearse outside of the studio. You'll also have to bring your own stuff, including plants, furniture, etc. The better prepared you are, the smoother the show runs and the more fun you will have. But, most importantly, you'll receive yet another credit. The three largest cable networks in the L.A. area are in our phone book.

As you can see from these first chapters, you've got a lot of work to do in preparing for a successful acting career. What with deciding on an image, getting good headshots, building an impressive resume, keeping your radar out for scam runners and getting into the right acting class . . . it might seem a little too much to even consider trying to find an acting job on your own.

Well, take a breath. Because now is the time to start delegating certain aspects of your career to professionals who can do the rest of the non-acting work for you better than you can. That's why actors have agents.

In the next chapter, I'll answer the question "Why do actors need agents?" in greater detail, show you how to distinguish a competent, reputable agent from an impostor, and coach you on how to keep an agent once you've gotten one. This is where your career moves to the next level. So, relax. This where the serious fun starts.

## AUDITION AND JOB TRACKING SHEET    DATE _____

Audition Date _____ Time_____

Name of Project _____

Contact Person: _____

Address _____

_____

Nearest Cross Street _____

Thomas Guide Coordinates _____

**Project:**

**COMMERCIAL**

**PILOT**

**EPISODIC**

**MOVIE OF WEEK**

**FEATURE FILM**

**MINI-SERIES**

**VOICE-OVER**

**1ST CALL**

**2ND CALL**

**PRODUCERS READ**

**SCREEN TEST**

Description of the Character:

_____

_____

_____

_____

_____

_____

_____

_____

_____

_____

Wardrobe and Special Instructions:

_____

_____

_____

_____

_____

Sides are at:

**SHOWFAX**

**AT CASTING OFFICE**

**AGENCY WILL FAX**

**PICK UP AT AGENCY**

**AVAILABLE NOW OR _____**

_____

# Chapter 8

# The Psychology of Acting

*It doesn't interest me what you do for a living. I want to know what you ache for, and if you dare to dream of meeting your heart's longing.  It doesn't interest me how old you are. I want to know if you will risk looking like a fool for love, for your dreams, for the adventure of being alive. It doesn't interest me what planets are squaring your moon. I want to know if you have touched the center of your own sorrow, if you have been opened by life's betrayals or have become shriveled and closed from fear of further pain? I want to know if you can sit with pain, mine or your own, without moving to hide it or fade it or fix it. I want to know if you can be with JOY, mine or your own, if you can dance with wildness and let the ecstasy fill you to the tips of your fingers and toes without cautioning us to be careful, be realistic, or to remember the limitations of being a human.*

**Oriah Mountain Dreamer**
**—"The Invitation"**

In Chapter 9, we will go over the audition process for all of the acting categories covered earlier in the previous chapter six I'll walk you step-by-step through each process so you won't feel overwhelmed when you're called upon to read for any role. The more you master this process, the more you will increase your probability of landing a role. With your anxiety properly channeled, you will virtually tap dance your way through these readings and have a good time during the process.

But, before we go into the audition process, let's spend some time talking about what I consider to be the single most important factor in achieving your career goals—getting your mental attitude in a good place. In this chapter, we will look at the obstacles that attempt to thwart us from the fulfillment of our dreams. Then, we will look at some of the qualities, concepts, techniques, and practices that successful actors have used to defeat those obstacles and keep themselves empowered. Finally, and maybe most importantly, use this chapter to remind yourself that you are only human and that you are not alone—even if, sometimes, it feels like it. Exercising acceptance regarding the moment-to-moment changes and rejections that are omnipresent in this industry, not to mention life itself, will strengthen your ability to persevere during those most difficult moments.

Since we are artists, we have an artistic temperament. You may be at the pinnacle of creativity and on top of the world one minute; then, in the depths of depression, thinking you'll never work again, the next. Just accept these as the natural cycles of an artist with an uncertain future. If you start to change the way you view success and failure you may find the the mood swings and fear stop visiting you. I choose to view success the way that Earl Nightengale does, "The progressive realization of a worthy ideal." That way if today something happens to upset my career plans I know that as long as I am in the game anything is possible. I listen to Tony Robbins Personal Power tapes and have redefined how I view failure. The only way I can fail is if I get up out of bed and decide, consciously decide not to be my best anymore.

Here is a list of ten secrets I use and some of the natural resources I work with to keep possibility alive in my heart.

1. **Passion**—Is there anything else you love to do more than acting? If not, you're on the right path. Being excited every day about what you're doing will carry you to places raw talent can't even touch.

2. **Perseverance**—Are you a fighter and a survivor? Great!!! Do battle with anyone who gets between you and your dreams. Challenge those people who tell you: "No, you're not right for the part." Ten years ago, Sharon Stone had a failed series called *BAY CITY BLUES.* She didn't let it stop her. Sharon went on to do *TOTAL RECALL* with Director Paul Verhouven but, after the release of that film, her career once again just seemed to fizzle and go nowhere. After every top-name actress in town turned down the lead in *BASIC INSTINCT*, Sharon began campaigning her old friend Paul. After a lot of initial resistance, Paul was finally convinced by Sharon that she was the perfect choice for the part. The rest, as they say,

is history. Superstardom followed for Sharon Stone! Can you imagine where you might wind up if you had the same drive that Sharon Stone has?

**3. Financial Support/Stability**—Don't be a here-today-gone-tomorrow kind of performer. Actors or models who won't take financial responsibility for themselves blow around town with no permanent or lasting address. It keeps them from finding out how successful they could be. This might seem like an exciting, romantic idea but, in reality, it only shows up that way in movies. Take a stand for yourself. Put down deep roots and declare: "I will only transplant my roots when my goals here are accomplished."

**4. Perspective**—After you finish this book, you will have the tools to accomplish your goals. How will you use them? What do you ultimately want out of life and out of your career? It's important to understand the difference between the two. Acting and modeling is a job, not an identity. And if we are not our jobs, then the quality of our lives should not be so attached to fame and success as an artist that we can't tell the difference between the two

I've seen too many actors and models who don't make that distinction. So, for example, when they enter a "dry spell" of work, which is normal, their entire life collapses because they are so convinced that if they're not acting or modeling, life is meaningless. If John Travolta had taken that attitude, he might have given up. Instead he hung in there and reinvented himself in *PULP FICTION.* Well-rounded people make better actors because they have more life experience on which to draw and a healthy perspective to keep themselves balanced and grounded in reali-

ty. You are, first and foremost, a human being. The people who know you and really care about you will know and remember you less for what you do than for who you are.

**5. Written Goals**—You build a ladder to your ultimate life and career goals. If you learn to prioritize opportunities, make commitments and manage your time effectively, the possibility of realizing your dreams turns into probabilities. What the mind can conceive, the body can achieve. What will you do this year to achieve your goal? What are you doing today to make your years goal happen? Where do you see yourself in three, five and ten years? .

**6. Support System**—Get a mentor and a confidant who understands the struggle and who will encourage you at those times when you feel stuck or filled with self-doubt. Surround yourself with people who are also taking action to pursue their dreams and are getting results. Cultivate people who nurture you. If your birth family does not understand your career choice, find an extended family who will support you.

**7. Publicity**—What do you say about yourself in public? Do you *"speak well about yourself"* with passion, enthusiasm, and self-confidence? Don't be afraid to acknowledge, in a non-egotistical way, the best in you: "Yes, I am a fine actor and I thought I did an excellent job in the role of Iago during the recent production of *'Othello'."* Use what you say about yourself publicly to attract attention and harness agreement from others. This way, your name will start getting known by people who don't even know you intimately; but, the word will spread: "Oh, yeah, I know him. He really is a fine actor! I heard he put on a wonderful performance as Iago in the latest production of **Othello.**" Who knows who might be listening in on these conversations! Models are complimented often on their beauty. Just remember it is a girl given to you and cherish it and the way it seems to other people smile. Until you get a bona fide professional company to manage your publicity, you could be your own best public relations agent.

8. **Packaging**—Remember in Chapter 2 when we talked about image, about how important it was to have a clear definition of who you are going to be selling to the world? Well, here's one of the benefits of that kind of clarity. When you know who it is that you are selling, others will start to see it in you, too. Look at your image or the person you present to the world. This is the most coveted acting job you might ever have to do. Speak, dress and groom yourself in a way that is conducive to your ultimate dreams.

Don't worry if, in the beginning, you don't feel like the image you are trying to project; act as if you already were the image you are trying to project. Hey! You're an performer and a professional model, aren't you? So, act the part; eventually, the feelings will follow. Or, to put it another way - fake—it 'till you make it.

9. **Self-Promotion**—Interact with as many people as you can but shy away from gossip; it encourages negativity and judgment. There's so much hype and gossip flying around at industry gatherings, I am convinced that the entertainment industry communicates almost entirely by rumor. Don't become a gossip. Meet and get to know lots of people. Experience them and let them experience you.

Be open, honest and sincere but, also, be discriminating. You don't have to confess everything about your life. By communicating in this way, you're the one who will stand out and gain the respect and attention you deserve. Be an introducer. If you know people with similar interests or projects, introduce them. Follow up with your new contacts. Plant a million seeds, tend to them and watch your abundant garden grow.

10. **The Media**—Magazines, newspapers, radio, TV and fan mail are what I referred to as "The Media." At the beginning of your career, you'll want to gather anything and everything that has ever been written about you and your work. Eventually, you will take the most outstanding written reviews and articles of your work and assemble them for use in your *"press kit."* A press kit is comprised of the following: newspaper article clippings written about you, reviews of movies and theater productions in which you appeared or modeling shots from runway show a short biography, and a photo.

A press kit is a promotional tool, the purpose of which is to bring public and industry attention to who you are and what you've done to date. These press kits are then distributed to the media either by your agent, your manager, or by your publicist. As you gain more and more attention in your career, be prepared for the onslaught of offers to interview you. Many actors and models are often caught off guard by this new experience and, consequently, do more to damage their career than they do to enhance it. But, if you followed my advice in the Packaging section, above, you'll already be behaving as if you are the successful artist you envision yourself to be. So, when those interviews come, here's my advice: Take a deep breath, trust your instincts when giving answers to an interviewer's questions, and remember: the difference between being open, being honest and confessing. And, have fun! The more fun you have, the more the audience will enjoy you as well.

# Actors are Notoriously Secretive

It's the funniest thing but actors and models don't customarily share information. The underlying fear from insecure professionals is that you will somehow ace them out of work, even if you are both up for totally different roles. or modeling assignments. The truth is, if everyone in the world had the same information, the most diligent people would still create the greatest possibility for succeeding. The odds are that the person who puts him or herself in the path of opportunity creates the highest probability of winning.

Below are a few other personal qualities I've developed in myself and have also seen work for other people. Disciplining oneself in these qualities can transform the possibility of success into a probability:

1. **Be Consistent**—I call it "Selling the Carrot." Each day I am the best carrot I can be. When Hollywood is buying carrots, they think of me first. So what? Let them typecast you. It propelled Arnold Schwarzenegger and Sylvester Stallone to stardom. You can show them your versatility when you get there.

2. **Go The Extra Mile and Have a Few Surprises**—If you give more to a role than is written, directors will take the credit, writers will love you and producers will hire you again and again and again. Give without being asked. Take risks. Follow the ideas that pop into your head in the moment. It will surprise everyone, maybe even you. Jack Nicholson said: "On the first take I always follow my instincts. If they don't like it, take two." The same holds true for auditions and readings as well as for performance in front of a camera.

   Do your homework and bring plenty of ideas to the audition or to the set. They don't just have to be acting ideas, they can be about the look and feel of the character, such as hair, wardrobe and make up ideas. Discuss them with your director. Bring whatever props aid you in building the character. Rehearse with and without your props. Dream up many ways of doing the same scene so no one idea gets locked in your head. Okay? You're a creative artist, aren't you? So . . . create!

3. **Learn From Defeat**—It's been said that what is important is not how one fails but how one recovers. Taking it one step further, it is moving from defeat to defeat without loss of enthusiasm that matters. Our strengths come from accepting and moving past our weakness. Let your anger drive you out of the pit, be a fighter!

4. **Go for It**—No balls, no blue chips. Be brave; be forward.

5. **Keep a Big Feeling** —A big feeling is just the conscious thought of unlimited possibilities. Be confident and spread it around. People gravitate to a person who knows how to be happy. Know what you want, keep your eyes on the prize, whether your personal circumstances are good or bad. It is especially important to keep a big feeling when you're feeling down. The person who has hope has everything.

6. **Learn to Handle People Well**—It is part of your job to make the people in the casting room feel comfortable and at ease, not the other way around. One feisty actor I know, when asked the standard audition line, "Do you have any questions?" responded in character, without missing a beat and said, "Yes, what is the capital of Ohio?" It cracked up the room, relieved the tension and put everyone at ease. This kind of disposition leaves the decision makers feeling confident that you can handle anything that comes your way, with all the pressure on the set.

Put everyone on the *same level* — When you walk into a room full of *"suits"* for a reading at the network or studio level, it is easy to be intimidated. Remember that you have already made bold acting choices that have gotten you this far. Trust yourself and stand tall. Upon meeting a network president, that same feisty actor I just mentioned was ushered into a large office with 15 Emmy's on display. The actor took one look at the Emmy's all lined up and asked, "Who's the bowler?" Once again he cracked up the room. Humor is the great equalizer.

7. **Make Wishes**—Focus on what you want. If you stay focused on even the most mundane, career-based activities, you will be so busy that you won't let the day-to-day time killers get in your way. You know what I mean, don't you? Like making unimportant phone calls for idle conversation during the time that should be set aside for mailing out pictures. Stuff like that. Your time is very valuable and should be spent on moving toward your biggest dreams. Otherwise, one day you'll wake up and find that there's no longer any time nor any room for what you want.

8. **Choose the Right Friends** —This doesn't necessarily mean choosing only people in high places or people who can advance your career. Certainly, successful, powerful people may be as nice to have as friends as anyone else. But rather, it means avoiding people I call psychic vampires— the negative people who feed off of your energy. These are people disguised as friends but who only call when they need something, or who have problems they want you to solve but contribute nothing themselves in return. These types of people are easy to spot. They always seem to be in crisis, or depressed about something, and rarely are seen smiling.

9. **Speak Up**—Assert yourself. Be appropriate to the moment but never be afraid to say who you are. When people ask you what you do, stand up proudly (figuratively or literally) and tell them you are an actor or model. Common comebacks I've heard to this response include: "Oh, really? How rare in Holly-

wood." Or worse, "So, what restaurant do you work at?" Don't ever take this from people, no matter who they are or how powerful their position. Although people have a right to their opinions, you also have the right to be treated and talked to with respect. If they can't respect you, all you need to do is step out of their way and let them go act out their personal flaws somewhere else.

10. **Luck**—Luck is being prepared when opportunity knocks. One wise golfer said "It's funny, the harder I work, the luckier I get."

11. **Youth is a State of Mind**—There will always be someone younger, tighter, or better-looking. But . . . there will never be another person who is uniquely you. You are not your body. You are not your age. You are not your face. Focus on the things in your soul that make you happy and you will be forever young. At my age, on a day when I am extremely happy, I will still get carded at nightclubs to see if I am really 21. My birth certificate tells me I am not, but my inner spirit, my bliss, says otherwise.

12. **Believe Your Own Press**—Ego and ambition are things I admire and possess. Ego teaches you to pursue greatness and ambition motivates you to get there, but never at the expense of other people. Ego misused becomes selfish and self-centered; ambition misused turns you into a human predator. These qualities will, ultimately, undo great acting and great actors.

13. **Make Other People Look Good**—A famous race car driver summed up the most important lesson of racing: "You can only win by winning, not by trying to make someone else lose. It's a matter of focus." If you obsess about your fellow actors' lack of generosity, personability, etc. then you aren't concentrating on your own dream. It's amazing how excited people get about a project when no one cares who gets the credit.

14. **Do Your Homework**—Some people can change bad habits or mind sets with a few affirmations. The rest of us have to work a little harder and make a conscious effort to change that bad habit. Embrace change as part of the great mystery and excitement of life. Use it to support yourself. Ayn Rand said: "Life is a process of self-sustaining and self-generated action and every value of life requires continuous actions to support and maintain it". Wow.

There is a lovely woman here in Hollywood to help you along the way with the mental struggle of being an actor. Her name is Linda Buzzell and she has written a book entitled *How To Make It In Hollywood— All the Right Moves.* She put on a seminar at **Women In Film** that gave me insight into sabotage and how to override the internal bullshit tapes. By actively engaging in these exercises and integrating them into your own consciousness, you, as a human being can train yourself to distinguish and focus on those thoughts that leave you with a sense that you can win and those that sabotage your ability to show up powerfully:

**To Win:** I know who I am and what I have to offer.
**Sabotage:** I try to be a chameleon and make everyone happy.

**To Win:** I know what I exude without me trying. (Image)
**Sabotage:** I must be a memorable.

**To Win:** I identify and acknowledge my weak points.
**Sabotage:** I hate it when I am weak.

**To Win:** I know what I bring to the party.and what I contribute.
**Sabotage:**I believe something outside of me is the answer or secret to my success.

**To Win:** I know what turns me on. I know what excites me and I brim with passion.
**Sabotage:** I'm a people pleaser and never have an opinion or enthusiasm of my own. I lack passion.

**To Win:** I know where I'm going. Clearly outline, in writing, what to shoot for.
**Sabotage:** I lack goals or direction and am controlled by other people.

**To Win:** I know that a "no" only means no today. (One actress kept getting called in for *CHEERS* and never got the role. They loved her work so much, the writers finally just wrote a part specifically for her.)
**Sabotage: I'm** being typecast.

**To Win:** I know now that I am already good enough.
**Sabotage:** I focus on how scared I am feeling.

**To Win:** I know that people will follow my vision. I'm clear, enthusiastic and firm about my passion.
**Sabotage:** I'm only mirror the politically correct opinions of the day.

## Making Others Shine at Work

Always look for opportunities to be interested—not interesting. Do your homework: go see films that casting directors and directors have done and refer to them in your audition, or interview. If you do not know their credits, use the books and film libraries covered in other chapters as a resource or call the respective guilds. Rent their movies and focus on what you like about the film. Find out the person's history. Read interviews in magazines and ask them about their personal lives. If you are genuinely interested in others, then you will be interesting.

Don't grovel in the presence of producers, directors, or studio executives or fashion designers. Remember: you are renting your services and talent out to somebody who needs you.

Problems are an opportunity to go beyond the places in your life where you've habitually been stuck. Don't see problems as problems. Make every obstacle is an opportunity.

Repeat the following: "I declare myself publicly to be _____ because it's true —even if there's no evidence to back it up at the moment. Don't brag to manipulate or psych people out. Bragging is a cover up for a lie.

Be bold right now. Don't be afraid of greatness. Use greatness and pride as part of the subtext in every audition.

Never believe what is on the surface. Living is finding the deeper truth.

## Turn Your Mental Tapes Around

Here are some ideas you can use to replace some of the most common, internal, destructive voices we hear in our heads. Be a detective and investigate your own life. Discover where you first began to believe these negative ideas and when you, ultimately, made the decision to accept them as your own personal "truth." Write these internal conversations down on paper—exactly as you hear them in your head. Once you've become clear and specific about those inner voices, use the following exercises to replace those negative thoughts with positive declarations. Don't wait around for your emotional body to catch up with your new declarations; that will take constant practice and lots of time. Instead . . . act as if those declarations were true (the same way you've been acting as if those historical negative thoughts were true); as though you were an actor playing a character.

The following are active exercises, so try them and see if it works for you.

## All About Sabotage

There are three indications that signal that a person is about to shoot him or herself in the foot:

1. Ignoring the rules. (Showing up late, not being prepared, coming in hung-over, etc.)
2. Complaining about the rules.
3. Becoming bitter.

The first step to stopping the behavior is recognizing it. You can get off the merry-go-round at any time and make a healthier choice.

## Handling Difficult People

It's not personal. These people are self absorbed and don't have an opinion about you. If they cross the line I always stand up to bullies. Some difficult people yell and scream, they are actually frightened and would like to cry but consider it to be weak. Women yell because it is what they do to fit in. They can't show fear. Be smarter, relax and exercise compassion until others are comfortable. If they have a track record, take what they are doing right and learn.

## On Perfectionism

There is a really dangerous kind of perfection. It manifests by you believing you are not really good enough, that if only your lines were just perfect, or you could just walk a certain way down the runway or achieve a look on your face in from of the camera then maybe you would be okay. This attitude halts spontaneity and enjoy life.

*To Win:* The critic in your mind who is hard on you is wrong and most of the time is not your voice but the voice of someone in your past you is haunting you today. I just say thank you and sssh ssh and tell the voice to be quiet.

Another type of toxic perfectionist believing that if it's not perfect, it's nothing. No two snowflakes in life are the same. Why would you ever want to take a step down from uniqueness to perfection?

## Snatching Defeat from Mouth of Success

It is very scary to be enormously successful. Shane Black graduated from USC and one year later wrote **LETHAL WEAPON**. It was sold for a record amount and then he became totally depressed. He was afraid he could never top his first career success. Rosanne Barr tainted her success with the rendition of the National Anthem and grabbing her crotch on national TV. Just another form of fear and self-sabotage. In these times I practice courage. Courage is being afraid and moving forward anyway. I start to believe I deserve my success. Each of us are a vehicle through which greatness flows. Acknowledge it and am grateful. I just let it flow and have no egotistical attachments to it. Accept that you had a lot to do with it, but not all to do with it.

## Being an Actor Can Be a Roller Coaster Ride

Let's face it, no matter how positive we try to be or how perfectly we follow the rules, some days things just go badly. It's particularly hard for me if I'm awaiting network approval on a series or I get put "on hold" for a commercial; or worse, if it comes down to myself and another actress for a role—and she gets chosen over me. Perceived rejection is a hard storm to weather for artistic emotional types like us. Also, my personal life can hurl me into "the pit" as well. On those days I batten down the hatches, hold onto furniture and hide all the sharp objects in the house. The cure for me is to play hooky during that day and go to see a movie matinee that makes me laugh or lifts my spirits. Go ahead and indulge yourself, get the popcorn, candy and a refreshing beverage. Hang on, don't make any decisions today because by tomorrow you will feel better and a lot more balanced because you took care of yourself today.

I learned a lesson from a wise friend of mine named Joe. One day, I was in a tizzy over a problem that involved having to choose among a sudden influx of agents who started wooing me to their agency and the accompanying roles for whom the agents were submitting (a rare, but enviable problem for actors to have). I was trying to solve the problem logically by using Joe as a sounding board. After I made my case, he said to me: "Acting is not an art of logic, it is an affair of the heart. If you try to make decisions solely based on reason, it will take you out of the natural flow of the process. And it will distract you from using the gifts that life has sent you." When you start to focus on your personal flaws and personal problems, you may miss the opportunity to express your greatness in the role that is on the table in front of you at that particular moment. Having become pre-

maturely and overly concerned with what wasn't happening or trying to overcompensate for a personal flaw (e.g., having passed up a great role because they weren't offered the money they wanted or believe they deserved), an actor might painfully discover that a loss of focus leaves him or her with the following consequences: offers stop coming, personal gifts atrophy, and eventually, the actor's art dries up and dies.

Joe worked on a soap opera and was challenged daily to bring daytime dramatic writing to life. It was his job, as a superb actor, to be committed to his art and elevate the words to an evocative level of performance, all within the confines of the hectic time restraints inherent to daytime shows—not to mention the disarming crises he had to deal with in his personal life. "If you focus on elevating the material," he said, "you can have a career for as long as you can remember your lines." He also reminded me that the nature of life is such that we are not necessarily meant to stay on top all the time. Success comes and goes, just as all things in life do.

Once again, John Travolta's career provides an example. The consistency that brings a certain level of mastery comes out of your desire to bring a piece of material to life with the very best of your abilities and the talents God gave you. Your talent is God's gift to you; what you do with it is your gift back. Ebb and flow. If you get no other message from this book, please try to grasp this one: Be faithful to your art, listen to your heart, and honor and express your gifts. The rest will take care of itself.

# Chapter 9

# The Audition Process

**Silent Pictures by Katie Maratta**

## How Casting Work

Before a project can be cast, agents and managers must know what the casting director is looking for. An entertainment industry script distribution company  known as **Breakdown Services** provides this very much needed and valuable service. The brain child of Gary Marsh, They originated in Los Angeles and now has offices in Toronto, Vancouver, New York and London.

Here's a simple overview of how their service works. Breakdown Service will go through a script and, then, create a *"breakdown"* of characters; i.e., a detailed description of each character's characteristics and qualities (hence the term breakdown). The description is written up and distributed to agents and managers who subscribe to the service.

Each breakdown listing is packed with important information. The name of the production company, network affiliation, name of the film, or the episodic show and the title of that show. Also on the page are the names of the executive producers, producers, the director, the casting director, and their associates. Also included is the start date of that project and the location where it is to be shotand where to send submissions for roles to be cast.

The final item in the listings is the character breakdown. The character description is including the name of the character,  a complete description of the  physical type, the age range, the psychological profile and what the character does in the story line and the page number in the script where the character first appears. If a star is already attached to a project, or if the part has been pre-cast, the character name and the word "cast" appears along with the star's name.

These breakdown listings are published daily and distributed to agents and managers all over town in the wee hours of the morning. The first order of the day for agents is reading through the listings and then compiling packets of actors' pictures  to submit to each casting director for their respective projects. Usually the agents with more clout and good casting director relationships will call on the phone to pitch their clients and secure audition times.

Breakdown Services also has a specialized service called comEx that delivers commercials via satellite to agents instantly throughout the day. Within minutes of a call being placed by a commercial casting director, all commercial agents receive the casting information simultaneously in Los Angeles.  Some sixty commercials per day are sent out to commercial talent agents this way.

Casting directors have the option of using Breakdown Services or going directly to the agents that they choose to work with.  However, Breakdown Services releases an overwhelming majority of the projects that are casting because of its 28 years of service, it has proven to be an effecient and easy way for casting directors to ge the word out to the legitimate representatives of talent. Here are a few other items that will help to learn about casting directors and approach them by mail.

## Casting By

This is a booklet that Breakdown Services prints in association with the **Casting Society of America.** It lists each casting director who is a member of the society and up-to-date, completed lists of each member's credits. You can use this booklet to find our the previous credits of a casting person you might be meeting for a reading. You can then rent their film and discuss their work intelligently while on your audition.

## Flyer Delivery

If you appear in a play or an industry welcome showcase, you'll need to get the word out. One way is by paying a fee to Breakdown Services to have your flyer included in their daily casting listings which are, in turn, delivered to all subscribers including agents, managers, producers and casting directors. Another way is by trying to get the Producer of the play to pay for the flyer delivery. If the producer will not, approach all the actors in the cast and get them to chip in. Whichever way you go about it, the cost will be about $70 per flyer. You must provide Breakdown Services with one flyer for each subscriber; so, you will have xeroxing costs as well. Print the flyers on bright paper so it stands out from the white casting listings.

Once the flyer is delivered, you can follow up with a phone call to offer tickets for your play to industry professionals. If complimentary tickets, food or wine are being provided, be sure to include that information on the flyer. Also, include the names of all the cast members, the names of the director and producers, and the dates and time of the play. Mini pictures of the cast are optional; however, if a casting director recognizes or is acquainted with one of the cast members, that might just be the enticement needed for the casting director to attend.

## Casting Director Labels

If you want to do a mass mailing to casting directors to let them know you are new in town or appearing on TV, in a play or other type of performance you will want to send a postcard. It is the way most casting directors perfer to receive these announcements. That way they can keep a stack of postcards on the corner of their desk and when they are looking for a role to fill they usually look there first. Hollywood, Here I Come! has the most up-to-date address labels to assist you. They are broken down into groups (casting directors and agents) and can be ordered already pre-printed on labels at our website http//www.hollywoodhereicome.com

## Mobile Mailbox

If you are physically right for a show and wish to get your picture to the casting director in a hurry without using a courier, you will want to know about **Mobile Mailbox.** It is the cheapest way to get your packet around town. This co-op messenger service has drop boxes all over the city with two pick-ups per day. Mobile Mailbox delivers submissions to studios and casting directors for $1 to $3. To get a list of drop boxes and rates by zip code and to pre-purchase their stickers (used like a postal stamp), call **Mobile Mailbox.** Using this service will save you from driving all over town with your submissions.

## Auditions At Studios

As our industry goes through the same economic turbulence as other industries, the major studios and production companies keep changing names or going out of business. A list of all the current studios in along with the most popular commercial casting houses in our phone directory at the back of this book. That way you can get to the right place for auditions. I have included the Thomas Brothers Guide coordinates so you can easily find them on your maps.

If you have an audition at a major studio, find out from your agent which gate to enter. Your parking pass or instructions will be at that gate. When you go to pick up your sides the day before, take the time to find the gate and get your bearings. This way, you won't be distracted on the day of the audition.

Once you get onto a studio lot, there is no rule about how long you can stay. It's okay to hang out, have lunch at the commissary and even go to a sound stage to see a shoot. More importantly, this is a great opportunity to visit other casting trailers and drop off your picture. It's called working the lot.

The casting people will assume that you are a busy actor if you're already on the lot. Just keep your stay in their office brief. Remember your 30-second pitch. Something like: "I was on the lot to read for so and so and I wanted to drop my picture by for your files." If you're new in town, be sure to mention this. Casting people are always looking for new faces. If they're away from the office and it is locked, leave your photo with a note. If you don't know which other casting people are on the lot you are visiting you can find out in The **CD Directory** also available on the website for your assistance..

# The Casting Director

Almost all casting directors are independent and are looking for their next job, just like you. They are an integral part of the movie-making process. Their responsibilities are complex, time consuming, and varied. Since you as an actor will be spending most of your career-building efforts with casting directors, I believe that it is very important for you to know the nature of their work. This kind of knowledge will enable you to conduct yourself more compassionately with them and, in the long run, be remembered as someone who shows respect and understanding for another person's skills. So, here is a list of just some of the things they need to contend with on a day-to-day basis:

1. Get hired; no time to celebrate.
2. Get the movie budget and see how much they have to work with.
3. Make up a wish list of actors for each of the larger roles.
4. Meet with producers and director to make casting suggestions and get their wish list.
5. Call agents and make offers.
6. Send out breakdowns to cast the roles that are left.
7. Sort through tons of submissions and hold readings.
8. Arrange callback readings with producers and director.
9. Call the union to see if all actors are members in good standing.
10. Publish the cast list for the production company.
11. Have scripts delivered to the actors.
12. Set wardrobe fitting times for the actors and director.
13. Type up contracts.
14. Give out the shooting schedule and call times.
15. Deal with any actor who is late or fired.
16. Wrap the job and go out and hustle for another one.

# A Day in the Life Of a Casting Director

Casting can often be a thankless job. A brief description of a casting director's day goes like this: Up early to go through the thousands of submissions they receive for each role and decide who will be set for *"pre-reads"* (a special reading for a casting director who isn't familiar with a particular actor's work) and which actors can go straight to producers. They are on the telephone all morning

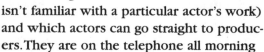

with agents pitching clients and setting appointments for auditions. Then they make copies of the *"sides"* (a few pages of the full script covering a specific character for auditions.

They almost never leave their offices for lunch and usually try to grab a bite while reading actors. (Don't be offended if they eat during the interview, but they shouldn't eat while you read. Just tell them you'd be happy to wait until they are done.) They preread about 40 to 60 people per role, so auditions often go into the early evening. Then it's off to meetings with the producers and director to suggest known actors for parts and to have *"concept meetings"* (where they try to achieve a meeting of the minds about the look and feel of a character) about other roles.

If, during these concept meetings, a casting director discovers that an actor is no longer with an agency or has changed agents, the casting director will use the **Academy Players Directory** or the **Agency Department** at **SAG** to track the actor being down. In the evening, casting directors grab dinner on their way to a theater, a cold reading workshop or a movie screening or they go home to view demo tapes or TV shows to catch an actor's performance. Finally, at day's end, they collapse and prepare to have more of the same again tomorrow.

## Casting Director Personalities

Some casting directors are former actors and, therefore, can easily empathize with a performer's sensitivity, drive, desire and passion to succeed. Most casting directors love actors and want us to be successful. However, it is important to remember that, even though we are on the same team, it is their job to judge your performance and bring to producers and directors the right actors for the right role.

Another thing to remember: just like you and me, they all have their own distinct personalities that are affected by circumstances that have nothing to do with you.

Some days a casting director may react to you lightheartedly and with warmth; the next time, distant with a cold-shoulder. Don't take it personally; it has nothing to do with your performance. Although you are on the same team as the casting director, you are being judged the minute you walk in the door. That's their job. So, make it work for you. You have their undivided attention for the first 30 seconds. Reach inside yourself and bring out that authentic quality of confidence within you.; not pushy, egotistical confidence but that of an actor who is at ease within his or herself and with his or her body.

## Getting the Sides or Script

As soon as you are notified that sides are available, go to the designated casting office or web site and get them right away. If you pick them up at the casting office stay there and read them in case you have questions. If, instead of sides, you are required to read the whole script, take it home and study it. Pay attention to what the other characters have to say about your character. Don't become discouraged if the character doesn't sound like your type; the producer and director may have decided to go a different direction with the role than is indicated in the script. In that case, ask the casting assistant about the character breakdown.

Incidentally, there are new services in town to help out busy actors who don't have the time to get across town through traffic to pick up sides. These services include picking up scripts from casting directors and faxing the available sides to your home or or posting the sides on the web. If you neither have a fax machine or computer of your own nor know anyone who has one, a nearby copy store or office supply store will receive the transmission for a fee. We have two companies who can get sides to you by fax or internet. Their numbers are in our phone book.

## Office Conduct

Be polite to everyone in the casting office. This week's secretary is next week's casting director. If your appointment is at 1:00 PM, that is what time you're expected to be there to read. Get there ahead of time so that you can relax and settle in. Sign in on the sheet or let the assistant know that you are there. **SAG** rules say they can make you wait up to one hour; after sign in then they have to pay you a penalty. At a normal audition, there will be usually about 10 to 20 people reading for the same role. From this group, three to five will go on to meet the producers and director. Don't become disheartened if the casting director seems to be acquainted with and, therefore, friendlier toward other actors waiting to read—it's the director who makes the final decision.

If you have a conflict with the audition time, have your agent call the casting director to notify them of the conflict. Alternately, you might consider showing up earlier and requesting to see if they can take you sooner than your scheduled appointment. Don't be overly demanding. Nobody like to feel bullied —especially when they are doing you a favor.

## Dressing for Auditions

Now, what about the proper attire for a reading? When auditioning for a feature film or a TV show, you don't necessarily have to dress like a waitress if you are reading for one but you should suggest the appearance of the character; e.g., in the situation of the waitress, you might allude to the character as a blue-collar woman by wearing a casual dress and flat shoes and chewing gum. On the other

hand, if it's a commercial audition, you are expected to dress just like the character.

## Audition Preparation

When you are called in to read, be professional and prepared: Have a varied inventory of things to talk about, if there is an interview before the reading. Have your picture and resume handy, even if you think they already have one. Know your lines (they don't have to be memorized at this stage of the process). Always keep the script in your hand in case you need to glance at it.

## The Audition Preliminaries

Most casting directors like to chat a little before the reading. They may ask you about credits on your resume, but most will ask you some personal questions, such as where you're from, what kind of hobbies and interests you might have outside of acting, etc. Don't direct the conversation back to acting so you can impress them with your list of credits; not only does it make you sound desperate but it gives them very little opportunity to see your passion. Talk about things that excite you: pets, children, vacations, etc. It will bring your body to life and be a good warm up for the reading. If a casting director does-

n't have time to chat, he or she will always ask if you have any questions about the script or the character. Here is your chance to clarify any doubts you have.

Remember: when you go to pick up the sides at the office, scan through them while you're there so that you can ask any questions before you go home to build the character. This way, when you arrive for the reading, you will walk in prepared, relaxed, on track and ready for any last-minute adjustments which might be thrown at you. You can take a moment to get into character before you start your reading. It's your audition. Take command of the room and the time. Don't rush. It's your shot and you have license to take all the time you need.

## Props, Guns and Touching Things

Never bring weapons into an office to use as a prop. It distracts the casting director from your good work and shifts attention onto the weapon and safety concerns. Props are usually a judgment call. I prefer to work without props unless it's something that particularly grounds me into the character.

As a rule, most casting directors I have interviewed do not like you to touch anything in their office—including them. If you have a very physical scene to do, you will just have to have the intensity and physicality in your body during the reading. With love scenes, you may have to create an intimate romantic moment with a casting director, often times a person of the same gender. One trick I have used success-  fully is to look deeply into the other person's eyes, so deeply that I can describe exactly their color, nuance and shape after I leave the office.

This gives me a focus and, more importantly, causes a reaction in myself and the casting director without requiring me to touch anybody. Of course, not all casting people are good readers or actors, so don't expect much interaction. Just carry the performance yourself.

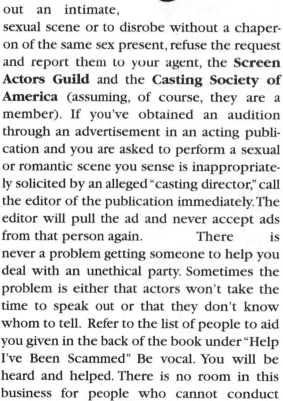

## Intimate Material

If anyone ever asks you to act out an intimate, sexual scene or to disrobe without a chaperon of the same sex present, refuse the request and report them to your agent, the **Screen Actors Guild** and the **Casting Society of America** (assuming, of course, they are a member). If you've obtained an audition through an advertisement in an acting publication and you are asked to perform a sexual or romantic scene you sense is inappropriately solicited by an alleged "casting director," call the editor of the publication immediately. The editor will pull the ad and never accept ads from that person again. There is never a problem getting someone to help you deal with an unethical party. Sometimes the problem is either that actors won't take the time to speak out or that they don't know whom to tell. Refer to the list of people to aid you given in the back of the book under "Help I've Been Scammed." Be vocal. You will be heard and helped. There is no room in this business for people who cannot conduct themselves professionally.

## That's a Wrap or Take Two

At the end of the reading, the only response you may get from a casting director is a simple "Thank you" or "Great." That's pretty typical. It has no bearing on how you did; it's just a way for them to indicate that the interview is over and they would like you to leave. If you blew the reading and are sure that you did, now's the time to speak up. Let them know you felt the reading was "off" and that you wish to read again. Nine times out of ten, a casting director will agree.

If, on the other hand, you are denied a second chance, it may be for other reasons, such as: they thought the reading was sufficient; or, although your reading was excellent, you're not physically right for the part; or, hundreds of other things. If you're curious, ask. But, don't pester them or beg; it makes you look inexperienced. If the casting person says the reading was fine, simply express your gratitude for their time, attention,  show good judgment and leave.

## Dealing With Nerves

The casting process can either be fraught with anxiety and rejection or it can be creative and fun. The choice is yours. If you go into a reading believing that you may be the answer to the casting directors' problems and that you are there to help him or her out, then any nervous energy you might have will be directed in a positive way and, in turn, will enable you to focus your attention on the casting director and his or her needs. You will be surprised at how much better your reading becomes when the attention is on something other than yourself. To this day, I still get nervous before every audition or performance. But when I consciously reinterpret the anxiety in my body from the fear of rejection to the possibility that something exciting is about to happen, I walk in fired up and confident. I am an adrenaline junky, so I love that feeling.

Now let's take a look at some of the different types of auditions you will inevitably walk into. In the following sections I have laid out each type of audition to

familiarize you with the nuances of the different processes.

## Theatrical or Television Auditions

The call will come from your Agent for you to read for a movie, a movie of the week or an episodic television show. Here are the things you need to find out or know ahead of time:

1. Date and time of the audition.
2. Name of the show or movie.
3. Casting director's name
4. Address where the reading will be held. (If it is at a studio, find out which gate to enter).
5. When the sides will be available and where. SAG rules say they have to be ready for pick up 24 hours ahead of time. (A full script also must be made handy to read in their office. If the part is small, don't worry about reading the full script.)
6. Name of the director and producers (only if you get a callback so that you can do your research on them).
7. The breakdown of the character. This is where you get an idea of the character's personality profile and some clue as to what to wear. If your agent says they are not handy, ask him or her to call you back with it but make sure you get this information, it really helps.

## Going Into the Room

When you're finally called into the casting room, you may find that you will be instructed to read either with the casting director or with a "*reader.*" A reader is usually another actor who is paid or who volunteers to help the casting office with the process.

Incidentally, you might consider assisting a casting director as a reader for the experience —when you're not showing up for your own auditions, of course. It's fun to do, if you have the time, and invaluable for you to see how a casting director chooses one actor out of many for one role.

If you do assist in the audition process often enough, you'll start to develop a sixth sense about which actors have that certain sort of "it" and which actors don't. You'll start to see clearly which ones are preordained to fail, which ones will get to a certain level of success but are locked into a type of role for the duration of their career, and which actors are destined to make all the way to the top.

## The Big Mystery

Which brings me to my next point—the Big Mystery. Why do certain actors rise to stardom and others don't? Well, the short answer is—nobody knows for sure. There are many stars with average talent whose rise to fame was manufactured (by expert public relations, master contract negotiators, etc.), or who were in the right place at the right time, or who knew the right person, or who benefitted for a number of other reasons unrelated to the mastery of their craft. Similarly, there are probably an  number of inordinately t ented actors who may never receive recogni- tion—for just as many baffling reasons. In the final analysis, I guess it's that ultimate, indefin- able quality which, all things being equal, make the difference between dom and obscurity.

Still, there are certai sional practices, certain qualities and attitudes you can cultivate for the audition process to make it possible for your own star quality to shine through. Next, I have out-

lined three role categories and their respective behavior qualities as they pertain to the audition process. If you are consistently cast in one type of role and want to move up, or if you're wondering why you keep getting stuck in one category, check your performance behavior.

## Bit Player—Five Lines and Under

1. Has all the words memorized and can read them with the inflection on a different word each time.
2. Never loses eye contact when reading.
3. Stays frozen to a single spot on the floor.

## Supporting Roles

1. Doesn't ever dominate the scene.
2. Doesn't risk too much.
3. Allows only a little bit of personality to sneak in.
4. Tends to rush the reading.

## Leading Ladies and Men

1. Make bold choices, whether right or wrong. (When Barbara Eden read for *I DREAM OF JEANNIE,* she came in and sat on top of the back of the chair, not in it. They knew right then, she was the gal for the part.)
2. Are interesting to watch as they struggle with conflicts.
3. Take advantage of the spaces between the lines.
4. Don't appear to know what they are going to say next.
5. Are keenly aware of everything in the room.
6. Take their time and feel free to move about the space.
7. Never refers to the character in the third person when discussing the role they are playing.

## Episodic Research

If you are reading for an episodic television show, take it upon yourself to see the program at least once. This way, when you walk in for an audition, you will already know the style of the show, the pace and the period. I tape the new fall line up every year just for this reason. It used to be that the casting period for new pilots was done every January; now, it happens all year long.

There is a new avenue for showcasing new programs called *"pilot presentations."* These presentations give the network an idea of what a show would look like without all the expense of a fully produced pilot. Pilot presentations are taped in one day. Actors are paid scale with no guarantee that they will get the role if the program is sold. Regular pilots differ in that they are fully produced (sets, costumes, props, etc.) and are used to create interest at the network.

With all the unique programming being made available on cable and the different ways in which they are cast, you never know where things will lead. An actor once told me that he heard a secretary booking another actor for the part he was about to audition for. Instead of getting mad, he decided to eliminate the pressure to do a perfect audition, since he knew he wasn't going to get the part anyway. So, he went in loose and relaxed, did a great reading, and two months later the same casting director called him in to read for a series regular on another project.

Finally, an important reminder about auditions: When you finish any audition, call your agent and to advise that you're done and are available to go out again. Sometimes there is another audition in the same neighborhood and you can save yourself a trip.

# Commercial Auditions

Commercials are made for one of the following markets: **National** (airing in the entire country); **Regional** (airing in part of the U.S.); **Local** (airing in only one city); **Class A Network Spots** (airing during prime time on a major network);or **Wild Spots** (air erratically, targeted for a certain audience or demographic); *Buyout* (unlimited use for one fee.)

So, what's the first thing you do when your agent calls for you to go on an audition? The first thing you do is to make sure that you get the following important information from him or her.:

1. Date and time of the audition
2. Location where interview will be held
3. Product name
4. Is there *"copy"* to learn? (Copy is the dialogue in commercials, usually not made available ahead of time, so go early to learn it.)
5. National, Regional, Local, Wild Spot or Buyout
6. Wardrobe (If you're not clear about this, get details. The often-used "nice, casual" is a common phrase that is still unclear to me. A nice, casual mom is different than a nice casual office worker.)

And remember your professional protocol: for commercials, dress for the part. Go to the audition well before your call time to see if there is copy to work on. You don't have to memorize the copy at an audition; they will have cue cards for you. When you arrive, chances are you'll have to hang out in the waiting room for a while until your name is called to go into the casting room.

## Signing In and Size Cards

While you're waiting, you'll need to sign in on the sheet marked **Exhibit E SAG/AFTRA Commercial Audition Report,** referred to as the *"sign-in sheet."* Always print the following mandatory information: your name, social security number (I always put "SS on file" because of identity theft, agency name, appointment time, actual time of arrival, and which number of audition or callback it is (usually numbered from 1 to 4). Then, initial it.

Be very exact about your appointment time because, if you're kept waiting longer than one hour, the production company is liable and might be obligated to compensate you with a small fee. The rest of the questions on the sign-in sheet are optional and are used by the unions to track casting trends. Next, you fill out what is commonly called a *"size card,"* if it is provided. A size-card asks for all kinds of information: your agent's name, your clothing sizes, and even physical attributes. Sometimes, they even ask seemingly wacky questions. For example, they might ask about your hands. I know what you're thinking but don't write in "two." What they want to know is what conditions your hands are in —excellent condition with an appealing appearance or poor condition with cuts and wrinkles. Fill out the sizes for the rest of your clothing measurements to the best of your ability. If you need to know your hat size, a trip to any western wear store can get you this information  comes down to a tings before shoot wardrobe person will doublecheck your sizes with you.

## Storyboards

After filling in your size card, start looking around to see if there is copy or a *"storyboard"* of the commercial available for you to examine. A storyboard is a series of hand-drawn pictures depicting the sequence in which the commercial will appear in its final form. One of the many purposes of a storyboard is to illustrate the look of the commercial.

When you get copy or a look at the storyboard, read everything on the page. It should tell you if the spot is 30 or 60 seconds in length. This way you can get an idea of the pacing of the commercial. If the person illustrated in the storyboard has a different hairstyle or color than you, don't panic; it's just a conceptual rendering. Besides, this is an arena where personality wins the day. If you do get ahold of the copy, rehearse while you're waiting to be called into the casting room. Practice the dialogue aloud by yourself or with a partner if they've paired you with one. If there is no copy, expect anything.

## Psychological Sabotage

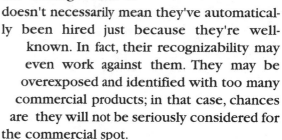

Incidentally, while you're waiting to be called in, don't be thrown if you see actors whose faces you recognize from commercials exiting the casting room. It doesn't necessarily mean they've automatically been hired just because they're well-known. In fact, their recognizability may even work against them. They may be overexposed and identified with too many commercial products; in that case, chances are they will not be seriously considered for the commercial spot.

Additionally, you may encounter some mean-spirited actors who gloatingly come out of the casting room boasting about how "they got the commercial." Believe me, they don't know any more at that point than the man in the moon. They are just trying to break your concentration.

## Polaroids

At some point — between the time you first sign in and the time your name is called — a Polaroid picture taken will be of you by the casting director or an assistant which will be stapled to your size card. Polaroids are taken most of the time for the purpose of expediency and to prepare the advertising company's wardrobe people for the kind of actors they will eventually be fitting. Even still, you will need to bring a head-shot for each audition.

## The Audition Itself

When your name is called, you go into the casting room. The first thing you'll do is greet the casting director. Next, you'll undoubtedly notice the camera person standing by the always-present video camera. (Commercial auditions are always taped. Theatrical auditions are never taped, according to union rules). Be gracious and greet them as well. Then find your *"mark."* A mark is a place designated on the floor (usually "marked" by an X or a strip of tape on the floor) where they would like you to stand; this is the distance to which the camera is pre-focused. If there is copy, check the cue cards to see where the words are located. The words are may be placed differently on the cue cards than on the copy you were initially given. It's okay to start mumbling your lines quietly to yourself.

Do not let anyone rush you. You can't do a good reading until you're comfortable with the cue cards. If you've learned the dialogue in the waiting room, you can refer to the camera more often and glance at the cue cards when you need a quick reminder. If there is a lot of dialogue, the casting director will have you direct your audition toward the cue cards and not the camera. Think of the camera or the cue cards as your best friend with whom you have something interesting to share. Touch them with the message.

## The Interview-Style Audition

But, what if there is no copy and no cue cards? Remember? Expect the unexpected! If that happens, you may be asked to do any number of things, like: work with whatever props they have available; or, improvise a scene; or, the casting director may even throw a question at you that you will have to answer off the top of your head. Don't freak out. Say the first thing that comes to mind. In fact, go in and have a ball. The more fun you have, the better your chances of being called back.

## And You Are?

When the camera starts rolling, you will be asked to *"slate."* This simply means for you to state your name out loud. If the casting people need the name of your agency and your profiles, they may or may not make these requests of you while the camera is rolling. When this information gathering part of the audition is complete, they may stop the tape before you proceed into the actual performance part of your audition or they may just keep the tape rolling.

Often times, after you've done your first take, the casting director may decide to do a *"second take"* (the second time in succession you are taped) so that he or she can direct you to alter your performance or make adjustments on your delivery. Perhaps the casting director wants to get a sense of the range and versatility of your performance capabilities; or they saw something about your delivery that stimulated an idea that was never considered before. In any event, when asked to do a second take, simply ask for a minute to digest the changes being asked of you in order to accommodate the new direction.

## Signing Out

When your audition is finished, the casting director will let you know. Thank both the casting director and the camera person for their time and interest—and be on your way. Don't ask for or expect an on-the-spot evaluation of your audition. Just leave the casting room, go  back to the Exhibit E sign-in sheet in the waiting room and record the time you are finished. This is called *"signing out."*

## The Odds

Commercials are a very lucrative way to make money from acting. Since they often pay significantly above scale rates and offer the possibility of maximum exposure for actors, competition is fierce. So, getting hired for a commercial becomes a numbers game. The average ratio between auditions and callbacks is 30:1. In other words, you'll probably wind up doing about 30 auditions before getting one callback. That's in the beginning of your career, of course. When you become more skilled at auditioning for commercials, callbacks numbers and chances for getting cast will increase.

Your look has more to do with being cast than your actual acting skills. To make things easier for the casting director, the production company and the advertising client, you will usually be put into categories, such as: Families—mom, dad, grandma, grandpa and cute little kids; Business—executives and office workers; Labor—plumbers, construction workers, etc.; Spokesperson—one person who presents the product; High fashion; or, the Brat Pack—hip, cool, young people.

## You Got the Job!

When you get hired, there are a couple of important things you should pay attention to. First of all, you will be paid for your work in one of two ways. Depending on your negotiated contract, you may receive either a *"buyout"* payment for your work or, alternately, a

*"pay-per-airing,"* where you receive a shooting fee and a steady income of residual payments. A buyout means you will receive a one-time payment fee for the shooting and airing of the your commercial. This usually happens when a commercial is sold to foreign markets. Residual payments, on the other hand, are paid out once for every 13 week cycle in which the commercial is aired in various markets. This is another reason why commercials for actors are so lucrative and competitive.

The second thing you need to watch out for is multiple commercial opportunities whereby you might be put in a situation resulting in a conflict of interest. For example,

if you shoot a spot for a car company that will air in the United States, you cannot do another car commercial until you are released from your current contract, since you would then have a conflict of interest representing two companies that make the same product. This is what the casting directors are referring to when they ask: "Do you have any conflicts?"

## Getting Into Unions Through Commercials

One final comment about commercials. Commercials are a great way to get into the **Screen Actors Guild.** If you are not a member of any union but you have a specific skill or look that the advertising people have to have, the production company—especially if the production company is a signatory to the Screen Actors Guild—will file papers and can still hire you by informing SAG of its intent to hire a non-union employee. The production company does this by filing a waiver called a Taft-Hartley. (See Chapter 11-"The Screen Actors Guild" for details on the **Taft-Hartley** laws.

## Print Auditions

Again, your agent will contact you. You need to know:

1. Where and when the audition is held.
2. Photographer or studio name.
3. The client or product.
4. How to dress.

## Dressing for Print Auditions

Here, again, it is essential that you dress for the part. Audition times for print are more flexible than audition times for other formats (e.g., theatrical, television, commercials, etc.). Your agent will give you the hours that casting for print will be taking place and you can drop by at your convenience anytime during that period. For example, if the call is from 2 to 4 PM, you can show up anytime within those two hours. However, I strongly recommend that you be there at two o'clock. A lot of models put off showing up until the last minute;

if you do the same, you might have to wait longer than you're able to or might even miss the opportunity altogether. Get there and sign in. Bring apicture,even though they will photograph you. There might be a size card to fill out as well. You don't have lines to worry about. There is never cop but that doesn't mean you can have a friendly interaction with the photographer. In fact, I think they hire the people who do.

## Say "Cheese" for Print Audition

When you go into the casting room, you will notice a photo shoot setup or a back-drop ready for Polaroids. When asked, step in front of the camera and have your photo taken. That's it! That's all there is to it! At some point, the photographer may want to see your photos you might have from other jobs, so you might want to have a portfolio available for their consideration, if you have one. This audition is based exclusively on a look and nothing else.

You might be asked to wear a swimsuit (both for print and commercials). Your agent will let you know ahead of time. Occasionally, these auditions are held in a hotel suite for foreign ad campaigns. My advice: if a situation like this comes up, bring someone with you for safety's sake.

## Rush Callbacks for Print

The time between callback and actual casting or even shooting can be very short. I have auditioned for a print job in the morning, been called back, hired and worked that same afternoon. If this is the case, the photographer will let you know so that you can check in with your agent or pager and be available at a moment's notice.

## Runway Auditions

Models who wish to audition for fashion shows are usually sent to a showroom at a local fashion mart or a designers showroom. Bring a pair of comfortable high heels that are very flattering to your legs. You will be asked to walk for them. You might want to bring some clothes to wear that accentuate your body and are as trendy as possible. Shoe models are asked to do the same thing and swimsuit models as well. Great shoes and clothes as well as a distinctive walk is the key here to being plucked out of the masses seeking these jobs. Usually when a designer finds a model they are happy with, that model is used over and over again.

## Voice-Over Auditions

The call for these auditions may come at the last minute, so a pager or cellphone is especially handy here. Ninety-nine percent of voice over auditions are held in your agent's office inside a soundproof booth. Pick up the copy as soon as it's available, especially those written as animation scripts. Animation scripts are accompanied by a drawing of the character or animal that needs a voice. The only limit to the character is the limit of your imagination. Again, ask how long the running time of the commercial is, in order to get an idea of the pacing. At the audition, you will be recorded on audio tape which will be shipped to the client.

## Industrial Auditions

Industrials are training films used by corporate America for instructional and educational purposes. Most franchised Los Angeles agents do not consider it worth their time to submit pictures for these jobs, preferring, instead, to focus on the more lucrative television and film auditions for their clients. But, there is a steady supply of work and income for any actor who pursues this avenue of work.

Agencies with offices in Orange County and San Diego, which are south of Los Angeles, actively pursue this market. You are permitted to have both a Los Angeles agent for theatrical or commercial work and an Orange County Agent for industrial work. You will either audition at your Orange County agent's office or at a corporate headquarters of the company making the educational film.

Because most metropolitan are so expansive geographically, it may not be possible to get the script the day before your audition. In that case, try to get your agent to fax the material to you. If your agent can't get the material delivered or faxed to you before your appointment time, arrive at the audition site an hour early to work on the material. If you use the earprompter, less rehearsal time may be necessary.

Dress for the part. You will either read for the client or be put on video tape, which will be used to make a decision. After you've performed in a few industrials, make it your business to get a copy of your industrial demo tape to your agent. Once they have a copy of your demo tape, your agent can use it for future industrial auditions and bookings, instead of having to go in person.

So, what specific information do you need from your Agent when auditioning for an industrial?

1.  Time and date of audition.
2.  Place to be held.
3.  Client or corporate employer.
4.  How to best to get the script.
5.  Wardrobe for part.
6.  Name of the casting director.

## Callbacks for Auditions

If the casting director wants you to read for the producer and director, they will give you a *"callback"* time. The process for a callback is much the same as the protocol for the initial audition. Get to the office and sign in. The casting director will bring you in and introduce you to all or some of the people in the room.

Expect to see a lot of people present: writer(s), director, producers and assistants. They are there to see if you are right for the part. You are there because you are absolutely right for the part. So, relax and have fun. Don't ever pull back out of fear. And don't change your wardrobe or the reading. The casting director is counting on you to deliver the same performance that wowed them the first time. If the director wants a different spin on the read, you'll be told.

## Callback Homework

A word of advice: before you show up for your callback time, do some homework. Find out who the producers and director are so you can rent their movies and become familiar with their work. If you've met or worked with any of them before, remind them when you're introduced. If the part come down to you and someone else, the actor with a past history of employment often has the advantage over those who don't.

On a film or TV series, you may be called back more than once, over a period of many months. Episodic callbacks usually happen during the same week of the initial audition because television shows move quickly and have to meet weekly deadlines. Just know that everyone in the room is pulling for you. An audition has less to do with whether or not a person likes your work than it does with an experience you may need to go through to determine whether or not you can collaborate together on a particular piece of work. Everyone in this process is your equal. Take the risk. Put yourself, your career, and your ass on the line and give them your best. Let go of your fear of rejection. Out of all of the hundreds of casting directors in town, you only need to know ten who like your work in order to keep working regularly, only ten.

## Doing Comedy

If you're reading for a comedy and no one laughs at your funny lines or falls over themselves to thank you, don't be thrown either way. These are busy executives who can be standoffish. Plus they have already heard the jokes a hundred times. While they're watching you with a smile on their face (or not), their minds are also on budget, production and writing problems. You are only a small part of their day, but you also have the power to make their day when you become the solution to their casting problem.

## Screentests

The powers that be want to see how you look on camera. This is the last step between you and the job. Relax and breathe easy because you've already charmed them. They may pick either you, a top-name actor, or someone who has *"TV Que"* (the measure of an actor's appeal to the general public), usually assigned to an actor by the network after the actor has appeared in a major role on a television series or movie-of-the-week).

No matter what you're auditioning for, remember this: Do your homework. Take risks. Have faith in your work. Don't judge yourself. Keep the channels open. And have a great time!

# Chapter 10

# Baby Steps for Child Actors

**Silent Pictures by Katie Maratta**

With more children's scripts than ever being written (*THE MIGHTY DUCKS, THE GRINCH, POKEMAN*) there is a huge demand for child actors. And if good fortune is on one's side, a child can continuing working until the teenage years (*PARTY OF FIVE, LIVING SINGLE, FRIENDS*) and, then, segue into adults roles much easier than ever before.

Just like their adult counterparts, children who wish to make it big must take many successful steps over a sustained period of time. There are no overnight success stories here. Any successful child actor must learn his or her craft and be ready when opportunity knocks. MacCauley Caulkin and Leonardo DiCaprio spent nearly a decade establishing their talent through commercials and guest roles. In 1990, MacCauley got a break in a John Hughes movie called *UNCLE BUCK* with John Candy and was paid a small five figure salary. Afterwards, Universal wasn't interested in signing him. But, after he hung in there for another year, Twentieth Century Fox launched him to superstardom in another John Hughes movie, *HOME ALONE*. The point being that success takes patience and persistence.

## Protecting Your Child and Yourself

If you're the parent of a child actor, you will often be battling many prejudices and pressures from within and without the industry. I'll give you an idea of what to expect and some pointers to assist you in protecting yourself and your child.

Every child is a human being—sensitive, inexperienced, and impressionable. Suddenly, a child is thrust into the new and unpredictable world of making movies and TV programming! A world very different than the stable one he or she is familiar with at home. A fledgling, child actor will be surrounded by adults working very hard and often under pressure to "get the job done" on time and under budget. Tempers can erupt out of nowhere and the child can, unintentionally, be rendered into a state of self-doubt. Or, at the other extreme, the people with whom children work can so overly indulge them as to leave the children thinking they are the Crowned Royalty of The World. In either case, it is very important that every successful child actor have at least one parent or grandparent who believes in the child and offers encouragement every step of the way while, at the same time ensuring that the child keeps both feet on the ground.

One of the prejudices you may encounter as a parent is people who believe that parents force their children into acting in order to live vicariously through them or even to steal their children's money. Once your child achieves notoriety, many people will even believe that the child got there on his or her own and that you are hanging on for the ride. Here are some ideas for countering this prejudice so that you can best protect yourself as well as the world's most valuable asset—the children.

Your first responsibility is to make sure that it is your child who wants the career, not you. Then, you must help your child develop the talent to back up that desire. Many parents become obsessed with having their child succeed. They wonder why some child Actors work all the time but theirs doesn't. The thing I have noticed from auditioning with many kids is the authenticity that some children exude when they are truly enjoying what they do. This love of their craft instills a confidence that lights up a room. They may have a strong personality but it's their naturalness and sincerity that sets them apart. A child's own enjoyment and dedication—not the parents'— is what opens many doors.

You, as a parent, have to be ready to make sacrifices as well as an honest commitment. For example, there is a large, initial monetary investment to be made on behalf of your child in photographs, resumes, and day care expenses. Or, you may have to leave work early at a moment's notice, drive across town in rush hour to an audition just to have your child say one word of dialogue or possibly no words at all. If your child gets the job, you'll be stuck sitting on a movie or commercial set all day and, then, have to make arrangements for yourself at work. At the end of a difficult shooting day, the child may abruptly decide that he or she doesn't want to be an actor anymore. So, these are the kind of experiences you will probably be confronted with as your child moves along in his or her career development. Let's now focus on a way to increase the probability of your child succeeding in the motion picture and television industry.

## Hedging Your Bets—Classes

The decision about whether your child is suited to an acting career can often be made by attending just one acting class. Furthermore, there are reputable, experienced professionals in the field who can help you decide if a career in acting is right for your child. And, there are a variety of venues that can help you determine whether or not your child has the aptitude for any or all of the performing arts. Acting, singing, and dancing are obviously the most sought after talents by agents. But, children can also study martial arts, play musical instruments, perform improvisational comedy or demonstrate athletic abilities and be just as valuable to an agent. My advice: Encourage your child to pursue any or all of these skills—but only if the child shows an authentic desire to do so. If not, don't force it. Don't make the mistake of trying to persuade your child to do your bidding because it secretly fulfills your needs; otherwise, this tactic will surely backfire and turn your happy child into a resentful little person who will, in turn, grow up to be an adult filled with rage. Care

for your child and be sensitive and attentive to his or her desires and needs, and go fulfill your own dreams somewhere else.

So, let's assume that your child not only expresses a genuine desire for acting or dancing or singing, etc., but also, exhibits some raw talent. Still undecided about whether or not to commit to an acting career, you wonder what to do next. This is the point where you should consider getting your child some training. Trained children are more in demand because they know what is expected of them. And, with a skilled trainer, you, as the parent, will find out whether your child has the disposition to adapt to the entertainment world.

It's important to get a good start for your children. In every large metropolitan city there exists a wide and varied group of professional trainers who coach children in specialized areas of talent. Ask anyone well known in the field of training children in the performing arts about career ideas. These are the people who can help you decide if a career in acting is right for your child. We have a list of great children's coaches for LA in the phone directory.

## Children's Coogan Law

This a new law that was instituted January 1, 2000. It protects the money earned by child actors. It was instituted because so many child actors find all their money has been spent by their parents when they reach 18 years of age. Parents must set up a special Coogan account at a bank or brokerage house that is insured by the government.

Any money that is earned by a child actors be it from commercials, acting, print, background and voice-overs must be deposited in this type of account. It does not matter what state or country the child is from or where they are employed.

You do not need a

lawyer or the approval of the courts to set up a Coogan Account. Once you set up said account you will be given a Deposit Authorization from the bank. This authorization has to be brought to every job for photocopying to be included with the childs other tax papers and contracts. If you have any questions about this or any issue to do with children call the Guild's Office Services listed in our phone book.

There is also a Young Performers Handbook that can be purchased or mailed for less than $5. It covers all kinds of questions about child performers and their parents duties.

## Children's Theater Groups

Most communities have many ongoing theater productions and are casting for new shows all the time. Try to find a group that takes children's productions out into the community. Most groups are open to children from kindergarten to high school level. It's a great way to see if your child has the discipline necessary to show up for the demands of a career. Sign your child up to audition. If accepted they will have to show up regularly for rehearsals and performances. That way you can see how they behave over the long haul do they show up with enthusiasm.

## Overview of Agents & Managers

Like all adult actors, children need support from managers and agents who know how to place the performing artist in an arena where success can occur. Let's take a look at

the proper function of these professionals so that you know what a children's manager or agent does as distinct from an adult actor's manager and agent.

## Children's Managers

Children's managers can and should open doors through their relationships with agents, casting directors, coaches, photographers, directors and producers. Their job is to assemble a support team to give your child every chance to succeed. A manager assesses your child's strength and weaknesses and suggests classes or exercises to help strengthen his or her talent. What managers, ultimately, look at is the big picture so that they know how to guide your child into the most productive areas.

Oftentimes parents confuse managers with baby-sitters. It is not a manager's job to take your children on auditions. That's your job. However, a manager will introduce you and your child to a prospective agent or agency. Another function of managers is to occasionally visit the final casting of a movie, TV show, or commercial; in this way, they can accomplish two tasks for your child's benefit: they can check up on your child's well-being while, at the same time, strengthening their professional relationships to a casting director. If you wind up hiring a manager for your child and he or she does decide to come on to the set to visit you and your child, introduce the manager to the director and producer. These are contacts your child's manager can use in the future to get your child another job with the same people.

Finding a list of good, competent managers can be as difficult for adults as it is for children; so, go to the Academy Players Directory for children and see who comes up frequently . Also check with the **Conference of Personal Manager** and ask them who might be good with kids. Also, see who are listed in our phone directory in the back..

# Children's Agents

While show business can be fun for your child and most certainly a lot of work for you, to an agent it's a livelihood. Before you make a decision to take your child to an agent, it's important for both of you to understand the kind of discipline and obligations that will be required of you. Signing with an agent means keeping your commitments to show up on time to auditions, interviews, set call times, etc. If you get into the bad habit of last-minute cancellations (for reasons other than illness) and continue doing that repeatedly, your agent will no longer support your child in the pursuit of a career. An agent can't afford to, neither financially nor professionally. So, before you even set up an appointment with a prospective agent, make an agreement between you and your child that you both will continue to do this until your child no longer enjoys it. But, please understand that once a child has made the decision to stop, he or she can't go back again.

Finding an agent who believes in your child is important; in fact, it's critical. From the minute you walk into an agency, the entire staff, from the receptionist to the agent him or herself will be evaluating not only your child's response to pressure, instructions, direction, etc. but, also, the manner in which you handle the child. So, come to the agency prepared to succeed. Dress your child in a clean, comfortable outfit for the interview and have photos and a resume ready to furnish the agent upon request.

# Photos

Because kids change so rapidly in their early careers (before 5 years of age), it is customary to use prints of a nice snapshot taken in your own backyard instead of costly photos. One good shot is all you need. Take as many rolls as necessary to get it. Agents and casting directors expect to get snapshots—not professional headshots. Photo scammers never tell parents this fact. Expensive photo shoots are the basis for most scams run against children and their parents. However, after your child has reached five years of age, you should get professional photos and have them redone every two years. You'll find a list of photographers in our phone directory.

# Resumes

A child's resume will look very similar to an adult actor's resume, with some exceptions. You can type in the color of hair and eyes because those attributes remain constant; but, the space for height and weight information should be left blank and filled in for each interview. Although you don't need to list current clothing sizes on the resume, you should bring along that information to place on the size card, which will be given to you at the agency. Most importantly, the resume must also contain your child's date of birth and Social Security number. Then, after you've done all of the above, you can format the rest of your child's resume in the manner I outlined in Chapter 5 ("The Rest of the Package") under the sections on credits and building a resume.

# Agent Interviews

Once you sit down for the interview in the agent's office, don't start gushing about your child's "extraordinary" talent. It's not helpful. It's okay to be enthusiastic; just don't take it to the obsessive extreme. Give the agent an honest assessment of your child's talents and experience and let the agent discover the singularity of your child's abilities for him or herself..

If, after the interview, you are turned down, don't take it personally. In all likelihood, the agency may decide that the category in which your child would have been placed is already filled. In that case, the agency is doing you a favor since competing for the same roles with an actor from the same agency would significantly diminish your child's chances for work and, ultimately, success.

On the other hand, if the agency accepts your child as a client and has you sign a contract, you could be well on your way to fulfilling your child's dream. Assuming you have found a good acting coach, the next step is having your new agent set up auditions. So, although your child will learn the techniques and protocol of auditioning through the acting coach, manager and/or agent.

There is a list of top children's agencies  available through any Film Commission office. We also have agents lists for major metropolitan areas on the web site. For a current address and phone number of any agency, get a copy of *The Agencies* on our web site www.hollywoodhereicome.com

## Auditions & Stage Fright

All right, now. Your child has an agent, which means that he or she will be getting ready to take that next step—auditions. Let's take a look at some of the things you both will need to be prepared for and some of the disciplines your child will need to have for the audition process.

If you can play make-believe and walk your child through a casting session, he or she won't be thrown off when actually doing the real thing. Kids are so lovable, but you have to help them put their best foot forward. The skill I find to be most valuable to children in auditions is that of observation. When a child is thrown into a strange room with strange people giving orders all at once, the child can become a bit overwhelmed, if not intimidated, during the first few times in a casting room. If a child is taught ahead of time to just observe and respond to the person giv-

ing directions, to fellow actors and to the camera, he or she will acclimate to this experience much more easily and, subsequently, give a much more relaxed audition.

Teach your child, first, to acknowledge the casting director or director when the child walks into the casting room. Then make sure the child remembers to look at the other actors and say "Hi!" Next, remind your child to look and see where the camera is so that they know where it is, and that they are probably going to be asked to do something for the casting director. That's it, that's all there is to it. Staying present and focused is the key.

Here's a good idea to help your child get over stage fright of the camera, assuming that is a problem, If you have a tripod and a video camera at home, set it up. Cut out a picture of your child's favorite cartoon or fantasy character and set it just above the lens. Tell your child to pretend that the camera is the cartoon character friend and persuade the child to talk to it that way.

## Helping Your Child to Light Up

Another thing that the two of you can do at home while waiting for that anticipated phone call from the agent is practicing how to *"slate."* Again, your child will probably learn about this procedure in acting classes, but, it is still a good idea to teach him or her about it. This is the word that the casting director will utter, probably within a few moments after your child has walked into the casting room. To slate means that, while the young performer is being filmed or videotaped, the casting director is simultaneously asking the child to state his/her name, age, or agent's name and whatever other pertinent information the casting director is attempting to gather. Practice asking your child questions in front of your home video camera: "What did you do this summer?" or "How's school going?" are common

questions one hears in the audition room. Teach your child to answer truthfully, and to keep answers simple. "School's great and I got a new kitten named Snowball." Then, your child can talk about things that interest him or her. If your kid doesn't care about school and doesn't they have a new kitten to talk about, suggest he or she talk about a favorite hobby. . . as long as the child answers the casting director's question first. An interested child is an interesting child to watch on camera. It sparks a casting director's enthusiasm.

## Preparing for an Audition

Finally, the much awaited phone call from your agent comes. Have a pen and paper handy and start writing the clear, specific information they will be giving you. If you're unclear about any of the information you're getting, ask again until you get it clear. And, here's an important tip: If no one's home to get the call except your answering machine, be mindful of your agent's efforts in setting up auditions. On any given day, your agent has multitudes of people to call with auditions. So, when your agent calls you with a confirmed audition appointment for your child, the last thing he or she has time for is an answering machine message with your tot singing a song or telling a "cute" story. Keep the outgoing message on your answering machine short and sweet.

Alright, get ready now, it's off to the audition! I have a survival pack that never leaves my car. That way I don't have to rush and gather things as I am running out the door to make my audition appointment. Since you, the parent, will be the designated driver, here are some suggestions for a survival pack of your own:

1. A *Thomas Guide* to guide you.
2. Brush, comb and hair things.
3. A change of clothes for the unexpected.
4. Pictures and resumes in a protective case (to keep gunk off of them).
5. Children's aspirin and a first aid kit.
6. A blanket and pillow for naps.
7. Pen and paper.
8. Beeper batteries.
9. Quarters for parking and pay phones.
10. An automobile emergency road service card in case your car breaks down.
11. Games and toys.

By putting together this survival pack, all you have to do is grab a beverage, your kid, and your appointment book with the address and directions for your audition and you're on your way. And, come to think of it, it wouldn't hurt to have a backup driver in case of last-minute emergencies.

## The Car Ride

In the car on the way to an audition play soft, soothing music. The Wave, 94.7 FM, plays great new age music here in Los Angeles and keep the trip anxiety free. No fighting or lecturing in the car. Just reassure your child how much you believe in him or her. If you are wound up during the car ride, you'll be sending a nervous and anxious child in to try and do his or her best work. Children who have a spiritual base in their lives can more readily respond to positive self-talk and creative visualization. So, if appropriate, use the car ride to play tapes of fun things they enjoy to keep your child as relaxed and confident as possible.

## Waiting Room Protocol

After you've arrived at the audition location and have signed in, you'll probably have some waiting time before your child is called into the casting room. Take advantage of that time. Can your child read? I know it sounds silly but most commercial copy and scripts can be tough for children to grasp on the first go around. So, spend the time in the waiting room helping your child master the dialogue that will be expected.

Whether or not the audition will require your child to read, the most important thing you could be doing as a parent is helping your child to stay focused. And, I guarantee you, while you're sitting in the waiting room, there will be plenty of distractions. For example, young actors might walk out of the audition room boasting about how they "got the part." Ignore them. Believe me . . . the actor doesn't have the role yet; that's not how the audition process works. Casting directors don't make a casting decision until after all the candidates have been seen. Such boastful kids are just trying to undermine you and your child's confidence. Another example: you might hear a lot of gossip in the waiting room about "all the jobs" and the booking ratio that someone's kid is getting. Trust me, most are probably exaggerating. Don't listen to or participating in the chatter.

What you should be doing is talking with your child. Encourage the child or work on outside activities such as homework. Emphasize: that this audition is one of many to come; that your child is at this audition to do the very best he or she can and most importantly to have fun. Say that whatever the outcome of this audition, you are already proud of who he or she is. Be careful not to distract your child's focus with admonishments, such as: "Don't fidget in there!" or "Don't talk fast!"— Stuff like that. "Don't" is a scary word that triggers a whole series of fears that will make your child tense and, subsequently, interfere with his or her best efforts. More important than talking is . . . listening. Listen to your child. If he or she is nervous, say it's okay to be nervous and to tell you about it. It is a very normal feeling. Let the child ramble on if need be. Be a committed listener. That is, don't render unsolicited advice; just be supportive and take in what they are saying. Let your child know that you understand without having to correct or criticize or evaluate. Being a committed listener for your child is one of the most powerful ways of enabling him or her to release tension. When that happens it's amazing how relaxed you can become and let your training and knowledge automatically be recalled.

## It's Show Time

Now, then. The door, finally, opens and the casting director calls the name of your child. It's show time! Parents rarely go into casting sessions with their children; so, it is important that your child feel supported. Send your child off with good wishes and emphasize that you'll be right there if your child needs you. Remind the child ahead of time that if anyone requests doing something that makes the child feel uncomfortable, he or she can say "No!" Furthermore, if that person persists, your child has the right to walk out the door and you will be right there to help. Children have great instincts and know when something or someone is dangerous or difficult to work with. It's your job to let your child know you are supportive and acknowledge these feelings. Give your child a big hug or a "high-five" slap on the palm before sending him or her in.

## Casting Office Tips

As you and your child approach the casting room together, here are some great tips for the proper etiquette with a casting director. Judy Belshe, longtime casting director, asked me to pass on these insights from her book *It's A Freeway Out There:*

1. Never ask a casting director for directions to the office; ask your agent.

2. Don't ask for feedback on how your child performed; casting directors don't have the time or the desire to talk about the results right then. Besides a callback audition is your answer.

3. Always bring a picture and resume, even if you think the casting director has one.

4. Don't let your children run around the

casting area causing a disturbance.

5. Never ask the casting director for advice on your child's career or a recommendation for a good agent.

6. Don't bring markers, food, color crayons or gum into the office; it destroys the furniture.

7. One parent, one child. Don't bring the entire family, friends and relatives to the audition.

8. Never ask to use a casting director's phone.

# Organizations

If you, as a parent, find yourself a bit overwhelmed or at a loss as to how to govern yourself in your child's career, contact the **Hollywood Screen Parents Association,** (818) 955-6510. This very supportive organization understands every problem you will face as a parent of a working child. They can provide you with lists of audition drivers and set sitters to help you with the workload. Additionally, they offer booklets on children's workshops, seminars, children's agents/managers and performance art programs to help you keep up with the competition.

# Your Child and the Law

Due to the horrendous abuses to children in the workplace that occurred in our nation's earlier history and the current abuses occurring around the world today, the United States Congress and all state governments have enacted a number of laws and regulations to protect a working child's well-being and interests. For the rest of this chapter, we will look at both federal and state laws and regulations to see how they specifically apply to your child in the entertainment industry.

# Work Permits

All minors working on the set must have a current **Entertainment Work Permit.** An Entertainment Work Permit must be given to the production company when your child goes to work on a film or television show. A permit can only be issued to children who have maintained a "C" average in their school studies. Once you've obtained the Permit, bring the original with you to the set. Employers, in turn, also must have a permit issued by the Department of Labor on file in order to employ minors. These DOL permits are issued and renewed every six months. A short list of Entertainment Work Permit offices are in the phone directory in the back of the book.

When a minor travels to another state to work in a motion picture, commercial, or television show, the California laws are still in effect. There must still be a certified studio teacher on the set. Any out-of-state child who comes to work in California must abide by the same California laws and obtain a work permit.

# Child Labor Laws

The purpose of the child labor laws is to protect your children while working. The laws clearly spell out working conditions for a child. Below is a distilled version of the labor laws delineating the limit: to the amount of time a child can work on the set; time for breaks; on-set schooling time required; time for meals; and, the maximum exposure time and distance a child is permitted under the hot lights. My research on all child labor laws is based on the best information I had available at the time of printing. To protect your child I would check with the Guilds, your child's agent, parent's' organizations and the State Labor Office to get the most up-to-date laws that apply.

# Minor Employment Rules

These following rules are enforced for both employee (your child) and employer under **California Child Labor Laws** anytime a minor is on the set:

SCHOOL MATERIALS: School-age minors are required to bring books, assignments, paper and writing utensils from regular school. Employers are required to provide adequate school facilities.

GUARDIAN OR PARENT: Must be within sight or sound for all minors under 16 years of age.

WELFARE WORKER/SCHOOL TEACHER: A welfare worker/school teacher must be provided for the education of all minors (up to 18 years) and has the responsibility for caring and attending to the health, safety and morals of all minors under 16 years of age. A studio teacher must be certified by the California Division of Labor Standards Enforcement (DLSE).

MINORS PER STUDIO TEACHER: One to ten minors on a school day, one to 20 on non-school days.

BABIES: For babies 15 days to six weeks a nurse and a studio teacher must be present for every three babies. For every ten babies of six weeks to six months, a nurse and a studio teacher must be provided.

TRAVEL TIME: Studio to location back to studio counts as part of a minor's work day. To minimize loss of work hours, children should report directly to local locations. When on a distant location with overnight, the grace period of 45 minutes each way from the hotel to the set is not counted toward work time.

TURN AROUND TIME: Twelve hours must elapse between minor's dismissal and the next days' call time or school start time. Otherwise, minors must be schooled at the employer's place of business.

WAIVERS: Minors aged 14 to 18 years may work up to eight hours a day for a maximum of two consecutive days with permission from school authorities.

EXTENSIONS: Requests must be submitted in writing to the DLSE. 48 hours in advance.

EMANCIPATION: Regulations are fully applicable to emancipated minors except for minors 16-17 years of age who have obtained a High School Proficiency Certificate. (Emancipation give the right to a minor to sign legal and binding contracts. The child still needs a work permit and schooling. A high school proficiency certificate is preferable as it enables a minor to work as an adult, not sign a contract but by choice can continue at school.)

NEW LAWS: As of January 1, 1993, important changes in the state's child labor law have taken effect. They impose greater limits on the hours that minors 14 to 17 may work.

CAMPBELL, 1992, AB 662: This legislation specifies that a minor 14 or 15 years of age may be issued a permit to work by a school official for not for not more than three hours in any day, and for not more than 18 hours in any week in which school is in session. It prohibits the employment of MINORS 15 years of age or younger for more than eight hours in one day or more than 40 hours in one week. It also prohibits the employment of minors 14 and 15 years of age during school hours, except as an adjunct to a school-supervised and school-administered work experience and career exploration program. If the student works under such a program, this new law provides for a maximum of 23 hours that may be worked during school.

The legislation imposes additional restrictions on the hours of work for minors 14 and 15 years of age by not permitting them to be employed before 7 AM. or after 7 PM, except for the summer months from June 1 though Labor Day, when they may be employed no later than 9 PM.

This new law also prohibits an employer from employing a minor 16 or 17 years of age for more than four hours in any school day, except as allowed under certain school-approved work experience or cooperative vocational education programs, or on any day that is immediately prior to a non-school day. The law further requires that minors 16 or 17 years of age may not be employed for more than eight  hours in one day or 48 hours in one week. Also such work may not begin before 5 AM or continue past 10 PM  on any day preceding a school day.

HORCHER AB 3143: Another new law that took effect January 1, 1993 is AB 3143 (Horcher, 1992). This provides a limited exemption to the work permit requirements for minors in the entertainment industry. Under this law, no work permit would be required to be obtained from the Labor Commissioner for a minor, providing that the appearance lasts four hours or less, is a single event within a calendar year, occurs on either a non-school day or the day immediately preceding a non-school day, the parent or guardian of minor is present at the appearance, and the minor does not directly or indirectly receive any compensation.

## Parental On-Set Tips

Some additional tips for parents who supervise their children on the set: On the first day of each new job, you or your child should bring the following:

1. Original work permit
2. Coogan Account Certificate
3. Passport or birth certificate
4. Social Security card
5. School work and books, if appropriate
6. Copy of *SAG-AFTRA Young Performers Handbook* & *The Blu Book**

*Blu Book* is published by The Studio Teachers Union with pertinent rules & regulations and can be found on the web site.

## Teachers on the Set

California law provides for a studio teacher to be present on the set, at the production company's expense, anytime a child is on the set. This applies to film, television, videos, and print work—whether union or non-union. Your child will be versed in all subjects that any child would normally take at his or her own school. During the shoot, a teacher does double duty as a social worker, whose job it is to protect the child's interests. Parents should speak to the teacher/social worker if the allowable work schedule is not enforced. The teacher/social worker will then, take up the proper issues with the director and to try to resolve the conflict.  It is the teacher/social workers responsibility to see that the child labor laws are enforced.

If you, as a parent, allow your child to be treated differently than is stipulated in the **child labor laws**, you are the one who can be fined and your child will lose his or her work permit. So, if  any work session runs over the allotted time, it is also your duty to see to it that the law is enforced. If a teacher fails to protect your child's interest or endangers your child in any way, ask the production company to replace that teacher.

Adherence to these laws is mandated. However, if on-set schooling becomes too unwieldy, there are alternatives available — especially for child Actors in high school — that will enable a student to complete  his or her educational studies.

## Independent Study Program

This is a program sponsored by the L.A. Unified School District that allows a child to study at home. The independent study program teacher meets with the student once a week to give assignments, and collect homework and tests. Your child can also enroll in classes at a local college on subjects the ISP teacher may not be qualified to teach. This way, a high school student can receive credit toward finishing high school.

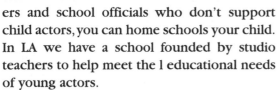

If you still want your child in a structured class environment and don't want to hassle with teachers and school officials who don't support child actors, you can home schools your child. In LA we have a school founded by studio teachers to help meet the l educational needs of young actors.

## High School Proficiency Exam (HSP)

This is a way to enable a teen to test out of high school. If a student passes the test, he or she receives a high school diploma and the permission to work an extra three hours on the set which would normally be used to be spent on school studies.

## Handling Producers

Finally, a word of caution to parents: Because producers are under constant pressure to make sure that their project is finished on time and under budget, some producers are inclined to take total control over children. Therefore, they expect parents not to interfere with the film making process, especially where it pertains to the child actor. To achieve this, many producers will treat parents like an unwanted guest or a troublemaker on the set, even if the parent has done or said nothing disruptive. There is often a thin line between the parent's proper role as caretaker for the child and the producer's province of caretaker for another kind of child (the project), which includes the actors. Unfortunately, that line is sometimes difficult to detect. However, in no case should you ever stand by and watch your child be mistreated. Speak out against situations that jeopardize the personal value, well-being, and self-worth of your child. Do not accept verbal abuse from anyone. On the other hand, if you really are intrusive, over-demanding, or egotistical, you'll get a call and a reprimand from your child's agent soon enough. So, don't push the envelope. For example, it is usually not permissible to bring your other, non-acting children to the set. If you and your acting child are going to be on location for a long period of time, ask the producer for permission to have your other children present on the set with you. The producer may not approve and, instead, ask you to leave your children in the dressing room or may politely request that you leave them at home with the other parent or grandparents. The point is: Be cooperative with and respectful of your child's employer, who has more to think about than just your child's well-being; if you act accordingly, you can probably expect to receive the same treatment in return.

## Other Children's Books

There are two books which I highly recommend that parents read: **Show Biz Kids— Quest for Success** by Ruthie O. Grant covers every aspect on more of a day to day level. This book is packed with advice, experience and positive thinking. Ruthie has two working children of her own and generously shares all of her wisdom. Another great book is written by Judy Belshe, entitled **It's a Freeway Out There**. A casting director for many decades, Judy shares her point of view from a casting director's perspective. It is on the web site as well.

The sky's the limit in a child's imagination. Children naturally believe they can do anything. So, it's important to remember that they will believe anything their parents tell them. Be conscious of the limits you verbalize to your child. If you don't rain on his or her parade with a shower of your own fears, little heroes will emerge.

# Chapter 11

# Contracts and the Job Itself

*There is a vitality, a life force, a quickening that is transmitted through you into action and because there is only one of you in all time, this expression is unique. And if you block it, it will never exist through any other medium and be lost. The world will not have it.*

*It is not your business to determine how good it is, not how valuable it is, not how it compares with other expressions. It is your business to keep it yours clearly and directly, to keep the channel open. You do not even have to believe in yourself or your work. You have to keep open and aware directly to the urges that motivate you. Keep the channel open.*

*No artists is pleased...there is no satisfaction whatever at any time. There is only a queer, divine dissatisfaction; a blessed unrest that keeps us marching and makes us more alive than the others.*

**-Martha Graham to Agnes DeMille**

You got a job, Yippee!!! Now the fun is about to start. But, wait! Not yet! Before we get to the fun stuff, we need to discuss two more items—paperwork and how a set operates. Understanding these two facets, though seemingly insignificant, is important because the more knowledge you have about any aspect of the film making process, the better able you will be to concentrate on and be effective in your performance once the director says "Action!"

For the first Third of this chapter, we're going to cover the following paperwork which you'll need in order to work and get paid: tax forms mandated by the federal government, the I-9 form required by Immigration and Naturalization, contracts required by your union, and, finally, industry-related documents. After we get through discussing paperwork, we're going to take a look at how a set operates and all the personnel involved in making a project come to life.

## Paperwork

Although dealing with different kinds of paperwork and their different procedures can be distracting and cumbersome, there is a very simple rule for you to remember: If you are working as a day player for one to three days, the paperwork will be given to you directly on the set. If the role you've been hired for is bigger, the paperwork goes directly to your agent.

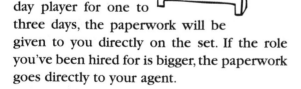

## Federal Tax Forms

### Tax Form W-4.

This is the form the IRS uses to determine how much tax to withhold from your paycheck. Unfortunately, they do not understand that actors and models may, from time to time, receive large sums of money only a few times throughout the year. So, for example, if you contracted to receive $5,000 per week for four weeks, the IRS assumes you will receive that amount for 52 weeks and bases your withholding on a yearly income; consequently, the IRS may insist that your employer withhold up to 50% of your salary. Of course, it is rare that an actor or model is contracted for 52 weeks; but, if you happen to be lucky enough to find yourself in that position, you should hire an accountant to assist you with your taxes.

Additionally, when you are filling out your W-4 form, I suggest you either ask an accountant or decide for yourself how many dependents you should claim so that you can put your withholding at a more manageable level. The more dependents you claim, the less money is withheld from your check. If you are given contracts to sign and a W-4 is not included, ask for one so that your paycheck will not be held up.

### Tax Form 1099.

If taxes are not withheld from your earnings and the amount is in excess of $600, you will receive a 1099 statement by January 31st of the following year. If the amount was under $600, the production company is not required to send you a 1099 statement; still, you must report the income on your taxes. Since withholding were not taken out of the paychecks, you can pay any taxes incurred with the money you set aside as described in Chapter 21 ("Uncle Sam—Your Taxes"). Hang onto your pay stubs to match them up with

HOLLYWOOD

1099 forms and W-4's. If you are missing any, or haven't received either the 1099 or W-4 by the first week in February, call the company and request that your forms be sent immediately so it won't hold you up from filing your tax return.

## Independent Contractors Invoice

You may be asked to sign an Independent Contractors Invoice. This form is basically your agreement to pay the taxes on the money you will be paid. If you work independently you may have to make one up yourself before you can be paid. Include name, address and phone of client, date and type of service along with the rate. I then staple a copy of the check to it when paid.

## The I-9 Form

Employment Eligibility Verification Form I-9. You are required by law, each time you are employed, to show proof of your citizenship and, subsequently, your right to work. Some people are apprehensive about disclosing this information because your actual age (as it appears on the form) may be different than the age a person can look and, therefore, might affect their ability to be hired for a particular role or modeling assignment. Let me assure you that kind of concern is not worth a moment's thought. I can tell you from personal experience that any paperwork or forms you fill out—either on the set or from your agent's office—goes directly to the production office. The casting director and director who hired you won't ever see it. I have often played women up to eight years younger than myself. Just remember: you are being hired for your talent and your body, whatever age it looks.

But this form is important. The actual document itself is included in the Appendix. Familiarize yourself with it and make copies from the book to use each time you are employed. Also in the Appendix is a complete list of acceptable documents to prove U. S. citizenship.

## Union Contracts

### Television Day Player Contracts.

Your day player contract will be signed on the set. Your tax forms should be attached. Check with your agent to find out what your pay rate will be. If you are working for scale, the production company must, by contract, add 10% of your contracted fee, which is to be paid to your agent; otherwise, you would be working for less than scale. If the negotiated pay rate is filled out incorrectly on your contract, speak up right away and get the contracts changed. Do not sign an incorrect contract with the promise it will be changed later. If there is anything in the contracts which you do not understand, ask either the assistant director who gives you the contracts, your agent, or the guild that governs your shoot. Do not sign anything until you understand it fully.

### Theatrical Day Player Contract.

The first contract I will talk about is an **Actors Television Motion Picture—Day Player Contract.** This contract is used for a number of day player jobs including: a day's work on a TV movie, a day's work on a television show shot on film, or for voice-over performers working in these mediums. Check each box at the top of the contract to see if the information is correct. In the body of the contract is a blank line for the amount of dollars you will earn if foreign broadcasting of the television show occurs and, also, a blank line for theatrical (movie the-

ater) release of the television show. Customarily, one or both blanks may have the letters N/A for not applicable typed in. In that case, just verify with the assistant director that the information is correct and sign your contract. The box at the bottom of the contract is for your initials, indicating that you have read and understand all that appears above it on the page. Make sure you do. At the bottom, print and sign your Screen Actors Guild name.

### Theatrical Day Player Contracts— Low Budget.

This next contract discussed is a **Screen Actors Guild Daily Contract for Theatrical Motion Pictures.** You will notice that there is a special provision clause added because the production company has qualified under the **SAG Low Budget Contract** (under $1,750,000) and, therefore, only has to pay actors $431 plus 10% per day. Attached to this contract, you may find a document called the *"rider to contract."* A rider is an addition to a union contract outlining any special circumstances for airing or payment.

This rider lays out specific clauses of the SAG Low Budget Contract which the guild wants to make the actor aware of. For example, one clause might designate that an actor has the right to additional money for working on a weekend. Or, in another example, a clause might insist that an actor waive the right to have all of his or her work days scheduled in a row. What this means is that a producer can work an actor one day here and one day there without having to pay for the days in between, thereby keeping that actor unavailable for other work.

## Billing

You should be given contracts when you arrive on the set. These contracts are sent to the production company's legal department and govern the rate at which you will be paid and your *"billing."* Billing is the size of the role (Starring, Co-Starring, Guest Starring, etc.) and where your name is placed in the

credits.. The production reports, which determine the amount, will be covered later. Chapter 11 ("Screen Actors Guild") lists the three day and weekly rates for film making.

## A.F.T.R.A. Prime Time Dramatic Television Employment of a Day Actor

These contracts cover all shows and commercials shot on tape. They differ a great deal from SAG contracts in format and layout. Read everything on the page. Here is the way the A.F.T.R.A. contract is laid out: First, at the top of the contract, is the name of the production company and date the contracts were filled out. On the top left side is production company information. First is the date your employment starts. Under that is "Part" where the name of the character you're playing appears. Next is the "Production Title," which is the name of show, and below that is the name of the specific episode or episode number in which you will be performing. The final line, designated as "Daily Rate," is where your salary per day will appear.

On the top right side of the contract is your personal information. The first line, "Name" is where you union name will be written. Next is your address followed by telephone number and Social Security number. Verify that all of these are correct so that you can receive your paycheck, residuals or any updated scripts. The final line is the weekly conversion rate. This is a rate the production company can choose to pay you if they work you more than three days.

The body of the contract has a blank line at the top where the production company name will be typed. In the middle of the contract are five blank lines. In most cases they will be left blank, but if they are filled in, ask the assistant director if you do not understand the special conditions you are agreeing to. It is okay to sign the contract if these lines are left blank. Near the bottom is a dollar sign and a blank area. It is rarely filled in and okay to sign if it is not. In the bottom right corner they ask for your initials indicating that you have read the entire contract and understand it. Then sign your name as it appears at the top of the contract.

Check everything carefully before signing and ask about anything you do not understand. A.F.T.R.A. has graciously agreed to let us print a copy of the **Day Player Contract** in the Appendix.

## Penalties

Whichever contract you are signing under, there are other items for which you should be financially compensated, according to the SAG or A.F.T.R.A. contract. Pay especially close attention to the following three areas:

On a daily contract, overtime starts after eight hours. The ninth and tenth hours are paid at time and one-half of your base rate. Double time is the pay rate after ten hours. If you have a three-day or weekly contract, overtime starts after ten hours at double time.

Meal penalties begin when you have not been fed six hours after your start time. The penalties are $25 for the first half hour, $35 for the second half hour and then $50 for each half hour.

## Wardrobe Pay

You are paid for a wardrobe fitting only if you are called in before the actual day of shooting. If you are hired under a SAG Day Player contract and are being paid $600 or less, the fitting rate is 1/8 of the daily rate. Often the costumer will call you directly for the fitting. Let the production company know so that any additional money you have coming to you from a wardrobe fitting will be included in your check. Your agent is entitled to 10% of the wardrobe pay, but not if you wear your own clothes. In that case, the pro-

duction company must then pay a cleaning fee. For SAG contracts it is about $11.50 and for A.F.T.R.A. over $10.

## Mileage

If you are required to drive to a location, the production company must pay you a *"drive to"* fee. Here's how the fee is determined: There is an area centered at Beverly Boulevard and LaCienega Boulevard extending out 30 miles in every direction known as the 30-Mile Zone. The fee paid to anyone driving to a location within the zone is calculated at $0.30 per mile regardless of which studio you are working out of. If you have to drive to a location outside the zone, not only do you get paid drive-to money but you should be on the clock from the time you leave your house. Be sure that this information is correctly reflected in your Production Time Report so you are paid correctly.

## Uniform Model Release

This type of documentation is used in modeling and industrial jobs. What distinguishes a release from a union contract is that the release is basically a time card not a contract. A model/actor release form usually spells out the amount to be paid and the length of time the company can use your likeness. It is as binding as any union contract, so if you do a non-union car commercial for a local market, you cannot audition for any other car commercials for the length of time spelled out in your model/actor release.

The voucher will be filled out by you and signed by the client. It specifies everything from client and billing information to times you break for meals and billing hours for fitting of wardrobe. See the Appendix.

## SAG or A.F.T.R.A. Production Time Report

This is the second most critical document you will sign, the first, of course, being your contract. The Production Time Report is the data that will be used to compute your pay. Make sure that the times of arrival, dismissal and meals are correct. Keep track of this yourself to make sure that they match with the Production Time Report. Lunch time begins when the first assistant director calls "Lunch"—not when you finally hear about it from someone else. Dismissal is when you have finished your work and you are officially released for the day (usually by the second assistant director). You change clothes, remove makeup and say your good-byes on your own time. Don't sign the production time report if it is not correct. A signature means you agree with all the information on it. If there are discrepancies on your time report, let your agent know about any disputes regarding "overtime" and "meal penalties." Let your agent haggle over the details so that you can continue to be the cooperative actor they wish to hire again.

## Deal Memos

A Deal Memo is a document that outlines the terms and conditions under which a production company is prepared to offer a role to an actor. It is used as a negotiating device before final contracts are drawn up. The agent and producer will haggle over money, on-screen billing, size of your trailer on the set and any other special perks. When they finally reach a conclusion to these negotiations with an agreement, the terms are spelled out in a deal memo and sent to the agent for the actors' approval. Actors generally don't see these forms or get a copy

of them but you should know they exist. Your agent will usually tell you the conditions over the phone. It is never an official deal until both parties have signed. If you have been offered a role, ask your agent if he or she has a deal memo yet to lock it down for you. If necessary, a deal memo can become critical proof in court or to the union if a production company decides to back out on a deal. In the case of union arbitration or a lawsuit, it helps you and your agent to document losses. A commitment—verbal or written—is binding for both parties. In the lawsuit of Kim Basinger vs. Orion, her verbal commitment to star in the movie *BOXING HELENA* was enough for the courts to award Orion $8 million when she reneged sending her off to the courts to declare bankruptcy.

## Shooting Schedule

A shooting schedule is yet another piece of paperwork you will be handed on the set. On this one piece of paper, you will have a load, some think an overload, of information for that day's work. You will see the shooting order for that day's scenes, such as: the order in which the scenes will be shot; which scene is scheduled to shoot first; which pages will be shot; whether the scene is an *"exterior shot"* (a scene done outside) or an *"interior shot"* (filmed on a sound stage or inside of some location site); whether the scene is a *"day shot"* or a *"night shot;"* etc. Most pertinent for you, the actor, on the shooting schedule is information that tells you: when your first scene is to be shot; which other actors are in the scene with you; on which page of the script the dialogue appears; and, most importantly, the times for your makeup call and when you are expected on the set. The Advance Schedule (also placed on the shooting schedule), helps you to stay abreast of scheduled work for the following few days. That way you can brush up on lines and figure out your sleeping schedule.

## A Script

Script changes occur frequently and, whenever there is a change in the script, a new one will be sent to your house by messenger. Every time there is a change in the script—whether it is a dialogue change, a change of sets, added or deleted scenes, added or deleted characters from the story—either the script or specific pages of the script are rewritten and printed on different color paper. You may receive written or verbal instructions with language like: "We'll be going off the pinks." This refers to the color of the script (or pages) that is most current and the one(s) that will be used for the day's scheduled filming.

If you have a small role with just a few lines, a shrunken, hand-size copy of your dialogue will be included with your contracts and paperwork at the beginning of the day. It is hand-size to make it easier for you to carry with you through makeup and wardrobe while you learn your lines. Check each script for changes in your dialogue, sometimes designated with an asterisk (*) at the margin of the page where the change has occurred.

So much for the paperwork. Now for the fun stuff. We'll go over how best to prepare to have the most amount of fun on the set. Also, I will teach you the titles and description of each type of job on the set.

## Preparation for the Job Itself

Before you begin the job, let's briefly review some preliminary reminders to help keep you from becoming distracted and some preparation tips to help you stay focused on your craft once you actually start working before the cameras: (1) check with your Agent to make sure the production company is a signatory of the proper union; (2) make sure you confirm your salary and billing; (3) double check your start date and time; (4) find out when the script will get to you; and, (5) make sure you are in the appropriate union for the production you're working on and that your dues are paid up. Borrow the money if you have to but don't make the deadly mistake of either not being in the proper union or not being in good standing because of unpaid dues. Because, sooner or later, someone will notice. And, if that happens, the production company will pass you over for the next person in line for that role. Time is money and no one will care about your problems.

Finally, the minute you get the script, start building a character. The clearer and more confident you get with your work, the more enjoyable shooting will be. Now, with your character tucked under your arm, set about making any physical changes you need to in order to visually portray your character before shooting. Getting your body toned up, changing facial hair, coloring or changing a hair style are choices you might need to consider, but never make them alone! You were hired partly for the way you look; so, before you change anything about your physical appearance, ask the director.

Another way to prepare is to get a good night's sleep for every day that you shoot. You may be wound up, excited or find it hard to doze off; in that case, I recommend some sleeping aids that you'll find in Chapter 17.

Before you leave for the set, pack the script and all changes, healthy snacks, a good book or paperwork, any wardrobe items you were asked to bring, extra headshots, a mobile phone if you have one and a pencil for last - minute notes.

## Collaborating On the Look of Your Character

Your first contract with the production before you arrive on the set is usually with **wardrobe.** If you go for costume fittings, share any ideas you have about the character's attire with the **costume designer** and the director. Most actors pay too little attention to this detail but it is one element of your character.

Next, if you have any unusual hair styling ideas, talk them over with the director and get in touch with the **hair stylist** so that any special products you might need can be purchased in plenty of time before you start shooting.

## Dressing Rooms

Before you go see the wardrobe and hair people on the day of shooting, you're off to your dressing room. A word about your dressing room. A dressing room is often referred to as a *"trailer"* because there is a bank of these very small rooms (including lavatories) attached together, all which are pulled by a trailer tractor. This whole long series of dressing rooms and lavatories is called a *"honey wagon."* The honey wagon is mostly used for location work: however, if there aren't enough dressing rooms available on the sound stage or on the studio lot, the honey wagon will be used to accommodate the additional actors.

In any event, if you wind up using a trailer from the honey wagon as your dressing room, your name will be inserted on the door. I know, it's great! Be careful going up and down the stairs as these dressing room trailers are usually set way up off the ground and the staircase is steep. The doors to the trailers are unlocked so don't leave any valuables inside. (If you have valuables you want baby-sat, give them to the prop master. I will explain who this person is later in this section.) Once you are inside, the door can be locked from within for your privacy. Most dressing rooms are equipped with couches, mirrors, radios, bathrooms, heaters and air conditioning. This is your home, so feel free to relax and nap if you like. If you are lucky enough to get a full-size room on the studio lot for your dressing room, you will find that it usually has a phone.

## On-Set Food

Now for breakfast. There are two groups of people in charge of food. The first is **craft services** people. They are part of the technical crew and are in charge of snacks on the set. Scheduled meals are done by a catering company. You can identify a caterer by the trucks that drive around town serving food. They can make you almost anything you want for breakfast. If there is no breakfast arrangements, then craft services will have coffee, juice, fruit, donuts, bagels, sodas and water on the set. The higher the budget the better the on-set beverages and food.

HOLLYWOOD

# Makeup and Wardrobe

After you've been fed, report to **make-up** and to **wardrobe**. These are two separate departments. Go to makeup first wearing no make-up and having clean hair. If your hair has special needs such as hot rollers, wear them to the set. If you wear contact lenses, tell the makeup artist before he or she starts painting. If your arms, legs or hands will be very visible, they may have to be made up as well. Wipe off any excess makeup on your palms before you touch anything, especially wardrobe.

**Wardrobe** may have you try on several outfits and walk you over to the director for approval, if you didn't have wardrobe fittings ahead of time. Be very careful not to get make-up on the clothes or to mess up the Make-up Department's handiwork. It is okay to leave tissues around the collar of a shirt until you are ready to shoot, protecting your wardrobe from make-up smears. The entire time you are going through this process, it's a good idea to be going over your lines for that day's shooting, so bring your script along. Don't let the costume designer give you clothes you dislike or aren't comfortable with. It is your character and ultimately you who will be seen in them. Be polite but hold your ground in these areas, unless the director overrides your choice.

# The Dialogue Coach

If there is a **dialogue coach,** go see him or her next before you get to the set. The dialogue coach's job is to check how well you know your lines, your believability and ease of delivery. Share your ideas about the character and ask for input. He or she is there to help with accents and to motivate actors. Your lines can be expanded or cut depending on whether or not you are having a great deal of success or a great deal of difficulty. Most sets do not have a dialogue coach; but, if the producers have hired one, use this person as you would an acting coach.

# Set Call Times

All of the above protocol should be completed before your *"set call time."* If your call to the set is 8:00 AM, that means you should have your make-up on, your wardrobe complete, your lines prepared and be physically standing on the set no later than 8:00 AM. Often, the time you are actually needed on the set sometimes fluctuates from the listed set call; in that case, tell the first assistant director that you will be waiting in your trailer when you are needed. Bring a book or personal work to do. It passes the time. I've spent many a rainy day playing cards with cast members or catching up on paperwork with my laptop. What other job do you know of where you get paid to do your personal business?

# Production Assistants to the Rescue

While last-minute lighting and camera changes are being made, you have time to sit in your dressing room and energize yourself. The first or second assistant directors. or production assistant (PA) will come to get you when they are ready to shoot. Production assistants help out on the set wherever needed, including walking you to the set. Waiting, anticipation and having to be ready at all times are what exhaust actors, not the actual work itself. Stay calm and relaxed. Once you are called to the set there will be plenty of time for make-up touch ups and *"run throughs"* (rehearsals before the actual filming of a scene).

# Professional Conduct

One final, important note about professional conduct and preparation before moving on to the next section: *know your lines and show up to the set on time.* Especially the latter. If, for example, your call time is 7:30 AM for makeup, arrive at 7:00 AM so that you have plenty of time to walk to the set, eat breakfast, settle into your dressing room and be sliding into the make-up chair on time (which is, also, a good place to go over your lines). Ignoring these two unspoken rules are the main reasons for getting fired as well as earning a reputation of being unprofessional. And don't think it can't happen—even if you're a star. Get ready…it's show time!

## Who's Who in Production Land

Now, let's get onto the set. Your first day on the job is very exciting with lots of new people to meet and lots of new things to learn. In this section, I will go over the job titles for some of the key craftspeople who work on the set, what their job entails, and how it relates to you. The information and description of these craftspeople in this section pertains to single-camera film projects. However, each format uses this basic crew structure. Variations occur from format to format (whether it is four camera sit-coms done on either videotape or film, or commercials or even industrials for that matter). Whichever medium you wind up working in, I would highly recommend that you write down the names of everyone you meet and work with on the crew. It will help you to blend in and feel at ease much quicker; besides, these people are going to become your family for the duration of the project . Some names are on the call sheet for you reference.

## The Director

You already know your director from the audition which landed you the job. He or she will approach and go over the scene with you including entrances, blocking, motivation and any special business you may do that will require a close-up to cover the action. If it is a large cast and your role is small, the director may not have to discuss any major character business with you but, instead, will glance at your hair and wardrobe. You may be instructed to do a final a walk through of the scene so

that additional marks can be placed on the ground, camera measurements taken and additional lighting set.

During the dress rehearsal the director may give you guidance for the motivation of your character. When the director gives you instructions, hear them out until they are done. Never criticize a director's ideas; on the other hand, if you have a good impulse, present it something like this: "What do you think of my character doing this?" If you have gotten to the set before your scene, you can often get a feel for the director's style and the mood on the set. Jack Nicholson said: "I always go with any impulse I have. If the director doesn't like it . . . take two."

Stay present and in the moment and magic will happen, I guarantee it. If you're totally confused about a role, call your coach. My coach and I fax script notes back and forth to the set. The bottom line: it's your face on the screen so make it the best and ask for any help you need. It's okay to be nervous,—that's just your impulses waiting to happen. Use everything you're feeling, even the nerves. Relax and let your instincts guide you. The camera eats you up when you are at your most exposed and vulnerable. It's what separates good from great.

## The First Assistant Director

The minute you arrive on the set, ask the first person you see to direct you to the **first assistant director (1st AD).** Next to the director, this is probably the most important person on the set because he or she is responsible for everything and everybody during principal photography. Additionally, the 1st AD is the liaison between the production office and the director; subsequently, an assistant director is responsible for: establishing call times, keeping the production moving according to schedule, and maintaining order and discipline on the set. More frequently than not, the 1st AD can be heard yelling: "Quiet on the set" and "Camera rolling" so that the director doesn't have to strain his or her voice and energy which would, otherwise, distract from the work ahead. When you meet with the 1st AD, after you have arrived he or she will tell you what to do next.

## The Second Assistant Director

The 1st AD has an assistant on the set called the **second assistant director (2nd AD)**. Either the 1st AD or the 2nd AD will check you in, give you the appropriate paperwork or forms (contracts, I-9's, W-4's), script updates, the order of shooting and show you to your dressing room. Be respectful of whomever holds these positions. They have to be attentive to everyone and everything happening on the set. They are usually the first ones there and the last ones to go home. It's not an easy job.

## Cinematographer

Walk carefully through the maze of thick, wire cables and standing lights and find your way to the camera. Then introduce yourself to the **Director of Photography (DP)**, also called the **Cinematographer.** The DP is considered the most important technical craftsperson on the set because he or she has the very important job of transforming the screenwriter's written word and the director's concepts into visual images. DP's determine camera angles and set ups for the movement of every shot. They make us actors look good. Frequently, you will be asked to run through your scene so that the cameraman can be sure that you are in focus through all of your movements.

## Cameramen and Focus Pullers

The cinematographer has a crew of two or three assistants: the camera operator, a **focus puller,** and a **first assistant cameraman**. The **camera operator** does the actual photography, panning or tilting or whatever directions the DP makes. The focus puller runs a measuring tape from the camera lens up to your face in order to get distance for camera focus; if the camera shot calls for movement (close-ups, pull backs, etc.), the focus puller makes sure that for every movement, the camera stays in focus. The first assistant cameraman (or loader) follows the camera around carrying empty magazines of film for those times when the camera needs reloading. Additionally, the first assistant is responsible for placing the exposed film securely in a case,  logging the information that's on that particular magazine, and then making sure the exposed film gets to the laboratory for processing.

## Steadi-Cam

Occasionally, a camera crew will use a special camera called a **steadi-cam,** which requires specialized training by a camera operator. This is a unique, self-balancing apparatus that is strapped onto the free-moving body of a camera operator. Because the camera is not fixed to a camera dolly, a camera operator can catch action in one, smooth motion without having to stop each shot and set up another camera angle. If you're watching a movie, you can often notice that a steadi-cam is being used when you see scenes of an actor running up two or three flights of stairs or winding through a crowded street or even in a scene that requires a long piece of dialogue while the actors are walking through a maze.

## An Actor's Best Friend

It's no wonder that an actor's best friend on the set often turns out to be the cinematographer. Part of their responsibilities include making you look great! And, as in any collaborative endeavor, your obligation to the DP is to cooperate. So, if a DP asks you not to not bob your head, or rock from side to side, or talk with your hands . . . listen to those instructions. The DP is there to make you look your best. My advice: get to know your cinematographers and their craft intimately (professionally speaking, of course).

## Lighting

Naturally, a cameraman can't take photographs without lighting. That's why there is a group of electrician's (or gaffers) on hand. Gaffers handle equipment such as: lights, reflectors, gels, scrims, bounce boards and an assortment of other accessories to create the most perfect lighting situations for every scene. The key electrician who confers with the director of photography about lighting is called the **head gaffer.** An actor's attention and interest in the electrical department's work is important. Just as with the camera crew, cooperation is a mutually supportive activity. If you are on the set being lit for a scene which is being set up to shoot, listen to the head gaffers instructions. You will be directed to a position where the scattered lights will make you look your best.

## The Grips

The people running around the edge of the set carrying equipment are grips, headed up by the **key grip.** Grips are responsible for moving heavy equipment, moving set walls, setting up overhangs for lights, setting dolly tracks for a camera, building and tearing down sets, etc. Although actors rarely have contact with these craftspeople, Grips can be useful to a performing artist. For example, if the shot being set up for a scene requires that an actor be a little taller for the sake of a particular camera angle, a grip also bring square wooden boxes called *"apple boxes"* for actors to stand on. The best way for you to cooperate with the Grip Department is to stay out of their way. They are always on the set quickly carrying out the wishes of the director, the cameraman or the production designer.

## Prop Master

All right. Let's say you're rehearsing and, at the last minute, the director decides that he or she would like you to be holding a glass of wine or a teddy bear or some other prop to enhance your character's action in the scene. Where do you get this prop? Especially if it wasn't written into the current pages of the script? Seek out the **property master.** The property master and his or her assistant (second property master) is responsible for providing any prop, large or small, which an actor or an extra is going to use in a scene.

Another one of the responsibilities of a prop master is what is referred to as *"continuity"* (or *"matching"*). Continuity is important because if a particular scene is going to be shot from different angles, all shots must match each other in terms of the way props are laid out. So, if you have a small prop of your own that you are going to use on the set to remind you of your character's motivation, let the prop masters know. They will position your prop carefully so that it is either out of camera sight or placed in such a way that the object can be matched for a different camera angle of the same scene.

HOLLYWOOD

Additionally, if you need some article to help your acting, ask the prop masters if they have it in their bag of tricks. However, don't think they are magicians. A property master spends a great deal of time going through the pages of a script to determine exactly which props are going to be used in the show. Then he or she spends more time driving all around town to gather those props for use in the show. Consequently, if called upon at the last second to provide a prop not called for in the script, he or she will look pretty bad and, further, it will cost the production company money if they are forced to take the time to go and look for the requested prop. The point is: A property master is not a mind reader. If you want or need a prop not called for in the script, respect the prop master enough to approach him or her early enough to make your request a reality.

## Firearms

The property master and second assistant prop mater are also responsible for handling weapons, firearms, etc. If a scene requires you to use or handle weapons, ask the prop master to instruct you in safely using your weapon. If you have to shoot a gun but have never fired blanks, meet up with the prop master before you start shooting and ask for some practice rounds and training. More on this later in this chapter.

## Testing One, Two

The Sound Department will become visible during the run throughs, and its craftspeople are another vital component of the on-set production crew. The Sound Department consists of the **recorder**, the **mixer** who sets the sound levels and is seated somewhere on the set with headphones on, and the **boom man** who "mikes" an actor (attaching a wire-less radio microphone and it's transmitter to a hidden area of the actor's body or clothing) or handles the "boom mike" (a microphone held on the end of a long pole close to actors heads to capture dialogue).

The purpose of being "miked" before your scene is to be shot is to make sure that you can be heard and that your voice levels are established during the rehearsals.

Typically, once you are miked, the mike is always on and, therefore, the sound man can hear everything you say. My advice: Turn the mike off when you use the restroom. However, when the camera is rolling, make sure your mike is on and see to it that you speak clearly. Even if you are doing an intimate scene, you must be heard. Just for fun, I like to whisper a joke into my mikes and watch the sound man crack up on the set. Naturally, everyone on the set turns to stare at him like he is out of his mind while I stand there and look like I have not idea what's going on. It's a good laugh.

## You Said Banana Not Orange!

The **script supervisor** is still another indispensable part of the crew. The script supervisor's responsibilities are manifold: keeping track of scenes; recording each shot and designating which ones are "circle takes" and which ones are simply unusable takes. Circle takes are usable shots as determined by the director which are, then, given to the editor who now has a place to start assembling the film or videotape. Script people assure a scenes continuity and make on-set dialogue changes as instructed by either the director or the production office.

Additionally, if you forget your lines, the script supervisor is there to help out. Or, if you change your dialogue, changes will be noted by the script supervisor to make sure you match your lines in the future. The script supervisor can also remind you about accessories, special effects makeup, or hair styles you previously used in different scenes.

You can almost always find the script supervisor seated in a chair as close to the camera as is allowable. The reason for this is they have to stay constantly within ear shot of any and all information that needs to be recorded from the key personnel on the crew, which usually means the director and the cinematographer. The camera itself, therefore, becomes the "central headquarters" of the set. You can stand near that area to observe and learn but be sure to stay out of the way.

## Sores, Cuts, Blood and Guts

With few exceptions, nearly every movie or television program produced today makes use of the specialized talents of a group technicians from the **Special Effects Department.**

There used to be a time that the activities of the on-set special effects people were restricted to making wounds, applying blood, attaching hatchets and knives to an actor's body and operating small gizmos on the set. Now that production budgets have increased and technologies of all kinds (computer, makeup, visual effects, etc.) have become so sophisticated, the skills of special effects craftspeople have expanded proportionately.

So, the special effects team continues to rig different special effects as called for in a script, they also work hand in hand with the property master when it comes to weapons. And firearms are a big part of most action scripts. So, if you are in a scene that calls for you to get shot by a gun, be prepared to be wired up with radio controlled packets with fake blood called *"squibs."* Make sure your skin is protected. One actor I know from **ROBOCOP** has scars from 200 squibs that were attached to his body for the movie.

## SAG's Firearm Guidelines

I've set down a list of SAG guidelines for using firearms on the set. A word of advice: be mindful, watch your back and take responsibility for your own safety, no matter who the expert is on a set. A fatal gunshot is a sad ending to a great career.

- Use simulated or dummy weapons whenever possible.
- Treat all guns as if they are loaded and deadly.
- Unless you are actually filming or rehearsing, all firearms must be secured by the prop master.
- Never engage in any horseplay with any firearms or other weapons.
- Do not let others handle the gun for any reason.
- Never point a firearm at anyone, including yourself.
- Always cheat the shot by aiming to the right or left of the target character.
- If asked to point and shoot directly at a living target, consult with the property master or armorer (firearms handler) for the prescribed safety procedures.
- If you are the intended target of a gunshot, make sure that the person firing at you has followed all of these safety procedures.
- If you are required to wear exploding blood squibs, make sure there is a bulletproof vest or other solid protection between you and the blast pack.
- Check the firearm every time you take possession of it.
- Blanks are extremely dangerous. Even though they do not fire bullets out of the gun barrel, they still have a powerful blast that can maim or kill.
- If you are on a set where shots are to be fired and there is no armorer or qualified prop master, go to the nearest phone and call the Guild. A union representative will make sure proper procedures are followed.

# Biff, Pow - It's Stunt Time!

Working in tandem with the special effects crew is the **stunt coordinator**. The stunt coordinator choreographs fight sequences, stages simple and complex "gags" (the industry term for falling over things), etc. Most importantly, the stunt coordinator works closely and tirelessly to rehearse a stunt if an actor has chosen to do the stunt his or herself. You will never be required to do heavy stunt work but may be asked to do fight sequences and simple falls. If, however, you are ever injured on the set, even minutely, let the AD know. There is a medic on the set at all times.

# Under the Hot Lights for Hours— the Stand-ins

After you have rehearsed a scene to the director's and cinematographer's satisfaction, you can either retire to your dressing room or sit in your on-stage director's chair to study your lines. While you're doing that, the rest of the crew goes to work setting lights, cameras, props, etc. That's when your **stand in** comes onto the set, stands on your "mark" (or beginning point), and walks through the scene so that the technicians can do their magic. In other words, your stand-in does the grunt work while you are relaxing in your trailer or finishing your makeup and wardrobe details. By necessity, your stand-in should be about your height and weight.

Stand-in's are also known as the *"second team."* You are a member of the first team. When the assistant director calls "First team! . . . "that means the director is now ready to film or tape your scene; so, drop whatever you're doing and go to your first mark. And while you're reaping all the glory, remember: stand-ins do you a great service so treat them with respect.

# On-Set Still Photographers

Frequently, a producer will hire an on-set still photographer who, during rehearsals and between takes, may take publicity pictures of the cast. Be cooperative and ask if you can get his or her card and purchase copies of the photos after the shoot. Try to stage a shot with yourself and any major star. You can use these in your publicity package and post-cards. If there is no on-set still photographer, bring your own camera loaded with black-and-white film. Shoot while the set is still lit, during a break. Try to grab the cameraman or someone you feel has a good eye and who is willing to take your photo. If you are using a camera with a flash attachment, always yell "Flashing!" before you take your picture to warn anyone who may be taking a light reading at the same time. Better yet, always get permission from the cameraman and head gaffer before you take any shot.

# The Rest of the Crew

So, these are some of the key personnel on a set during principal photography. There are other members of the production crew who may pop in and out of the set occasionally, such as: **production manager, production designer, set decorators, set dressers, nurse, teamsters, generator operators,** and many more depending on the size of the project being produced. Take the time to find out who these people are and what they do.

And, still, there a few more people who you will rarely see on the set at all; and, if you do, they keep a low profile. Let's take a look at some of the essential off-set production staff.

# The Money Magnet

The **executive producer** is the person who customarily arranges for the financing of a project, unless he or she actually finances the project and establishes distribution after the project is completed. They then hires a producer to run the show. On an independently made picture, the executive producer is the liaison between the financier and the producer. In the case of a studio- made picture, the executive producer is the liaison between the studio and key people at the production company. They keep everything on track.

# The Nail Biter

The **producer's** job is to make sure that the production is finished on time and on budget. Once a project is financed, and cast, the producer becomes the most important person on the whole project because he or she runs the whole show. Consequently, a producer carries and is responsible for everybody and everything involved, not just one specific task, in the successful production of that particular project. So, if you happen to see some nervous person standing in the corner of the sound stage eating Tums, that's probably the producer.

# Off Set Production Office

The brain center from which all production operations and decisions flow is the production office. The production office houses the executive producer, producer, and their support personnel, an indispensable group of people known as the **production staff.** The production staff is comprised of secretaries, production assistants, production coordinators, writers, and associate producers. These people perform hours of tasks, often above and beyond the call of duty, just to lighten the load of the Producers as much as possible. Unfortunately, of the scores of people working on any particular project, the production staff is even less visible than the executive producer and producer; subsequently, the only acknowledgment they

receive is an occasional thanks from their bosses. So, if you ever get a few minutes, go up to the production offices, familiarize yourself with the staff, and let them know that you know how good a job they're doing.

# That's a Wrap!

When you are wrapped each day, you are not considered officially released until you sign out with the 1st or 2nd AD. At that point, you'll be given a call time for the next day. If you're released early in the day and the call times haven't been set, you will receive word at home or through your agent.

Depending on either the established shooting timetable or unforeseen circumstances, you may be re-scheduled to shoot your scenes under different scenarios:

# Holds and Carry Overs

If you are told you are *"on hold,"* that means although you are contracted to be available for the next day's shoot, you won't have to report to the set until you are called. This is where pagers and cellphones come in handy so you don't have to sit at home.

Another situation in which re-scheduling of your scenes can occur is when you are placed on a *"hold-over"* or *"carry-over"* day. A hold-over day is something completely different than being placed on hold. In this situation, the director has decided to use you for an extra day which you weren't originally scheduled for. If, for one reason or another, the production company ends up keeping you for three days and you were only hired for one, the pay may be changed to a *"conversion rate."* This is a lower rate than your daily pay but includes more days. Ask your agent if he or she can help raise the conversion rate so you can get more money.

Still another case in which re-scheduling may occur is when the director may decide to *"shoot around you."* This means the director will shoot other scenes until you are available again.

If any of these predicaments occur and present a conflict for you, communicate your problem to the director, producer and your agent right away. Especially your agent. Agents are great at working these things out.

## When Your Job Is Done

When you finally finish your last day of shooting, thank everyone. Expressing gratitude and acknowledging others for their good work goes a long way. Many directors and producers will remember you for your professionalism and cooperation. It's not unusual for directors and producers to re-hire cast members with whom they've had an extraordinarily good working relationship. If you're easy to work with, chances are you'll get invited back. So, give everybody on the cast, crew, and production staff one of those "Until-I-see-you-again" smiles and a warm handshake. You'll be remembered. It's a nice way to say good-bye.

## Post-Production Work

Well, now, that was fun, wasn't it? It's on to the next job. Right? Guess again. Just when you think your job is over . . . it's not. There still may be more to do. After your job in principal photography is completed, you may be asked to do some post-production work. For example, you may be required to do some looping in order to dub in some dialogue that somehow got ruined when one of your scenes was originally shot. Or, you may be asked to do some contracted publicity work on behalf of the studio or television network that financed your project and paid your salary.

So, let's talk a little bit about post-production. Here is where you'll meet scores of other people who are working on your project but whom you will never, ever see on a sound stage. They live in a world all of their own. Some of the people who work in post-production are: the **sound editors** and **technicians,** the **ADR people, computer graphic imaging personnel, visual** and **optical effects technicians, composers** and **arrangers, musicians** and scores of others. Without these master crafts people, the final product would end up looking and sounding like an amateur home movie.

Two of these skilled professionals are worth mentioning here, particularly because they both have a direct impact on your work:

## A Bad Chinese Movie or Not?

*"Looping"* also known as automated dialogue replacement (ADR) is the art and skill of matching your vocal vitality, pace, meter, character delivery and lip movements to the footage shot for a specific scene. Looping is an essential part of your acting skills.

If the sound recording of your performance is not usable, you may be required to develop this skill called looping. When a scene is first being recorded on the set by the sound man, it is not uncommon for extraneous noises or technical problems to produce an unusable recording of whatever sounds or dialogue may have been needed for that scene. And, if there is no time to reshoot the scene or if the visual imagery in the scene is so perfect that the director insists on using that take, you may be paid at some point to go to a special recording stage and loop your own dialogue.

## Center Stage on a Dark Sound Stage

During your first visit to a looping stage, you might feel intimidated by the massive, empty, and darkened space which seems to swallow up your entire being. Don't be intimidated and don't feel embarrassed to tell anyone you have never looped before. There are professionals there to assist you and to make you look good. The director will be there to guide you with your performance. The director works side-by-side with the **engineer**, a technician responsible for cueing up the scenes on the large screen in front of you. Both the director and the engineer sit up in the *"control booth,"* a room with glass windows and technical equipment that looks out over the sound stage where you will be standing with a music stand to hold the script.

You stand at a spot in the room where the engineer has set up a microphone and a music stand facing the screen. The dialogue you are to record will be written on a page sitting on a music stand for you to look at. There are headphones available so that you can hear any of the other characters' dialogue spoken.

Ask the engineer to run the footage a few times on the screen in front of you so that you can rehearse matching the lip movements. Say the words out loud so that the levels can be set to suit your voice. Although the sound stage may be massive, you don't have to yell. The mike level will be adjusted by the Engineer to your vocal level. When you are ready to do a "take," you will hear a series of three beeps at the beginning of each section that needs to be *"revoiced."* These beeps alert you to get ready to speak. Silently count the three beeps and start speaking at the time when the imaginary fourth beep would take place. It may take several passes for you to master this easy process. Don't panic. This is normal for novice and veteran actors alike.

## Oh My God, I Hate My Hair!

Someone else from the post-production team whom you'll **never** meet on a set but who nonetheless has a direct impact on your career is the film or videotape **editor.** Editors assemble the scattered pieces of film or videotape, often given to them out of sequence, from a movie or TV show and splice them together to produce a seamless, continuous story. A seasoned editor can make an adequate looking show look great as easily as an inexperienced editor can make the same show look amateurish.

Similarly, an editor can make an actor look extraordinary, depending on the quality of the performance. If you are giving an interesting performance, the editor will use your cut often; if not, your scenes could wind up on the cutting room floor.

## How to Make an Editor Frown

Here are some of the pitfalls to avoid as a performer which can cause the editor or director to cut your scenes from a motion picture or television show .

- Fidgeting or tapping your feet when shooting your close ups.
- Weaving, drifting, bouncing or having jerky movements.
- Physically blocking your fellow actors from being seen on camera.
- Inaudibility. Speak up even when intimately whispering.
- Moving on another actors' lines. It pulls the focus off the person speaking.
- Volume level. Because stage actors are trained to project their voices due to the absence of sound amplification equipment, they oftentimes blow the sound guy's ears out when they are working on a movie or TV show that uses sound recording equipment.
- Talking with your hands.
- When exiting a scene, you stop before you are out of frame and, consequently,

ruin your scene. Ask the cameraman to tell you when you're out of frame. Stand still quietly until "Cut!" is called.

- Going out of character. You never know when the camera will pick up what you are doing. If you're horsing around and it doesn't suit your character, they'll have to reshoot the scene which, in turn, costs a lot of money which, in turn, can make you look bad.

## Your Job After the Job

Well, it looks like our work here is done. But . . . not really. Technically, when your principal photography and post-production work are completed, you no longer have to account to anyone else for that project. However, there is still one person left to whom you need to be accountable. That person is you. If you want to keep moving your career forward motion, and to rise to the heights you've hoped for, there is still work to be done. That's why I call it "your job after the job." After you walk off the set there are many steps to maximizing your newly acquired acting credit unless, of course, you've decided that your last job is just that . . . your last professional job.

## Resumes

Update your resume first. Tell your agent you would like to come in and exchange your resume on the headshots with ones that include your newest credit. Your agent will always appreciate this conscientious effort on your own behalf.

Updating your resume is a four -step process: (1) unless you have a home computer and can do it yourself, go to the typesetter who printed your resume and have your changes made there; (2) then go off to a copier to make multiple copies of your updated resume; (3) cut them to the proper size—8" x 10"; and, (4) take a staple remover, remove all the old resumes from your headshots and attach the new ones.

You will have to update your resume in this manner every time you complete a work assignment and receive a credit. And make sure you follow this process. Credits that are written in by hand look sloppy. You can, however, do it in an emergency situation. If the added credit is a film that has not yet been released, put the expected time of release by the title (e.g., Fall 1997) to let everyone know you've received a new credit on a product not yet available for viewing.

## Thanks for the Job!

Send your agent a handwritten thank-you note to say how much you appreciate his or her support and efforts on your behalf. Invite your agent to the set, to the screening and out for a celebratory lunch. This is called romancing an agent. This is a relationship like any other and you will reap untold benefits by consciously nurturing this one.

Call the casting director who hired you and ask for referrals to other casting directors. You never know who is friends with whom. Incidentally, casting directors are often forgotten on actors' thank-you note lists; so, send them one as well. This way, when you send your demo tape to that casting director, he or she will remember your gesture of appreciation and will be more inclined to give your demo reel the attention you want.

## Still Photographer

Pull out the business card of the Still photographer you met on the set and call to review the slides or contact sheets. See if any photographs taken of you would be suitable for use as publicity postcards. If there are any shots of you with a recognizable star, use those. Always offer to pay for any useable on-set photographs.

## Postcards

Decide ahead of time preferably, with input from your agent, what you would like to have written on your postcard. Then, while the typesetter is updating your resume, have the message for your postcard typeset at the same time. Review Chapter 13, on publicity, for lists of places to print postcards or add a message to existing postcards. When you have completed a film that is not yet released, you can do a mailing that announces **"Principal Photography Completed."** Later, you can do another mailing when the film comes to the theaters. Principal Photography Completed means that you are done shooting the film but it has not been edited and is not available for release yet.

You will then want to get labels from our order sheet at the back of this book so that you can make an annoucement to all casting directors in Los Angeles or New York that you are working. Also mail these postcards to your director, producer, casting director and agent to let them know you are doing publicity. They love it when actors take pride in their work and use it in a professional way. Also, mail your postcard to anyone in the rolodex file that you are building, especially to all casting directors, whether you know them or not. This lets them know you're working and when they can see you. They may not go and see the movie nor watch the TV show you're appearing in but they will remember you as a working actor who conducts him or herself in a professional manner.

## Publicity

If your role was sizable, let the unit publicist hired by the production company and the producer of your project know that you are available for publicity. During photo opportunities at publicity events, try to position yourself next to a major star. If you would like to use a still photograph from the shoot, get permission from the production company.

## Ads in the Trades

Ask your agent or manager to place a thank-you ad in the trades acknowledging the director, producer or the production company for the extraordinary and unique experience you had working on their project. You pay for the ad. See more about this in the chapter on Publicity.

## Cast and Crew Screenings

Ask to be invited to the cast and crew screening of the movie. If your work is for television, get an air date from the production company so you can announce it in your publicity. Be sure to invite your agent so they can see your latest piece of work. They will start to talk about it right away when selling you to other producers, directors and casting directors. They can also use the screening to smooze directors and producers for future on your behalf. That it let's quickly move on.

# Chapter 12
## Screen Actors Guild

**T**his is the union established for the protection and enhancement of conditions for all 90,000 members working on 35-mm film, television shows, commercials and interactive CDs. The Guild also functions to negotiate contracts and process residuals. Most actors thinks of this entity as the "thing" to which they pay dues. In this chapter, we will explore the treasure chest of services available to you once you become a member.

The Screen Actors Guild also collects information from casting and work figures data. For example, 78,000 members (nearly 80%) earned less than $5,000 last year and fewer than 3,500 members (less than 5%) earned more than $50,000. Sound discouraging? Forget about it! Contrary to popular belief, the older you get the more money you make. It is a common thought that youth is the key to working but a recent graph shows that the top wage earners for both men and women are the 50-plus age group. The second most successful group is men and women aged 40 to 50. So don't worry about aging or not getting an early start with your career.

One of the reasons I wrote this book was to make it possible for you to boost your chances of making it into the money earning group. By providing you with information, strategies, proven techniques, encouragement, and a specific game plan, I intend for you to fulfill your dreams as a successful working actor.

# Nationwide Offices

The Screen Actors Guild national headquarters is in Los Angeles with branch offices all over the country. A list of all the branch offices is in our telephone directory located in the back of this book so you can locate the one closest to you. The asterisk (*) denotes A.F.T.R.A. offices that also handle SAG business in their area.

# Qualifications for Joining

This union has very strict requirements for joining as outlined on the next pages, and a performer may become eligible under one of the following conditions:

### 1.) Proof of SAG Employment
### A. Principal Performer Employment

Performers may join SAG upon proof of employment or prospective employment within two weeks or less by a SAG signatory company. Employment must be in a principal or speaking role in a SAG film, videotape, television program or commercial. Proof of such employment may be in the form of a signed contract, a payroll check or check stub, or a letter from the company, on company letterhead stationary. The document proving employment must provide the following information: applicant's name, Social Security number, the name of the production or the commercial (the product's name), the salary paid in dollar amount; and the specific date(s) worked.

### B. Extra Players Employment

Performers may join SAG upon proof of employment as a SAG covered extra player at full SAG rates and conditions for a MINIMUM of three work days subsequent to March 25, 1990. Employment must be by a company signed to a SAG Extra Players Agreement, and in a SAG film, videotape, television program or commercial. Proof of such employment must be in the form of a signed employment voucher (or time card); plus a payroll check or check stub. Such documents must provide the same information listed under SAG Principal Performer Employment in the previous section.

### 2. Employment Under an Affiliated Performer' Union

Performer may join SAG if the applicant is a paid up member of an affiliated performers' union (A.F.T.R.A., AEA, AGVA, AGMA or ACTRA) for a period of at least one year AND has worked at least once as a principal performer in that union's jurisdiction.

### Taft-Hartley Waivers.

You are not required to join a union to work as an actor, but it is an asset you will want if you plan to make acting a career. But getting into the Screen Actors Guild can be a true catch-22 situation. As an actor, you cannot get into the union without a union job and you cannot get a union job without being a member of the union.

The easiest way around this quandary is to get a waiver known as the Taft-Hartley waiver. This is the way the process works: If a director and producer, for example, want you for a television commercial bad enough and you are not yet a member of SAG, they will file a Taft-Hartley waiver form (provided by SAG). Under the Taft-Hartley Act enacted by Congress in 1947, an employer is free to hire a person who does not belong to the union. But, that person must join the union after a specified period of time (for actors, the period is 30 calendar days). When you work again after the 30 days have elapsed, you will be required to join, and pay both the initiation fee and the first six months' dues in advance. Those fees currently run about $1,400 and can be paid by either cashier's check or money order. If the employee fails to join the union after that specified period of time, the employer must discharge the actor. The employee must join or they can never work under a union jurisdiction again. This filing, then, makes an actor eligible to join the Screen Actors Guild. For further details about the Taft-Hartley laws, contact SAG, Membership Services or, get a copy of *Readers Digest's You and the Law*, p. 477.

# New Application Review

SAG closely scrutinizes new applications. Although anyone under 18 years of age is easily "Taft-Hartlied" since SAG has no requirements for minors, a more rigorous examination by SAG often makes production companies reluctant to use the Taft-Hartley wavier for new adults since the production company may become subject to a fine if the Guild rejects the request. The guidelines for new applicants are: (a) that you must have studied acting for at least a year; (b) that you plan on making the industry your main focus; and, (c) that none of the current guild membership would have been able to do the job you were hired for. The last part (item c) is the stickler; so, I will clarify the meaning of this particular requirement in the next section and, also, give you some other ideas as to how you might find your way into SAG.

# All Roads Lead to Rome

The most unique way of getting into the Guild is by one of the following avenues: having a skill (martial arts, juggling, singing, etc.); being of an unusual physical size; or, speaking a language that is needed but in short supply among the union members. This is what I was referring to in item (c), above.

Still another way of getting into SAG is to join sister unions and wait the required period. For example, if you land a speaking role of five lines or less on a soap opera, you can then join the American Federation of Radio and Television Artists (AFTRA), SAG's sister union. Then, after one year, you become eligible to join SAG. Hang onto your paperwork from the soap and AFTRA. You will need it to be admitted to SAG. Here's another example: If you are a clown or entertain at children's parties, you can be admitted through The American Guild of Variety Artists, another sister union, after waiting one year. Here again, hang onto your paperwork. Requirements for joining these other unions are covered in the next chapter.

Finally, the last way to get into SAG is to work as an Extra by collecting three SAG vouchers or by being upgraded from an Extra to a Speaking Role. This action is authorized by the director and is called a *"bump up."* Once again, hang onto all paperwork for each upgrade and get a copy of the paycheck and stubs.

## Once You Get to Rome

After you pass the hurdle of getting in, you will be invited to an orientation. While attending the orientation, you can pick up the booklets entitled *Contract Summary—Theatrical Motion Pictures and Television; Extra Performers Theatrical Films and Television Digest; Stunt Performers; Theatrical Films and Television Digest; Commercials Contract Digest.* These digests contain synopses of the SAG contracts as well as a truck-load of information covering all aspects of an actor's career in the entertainment industry. These booklets should answer a great many of your questions; however, if you find that you have a question that is not covered, you can call the individual departments at SAG for assistance to get your questions answered. The staff at SAG are happy and willing to serve you. Our union serves it's members, not vise versa.

## SAG Departments

There are many departments at SAG to help you too. There is a list of the direct dial phone numbers for every possible service you might need. It is located in the back of this book. We will discuss, in detail, each one of the services and the types of questions each can answer. OK. Let's go over the services and kinds of questions each department can address.

## Main Switchboard

Like all businesses moving in to the 21st century, SAG uses an automated system that answers the main phone number; however, a menu is presented for your choice. If the department you need isn't listed press "0," to talk to an operator who will direct your request or problem to the proper department. It is

an easy number to remember, one that you will want to commit to memory in case you ever need help.

## Address Changes

If SAG doesn't have your current address, you won't receive your dues statement. If left unpaid, your membership will lapse and you will have to pay extra charges to be reinstated. Also, remember: no address, no residual checks.

## Affirmative Action Department

This department works with four target groups: Seniors, Performers With Disability, Women, and Equal Employment Opportunity for Performers of Color. This department tracks casting statistics to make sure that the proper number of target group members have been seen for projects. The Affirmative Action Department also offers a great many seminars, symposiums, showcases and a Career Day at the Directors Guild of America with many of this businesses' top directors. Call the office for a schedule of events.

Another way this office supports actors is in the area of sexual harassment. If you run into any problem in this area the people in the Affirmative Action Department can help you through this sort of dilemma. The area of abuse is so important to the Guild that it is the second item announced on the automated answering system. Most actors are hesitate to report perpetrators because they are afraid they may get themselves blackballed. Trust me, it's a myth. And consider this: if you are attacked, intimidated or pressured to have sex, why would you want to work with such a person to begin with. Your strength and self-respect lie in the reporting such people.

# A.F.T.R.A.-SAG Federal Credit Union.

The main branch of the Credit Union is located in the heart of Hollywood with other locations in Los Angeles and around the country. These banking services are open to anyone in either of these unions and AGVA. Here are some of the many services that the Credit Union offers:

* An interest-bearing checking and savings account free of monthly charges.
* A Take One ATM card adjoining your checking and/or savings account. This way, you can make withdrawals at any ATM bearing the Star or Plus symbol. ATM deposits can be made at deposit network ATM. (they will provide you with a list.)
* If you have questions about your accounts, anytime day or night, the Credit Union's 24-hour Steller Teller can help. By using the Steller Teller, you can access current balances, loan amounts, due dates, payoff amounts, transfer funds between accounts, inquire about loan rates and much, much more.
* Regular Visa cards and secured Visa cards for those of you establishing or cleaning up credit.
* Low-cost auto, home (1st or 2nd Trust Deeds) or home equity unsecured personal loan. Imagine applying for a loan without the banker hassling you about being employed as an Actor.
* High-yielding share certificates.
* There is also a service available whereby your residual checks can be directly deposited into your accounts.

Every quarter, the Credit Union publishes a newsletter called *Que Sheet*. In it, you will find articles ranging from current interest rates to money-saving tips to upcoming special events. One such event recently offered the services of an attorney to prepare your Will. Normally this would cost $150 but, through the Credit Union, it was made available for $55.

# Agency Department & Actor Locate Service.

If you are considering signing with an agent and want to see how many clients that particular agency has signed to contracts and who is on the agency's client list, go see the gals in the Agency Department. They have the agent's full contracts lists along with current copies of the *Academy Players Directory*. This way, you can see if you recognize any faces or if there is a possible conflict with your type within the agency you are considering. Conversely, this department has your name and agency will representation on computer which they make available to any producer, casting director or production company trying to locate you for a project. If you are not signed to a contract with an agent or an agency, you will not be listed. That is why it is so important to have an agent, not just agree to represent you but to sign you to a contract. Managers and answering services are also listed. Let them know when you change agencies.

## Agents List

When you contact this particular service by phone, you will get a recorded message telling you that, if you wish to receive a list of all Los Angeles SAG franchised agents, addresses, phone numbers and the categories they represent, then you must send a self-addressed stamped envelope to the SAG office. If you are not a Guild member, send your SASE envelope to the address listed at the beginning of this chapter along with a $3.00 check or cash. Or, you may drop by their offices to purchase one. If you are a Guild member, the list is free.

## Casting Seminars and Showcases

Every month SAG offers a free forum for members to work in front of top-rated casting directors. The scenes must be no longer than three minutes in length. No monologues are accepted. You will be instructed as to which day the phone lines are open for reservations. These forums fill up quickly, so call first thing in the morning. If you have a partner for your scene, you will be asked for both your own and your partner's SAG registered names and guild card numbers. Both performers must be paid-up members. A recorded message with the date of upcoming SAG Showcases is given at the end of the Casting Hotline discussed next.

## Casting Hotline

The Hotline is a recorded message of all casting notices given to the Guild, usually by out-of-state production companies looking for union talent and some local projects as well. The recorded message also includes a character breakdown of age and description along with a mailing address to which your picture and resume should be sent. Be sure to check that the production company has completed its SAG Guild signatory papers before you begin work.

## Committee Office

If you wish to take action on a particular issue over which the Guild has jurisdiction over and put a voice to your opinions, the SAG Committee is for you. There are 17 National and eight Local Committees. Any paid-up member may serve on a Committee provided you do not have a conflict of interest. New members are added at the beginning of each year. Call the Committee Office for a list of each committee with a description of its function and get involved.

## Communications & Publications Department

This group publishes *Call Sheet* and *Screen Actor* magazine. Both publications are packed full of news and updates about the Guild. You will be kept abreast of changes to contracts, outcomes of committee meetings, facts and figures on earnings, etc. If you have an idea for an article, let them know.

## Contracts

Should you ever have a question or a problem with a contract look over the list of departments and call the direct number for the office that oversees that area for assistance. Two of the departments on this list and the services they provide require your attention. Production Services is the office producers call to determine if you are a paid-up member in standing before they employ you; otherwise, they can be fined for using non-eligible talent. Through the Production Services office, you can also get copies of the Series casting directors List (all Casting Directors working on episodic shows) and a list of production companies that have recently signed their SAG agreements. Some people use this list to send pictures, unsolicited, for casting.

Signatory Records is the office you call before accepting employment to verify that the production company employing you has signed their SAG agreement to abide by the regulations for working conditions and pay. When you join the Guild, you agree to abide by the Constitution and By-Laws. The most important of these rules is Number One: "No SAG member shall work as an Actor or make an agreement to work as an Actor for any producer who has not executed a basic minimum agreement with the Guild which is in full force and effect." If you accept employment without checking on the production company's status with the Guild and, later, discover that they are not a signatory, you will be fined or expelled from the union.

The function of the Contracts Department that most concerns actors, though, is the union minimum scale. The most current figures for these minimums are in the telephone directory in the back.

## Dues Information

Three times a year you will receive a statement from SAG indicating the amount you owe in dues. The amount due is based on your salary earned the previous year. Any questions or disputes you might have can be addressed by this office. Also, if SAG is not your parent union (because you joined A.F.T.R.A., AEA or AGVA first) and you made less than $25,000 last year as an actor, you are eligible for a $10 discount on your dues. Make the appropriate arrangements through this office.

## Emergency Fund

This is a fund that has been set up for members in dire financial need. If you made less than $5,000 during the last three out of five years, you qualify. Your application is reviewed by the Board of Directors and checks are issued to your creditors for basic survival. This includes rent, utilities, doctor bills and insurance premiums. The maximum amount an actor can receive is $2,250 per lifetime. This fund is administered by The Screen Actors Guild Foundation.

## Executive Offices.

If you have a burning SAG issue on your mind and wish to bring it to the attention of either the national or Hollywood director, this is to whom you make your call or address mail.

## Film Society.

Every year members of the Guild are invited to join the Film Society at a cost of about $105, including parking pass. The appli-

cations appear in the Spring issue of **Screen Actor** magazine. If you are accepted, you will receive a pass for two people per screening inviting you to about 40 movies a year (usually screened at the Directors Guild of America Theater), plus bonus screenings. Competition to get in on this deal is fierce so follow the mailing instructions carefully and hope you get picked out of the barrel. You can call the office if you lose your screening pass and find out what to do to replace it. If you lose your parking pass, the Film Society will not replace it; however, you can purchase parking stickers at an additional fee. A complete list of rules will be sent to you. Caution: you can be thrown out of the Film Society for giving your pass to another party or for eating in the theater. The telephone recording line has a list of u p c o m i n g movies to be screened with the dates and times.

## Legal Affairs

This office is here to help with the tougher problems faced by the membership, such as: sexual harassment; what to do if you have not been paid by a signatory company; bankruptcy negotiations between production companies; actors who are owed money; etc. If you have a problem of this nature, give them a call for help.

## Membership Assistance/ Leniency Committee

If your dues are not paid for a period of 1 1/2 years, your membership in the Guild is terminated. To reinstate yourself, you must rejoin by paying full, new membership fees (currently about $1,400). If there are extenuating circumstances that caused you to default on payment, you can talk to this office about applying for leniency in the form of a monetary reduction and reinstatement, rather than having to rejoin.

## Membership Services

This is the office production companies call to see if an Extra is paid up and, therefore, employable. The reason I list this number is that Membership Services seems to be the catch-all for Extras who have questions regarding money, working conditions and contracts. Be easy on these people, they are very kind but overworked.

## New Membership

The staff in this department can give you all the information you will need to join the Guild. When you first become a member of the Guild, it is important for you to pick a name to use that does not conflict with any other current Guild member. They will assist you to see if your name is already being used. If so, you must choose a new one or change the spelling of the one you're going to use. Eventually, the staff will set up your intake appointment where you pay your initiation dues and sign your application for membership. Once accepted, this office will let you know when the next orientation for new members will be held.

## Pension and Health

One of the primary benefits of working under SAG contracts is participation in the Screen Actors Guild—Producers Pension and Health Plans. Performers who earn a minimum SAG income of $5,000 a year are automatically enrolled for 12 months in the health plan. Effective January 1, 1993 the Health Plan has two different levels: Plan I and II. Your covered earnings and previous years of health plan eligibility determine which plan you qualify for. Both of these Plans cover your spouse and your dependent children. They also cover dental care and hospitalization. For $5 and the cost of a stamp, you can mail any

prescription to a national service at a huge savings to you. If you are in the health plan but will not qualify for the next year, the same coverage will be offered at a cost to you and your family. The rates are very competitive. You must contact this office within 60 days after they offer you this option, or your health coverage will lapse. After the 60-day period, you cannot buy this insurance, even if you intended to do so. Most private hospitals and physicians accept the insurance.

About pension. If you earn $5,000 annually or more, you earn one Pension Credit for each calendar year in which you make this minimum (and $2,000 annually prior to January 1, 1992) in SAG employment. Once you have earned 10 Pension Credits, you become vested and qualify for a pension upon retirement. There are currently 3,600 SAG pensioners who receive monthly payments ranging from a minimum of $220 to a maximum of $4,000, depending on past income. The Pension and Health office can answer a vast array of questions about the health and pension plans as well as helping you to fill out your paperwork.

## President's Office

The buck stops here. If you cannot get needed action on a matter at any of the lower committee levels, contact this office for assistance. The President is an elected official and, also, a working actor; so, be patient.

HOLLYWOOD

# Residuals/Residual Claims Department

Residuals are fees that are paid by productions companies to actors based on any number of specific exhibition scenarios. An example of a situation in which an actor might receive a residual payment is when a TV show is rerun or sold to a foreign or cable market. Another example is when a movie in which the actor appeared airs on cable TV or is sold to video retailers. Still another is TV commercials. This is a venue where big money can be made because residuals are paid to an actor each time the commercial airs. Initially the actor is paid a booking fee to shoot the commercial. *"Usage fees"* (points assigned to each city in the U.S. based on population, which are tallied to determine residuals) are then calculated and the actor earns money for every airing of that commercial.

Residual checks usually are issued in 13-week cycles for commercials. These checks will continue to show up in the mail years after the actor has completed the work. I recently received a residual for a TV movie I shot 12 years ago, which reaired recently. For tax purposes, hang onto the pay stub or the payment outline sleeve in which the checks are delivered. If you see a movie of yours airing, expect a check. If it airs in prime time, the production company has 30 days to get the check to SAG and, from there, it takes about 10 days for SAG to process it. If a show airs on cable, SAG pays out every quarter, ending March 31st, June 30th, September 30th and December 31st. The producers then have 60 days after the end of the quarter to get the checks to the Guild for processing. The Guild has one of the best tracking systems for monitoring every TV show, commercial, etc.; so, even if you aren't aware that one of your shows has been broadcast, don't worry; you have someone looking out for you. If you have a problem or question with residual pay-

ments, call the Residuals Claim Department. But remember: if they don't have your current address you'll never receive these pennies from heaven.

## SAG Conservatory at the American Film Institute

This is a place where actors can go to hone their craft at a cost of $10 per year. Classes are taught by casting directors, agents, directors, voice coaches, etc. The classes fill up quickly. You will be mailed a schedule and if you want to enroll, instructions how and when to register by phone are included. Also, if you wish, you can include your picture in the casting books which are, in turn, made available to directors and producers attending AFI for their student projects.

Each summer the Conservatory offers a weekend seminar. They attract some of the top people in each area of film to teach these classes. You must be a member of SAG in good standing to join. Call this office for an Conservatory application.

## SAG Foundation and Book Pals

The SAG Foundation embodies the most generous and supportive spirit of the Guild. Just get a load of some of the services they provide under the SAG umbrella: The Foundation offers a fee-free consultation service —available at any point throughout an actor's career—to both union and non-union actors. The consultation consists of advice on issues ranging from educa-

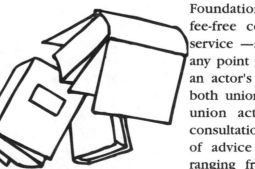

tion to transitioning out of the performance arts. Next, the Foundation provides a list of addresses for companies and organizations that will hire performers for part-time and/or flexible, full-time survival jobs. Also, there is the professional actors seminar entitled "No Illusions," which provides a common sense lesson on the business of acting.

The philanthropic spirit of the SAG Foundation has established two financial assistance programs: (1) The Emergency Fund, which provides emergency relief (the details of this fund are outlined in this section under Emergency Fund); and, (2) The John L. Dales Scholarship Fund, which offers educational loans to be used for further artistic training or to get needed training to transition out of the entertainment field.

The SAG Foundation also has a program called Book Pals. PALS is an acronym for Performing Actors for Literacy in Schools. Under the aegis of Book Pals, actors can be in service to others by volunteering to read to school children. Several cities have Book Pals programs, including: Albuquerque, Chicago, Dallas/Ft. Worth, Detroit, Houston, Los Angeles, New York, Arizona, San Francisco or Washington D.C. Contact these A.F.T.R.A. or SAG offices for participation in this wonderful children's program.

# TDD Line for Hearing Impaired Members

This is a service telephone line available to any Guild member with a hearing impairment. You may link your TDD line to the Guild's or have a Pacific Bell operator assist you if you do not have your own equipment.

Hopefully, I have helped clarify some of the ways in which the Guild is here to help you. If there is an area or question that was not covered in this chapter, call the main switchboard and briefly describe your query to the operator. She can then direct you to the proper department. The only foolish question is the one you didn't ask.

Recently, the Guild began presenting the Actor Award, given to actors in many categories who embody the spirit of the Union. In his acceptance speech, Tom Hanks produced and displayed the very first Screen Actors Guild union card he ever received. He still has it and treasures it to this day. All of the big stars on Oscar night started out just like you —no credits, no agent and no union affiliations. Follow your dream, live your vision and remember that perseverance and dedication are an important part of any choice you make!

# Chapter 13
# AFTRA, AEA and AGVA

In the previous chapter, we covered, in detail, information pertaining to the Screen Actors Guild - the largest and most prestigious performing artists trade union in the entertainment industry. In this chapter, we will discuss, in equal detail, the remaining unions for all performing artists.

# A.F.T.R.A.

The American Federation of Television and Radio Artists is the union that has jurisdiction over all live or recorded television, live or recorded radio, talk shows, soap operas, cartoons and some musical recordings.

The information in this section about AFTRA pertains to the all the offices all over the country Each one services member in that area. There is a list to assist you in locating the local chapter closest to you in the phone directory under AFTRA Regional Offices.

The biggest difference between joining AFTRA as distinct from SAG is the fact that you do not have to be Taft-Hartlied into AFTRA. If you have a desire and the financial ability to join, you may join AFTRA at any time by paying the initiation fee and six months dues. Whichever union you first join becomes your *"parent union"*. Any other unions you join subsequent to joining the parent union become your *"sister union."* AFTRA will knock $10 off from your yearly dues if they are your sister union and the same applies to SAG. Just let them know when you sign up. At the time of publication for this book, the total amount of both initiation fee and six months dues comes to well over $1,000.

AFTRA employs a system which makes it financially viable to join the guild while, simultaneously, securing work as an Actor; this is known as the 30-day grace period. Quite a few Actors use this thirty day grace period to work as much as possible and apply the money they earn toward their initiation money. It works like this: You may call in each day to AFTRA-affiliated shows and soap operas trying to secure extra work. From your first date of employment, you can work as often as you wish without being required to join. Thirty days, after your first day of employment you become what is called a *"must join"* and cannot work another job without first paying the initiation fee. You should know this, however: competition for these jobs is fierce. On the other hand, if you're fortunate to get work as an Extra on an AFTRA-affiliated show, you can still get bumped up to a speaking role and, subsequently, become SAG eligible one year later. That's why you should hold on to your contract, pay stub and AFTRA initiation paperwork so that you can give it to the good people at SAG when you become eligible.

Since AFTRA's doors are open to any actor or model, I strongly urge you to start getting seriously involved in your career immediately by signing up as a member of AFTRA at the chapter nearest you. Call or write them and ask that an application be sent to you. Just being a part of a local AFTRA union and participating in its meetings will give you a leg up on bringing your dreams closer to a reality.

For one thing, attending union meetings will put you in touch with other working Actors who can offer you hints on how to earn a living in your local market. Or, you might get a good lead on the names of reputable acting coaches, photographers and Agents. In fact, AFTRA makes lists available to its members itemizing all of the AFTRA Franchised Agents, shows, radio stations and production companies in your area so that members can seek employment with reputable companies who are union signatories honoring AFTRA's contract. So avail yourself of this powerful affiliation, you never know where it is going to lead. Best of all you are a card carrying, union member who takes their career seriously and can list it on your resume right away.

## Services and Departments of A.F.T.R.A.

Now let's take a look at how this union operates and what services are available to its members. In the back of this book is a copy of the directory to the different departments at AFTRA. This list is re-published from time to time it because of continuing personnel changes. The **AFTRA Telephone Directory,** in the back of this book has the most comprehensive list of departments to help you get in touch with the right person to answer your questions. The names may change but the extension will remain the same. If that persons no longer there ask who took their place.

## Agency Department

The Agency Department manages all Agency problems, franchise questions, and Performer/Agent contracts. Furthermore, this department provides contract information for bona-fide Producers and Casting Directors who want to hire AFTRA members.

The Agency Department keeps a computer file on each actor or model and his/her Agent. So, it is very important that, when you sign with an Agent, that you make sure to send the Agency Department a copy of any AFTRA Agency contract you sign; similarly, should you part company with an Agent, the Agency Department should also get a copy of any termination letter you send to your Agent. If you're in search of representation, the *Franchised Agents List* is available at the front counter of any AFTRA Office. Or, you can request that the list be sent to you by calling the office nearest you

## Broadcast Representatives

Broadcast Reps assist on-air television reporters, television news anchors, radio DJ's, staff announcers and any actor who records syndicated radio dramas by negotiating a contract with each performer's respective station.

Additionally, a Broadcast Representative's work also includes organizing those radio and television stations which do not have collective bargaining agreements with AFTRA and negotiating a mutually acceptable contract between two entities.

The Broadcast reps visit AFTRA stations on a regular basis in order to process grievances, negotiate station contracts and stay abreast of current rate information. You may call this department's representatives at their individual extensions anytime between the hours of 9:30 AM and 5:30 PM.

## Cast Clearance

Cast Clearance is the division which a production company contacts prior to hiring an AFTRA member. They do this in order to verify that the prospective performer is a paid up member in good standing and consequently available for hire. That why it is imperative to keep up with dues. If you are in financial difficulty please read Honorary Withdrawal rather than just stop paying.

## Communications/Member Services

The Member Services/Public Relations Department implements all of AFTRA's Actor support and information disbursement services, including: showcases, workshops, rap sessions, seminars, committee meetings and events, the Extra Casting file, Casting Access program, and membership meetings. One of the most highly-attended events is the Member Services monthly Casting Showcases which pull in some of the industry's top names and they

are available free to all members. Next, are the guidelines if you wish to attend any of the Casting Showcases. Reviewed the list before you begin rehearsals with your partner.

1. Scenes are performed privated for franchised agents and casting representatives from AFTRA television programs, commercials or broadcast industrials and are an opportunity for two members of AFTRA to perform.

2. Both performers must be paid-up members of the Los Angeles Local. Only two-person scenes are permitted, no monologues. AFTRA cannot help you find a partner.

3. The two Actors are responsible for selection and rehersal of material. You may gear your scene to be appropriate to the particular Casting Director or Talent Agent present. Scenes may not exceed three minutes and will be timed and stopped. No firearms or nudity will be permitted.

4. All showcases take place at the AFTRA offices. Props should be kept simple and AFTRA will provide a table and chairs.

5. Call your local office to find out when the next showcase will be held and who is attending. Every effort will be made to announce the casting representatives and franchised Agents in advance but last minute changes are always possible.

6. Teams are signed up on a first-come, first-served basis. When signing up you will need the name and social security number of both scene partners.

The Commiunications/Member Services Department also publishes **Diallog** - AFTRA's quarterly newsletter. It is packed with information containing: listings for special events, changes in AFTRA contracts, a list of AFTRA signatory Production Companies along with their respective address and phone numbers, Game Show listings, Soap Opera lists with Extra Casting Hotline numbers, Studio Lists, AFTRA Radio Station listings and all the day-to-day tidbits of news from the union.

The TV Department also compiles an additional roster called the **Show Sheet** which is simply a listing of shows you can use to find work. One section of **Show Sheet** lists all AFTRA-sanctioned shows, identifies the person in charge of principal and extra casting along with contact phone numbers. In another section, game shows are listed. There is also a studio list and digest of rates for all different categories of AFTRA's jurisdiction.

Finally, **Show Sheet** has a list of all members who have not notified AFTRA of a change of address and who might have checks sitting at the AFTRA office waiting to be picked up. The number of people on this list continues to baffle me. You can get a copy of **Show Sheet** as an addendum to **Diallog** or you can get it as a separate copy. Both are available at the front counter at any AFTRA regional office.

The New York office of Communications/Member Services publishes **AFTRA Magazine.** This magazine has killer articles ranging from survival in this business to profiles of successful members to updates from every local chapter around the country to articles concerning national issues affecting our livelihood. Check it out it will not only keep you up to date but it is a good read.

# Executive Offices and Directors

If you have an idea regarding contract negotiations or the governing function of the guild, contact this office. Inquire as to who is the national director for your area and direct your calls and correspondence to that person.

## Membership Department

The membership counter is open from 9:00 AM to 5:30 PM, Monday through Friday, to serve AFTRA members. Membership Representatives process both new AFTRA members and dues payments. New members applications are accepted between 9:00 AM - 4:00 PM daily. Call and get a list of all documents you will need to bring. Then, schedule an appointment. If you are already in a sister union, make sure you convey that information at the time you are making your appointment. Find out which paperwork they will need from that respective union. This is why you must hang on to your first pay stubs and contracts from all production companies you have worked for and any unions you have joined prior to this one.

In addition to answering inquiries regarding dues, the Membership Department also processes name and address changes. The best time to call this department is anytime between 12:00 Noon and 2:00 PM.

## National Singers Representatives

This office is tied into the AFTRA computer system for Los Angeles enabling them to access current membership data and contracts along with rate information regarding Sound Recordings. If one of the local offices across the country cannot answer your question about sound recordings, this office can research it and give you the answer..

## New Technologies/Information Systems

If you work on an interactive project (e.g., interactive movies or video games) and need some assistance or have a question, call the Interactive Media and Information Systems department. They have current rate and contract information.

## Non-Broadcast

The Non-Broadcast Department handles questions about video and audio contracts for industrials, in-store promotions, talking toys and recordings for automated telephone answering systems. The Department can answer all your pay rate and contract questions cover under the **National Code of Fair Practices for Non-Broadcast -Educational Recorded Material.**

## Residuals

The residuals division administers the disbursement of residual payments to its members. Everyone loves to get mail from this department because they are responsible for monitoring, receiving and distributing all residuals for domestic and foreign television, pay TV and home videocassettes. Since all of these residuals are sent directly to AFTRA, this is usually the busiest department in the entire AFTRA Union.

If you do not receive a residual payment due to any of the trouble situations mentioned in this chapter, call the Residuals Department, have all of your paperwork at hand before you call so you can answer any requests for information.

## Sound Recordings Department

If you are a singer or back-up singer working on an album/CD, or an actor recording books on tape, this is the department for you. Much like the TV & Radio Contracts Administrators  Department for visual performers, the Sound Recordings Department processes talent payments. They also pursue and collects penalties and claims, distributes talent checks, answers question from members and recording companies. Sound Recordings processes member reports and phone reports for sound recording performers.

In addition to phonograph recordings (records, audio tapes and compact discs), this department covers music videos and books on tape. The Sound Recording Department's most frequently asked questions are about contracts, rates, how a performer will be paid and the time frame for payment specified in the current negotiated union contracts. If you are negotiating a deal with a record company, this department can be of assistance in helping you get a fair rate of pay for your services.

The Director of the Sound Recordings Department attends to those above-mentioned duties, visits recording sessions and supervises the department. The best time to call the Sound Recording Department is in the afternoon.

## Television Department

The Television Department is responsible for payment and working conditions on all AFTRA television programs, pay television shows, non-broadcast video industrials, video home cassettes and infomercials.

The Television Department assigns Television Field Representatives, referred to as "TV Reps," to attend to a variety of matters: visiting the sets of AFTRA TV shows to ensure that their AFTRA members are being treated properly and legally (e.g., being paid correctly and in a timely manner); answering questions for both AFTRA members and producers. They provide information for contract negotiations; and, finally, TV Reps pursue and collect any claims which might be called into question pertaining to an AFTRA show. If any of these situations should ever arise, an AFTRA member should call a TV Rep.

The Television Field Representatives are each assigned to specific programs. These assignments are usually determined by the facility at which the program is taped. This allows the representatives to visit several sets in any day. Since TV Reps often visit the sets in the afternoon, the best time to call the TV Department is in the morning between 9:30 AM and 12:00 Noon. You can leave a message 24 hours a day on their voice mail box. The direct numbers for each TV Rep is listed in the phone directory for your convenience.

## TV & Radio Commercials Contract Administrators

Probably one of the more challenging departments in AFTRA, the Commercial Contract Administrators Department, has its tentacles stretched out into many critical areas. This department is responsible for: collecting fees for AFTRA television commercials, radio commercials and promos; pursuing and collecting penalties and claims; and, distributing payments for commercials. They also mediate contract questions from members and producers.

Each Contract Administrator covers an assigned group of advertising agencies based on the first letter in the agency's name. If there is a radio or television commercial problem with a specific ad agency, a telephone call should be directed to the Contract Administrator who is assigned to the agency in question.

Contract Administrators keep track of commercial cycles and notify companies when additional payments are due. Since all commercial talent payments are sent directly to AFTRA with the exception of major payroll companies your payments will be monitored by and sent from the Guild. Finally, Contract Administrators also compare amounts of checks to the member reports and file claims on your behalf when necessary.

The best time to call the Commercial TV & Radio TV & Radio Contract Administrator Department is anytime between 9:30 AM and 5:30 PM, except during lunch time.

Commercial Contract Administrators and their agency designations are in the AFTRA directory in the back of book.

## Benefits Provided by AFTRA

That's basically it as far as departments go. Now, let's take a look at some of the benefits available or some of the situations you might find yourself in. This is by no means meant to be a list of all of the services offered by AFTRA. I have just tried to touch on some of the most frequently asked questions. If you need help of any kind, never hesitate to call AFTRA, they are ready and most willing to help their members..

## Agent Search

To assist you in your search for an Agent, the Agency Department at AFTRA has printed up a handout entitled Tips on Getting An Agent. It has a lot of really good ideas on how to land an Agent you will be happy with. Here

are my tips to remember. All Agents should be franchised Only a 10% commission on your wages can be collected by Agents. If you wish to limit an Agents area of representation contact AFTRA on how best to contractually facilitate that. Agents cannot request fees for headsheets, portfolios or any other tools from them to secure you employment. Nor can they insist you use a specific photographer for headshots. You can submit a written request to your Agent once every four weeks for information on what efforts the Agent has rendered on your behalf.

Hopefully, you'll have a closer relationship and will know what your Agent is doing. All payments will be made directly to you unless you give your Agent written authorization to cash your checks and subtract commissions. That authorization remains in effect until you rescind it in writing. Once you've

landed an Agent, you must let AFTRA know so that they can update their records. They have a specific representation form you can fill out at the AFTRA Offices.

## Terminating an Agent

Somewhere down the road, if you wish to change to a different Agency, it is possible to do so under **Rule 12-B** of the **Standard AFTRA Exclusive Agency Contract.** Here is how that rule reads....

From time to time AFTRA Members who are not receiving satisfactory representation from Agents with whom they have Exclusive Agency contracts, inquire how they may terminate such agreements. In all cases of termination by the performer, the following procedures apply as provided in **Paragraph six (6)** of the AFTRA Exclusive Agency Contract:

In any ninety-one (91) day period before serving termination notice;

If you are not employed, being paid, or entitled to be paid for fifteen (15) days' work in AFTRA's field or any other entertainment branch for which this Agent is authorized by written contract to represent you;

and you are not working under a written contract quarantining you employment for at least one program each week for thirteen (13) consecutive weeks;

or do not have such a written contract under which you will being working within forty-five (45) days;

or do not have such a written contract beginning no later than October 15–if you are terminating in August or September;

and you are not working under a written contract guaranteeing you employment for at least one (1) television program every other week in a cycle of thirteen (13), broadcast on an alternate week basis, or eight (8) within thirty-nine (39) weeks on a one (1) show per month basis;

and you do not have a contract guaranteeing you compensation of $20,000.00 in the next one hundred eight-two (182) days for performances in radio, television or phonograph recordings;

or do not have a contract guaranteeing you compensation of $25,000.00 in the next one hundred eighty-two (182) days for performances in any entertainment field for which this Agent represents you;

and you are not physically or mentally incapable of performing;

and you are available for calls at you customary compensation and conditions (commensurate with your prestige and usual standards);

you may terminate your Exclusive Agency Contract by simply notifying your Agent in writing (with a copy sent to AFTRA).

Keep the following points in mind (Ninety-one (91) days are computed on this basis):

Two and one-half (2 1/2) days counted for each television broadcast except during June, July or August, when each day's employment in the television broadcasting field counts as three and three-fourths (3 3/4) days;

One (1) day counted for each radio broadcast and transcribed program except during June, July or August, when each day's employment in the radio broadcasting field counts as one and one-half (1 1/2) days:

One (1) day counted for each master phonograph record;

but if your television performance exceeds three (3) days (including show day) or you have exclusivity in excess of three (3) days (including show day) the 91-day period is extended by the number of television days in excess of three (3) days.

Likewise, you do not count days:

• during which you have formally declared yourself unavailable;
• or are incapacitated;
• or are at work in an entertainment field in which your Agent does not represent you;

You do count:

the period of guaranteed employment specified in an actual bona fide offer of employment (at your customary salary, usual terms and commensurate with your prestige) which you refuse; or a broadcast for which you are paid even when you do not perform.

As you can see, the conditions under which you can leave an Agent or Agency are spelled out very clearly. You should write a letter to your Agent, including the sentence: "I am terminating our contract as per Paragraph 6 of AFTRA's Rule 12B." It should also include your name (and any a.k.a's), address, social security number, the name of the Agency being terminated, and any new Agency you may have. Mail the original to the Agent and send a copy to AFTRA Agency Department.

## Benefit Performance

If you are asked to appear in a Benefit Performance, clearance must be obtained from Theater Authority West. This is an organization handles clearances for all talent unions. All charity and benefit functions must clear through them.

A portion of the receipt from such benefits is distributed by Theater Authority to AFTRA's Sick and Benefit Fund The Fund uses the contributions for the relief of members who have an emergency need for aid because of health, personal crisis or economic stress. As always, check with the AFTRA office prior to working to make sure everything is in order.. The Theater Authority West number is listed in our directory under Professional Organizations.

## Digest of Rates

For the most up-to-date rates for any type of AFTRA job, please contact the guild. For wardrobe fitting and overtime rates in every category, contact The Television Department. The current rates are available in the phone directory in the back of the book under AFTRA Digest of Rates.

Commercials are negotiated on a individual basis by your Agent. There are so many different markets and types of spots (i.e. primetime, late-night, daytime, etc) that the rates are too complicated to go in to. Call the Commercials Department for specific rate quote. Basically, you receive a shooting fee for the actual taping of the shot. After that, a residual check will appear in your mailbox every cycle, usually thirteen weeks. That is why commercials are so fun and lucrative. You work a few days shooting the spot and it keeps earning you money as long as the commercial continues to air.

## Health Plans

Effective January 1, 1994 the Health Fund will introduce two benefit plans: 1) the Individual Plan, and 2) the Family Plan. You must earn $7,500 in AFTRA to qualify for the Individual Plan and $15,000 to qualify for the Family Plan. Each plan offers a wide variety of coverage. Contact the Health and Retirement Department listed in the AFTRA Directory in the back of our book for more details.

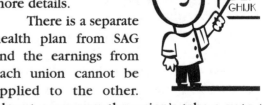

There is a separate health plan from SAG and the earnings from each union cannot be applied to the other. Almost every year the union's take a vote to see about merging but, as of this date, it has not as yet happened.

## Honorable Withdrawal

If you run into hard financial times and are unable to pay your AFTRA dues, measures can be taken to insure your continued good standing in the union. An Honorable Withdrawal Card will suspend your dues payments when you are not actively working under AFTRA's jurisdiction. To be eligible for Honorable Withdrawal, you must have paid dues for the previous 12 months. Requests for Withdrawal must be made in writing and postmarked no later than May 15 or November 15 in order for your membership to be effective for that particular dues period. A Withdrawal **card must be held for at least six months.** If you should work under AFTRA jurisdiction within this initial six-month period, you must pay full  dues to date and your Withdrawal will, then, be canceled. If you hold your Honorable Withdrawal for the initial six months, you may reactivate with AFTRA at any time after that period by paying current dues.

## Retirement Fund

Currently, the Retirement Plan is fully funded and has assets of $838 million, enough - according to the Funds' actuary - to meet all obligations. That is good news since many large corporations are realizing their retirement plans are unfunded. To qualify, you must make $5,000 for a period of five years to receive a monthly check at age 65. Since this is a seperate office from AFTRA, if you have a change of address, make sure that you take it upon yourself to notify both the Retirement Fund office as well as AFTRA. Their telephone number is in the back of this book.

## SAG/AFTRA Credit Union

The fantastic thing about this federal bank is they will never look down on your irradic work record as an as like it is a bad thing. They understand we often have to have an additional survival job. They offer a variety of services for your home, car and personal finances. They have offices all over LA and some in other cities. A list of branches is listed in our telephone directory under AFTRA/SAG Federal Credit Union.

## Sexual Harassment/ Discrimination

If you encounter any discrimination or sexual harassment on an AFTRA audition or job, don't pout, just speak out! Immediately talk to this union office. They will send someone right away to help you and give you a plan of action to take care of yourself.

## Talent Payments

Checks must be received by you, your Agent or AFTRA within 12 working days of employment. Any infraction must be reported to your AFTRA office promptly. AFTRA will process claims on your behalf in a completely confidential manner.

## AFTRA Committe

The guild has twelve different committees that work to improve conditions for special interest groups covered under AFTRA jurisdiction. Any paid up member of the union can volunteer on a committee. To participate just write to the chair of the committee in care of the AFTRA Los  Angeles Offices. There is a list of the committees and their current chairperson.is listed in the back of this book. Look in our Hollywood Little Black Phone Book under AFTRA Committees.

# AEA - ACTORS EQUITY ASSOCIATION

This union covers theater performers, including: principals, singers, dancers, chorus and stage managers. Equity has four offices located across the country that are listed in the phone directory under Actors Equity Assn.

## Enrollment

In order to apply for membership in Actors' Equity Association, you must meet one of the following three requirements:

1. Signing an Equity Contract. If you have been signed to one of the standard Equity contracts (Production. LORT, Stock, Dinner Theatre, TYA, LOA, SPT, etc.), you are eligible to join AEA from the date of the contract signing. However, certain LOA, SPT, TYA and Mini contracts have additional requirements which must be met before applications can be accepted. Check with the Business Representative for the specific contract to find out these requirements.

2. Membership Candidate Program. The Member-ship Candidate Program allows non-professional Actors to credit their work toward Equity membership. After 50 weeks at accredited theatres, the registered Membership Candidate may join the union. The Program is in effect in Equity LORT, Stock, and Dinner Theatre companies as well as some of the Equity Developing Theatres. For more information, contact the Membership Candidate Representative and ask for the Membership Candidate information sheet.

3. Open Door Admissions. If you are a member of any 4A's union (AFTRA, SAG, AGMA, AGVA, AGMA,, HAU, IAU or APATE), you must meet all of the following requirements to apply for membership in AEA:

A. You must be a member for a least one (1) year.

B. You must be an active member in good standing paid in full through the current dues period.

C. You must have worked under union jurisdiction on either one principal, one "under-five", or three days of extra contracts. If your parent union is AFTRA, SAG or AGVA you must supply proof of work in the form of a copy of the contracts(s) or a letter from the parent union certifying the proof of work.

The initiation fee is $800 and will be reduced by up to $400 based upon the initiation fees paid to another parent union. Basic dues are $39 every six months less if you are a member of a sister union and are pro-rated depending upon the month in which you join. One year after admission to Equity, you are eligible to join the Screen Actors Guild.

## Membership Candidate Program

This program allows non-professional Actors to gain membership into AEA by working as apprentices at specific Equity theaters. To become a candidate, you must first secure a non-professional position at any Equity theater that offers the Membership Candidate Program. The theater will have the registration form and you must pay them a $100 fee. You must complete fifty weeks of work and take a written test  after forty weeks; if you pass, you are eligible to join Equity. If you are or have been a member of another entertainment union, a special request along with a copy of your resume and a detailed description of work must be approved by AEA to join this program. For a full outline of this program, contact the AEA office nearest you by phone or by mail and ask for the Membership Candidate Representative.

## Auditions

There are two basic types of Equity shows. The 99 Seat Equity Wavier shows which are produced all over town and pay Actors little or no money. The listings for auditions for the 99 Seat Equity Waiver shows can be found on the hotline at the AEA offices as well as in *Backstage* and *Backstage West.*

The other type of show is Equity paying productions. Since there are so few Equity houses and so many Actors wanting the roles, competition is stiff. The calls go out through **B r e a k d o w n Services** and the **Equity Hotline.** If an open call starts at 10:00 A.M., it is not unusual for Actors to start lining up at 6:00 A.M. Get to the audition early and be prepared to wait.

Equity has a program where performers from other unions can qualify to audition for Equity shows. If you wish to look into the qualification requirements call the Equity Office and ask for the **Auditions Information and Procedures** handout. It is a three page outline of every scenario under which you would be allowed to audition for Equity shows without actually being a member of AEA.

## Equity News

This publication comes out each month and has information about meetings for each region. Additionally, Equity News covers items such as Equity updates, financial reports, events and newsworthy info occurring inside the union. A subscription to Equity News is available at each regional office .

## Bulletin Board

In the lobby of the L.A. Office is the bulletin board, always teeming with a ton of information. Here you can find lists of local theaters, notices for available apartments on both the east and west coast, casting notices, official information and listings of survival jobs. Y'know, stuff like that.

## SAG Eligible

As with the other unions, after securing a job in Equity, you are eligible to join SAG after a period of one year. Keep you paperwork handy to give to SAG when you join.

## Casting Books and Hotlines

There are casting books in the L.A. Office, with lists of shows auditioning in New York, Chicago and Los Angeles. Here are the hotline numbers for cities across America:

## AMERICAN GUILD OF VARIETY ARTISTS

AGVA was chartered by the Associated Actors and Artistes of America in 1939. Their jurisdiction encompasses variety shows and performers of all kinds. Currently, under the AGVA contracts, members consist of artists who perform at theme parks like those at Disneyland, Universal Studios Hollywood as well as performance arenas like Radio City Music Hall. AGVA also represent performing artists who appear on Broadway, Off-Broadway and cabaret productions around the country. Many of the membership are Casual and Club date performers. Member performers are Artists such as singers, dancers, comics, magicians and clowns who perform individually in hotels, nightclubs, theatrical reviews, live industrial shows and private parties.

AGVA's national headquarters is in New York with renowned poet, Mr. Rod McKuen, currently serving as the President. They also have a The West Coast office is headed by Ron

Luber. The addresses are in the phone directory under American Guild of Variety Artists Regional Office.:

## Membership

Any Artist may apply to join AGVA. Prospective members should submit a copy of their current picture and resume for AGVA's files, along with a letter requesting a membership application. AGVA's membership department reviews each application and determines eligibility. After one year's membership, members may be entitled to join AEA or SAG.

The initiation fee for AGVA is presently less than $1,000.. Dues are billed three times a year and are based on a sliding scale according to income, starting at a base of $24.

## Jurisdiction

AGVA, in accordance with industry standards, sets and enforces salary minimums as well as conditions of employment, such as: rehearsal hours, overtime, safe and sanitary theater conditions, travel stipulations, etc.

## Salary Protection

AGVA requires all Producers to post a salary bond through their Bonding Secretary before beginning rehearsals. In this way, each Artist is insured his or her salary regardless of the financial state of their production.

## Minimum and Coverage

AGVA minimum wage is $125 per day and is covered under their standard contract. When you contract for work with an employer, you must also get that employer to send a check to the union office in the amount of $10 for Workers Compensation Insurance. This policy covers you from the period 24 hours prior to the contracted performance, through your performance, to 24 hours afterward. If someone contracts with you and breaks that contract, AGVA will pursue payment and sue on your behalf, if necessary.

## Health Insurance

If you are employed under an AGVA Collective Bargaining Agreement or Casual/Club Date Contract, you may accrue medical coverage. This coverage is provided by the **AGVA Welfare Trust Fund**. If you fulfill eligibility requirements you are entitled to General Coverage Plans A and B that cover hospitalization, major medical, dental, and optical care. These Plans also offer medicare Supplemental Coverage and Occupational Coverage. Details of these plans are available by calling or writing to office the Welfare Trust Fund.

To qualify for Plan A, an Artist must accrue fifteen (15) days or three (3) weeks of employment. Every calendar year there is a $250 medical and $200 dental deductible requirement before reimbursement is possible. To qualify for Plan B, all you need is three (3) days of employment. Claim forms must be received by AGVA Welfare Trust Fund within 120 days from the date of treatment to be eligible for reimbursement.

You will receive an identification card at the time that eligibility begins. Coverage runs throughout continuous employment and for approximately five months following the last day of employment. If you work on a limited or short run show of less than eight weeks, you will receive one week of insurance coverage for each week employed. The addresses for all the AGVA Welfare Trust Fund are located in the back of this book in our Hollywood Little Black Book.

## Margie Coate Sick & Relief Funds

All members of AGVA, whether active or inactive, in need of assistance may receive benefits from this fund. The fund can assist in emergency relief of unpaid bills such as: rent, utilities, hospital, medical, and dental. This money is "granted" and need never be repaid. Members are bound by law to establish "need" by filling out a form and returning it to the Administrator.

The money for this fund is raised by performers through telethons and other charity affairs that are cleared by the Theater Authority. The Theater Authority, Inc. and the Theater Authority West, Inc. provide all the money for this fund. No dues or initiation fees are used to support this Fund. The money is

earned by performers, belongs to performers and are there for performers when they are in need; so, you should never be embarrassed when applying for assistance. The Fund office and Administrators are here to help.

The names, addresses and phone numbers for both AGVA Sick & Relief Fund offices are in the phone directory under the same.

## Community Outreach

Each month AGVA puts together a show to take to area hospitals, institutions and senior citizens centers. It is a win-win situation. The performers have a chance to try new material and give back to their community. The audience members include people who would not otherwise be able to attend such a performance due to illness, financial inability or restricted mobility. Interested members of this union can contact the union office to participate in these performances.

## Discounts

AGVA offers its member a wide variety of discounts on goods and services. In addition to health care (dental care, vision care, hearing care and prescription discounts), AGVA has arranged for its members to get consumer discounts at some of the local merchant outlet stores. Members can get such items as: tires, paint, furniture, window coverings, electronic equipment, health club memberships and even a membership at Price Club. Furthermore, as a member of AGVA, movie discounts are available at AMC and other well known theaters. Finally, AGVA also offers substantial savings on travel, cruises and hotels. This last one, for me, is one of the really fun benefits of this great union.

All of these unions - AFTRA, Actors Equity, and AGVA - were formed for the protection and service of its members. They keep us safe on the job and make sure we get paid what we deserve. If you have any problems whatsoever, the staff for each one of these unions is there for you. Use them.

# Chapter 14

# Publicity and the Trades

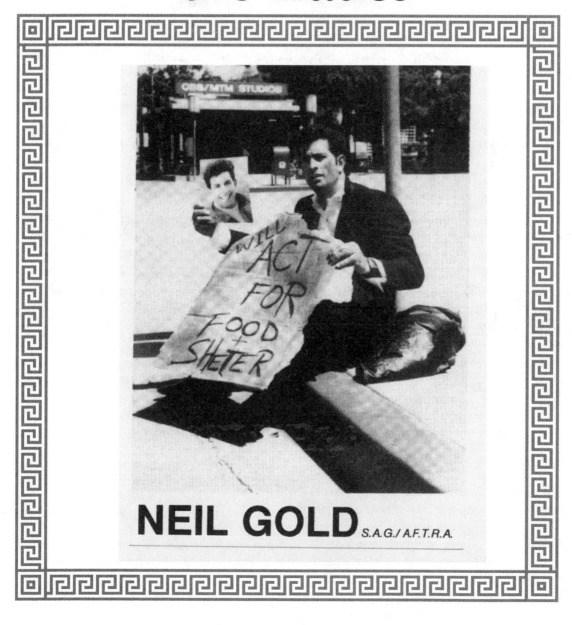

Since the very first actor was required to perform a *"stunt,"* Hollywood studios realized the value of publicity and you should too! When Meryl Streep graduated from Yale Drama School, she hired a $2,000-a-month publicist to help launch her professional acting career. Even though $2,000 was a lot of money, Ms. Streep recognized the critical importance of public relations. If you can possibly afford publicity, you can move your career to the next level.

In this chapter, I'll explain the importance of publicity, describe the components of an effective publicity package, and teach you how to get the most bang for your buck. Talent is not enough to make it to the top. Your talent will sustain a career once you are at the top but the number of talented unknowns in Hollywood is the great tragedy. Moving your career along is based on your strategy for making industry people aware of your reputation. If industry pros have never seen your work but become aware of you through effective publicity, they will assume good faith in your work as well.

## Publicists

If you don't have a steady acting job that generates income to pay for a publicist, you will have to act as your own promotional agent. Whether you can afford to hire a publicist or are forced to be your own, take a close look at this section so that you will understand some of the functions in which publicists seeks to gain attention for their client.

A publicist's job is to get a client's face and name in as many publications as possible. After you've gotten a noteworthy role in a movie or television show, you can hire a publicist for a couple of months to promote the work you've just done. When your finances permit, you can retain a publicist on a permanent basis.

When hiring your own publicist, have a clear idea of the image you are selling. Meet with several and find out what contacts they have, who their clients are, and what their strategy is for getting your name out there and into the public's consciousness. This will give you an idea how connected they may be on a national level and, therefore, how effective they will be for you. Before you decide on a particular publicist, make sure he or she shares or understands your views and speaks the way you would because, in due time, your publicist will become your mouthpiece.

## The Unit Publicist Can Help

If you have a sizable role in a movie or a role on a television show, you have an additional opportunity to enhance your exposure possibilities: meet the unit publicist for the film or TV show and let them know you are available for any kind of promotion or interviews. It is their job to publicize the entire project and you can benefit from this opportunity.

Since the production company is paying for the unit publicist's salary, this is free publicity for you. Take full advantage of this situation. Contact the publicist with enough lead time for them to get you booked on talk shows and in magazines before your show is aired or your movie is released. Let the publicist know about any affiliations you have with charities so that they can create goodwill for you. Once your articles come out in print, you can send them to people on your mailing list as a clever way to keep in touch.

## Where to Find a Publicist

Like any other support service in the entertainment industry, publicists come in all kinds of packages. Some are more affordable than others. From time to time in **Backstage West** there are ads for more affordable publicists. Whether you're interested in or in need of a particular PR company or not at the time, it might be good practice for you to find out what services are offered at what cost. The **Working Actors Guide** has a whole section called "Public Relations." It tells you the length of a commitment each company asks for, the type of clients they handle, some of their approaches to publicity and how long they have been in business. There is a list of some firms and the celebrity clients they have handled in our phone book under Publicity.

We've used these particular agencies as examples of the kind of companies that already have good, national contacts which can be used to promote any of their clients, including you. These companies have the expertise and ability to get their clients on **ENTERTAINMENT TONIGHT, EXTRA** or **CNN ENTERTAINMENT NEWS.**

## Gathering a Portfolio of Attention-getting Material

Use smaller roles such as cops, reporters, doctors, office workers, lawyers and the like to climb the ladders of success. Remember Bronson Pinchot's very small but memorable role in **BEVERLY HILLS COP?** That's how he launched his career. If you are a classic leading man or woman, your career can be launched through leads in low-budget features, such as Jennifer Jason Leigh's first lead in a little cult classic **THE HITCHER.**

You can even use publicity shots of you doing a runway fashion show. When you are thinking of doing some publicity, look for photographs and film clips from your work that radiate charisma, charm and intensity in personality. The purpose is to distinguish yourself from the masses. You are looking for your unique selling point.

## What Publicity Stuff to Gather

Throughout your career keep a file of reviews, publicity stills and film clips to use in your *"press package"*. A press package is a collection of photos, biography, reviews of your work and interesting facts about yourself. A press package is sent to anyone who might write an article about you or interview you so he or she have an idea of who you are, what makes you unique and what project you are currently publicizing.

If you work on a movie set, you can get access to the stills taken on the set which are already paid for by the production company by befriending the still photographer. Get the photographer's business card and let him or her know that you would like to buy some action photos of yourself and any shots of you with a major star of the picture. Always offer to pay. These shots rarely cost over $10 per photo and are sometimes free.

When you're working on a television show, chances are that the producers won't be hiring a still photographer. So, do the next best thing: load your own camera with black-and-white film. During a break, ask a recognizable cast member to stage a scene from the script and use the existing set and lighting to have some photographs taken. Always get permission from you fellow actors, especially famous ones, to use their likeness in your publicity. The cameraman is the best person to ask to snap the photo, since he or she knows how to frame a shot and how to get good lighting.

In the case of fashion shows make sure you get access for a friend of yours. Give them a camera loaded with color film and hand them a roll of black and white to shoot when the color is done. These great shots can not only be used for publicity but in your portfolio to show other clients,so it has the desired effective of hi I am modeling all the time.

## Postcards

After you've developed and printed the contact sheets, select the best photos for your postcards and press kits. When I asked a number of casting directors about their preference, most indicated to me that postcards are their favorite way of being notified of upcoming TV and movie performances.

At the end of the chapter are some great examples of publicity postcards. Notice the Neil Gold (chapter cover) clever use of humor. Or you can learn a lesson on the use of quotes from Sibel. Bob Sky's makes you feel like it's your responsibility not to break the chain by hiring him. Kevin Page action shot taken on the set just grabs your attention.

## The One-Man Publicity Machine

Use your imagination because you are going to be a one-man publicity office until you can afford a larger, professional PR firm. Once you've selected a photo, decide what

sort of spin or slant you want in the message of your postcard. Be clear and certain about the image you intend to project. On the postcard, include your name, an agency or answering service contact and your union affiliations, if you wish. Just before you go to press for any last-minute changes, check with the production company for the TV show air dates or the release date of a film in which you appear. You will definitely want to include this information on your printed postcards so if they don't tune in will at least realized that you are a working professional.

## Printing Postcards

Now we go to press. The lithograph process is always used for postcards. Each of the designated companies under Lithographers in our Little Black Book manufacture postcards with various prices and production turn around times. Whichever way you decide to go, be sure to bring the original photograph you wish to use and your message written or typed out.

## Printing Messages on Existing Postcards

If, after you've done a mailing, you have some remaining postcards with no message printed on them and you would like to use them up, there is a company that will print messages, after the fact, on your blank surplus postcards. This company in our phone directory under Lithography - Adding Typesetting is a Los Angeles based company but if you check around in the printing community listed in your yellow pages you will find someone who can do this for you. That way if you want to print up 500 postcards with a message on it and then 500 with just a photo and add a message after you get your next job, you can. It will help you to save a little cash.

## Mailing Labels

Now to get your postcards addressed. You can buy the commercial and theatrical casting directors labels on the last page of this book off the order form or on our web site. This will run you $20 for the combined list. All 360 plus Los Angeles SAG agents go for $20. For $15 you can get either the agents or the casting directors list from New York. If you own a home computer with the ability to print labels, you can do it yourself. However, if you decide to do label printing yourself, you should subscribe to the **CD Directory** from our web site and diligently keep up with the changes they will mail to you every two weeks. When your mailing list gets too large or you have no time to update, there are people who can do the job for you. In our phone directory there is a list under Typesetters.

## Personalizing Postcards

If you decide to include a handwritten message on the postcard, be sure to vary the wording when mailing to several people in the same casting office; otherwise, it will lose the personal touch. If you include your return address (use P.O. Boxes only), it will help you keep your home computer list current because the postcards will be returned to you if the party has moved on.

## Post Office Mailing Sizes

When you print up 4 1/4" x 6" postcards, the post office will let you mail them and only charge you the postcard rate but, if you go to a larger-sized postcard, the postage jumps to the first class letter rate. This comes out to be a huge dollar difference per 500 postcards mailed.

## Press Releases

If there is something very unusual currently going on in your life or in your career, this is an opportune time for you to send out a press release. Since press releases are by their nature designed to be sent to newspapers and magazines, you must have something to say that will capture their attention. Decide what you want to achieve with this kind of publicity. In the beginning, for example, it may be that you just want to let the public know of your play, or the premier of your movie.

When some actors recently started a theater for inner-city children, they designed a press release and were written up in the *Los Angeles Times*. Since newspapers have pages to fill daily, they are grateful for the help. Whatever you're publicizing should be noteworthy. They would not, for instance, write an article about someone who has moved to L.A. and decided to be an actor. But probably would give you coverage if you were a person who moved to L.A., decided to be an actor and were responsible for the inner-city theater group I mentioned above. Look for a hook; find an interesting angle.

Always mail press releases to your hometown newspaper. They often do hometown-actor or model - makes-good stories. Press releases must be in a particular format with the following information:

1. Name of the company sending the release (on their letterhead).
2. The date the release is being sent and when it is to be released.
3. The who, what, why, when and how of the "event" or information that is being publicized.

Here is a sample press release for a play entitled **SHAKEN, NOT STIRRED**. It should give you a few ideas to help you write your own press releases.

**FOR IMMEDIATE RELEASE**
Big Mouth Productions

SHAKEN, NOT STIRRED
An evening of sex, comedy and a touch of vermouth

Six ten-minute plays written by such diverse and prolific playwrights as: Christopher Durang, David Ives, Joe Pintauro, Steven Dietz, Glen Merzer and Murphy Guyer will be presented at the Fountainhead Theatre in an evening entitled: **SHAKEN, NOT STIRRED.** Opening night is Monday, May 3, 1998 at 8:00 PM. Performances continue Mondays and Tuesdays through Tuesday, June 8, 2000.

With the talents of five directors, six plays, seven actors and a fantastic production design team, **SHAKEN, NOT STIRRED** has more than 350 years of theatrical experience upon which to draw.

Along with the six plays, all of which present a view of life and relationships in an amusing if somewhat unconventional manner, there will be live music and some performance surprises to amaze and delight.

Admission for **SHAKEN, NOT STIRRED** is $10. The Fountainhead Theatre is located at 1110 N. Hudson, at the corner of Hudson and Santa Monica Boulevard, just off Theatre Row in Hollywood. Valet Parking is available for $2.00. Reservations can be made by calling (310) 555-1212

Bigmouth Productions extends an invitation to our Gala Opening, Monday, May 3, directly following the performance. Gourmet refreshments will be served. Perhaps, a dry martini, up, with a twist?

March 25, 2000

# How to Write a Bio

No press kit is complete without a bio of the artist and publicity photos. Fred Rogers' bio below gives you an idea of how to write one. The pictures for the press kit are more easily printed in newspapers and magazine if they are photos—not lithos—and it's best if you can include a studio or network logo on the material, if there is such an affiliation. If you are in a play, take black-and-white stills during a dress rehearsal and enclose tickets to the performance in your press kit. The more professional the package, the better your chances of getting it published. Here is Fred Rogers' bio:

### Fred Rogers Bio

One of TV's most familiar faces, Fred appears almost daily as a spokesman for some of America's leading advertisers, or as a Guest Star on such series as *DYNASTY, FALCON CREST, OUR HOUSE, FACTS OF LIFE, GIMME A BREAK, LOVE BOAT* or *RIPTIDE.* He's had recurring roles on *HARPER VALLEY PTA, GALACTICA, MEDICAL CENTER* and *THE F.B.I.*

Fred has been featured in over 615 commercials! Everything from appliances to automobiles, cough relief to copier machines, laundry aids to long-distance phone service, instant cameras to instant coffee. Recognize the "Airline Pilot" from the current *NUPRIN* spots, or the *NAPA MAN?*

A versatile talent, Fred hosted the popular daytime program, *THE GIRL IN MY LIFE* on **ABC** for 18 months. He traveled to Europe to host an hour-long pilot for **20th Century Fox,** *THE INSIDE GUIDE TO PARIS* and last summer was called to Spain to co-star in the feature, *EDGE OF THE AXE.* He co-hosted ON-TV's monthly program for subscribers, *ON THE MOVE* and currently hosts Video Marketing Networks' *HOME SHOPPING SERIES.* He produced and hosted the video celebration of *THE CALIFORNIA ANGELS 25th ANNIVERSARY OLD-TIMERS GAME.*

In the Industrial Film arena, Fred Rogers' been chosen to host and narrate training and informational programs for: **Mastercard, IBM, Chrysler, Bank of America, McGraw-Hill,** and hundreds of other clients.

## Writing a Bio for Playbills

Whenever you get involved in a production of a play there is always a concern about what to say about yourself in the program, otherwise known as the *"playbill."* There are many ways to go with these generally short blurbs. You can be comedic, make a statement or be straightforward. Below you will find three different styles of bios. Two things to consider when writing a bio are the image you are projecting and the image of the character you are playing. Either will work. Here are your samples:

**Cameron Thor (Jim)** has appeared in and directed a number of plays in Los Angeles, most recently, last year's award winning *PVT WARS.* He has worked extensively in both television and film, including *CURLY SUE, A FEW GOOD MEN,* and Steven Speilberg's *JURASSIC PARK.* He co-founded the Actors' Gang, studied under George Bigot of the the **Theatre De Soleil,** and currently studies with Roy London. Many AIDS organizations need your money. I'm donating my salary and urge to you to send what you can to: All Saints AIDS Service, 126 West Del Mar Blvd.,

Pasadena, CA 91105, or call 818-796-5633. They're particularly in need of funds for their work with AIDS victims, children, and their families. This is for you Max. I miss you.

**Cynthia Ettinger (Maggie)** spent eight years as a member of the Actors' Gang including performances in San Francisco, New York and Scotland. This marks her third production with Ebbe Roe Smith and Lisa Sandman. She has appeared in The Brides productions of Ebbe Roe Smith's *HOW MUCH WOULD CHUCK?* and Len Jenkins' *GOGOL* at LATC. Some of her television credits include *SEINFELD* and *REASONABLE DOUBTS.* Cynthia was also seen in Jonathan Demme's Academy Award-winning *SILENCE OF THE LAMBS* and *ARMAGEDDON.*

**Tom Booker (Bobby)** is a former mascot from the University of Oklahoma. He found himself stranded in Chicago during a beer run gone bad. Tom has appeared in the Annoyance Theatre productions of *SPLATTER THEATRE II, COED PRISON SLUTS, THAT DARNED ANTICHRIST and YOUR BUTT.* He has also directed Annoyance Theatre productions of *MANSON: THE MUSICAL* and William Shakespeare's *SID and NANCY.* He used to perform with the improvisation group Blue Velveeta but he doesn't anymore. Look for Tom in the film *THE BABE.* He's the one with the megaphone. He spends most of his spare time experimenting with hair care products and teaching his dog the fundamentals of field hockey.

## Press Conferences

If you are announcing some spectacular event related to your career, you can hold a press conference at your local press club. The ones in LA are listed as Publicity-Press Clubs.

## Newsletters

This is a great way to keep your family, friends, colleagues and Agents or Managers apprised of your success. Casting directors and other busy industry professionals rarely have time to read newsletters; but, if they contain a picture of you with a celebrity and a brief caption, chances are you'll get their attention. Although postcards are cheaper to print and mail, including a newsletters in your press pack is a much more effective way to give the reader an idea of your personality.

If you want to make a big impression, send an announcement of a great role on attractive stationary that resembles a wedding invitations; if you hand address them, they will almost immediately get opened because they look like an invitation to a party.

## Let's Get on TV

A little known fact is that all of the magazine shows and the trade publications are very open to receiving Actor-submitted material. They have segments and sections that must be filled daily. If you have a big deal event or fashion show, movie or mini-series you need to publicize, take a closer look at these outlets for publicity. The current hot shows are listed in our phone directory under Publicity - Magazine Shows.

## Calendar & Theater Section

The Theater Desk of the most major newspapers are constantly looking for stories. If you want to have your play reviewed, send a complete press release, including a contact phone number to the Theater Desk. If they plan to attend your event they will let you know one week in advance, if your play is going to be reviewed. If you have an idea for an article or a desire to be interviewed for a feature article on your play, movie or TV show, send your information to them. Try to find an angle that will grab their interest. Be make sure to include a contact phone number so they know who to contact for the interview or review. The calendar section contact at the LA Times is in our phone directory under Publicity - Newspaper.

## The Trades

This is the slang term for the newspapers that just cover the entertainment industry. One is published in New York but most are published in Los Angeles. Here is how they work and who to contact.

## Backstage & Backstage West

**Backstage West** is, also, a publication mainly for actors. In one section, there is a column called "Opening This Week" where freelance writers cover theater performances and offers their favorite pick. In another section, there is a column called "Review." This is a column written by many different freelance writers who also award a critics' pick for theater. To submit a play, musical performance or stand-up act for review, fax a flyer to them and then send a press kit, if you have one to the address under Industry Newspapers in our phone directory in the back of the book.

## Hollywood Reporter

This trade magazine comes out daily and is read by people in every area of the entertainment industry. As a user-friendly publication, The **Hollywood Reporter** encourages actors to submit news items that can be read by their 32,000 subscribers ensuring that the entire industry knows when you are cast in a new role. It gives casting people, directors and producers an opportunity to view your work in television, film or plays. Send your photo and casting information to either their film or television department.

There is always a lot going on in this town so critical acclaim is one of the most vital elements of the acting professional. The **Hollywood Reporter** previews and reviews new plays, television shows and films all the time. Make sure to let the **Hollywood**

*Reporter* know about your next opening, air date or screening by faxing the information to the phone number under Industry Newspapers in our phone book in the back. When you sign with a new agent, manager or publicist, let everyone in the entertainment industry know by sending them a fax. After you have given the details, the staff at the trades will decide if you or the new agent or manager is a big enough name or newsworthy item to write about.

Throughout the year, the *Hollywood Reporter* prints a number of "special issues," usually centered on a particular upcoming event like the Academy Awards, the American Film Market, the Cannes Festival Film Festival, etc. Check with them for a list of these special issues. This is a great opportunity to bring the attention of your talents to a specialized audience: You can do this by taking out a paid advertisement in any one of these "special issues." The pricing structure is in our phone directory as well.

**Hollywood Reporter's Special Issues.**

If you feel that you need some assistance in getting your ad placed, I highly recommend that you contact the Talent Specialist at the *Hollywood Reporter.* They are very intelligent, compassionate and supportive people who will take you by the hand and guide you with the placement of your ads.

## Daily Variety

The *Daily Variety,* with a circulation of 25,000, is the *Hollywood Reporter's* competitor. They do not offer any columns for actor-submitted material. The only way to

appear in **Variety** is to take out a paid advertisement. You can contact talent representatives for ad design. Their current rates are in the telephone directory in the back.

## Tips for Paid Advertisements

When placing your ads in either the *"the trades",* bring the original photograph. Provide each publication with all agency, publicist and manager names and telephone numbers. For television, include: air date, time and network. If your role was large, add the billing.

Although you will place your own ads in the trades, the best and most professional way of writing your ad is to make it sound as though your Agency or the production company are making the announcement to congratulate you. The announcement should read something like this: "The Artists Company is proud to announce" Try to make an enticing statement about the character you played to get people to watch the show or film.

A final note on paid advertisements: With any paid advertisement, there are a couple of guidelines on the size of ads. Take out a 1/8 page ad for smaller roles, just to let people know you are working. If you have a sizable role that shows off your talent and can afford it, don't be small time in advertising. Take out a 1/2 page or full-page ad.

The thing to remember about publicity is that life will provide you with opportunities and contacts. It's up to you to stay in touch and keep them alive!

Don't Break the Chain...
Of Continued Success!

Secure the Voice Talent
of Bob Sky!

...Link Up Today
SPECIAL ARTIST AGENCY
8730 SUNSET BOULEVARD
LOS ANGELES, CA 90069
(213) 855-1803

In the lead, Ergener brings a truthful dose of despair, nerves, and triumph...**Her closing song is a stunner.**
   **--Backstage West**

...the captivating **Sibel Ergener** plays an unknown, terrified, coke-snorting actor...One of the most entertaining plays I can remember...This 22-member cast is very strong.
   **--L.A. Weekly**

**Sibel Ergener** emerges triumphantly as the talented but troubled Christine Farley...the show is irresistible fun...a well written and solidly acted comedy.
   **--Los Angeles View**

SIBEL ERGENER

**"NYPD Blue"**

**Co-stars**

# KEVIN PAGE

**(Robocop, Fear No Evil, Brotherhood)**

# Chapter 15
# Building a Demo Tape

The days following your gig can be a wonderfully exciting time. You get to run around updating your resume, building a hot publicity campaign, thanking everyone who helped you get there—all with the warm afterglow that comes from working at a craft you love.

But . . . wait! Not so fast! There's still more work to do before you can bask in the glory of your first success, like building a good demo reel, which is the topic of this chapter.

## The Demo Tape

Now let's get down to the how's, what's, and why's of building a demo tape for theatrical, commercial, talk shows, game shows, stand-up, industrials, fashion shows and voice-over.

So, why the need for a demo tape? Your 8" x 10" headshot and Zed Card opens the door to opportunity and the demo reel enables you to pass through. I always assumed that, if I was auditioning for parts, I would never need a demo tape unless I was trying to land a bigger agent. Not true. In the summer, some casting directors will view tapes of actors that are being pushed by powerful agents. The summer is traditionally *"hiatus"* time (that part of the year when television shows are on vacation and the fewest projects are in production); so, most casting directors have the time, and they love to discover new talent. Busy fashion designers may not have time to meet every new model but would rather look at a tape in the privacy of their own office or home.

Consider another reason why you should have a demo tape: what happens if you are out of town on vacation or working on a show in some distant, foreign land? A director unfamiliar with your work wants to see who you are and what you are capable of. The demo tape then becomes invaluable because the director and producer can review your work and make an expeditious decision. The same thing holds true if the fashion designer or director is on location and can't meet and audition you.

## To Be Competitive

Now for the "what's" of demo tapes, as in what you should do and what you should know about demo reels. It's important that the quality of your demo tape be of broadcast quality. Thousands of dollars and valuable time are on the line for producers and directors who have scant time to waste on amateurish efforts. Nothing less than a broadcast quality camera will be acceptable. So, when you are advised to go out with your video camera or even a High 8 camera (slightly more professional than the home models) to shoot your demo, your knowledge of this fact will reflect your professionalism and respect back to those who are using their precious time to view your tape. The new DVD cameras seem to work very well though.

Demo tapes come in two different sizes. Your *"master demo"* reel will be assembled on a 3/4" tape and *"dubs"* will be copied onto 1/2" VHS size tapes. A master demo reel is the reel on which you assemble all of your film clips. It is the finished product ready for professional viewing. The reason that 3/4" tape is used is because the quality of the resolution is vastly superior to that of 1/2" tape due to the extra surface space on the tape itself. Also, most production companies and post-production companies use a 3/4" video tape recorder in their offices or studio; the 1/2" videotape recorders are customarily for use in the home.

But, if you ever wanted to make a 1/2" copy (called a "dub") from the 3/4" master reel, you will be more than satisfied at the resulting quality. To start collecting samples of my work, I purchased several 3/4" 20-minute tapes to hand out to production companies. Then, after final shooting and editing was completed, the editor who worked on my show would dub a copy of my work onto 3/4" tape for me.

Now, for the "how's." To start off you will need two 20-minute 3/4" tapes, ten 1/2" VHS tapes and ten plastic cases for the VHS tapes with full sleeves (a clear plastic outside liner into which you slide artwork).

There are a couple of places in most cities where you can purchase professional tape. Get a one 3/4" to start.

## Gathering Material for Your Demo Reel From Television

If the television production company cannot or will not provide you with a copy of your work, there is another way to get it. Find out what day and time the program on which you appeared will be airing and call a

company that does *"air checks."* An air check is a copy made of the broadcast from a televised show directly onto a 3/4" tape. At the same time I have the company make a 1/2" dub so that I can sit at home and watch the show to decide which scenes might be appropriate and powerful for my demo reel. I watch the tape over and over again to ascertain which part of the scene really cooks.

There is a list of companies that do air checks and that are affordable to actors in the phone directory under Demo Reel - Air checks.. The price is for an hour long show and does not include 3/4" tape stock. If you don't bring your own tape, you will be charged a retail price for the same tape you can buy for wholesale.

## Getting Material Feature Films

Getting a copy of your movie work is a little bit harder. Here are a few ways I personally have successfully gotten tape. Stay in touch with the director. Directors often make copies to show distributors, investors, etc. Ask them for a VHS 3/4" copy as soon as they have one available. If you are polite and offer to pay. They usually comply free of charge.

Another way to obtain a copy of your work is by calling the production office and asking them to put you in touch with the Editors. When you contact the editors, identify yourself by your character's name. Ask them if they expect to have any *"out takes"* (takes that will not be used in the final print) of your performance which you could obtain for your demo reel. If they say yes, make arrangements to go by and pick up the film. Take the film to a processor and have it transferred onto 3/4" video tape. Just remember that the out takes you get from the editors are the rejected takes, so it may not be your best work.

The final method for getting a copy of your work takes the longest: Either wait for your movie to go to cable TV and get an air check or wait until it goes to home video and have it transferred from 1/2" to 3/4".

## What If You Have No Tape?

If you are just beginning and have no tape of yourself, there are lots of companies that will offer their services to film you doing a monologue or in a scene. These companies will be happy to charge you large sums of money to do this. I would rather you do a no-budget, low-budget or student film than have you pay to get something that will not be acceptable .

If you haven't yet gotten work on a feature, TV show or commercial from which you can get clips of your work, there is another way to get material for your demo reel. Call on some friends or acquaintances who work as industry professionals and ask them to volunteer their time and expertise to assist you in filming or tap-ing yourself doing a scene or two. This may run into some expense. But, if you're really lucky you can keep expenses to a minimum, paying only for some equipment. If you're really, really, really lucky . . . it may cost you next to nothing. Use favors if necessary. You can probably see where I'm going with this strategy. That's right! Just think—you'll actually be taking on the dual role of actor and Producer.

# Producing Your Own Demo Reel

So, if you decide to go this route alto-gether, here are some tips to assist you in cre-ating a great shooting experience as well as turning out the desired result for your demo reel:

**As the producer:**

1. You may want to assume the role of executive producer and "hire" a produc-er to attend to all of the details of the actual production. This way, you'll have someone looking out for your interests which, in turn, will enable you to focus on your work as an actor. Incidentally I use the word "hire" here as an opera-tional term. Whether you have to shell out any money is something you will have to determine ahead of time.

2. Everyone knows someone who has or would like to direct. Choose someone you trust and someone who believes in you., who has some experi-ence and can guide you. Sit down together and discuss the scene(s) you intend to do. Find out how he or she envisions the scene(s). Encourage the director to shoot the scene from many different angles, so it can be edited together later to look as pro-fessional as possible. Do the same with the cameraman whom you hire. In fact, all

three of you should sit down at the same time and discuss these matters. This is a mini-production meeting.

3. Consider shooting the scene(s) in an outdoor setting to avoid complicated lighting.

4. If you're going to use an existing loca-tion, find out how many hours you can use it. Shoots usually go over budget for one reason or another. Because this may be your first time out on a venture such as this and, also, for sanity's sake, figure that it will take twice as long to shoot as you think it will.

5. Check with the owner of your location to find out about the availability of power sources to run camera, sound and lighting equipment. An outside loca-tion is great but if there isn't any power nearby, you will have all the equipment you need but no ability to shoot the scene(s). Have the cameraman approve location before the shoot date, in case of any lighting difficulties.

6. Ask other actors to play the other roles including background. Use up favors if necessary. Overbook the number of extra actors and crew in case someone either can't or doesn't show up at the last minute. Confirm everyone on cast and crew the day before shooting.

7. Confirm that someone is bringing the tape stock or film.

8. Have everyone ready to go when the director arrives on the set. This means the crew should be on the set and all actors in wardrobe and makeup. With respect to actors in wardrobe, no one appearing on camera should wear white, black, checks, or swirls because of the difficulty in lighting these appar-el patterns and because of visual distor-tions, which show up on the screen and can easily distract the viewer from the main action. Deep, rich colors are best.

9. Above all, make sure that someone keeps track of which takes you are going to use and which ones you are going to discard. This way, you won't waste time or money when it comes time to review the tape and locate a specific take to edit into your master demo reel.

10. Treat your cast and crew like gold. Bring food to eat and plenty of soda and water.

**Now, as an actor:**

1. Do not do a monologue. agents want to see if you can act and react to another actor.

2. Pick a scene from a play or movie that is not very common.

3. If you have any well-known actor friends, ask them to do the scene with you. This will give your reel credibility.

4. Rehearse the scene for several weeks and work with your acting coach on the piece. Invite your director to rehearsals, so he can start thinking about camera angles for shooting the scene.

5. Employ a professional makeup artist.

The more you can make the final result look like a professional shoot, the more useful the demo tape will be.

# How to Get a Script for Your Shoot

If you see a scene from a movie you would like to use, you can obtain the scene in any of three ways:. The first one you can go to the video store and rent the tape and audio record it off the VCR and transcribe it later. Go to the local university film school and see if they have scripts. The last way only works if you live or call LA

and ask for a script to be sent. Nu Print Stationary has a library of scripts at a cost about $20. They are listed in the directory under Demo Reels - Shooting

# Do Not Reinvent the Wheel if You Can Help It

Now let's say that you don't know enough people to assist you in self-producing your scene. What can you do? Well, there are small production companies in large cities can actually specialize in this area of demo reels for actors. In our phone directory under Demo Reels - Shooting are two production companies that have a good deal of experience in shooting actors' reels and in making the final result look professional for a great price.

All the companies should use broadcast quality cameras, lighting packages and microphones which gives them the capability to shoot indoors or out. It may cost more to light a scene inside because more lighting is required. So, be mindful: the more complicated the setup, the more money you will have to spend. Call and discuss your ideas with all of them and get a ballpark figure.

Now that you have all the tools to gather pieces of your work, let's talk about assembling them into a demo reel.

# Tailoring Your Theatrical Demo Tape

The demo tape you will assemble to get work in theatrical feature films will contain clips of your work from movies, television shows, stand-up comedy acts, student films, fashion shows and taped plays. If you're just starting out and have none of the above, use any tape that you might be able to get from your acting class. Keep it short. Five minutes is okay; three is better. I always put the running time on the outside of the tape box.

When the tape begins to roll for viewing, the first thing that should appear is your name. Then you can get creative about the presentation of your work. The first scene to open the tape with, after your name, should be your most impressive work. Following that first scene should be two or three more scenes that best depict your range as an actor. Most actors think they need to set up the story line of a movie for the viewer. Agents and casting people are not interested in the story. They just want to see if you can act. One of the more popular ideas currently circulat-

ing the actors' community is that of building a collage using clips of all your character looks with music laid over the visuals. Kind of like a music video. Tape from any or all of your work (music video's, acting class, commercials, etc.) will work for the collage, as it is just a glimpse of that look. You slam several of these looks together and the viewer can get an idea of your diversity.

If you notice, at the **Academy Awards** they show only 15-second clips of the biggest stars having a special moment. For your demo reel, the scenes don't have to make sense. I think short and strong is the key here. Any reputable editing facility you use to assemble your master demo reel will provide experienced people to guide you. Follow your heart and creativity. Make sure you use good visuals and sound quality. Nothing says amateur like poor quality film.

Finally, end the tape with your name. Don't include a contact number, put that on the box in case you change agents or voice mail boxes.

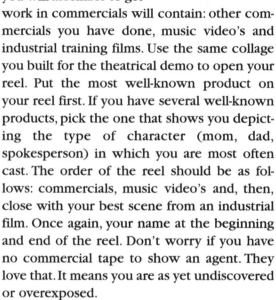

## Commercial Demos

The demo tape you will assemble to get work in commercials will contain: other commercials you have done, music video's and industrial training films. Use the same collage you built for the theatrical demo to open your reel. Put the most well-known product on your reel first. If you have several well-known products, pick the one that shows you depicting the type of character (mom, dad, spokesperson) in which you are most often cast. The order of the reel should be as follows: commercials, music video's and, then, close with your best scene from an industrial film. Once again, your name at the beginning and end of the reel. Don't worry if you have no commercial tape to show an agent. They love that. It means you are as yet undiscovered or overexposed.

## Your Game Show and Talk Show Demo

Demo reels for game shows and talk shows are assembled the same way. If you've previously done a talk show, open your reel with a clip of you introducing yourself from one of the shows you've hosted. It is optional at this point whether or not you want to build a montage from the shows you have hosted. If you do, pick highlights of shows that feature various personal qualities (e.g., high energy, comedy, vulnerable, compassionate). Close with a wrap up from an actual show.

If you haven't any tape of yourself to compete in this arena, you still have some choices. Either you can get your own public access cable show (covered in Chapter 7), or call cable companies to see if they need any-

one to host their public service shows. If not you can try to rent a small studio with cameras and shoot a short tape with interviews., Be prepared just as you would for shooting a scene earlier in this chapter. Have everyone confirmed and standing by. Rehearse the entire show ahead of time so the taping goes smoothly. In our phone book I have a facility you can rent listed under Demo Reel - Shooting. With talk shows you are not limited to shooting indoors. Take the show on the road just like Access Hollywood or Good Morning America. You pick the style that best suits you. We have a book on the web site to help you. It is called **How to Star in Your Own TV Show for $50 or less.** Give it a look this guide is full of great ideas and helpful phone numbers as well.

## Your Stand-up Comedy Demo

If you've been doing a lot of stand-up comedy, building a demo tape is relatively easy. Most comedy clubs have a camera mounted on the wall in the main room to tape performances; this way, comedy club owner s around the country can view the tapes prior to hiring you for road trips. But, to ensure that you get the kind of material you want of yourself, bring your own high quality 1/2" VHS tape and record your act (with the owner's permission, of course) on a night when you're hot and the audience is responsive. If there is no taping system at your favorite club, arrange for a professional with a DVD camera to come out and shoot your act.

Because some comedy clubs have their own television shows, you can order an air check of these performances. These tapes cover your full act in its entirety. When you get the tape, make some copies and send them to

your agent so he or she can distribute them to sit-com casting directors for Series Regular consideration. Program Development departments of each network will also view your tape to consider you for talent around which to build shows. If you are going to use your demo reel to seek representation, be aware that prospective agents seeking clients to sign for stand-up will seldom come to see your act in person; they customarily only see tape. If they are still interested after that, they will then come to see you live.

## Your Industrials Demo

If you are employed often in industrial films, you may want to build a demo tape specifically for this medium. On an industrial demo reel, you can open this tape with that same infamous montage we talked about earlier or just go right to the work. Insert an opening to a film where you introduce yourself. Next, cut in a scene of you demonstrating the product. Also, add an action scene showing you walking and talking or some kind of movement of that nature. Finally, close with a wrap-up from an actual show. Only people who are employed frequently, who can use the ear prompter and who have at least a couple of good suits need worry about a demo in this area.

## Assembling Your Demo Reel

So far, I have directed you to use different types of clips and suggested an assortment of ways for obtaining them. We, further, discussed the best way to format your demo reel for viewing depending on the particular area for which you are building your demo reel. Once you have all the clips on tape, you

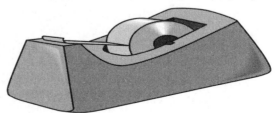

need someone to organize them into your demo reel and build your montage, if you decide to use one.

## Editing Video Demos

One way to save yourself some money before you bring your clips to an editor, is to have the tape *"queued up"* (pre-viewing the tape and having the tape set up to start playing beginning with the scene to be transferred) to the place where you would like each edit to begin. If the clips you intend to edit onto your master reel are on a 3/4" tapes and you don't have access to a machine to queue them up, there are things you can still do. Get a 1/2" dub and start running the tape from the beginning of the action. Then, by using an accurate stop watch, time how long it takes to get to the point of usable tape. Write this down and go on to the next clip. The editor can then use this information to find the clip quickly. Have an idea in your head of the order of film clips and how the tape should flow.

Let me explain a little about the nuts and bolts of editing. Until recently your tape had to be put together in chronological (linear) order. Each clip was copied by a computer and transferred onto a master tape. The drawback to this process was that each time you copied a piece of tape, it lost a *"generation"* of quality. A generation is the deterioration of audio and video quality that happens with each copy of a copy of tape.

Now, there is a special effects system that can copy your tape onto a computer's hard drive as well as add all kinds of jazz to your demo. It is called the *"Video Toaster."* The toaster can flip the entire screen, make it fly away, fade out and fragment the screen into squares that fly away. The makers of the Video Toaster have come up with a new editing system called the **Video Flyer.** It is used in conjunction with the Toaster. You can use any size tape (1/2", 3/4", beta, high 8 and 16 mm). The sections of tape can be moved around inside the computer to achieve any order you wish. This is called *"non-linear"* editing. The hourly cost for this type of editing is higher but it takes half the time or less to build a demo tape. Some editors in town are using a system called **DAT**. It is a digital computer system through which tapes can be edited out of sequence and then assembled. This method of editing tends to be very expensive and you lose some of your crisp, clear images. I would stay away from this type of editing.

## Running Off Copies of Your Demo Reel

If you use the Video Flyer for dubbing, there is no generation loss if you choose to make copies for you to distribute to agents and casting directors. Get one 3/4" copy of the demo and take it to a dubbing company. It really doesn't matter if you go for the hard case or paper sleeve. Whichever way you decide to go, keep your master stored in a fireproof safe at home or in a safe-deposit box. It is a very valuable asset and should be treated as such. There's two dubbing companies listed in the back under Demo Reels - Editing.

## Artwork

Earlier, I instructed you to purchase tape boxes with a clear sleeve or paper cover. .The sleeve is to hold artwork. The front cover traditionally contains your headshot, but if you have a great action shot from a film or television show, by all means use it. Your shot can also be glued to a paper sleeve. The "spine" (the part of the box between the front and back) should have your name in large letters. You can cut your name off of old headshots or print it out on a computer. The back is a perfect spot for your resume, but it will have to be reduced in size. On the bottom of the resume, put: "FOR PICK UP, CONTACT: (your service number)". Inside the box, on the tape itself, more labeling is necessary. Put your name and your agency telephone number, just in case the tape is separated from the box. You can do all of this yourself and paste it up or have the editor do it when finishing the reel.

## The Return of the Wayward Demo Tape

Be in charge of your demo tapes. If you know that your agent is too busy to attend to retrieving and returning your tapes, make the offer to drop off and pick up your own reels. If the tapes are left at your agent's office for too long, they will probably get thrown away. That is why the offer to pick them up is the wise thing to do.

If you send out your tape to a casting director or a prospective agent and want to know if your reel has actually been viewed, pre-set your tape at a spot other than the

beginning. When you get your tape back, check to see if it is in the same spot. If it is, it was never viewed. Incidentally, if you are

called to pick up your tape, you do not have to go in person. Get the name and address of the person calling and explain that he or she will receive a self-addressed stamped envelope in the mail within two days. Or, alternately, if you've mailed your demo reel to a prospective agent or casting director, make sure you've included a self-addressed, postage pre-paid manila envelope in the business envelope addressed to the them. Naturally, before you mail your package, you will have to take it to the post office and have it weighed so that you can have enough postage attached to the manila envelope to cover the cost of the return of your demo tape. Fold up the manila envelope with postage and attach a Post-it note asking for the return of your demo tape. Place the entire package in a business envelope and mail. The whole process costs less than three dollars and saves you a drive across town.

Do not drop tapes by a casting director's offices unless it has been requested. A casting director works on a project-by-project basis and doesn't always have time to view your tape to determine where it might fit into his or her casting agenda. Have your agent promote you to a casting director and, then, deliver the tape to the casting director.

## Voice-Over Demos

The voice-over demo tapes look different than the tapes you use to build your visual scenes with. Actually, a voice-over tape is nothing more than a high-quality audio cassette, the kind you buy in any music store.

Voice-over demos fall into three categories: commercial, animation and industrial. Masters are assembled on **DAT** (a digital sound recording process) reels and the dubs made onto cassette tapes. The person who builds your demo reel will provide you with the DAT. So, no pre-purchase of tapes is necessary.

Before you run out and hire a person to build your voice-over tape, do a little market research. Start listening to radio & television commercials and Saturday morning cartoons. Does your voice fall into an identifiable group? Consider the following voice qualities and their respective categories: Honest and believable for banking commercials and cartoon heroes; dangerous and defiant for truck drivers and cartoon villains; soft and seductive for perfumes and cartoon damsels in distress; tough and headstrong for kids' advertising and playing cartoon kids. Most cartoon boys are played by women. Infants and toddlers are also played by women.

Another way to do research is to purchase popular magazines and practice the written copy in the advertisements contained in them. These will become the scripts off of which you will build your demo reel. If you find a commercial advertisement that you think you would sound perfect for, tape it.

Find as much variety in your niche as possible. Feel free to write your own animated adventure in which you play all the characters. Practice the script so that you can switch from one character's voice to the next in your sleep.

You might want to try your hand (or voice) at industrials. Usually, industrial voice-overs are comprised of technically oriented data that will teach the listener a new skill or impart knowledge of a product. If you don't want to write an original industrial script yourself, use any instruction manual.

## Preparing for the Voice-Over Demo

If necessary, go to one of the voice classes in your area or listed in our phone directory to brush up on your technique. It'll be your dime paying for the time in the recording studio, so, be prepared and do your rehearsing in class or at home. By the time you walk into the studio to record your demo, having a microphone stuck in your face and reading copy off a music stand should be a very familiar drill and you will take less time.

## Cutting the Voice-Over Demo Tape

Once you are ready to cut the demo tape, call around to the recording studios and ask who is the experts. See if the same names keep coming up. The cost for the demo will be between $300-$500. Prospective companies or directors should meet with you, assess your talent, pull some of their scripts and direct you through the recording session. A tape will be edited from that. We have two

great ones listed in the directory under Demo Reels - Voice Over.

## Dubs of Your Voice-Over Demo

Once the tape is cut, you will need about 50 dubs to circulate to Agents and a stack to give them once they have signed you. They should be real time dubs which are better quality. Assuming you have about a six minute or shorter reel they should cost less than $2.00 each. Check out our Dubbing list in the directory under Demo Reels - Dubbing.

## Animation

Usually the call for a voice-over artists goes out to all the voice-over agents along with a drawing of the character. So, it is a tough nut to crack without an a Agent. But if you want to mail your animation reel directly to the person who casts the shows, there is a list of the players in our telephone directory under Animation Houses.

## Voice-Over Demo Artwork

There's still more work to do. The box that holds the audio cassette has artwork called a *"J-card"* because of the shape it makes when folded to fit the box. The cassettes will need a label with your name on it. Your name needs to go on the spine of the J-card. Your Agent's phone number or a contact name must be listed on the outside of the J-card. If you choose, you can add an index of commercials you have done to the inside of the J-card. Additionally, with a home computer or with the aid of a typesetter, you can lay out the lettering on the guide that is included in the box. You may want to add a personal touch by using clip art—graphics software for computers which is available at art, computer, or office supply stores. You could also use old headshots or unused postcards. Cut them down to size to fit in the cassette boxes. Glue your name perpendicularly onto the headshot so it visible when the cassettes are stacked on it's spine. You can save quite a bit of money with ideas, ingenuity and a good office supply store. If you get your tape done professionally ask the Dubbing House to do your J-card or look in our phone book under Demo Reel - Voice Over.

Once you have landed an agent, he or she may have you mail a tape to each of the agent's clients. This should be done only when it is economically possible and you have the time. Most clients don't pick voices that way but in an emergency situation you could be booked from your tape.

## Voice-Over Agency Reels

Each year most agencies record all of their top voice talent on reels or cassettes to be sent out to lots of clients. This entire process is done either from an agency's office or at an outside recording studio, at **no cost** to the actor. The agency pays for everything. It is their cost of advertising to get their stable of talent known around town. If an agent ever asks you to record an agency reel at your own expense, just decline.

Now you are as well versed on how to build a demo reel as anybody in town. Start gathering pieces of tape back home, if you can, before coming to Hollywood. Don't judge your work. Few of us like the way we look or sound on tape. Be ingenious. Go with your instincts. And, remember, when you're out there pounding the pavement, you'll never get a second chance to make a first impression.

*"If only I'd known that one day my differences would be an asset, then my early life would have been much easier."*

---Bette Midler

# Chapter 16
## Moving to LA
## Home Sweet Home

It is my desire in this chapter to facilitate your move from your hometown to Los Angeles. After reading through this chapter, review the checklists in Chapter 1 to see that you have everything you'll need before leaving your hometown. This chapter will cover the following topics: various ways you might consider traveling to Los Angeles and what to do once you get here; easy access to temporary housing; general information about the city; and, finally ways to find a permanent residence and furnish your new apartment or home.

Before you move to L.A.—whether you're coming by plane or by car—you'll need a map to get around. The most comprehensive one is *The Thomas Guide*® by *Thomas Bros. Maps* ®. To obtain one, fill out the order form on the last page of this book or log on our web site. The cost is approximately $25. This map will help you find the exact locations for everything and some agents give audition locations by these coordinates. I refer to all of the studios listed in our Little Black Book in the back by using *The Thomas® Maps Page & Grid*. For example, the designation "TBG 631 H-5" refers to the following:

TBG-*Thomas Bros. Guide*®
631—Page 631 in the map book H-5
The intersection of grids
H and 5; the square        w h e r e
your destination is located.
*T h o m a s   Bros. Maps Page  & Grid* used with permission granted by *Thomas Bros. Maps.* It is unlawful to use any part thereof, whether for personal use or resale, without permission. All rights reserved.

Welcome to sunny Southern California! Probably the first thing you will notice is the traffic. Try to plan your arrival during non-rush hour times. The morning rush begins at 7:00 AM and lasts until 10:00 AM; the afternoon rush goes from 4:00 PM until 7:00 PM.

The city is ringed by four major freeways: the **Santa Monica Freeway** (Interstate 405) to the west; the **Ventura Freeway** (101 &134) to the north; and the **Golden State Freeway** (Interstate 5) to the east. Morning traffic moves east from the beaches into L.A.; southeast from the San Fernando Valley into L.A.; west from **San Bernardino** into L.A.; and, north from **Orange County** into L.A. During the evening, the process reverses.

Drivers are notoriously impatient and, often, downright dangerous on Los Angeles freeways. Don't let it rattle you. Just stay conscious and drive defensively. Providing there are no jam-ups, the traffic moves from moderately fast to very fast on the freeways. The slow lane averages 55 mph and goes up to about 80 mph as you move to the fast lane. If cars come up behind you and flash their lights, they want you to move over to a slower lane. Just change lanes when it's safe to do so. This will be your first challenge by a city that will try to change the way you do things. If you're a courteous driver, continue this practice. If you're not, better get plenty of car insurance. It's a jungle out there.

The names of some of the streets and the directions in which they flow in this town can be pretty perplexing. To avoid confusion, make sure that you check to see whether your destination street has the word Drive, Boulevard, North or South attached to it. An example of this confusion is **Beverly Boulevard** and **Beverly Drive**. Beverly Boulevard runs east and west starting in West Hollywood and terminates in downtown L.A. Nearby Beverly Drive, however, runs north and south through Beverly Hills. Another problem is two streets with similar names. **San Vicente Boulevard** starts on Pico Boulevard in the Crenshaw District and runs diagonally through West Hollywood ending on Sunset Boulevard. **San Vincente** begins on Wilshire Boulevard just west of Interstate 405 and then turns west through Brentwood and ends at the beach. If you ask about the nearest major cross street when getting directions, you'll have a better chance of finding your final destination.

Read all the posted parking signs carefully including street cleaning, permit parking and tow away traffic times. Parking at meters on many main streets is prohibited after 3:00 PM. The parking lane must be cleared to be used as an additional traffic lane. So, the police don't just ticket your car, they tow it away. And they **will** tow your car! The fees to get your car back are pretty steep and to add insult to injury they make you pay a parking ticket and tow fee.

## Arriving in Los Angeles

Depending on your means of getting to Los Angeles, I recommend the following guidelines to facilitate your arrival:

**By Car:** If you're driving to Los Angeles in your car, I highly recommend that you now begin thinking about your protecting your vehicle. Ideally, your car should be paid for, insured, and economical to operate because drive you will. Once you arrive, you'll be amazed at the excessive amount of cars in this city. People in Los Angeles love their cars and would drive to their refrigerator if the hallway was wide enough. Public transportation is hard to access and time consuming for a large sprawling city like Los Angeles.

If you want to start learning the shortcuts around town, get a copy of *L.A. Shortcuts—The Guide Book for Drivers Who Hate to Wait* by Brian Roberts & Richard Schwadel. This book is available at Los Angeles area bookstores.

Most importantly, you are going to be in a major metropolitan city with a high crime rate. Never leave your keys in the car. Always lock it whether you're in or out of your vehicle. Use all the anti-theft devices you own.

Because car jacking is very prevalent. The single safest precaution to take is always be aware of what is going on around you.

**By Plane:** If you're coming here by plane, follow these simple guidelines to get you where you want to go. After picking up your suitcase at the airport's baggage claim, proceed outside to the curb. Out by the curbs, there are various buses which will take you to car rental agencies. There are, also, private transport vans to take you either to hotels and residences for a flat rate, or to transport you to the bus terminal near the airport. If you can't locate the ground transportation you need, there are booths marked "INFO" at each baggage claim curb to help you out. Or., alternately, **Travelers Aid** has a booth in the baggage claim area by **American Airlines in Terminal 4** to assist you. Keep a close eye on your bags as well.

**By Greyhound Bus:** If you're traveling cross-country by bus, don't even think about making your final destination downtown Los Angeles. It is in a dangerous part of town. You should choose either the brand new Hollywood Terminal, a short cab or bus ride from some of residence

hotels I recommend or the North Hollywood Terminal, next door to a theater. Again, watch your bags.

## Rental Cars

If you're traveling here either by plane, train or bus, you'll probably need to rent a car for a short time period after you've settled in. Geographically, Los Angeles is the most expansive city in the entire county. And, it will be a long, long walk to get anywhere you want to go. So, I highly recommend renting a car if you didn't bring one with you.

The two car rental agencies I found to be the least expensive, as of this printing, and are listed in the directory under Car Rental. Both agencies are located near the airport on Century Boulevard, require a major credit card for rental, advance reservations and offer these rates for drivers over 25 years of age. From the car rental agencies, go east on **Century Boulevard,** get on the Interstate 405 freeway going north and follow your Thomas Brothers Guide to the temporary motel of your choice.

## Local Buses

If you decide to use the city's public bus transportation, the **Metro Rapid Transit District** which is the combination L.A. area bus company and Metro Rail System has set up an info line to help you. Call between 5:30 AM and midnight, 7 days a week. Have a pen ready and be prepared to be put on hold.

When you finally talk to someone, tell them where you are, where you want to go by either address or cross streets and what time you hope to get there. They will tell you where to catch the bus and all other pertinent information, such as: connecting buses or trains and their respective route numbers, scheduled times of arrival, etc. The number is located in our phone book in the back. Most area buses are very safe so don't worry.

## Temporary Housing

I have searched out area motels for you in different parts of the city that are clean, safe and offer a variety of services. All are within the same price range. To pick the motel best suited to you, we'll examine the different areas of Los Angeles and find a location where you would feel most comfortable. Any one of these motels will provide a good, temporary home base from which you can begin searching for an apartment or a house in which to establish your permanent residence.

## Safe Beach Areas

If you are considering a permanent residence at one of the beach cities, consider the following:

**Malibu:**
Very pricey. Far from movie & TV studios.

**Pacific Palisades:**
Slightly less pricey than Malibu & landlocked.

**Santa Monica*:**
Rent controlled, lots of competition for units

**Venice*:**
Careful, lots of gangs! Canal area is good.

**Marina del Rey:**
Upscale, trendy, a bit more expensive.

**\*WARNING: Never** go to the beach at night. The area has been taken over by gangs, addicts and the homeless. It's okay to go to the Santa Monica shops and restaurants but be aware of the other people on the street.

For the most part, the beach communities have a very casual and relaxed atmosphere. Most people living there are very outdoorsy, into all sports and very healthy lifestyles. In the Santa Monica/Venice area, you will find the more popular shops and restaurants open on **Main Street** by the beach. On the weekends, the **Third Street Promenade** has a great Open Market and Fair with street performers. The beach communities are close to: **Sony Pictures, Metro-Goldwyn-Mayer, Culver Studios** and **20th Century Fox.**

## Looking for a Beach Apartment

One of the most charming aspects about living in Santa Monica is the many streets teeming with older, spacious apartment and character laden residential buildings. Nearly all rental properties are under rent control; so, competition among renters is fierce.

There are many different ways to seek out and locate the areas in which you are considering permanent residency. To find your new home start driving systematically through the streets of Santa Monica and look for the "FOR RENT" signs usually posted somewhere outside in the front of the buildings. Circle the neighborhoods that seem appealing to you. The neighborhoods tend to get less desirable as you get closer to **Ocean Park Boulevard** to the south.

Still another way to find your permanent residence is to get a copy of *The Argonaut.* Although *The Argonaut* is available at most busy street corners, you can always be sure to find one at the 7-11 on Wilshire Boulevard and Barry Avenue or at the **Wilshire International News** at Centinela. I have been told that the best days to look for new listings for apartments are Saturdays and Sundays.

If you don't feel comfortable looking for a place on your own or don't have the time, there is a company who, for a pretty hefty fee, helps people find places to live near the beach. The name of the company is **Wellman Realty Company.** Their fee is based on calculating the difference between the discounted rent they can negotiate and the fair market value of the same unit on the open market. The fee you are charged is three times the amount of the difference. Generally, they will show you the best they have to offer right away; so, if you like the place . . . go for it! Wellman Realty Company is located at in Santa Monica and they are listed in our phone directory under Temporary Housing.

## Safe Areas in Los Angeles

The **Los Angeles cities** where you should consider living include:

**Westwood & West L.A.:**
Young professionals and UCLA students; good price.

**Beverly Hills:**
Great address, smaller apartments, more money.

**Beverly Hills Adjacent:**
Some great places but read the warning.

**West Hollywood:**
Centrally located, safe and affordable; strong alternative lifestyle community.

**Fairfax Area:**
Strong ethnic influence; large, safe apartments.

**Miracle Mile:**
Older interesting buildings; be sure to check for parking.

**Melrose Avenue:**
Very hip and trendy; affordable.

**Hollywood Hills:**
Great views, slightly pricey.

**Beachwood Canyon & Los Feliz:**
Below the Hollywood sign; affordable but not safe south of Franklin.

**Warning:** Anything south of Olympic and east of LaBrea is chancy and consequently cheaper.

The parts of the city most people refer to as "Los Angeles" are nowhere near downtown. Rather, what most people mean are the parts of Los Angeles I've listed above, which are considered to be very safe areas. Unfortunately, Hollywood is not included among them. It's a fun place to visit but you wouldn't want to live there. More about that later. You might eventually go downtown to visit **The Dorothy Chandler Pavilion, Music Center, Dodger Stadium, Convention Center** and the **Los Angeles Courts.**

The Los Angeles cities are faster paced and more congested than the beach. They offer a more cosmopolitan lifestyle with a wide array of restaurants, shopping boutiques (**Rodeo Drive and Melrose Avenue**) and cultural centers (**Theater Row, CBS Television Center** and **Farmers Market,** )an international open air market. You won't want to miss the "**Hollywood**" sign at the top of **Beachwood Canyon**; or, **Mann's Chinese Theater** on **Hollywood Boulevard** near **Highland Avenue** to check out hand and footprints of **Hollywood's** legends; or, the **Hollywood Walk of Fame** all along **Hollywood Boulevard** to find your hero's star. The area also includes: **Fox Television, Warner Hollywood Studios, Raleigh Studios, Paramount Pictures, Sunset-Gower Studios** as well as many production companies and casting offices.

# Finding a Los Angeles Apartment

If you're looking for a place to live, one of the better ways is to purchase the Los Angeles *Recycler* available at all newsstands, convenience stores and gas stations. It comes out every Thursday and costs less than $2. On-line listings come out Wednesday night. You will find lots of housing broken down by areas. Or, you can also drive through selected streets in any area and try to narrow down the field.

If you decide you need some outside assistance, there are companies from which you can purchase "listings" to help you locate available apartments in your price range. In addition to regular apartment listings, these companies list rooms for rent in stately homes, work-for-rent opportunities and, also, "roommate wanted" situations. Both company's lists and web sites are updated on a regular basis. You can find their information under Housing - Temporary in our phone book.

# Safe Areas in the San Fernando Valley

The San Fernando Valley cities where you should consider living include:

**Sherman Oaks:**
Lots of houses and larger apartments.

**Studio City:**
Convenient to studios and freeways.

**North Hollywood:**
Family & singles area, affordable.

**Toluca Lake:**
Great location, slight higher rent.

**Burbank:**
Near major studios and affordable.

**Warning:** The further north from the Ventura Freeway the more dangerous and less desirable.

# Finding a San Fernando Valley Apartment

The **"Valley,"** as it is referred to, has a small-town, family-oriented kind of feel. The pace in the Valley is slower here and you'll find a kinder, gentler Los Angelino. There is a full array of restaurants, shopping malls and boulevards (the **Sherman Oaks** and **Glendale Galleries** as well as **Ventura Boulevard**), and some theater. At various times of the year you'll see small circuses and street fairs in your neighborhood. The motion picture studios and television studios in the Valley include: **Universal Studios, CBS/MTM, Warner Brothers, Lorimar** and **Disney Studios, Columbia Pictures Television, Viacom** and **NBC Productions.**

If you're interested in living in the Valley, I'm going to refer back to *The Recycler— San Fernando Valley Edition,* which comes out on Thursday. There is, also, a newspaper based in the San Fernando Valley called *The Daily News* where you'll find quite a few listings as well.

On the first Sunday of each month is the **Rose Bowl Swap Meet** in Pasadena, a must see to find the special items for your new place! Be forewarned: although the Los Angeles cities and the San Fernando Valley are only separated by a "hill," the summer temperatures can run 10 to 20 degrees hotter in the Valley.

## Other Resources for Apartments

Two other great resources for finding you new home—either for the Los Angeles cities or the Valley—are located at the main office of the three major actor's' guilds: the **Screen Actors Guild** and **A.F.T.R.A.** SAG's bulletin board is in the first floor lobby, while A.F.T.R.A. is on the 9th floor. **Equity** can be found on the 1st floor at 5757 Wilshire Boulevard. All have bulletin boards with listings for all kinds of living situations: Actors who want to sublease their place, actors looking for roommates, etc. Guild members can put up info here. You can look at the bulletin boards whether you're a card carrying member of these guilds or not.

## Month to Month Housing

If you can afford temporary housing and really take your time to search for a great apartment, I suggest you look at these places, **Oakwood Apartments and the Heritage Motel** Each offers a month-to-month leasing arrangements. The Oakwood location I recommend is in **Toluca Lake**, just blocks from Warner Brothers and Universal Studios. The monthly rates for a furnished studio apartment includes utilities, local telephone service, voice-mail, cable television, pool and spa. There is a one-time credit check and administration fee.

The Heritage Motel requires no credit check and a small security deposit to move in.

## Tips for Apartment Hunting

Currently, all of Los Angeles is experiencing a rental "glut" and this trend will probably continue for quite some time. You'll want to get a copy of *The Working Actors Guide* to assist in your search. The *WAG* is an amazing book that has lists and ads of goods and services to help actors. It has a great description of neighborhoods under the "Housing" section. Drive through your prospective neighborhood at night and ask yourself this. Does it feel safe? Is there vandalism or graffiti? The best time to look for an apartment is during the last week and the first week of each month because a tenant usually gives notice to vacate around the first of each month

Since I want you to have all the tools you need prior to your journey to Los Angeles, I have arranged for most of the books I will recommend to be readily available to you.

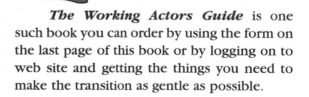

*The Working Actors Guide* is one such book you can order by using the form on the last page of this book or by logging on to web site and getting the things you need to make the transition as gentle as possible.

## Overall Apt. Shopping Tips

Some general tips to remember when apartment shopping: Make a checklist so you know what each apartment offers and can compare them easily. It also fools the apartment owner into thinking that you know your market. This will get them to negotiate with you more readily. Set a limit on price (no more than one-quarter of your income) and stick to it. Get everything you want; e.g. parking, hardwood floors, etc. Additionally, if you have to pay the utilities in your apartment, they will cost about $100.00 a month, not including telephone and cable.

## Furnishing Your Apartment

If you're on a real tight budget, shopping neighborhood garage sales and thrift shops are a great way to furnish your home. Another place for basic furnishings from bedding to flatware, IKEA is the ticket. IKEA is an affordable home furnishing store and is your bargain find. There are two locations under Housing - Furnishing

## Apartment Renting Laws

If, after having settled in an apartment for awhile, you later find a better place to live and decide to relocate, please consider the following financial costs in your decision: Not only might you have to sacrifice the installation fee for your phone in your current apartment but you will have to pay it again when you relocate to your new apartment. Similarly, your apartment security deposit, equal to one month's rent, will be forfeited unless you've completed your lease. If the lease is up, the deposit will be returned to you, but only if the apartment building manager or owner decides that there was no damage done to the place while you stayed there. The process of returning your security deposit could take up to three weeks after vacating the apartment so, have plenty of money in reserve to facilitate this decision.

Although all rental deals are different, you shouldn't have to put up more than first month's rent plus a security deposit usually equal to one month's rent. California law requires that your deposit, less any damages, be returned to you no later than 14 business days after vacating an apartment. The **Department of Housing** can help you with any unethical landlord or the return of a security deposit. In the phone book under Housing - Temporary.

Actors, on an average, move four times in their first two years in L.A. Financially, this can be very costly, what with the loss of security deposits. Emotionally, it's disruptive to your lifestyle, ultimately pulling the focus off your career. So, choose carefully. Pick a place you'll be comfortable and happy in for a long time.

---

**MONTHLY BUDGET TO LIVE IN L.A.**

_____Monthly Rent
(1/4 of take-home pay)
_____Utilities
_____Gas
_____Car Insurance
_____Food
_____Entertainment
_____Acting Classes
_____P.O. Boxes &
Voice Mail

$_____ TOTAL

# Chapter 17

# Your
# Survival Job

*"It's the old story. I was in the middle of a successful acting career when I was bitten by the accounting bug."*

Drawing by Leo Cullum;©1992 The New Yorker Magazine, Inc.

Now for finding you the kind of job that will sustain you while you're climbing the ladder to stardom. When you get to Los Angeles, you will notice there is a lot of glitz, glamour and all that jazz. You'll meet people with fancy houses, expensive cars, car phones, and lots of cash in their pockets. This is one way the city will try to distract and tempt you away from your purpose. You came here to start a career and suddenly you find yourself obsessed with all the toys. If you focus on material things, you'll be prey to every "get rich quick" or "I-can-make-you-a-star" scheme around. And, believe me, there are tons of them. Instead, focusing on your career and a job that will move you toward your professional goals, coupled with a lot of hard work, you can eventually have all the bells and whistles. The point is, stay focused, remember your purpose, do what you love . . . and the money will follow.

## Job Flexibility

Any job you take on in order to support yourself financially has to be fairly flexible. The ideal situation would be to develop an income-producing activity or a successful business where you live now so that you could use it to sustain you financially in L.A. During my summer before I went to Hollywood, I learned how to tint windows on cars. When I arrived in L.A., I approached a few new car dealers with some samples of my expertise, negotiated a couple of deals and created a successful business. It didn't give me a lot of frills but it paid the bills and, more importantly, it gave me the flexibility I needed to go on auditions.

One gal I know loves to paint ceramic angels. She started a home business by selling them to boutiques on Melrose Avenue (famous for its eclectic shops). Another actor makes furniture and is a handyman in apartment buildings. Yet another repairs cars. An actress

I know kept her flight attendant job right up until the day she landed her first series. What is your hobby? Would it make a good home business? Or, as an alternative to your own business, consider keeping your current job and asking for a transfer to Los Angeles.

Get the training and job experience before leaving for L.A. If you train for a marketable job now, while you're still living in your hometown, it will cost you less emotionally and financially once you get here. Unemployment in California is very low and competition for jobs, even as a waiter, can be fierce without prior experience and letters of recommendations. Get your letters from employers before leaving for California and make copies of them to include with all job applications. It will be a huge asset.

## Job Opportunities for Actors in Los Angeles

As a fledgling actor in Hollywood, you may work erratically throughout the year but not continuously enough to quit your day job. Your job may be something you can do at night to leave your days free, like: bartending, being a bouncer, waiting on tables, servicing guests as a hotel clerk, providing health care, driving a taxi, working as a disc jockey at clubs or private parties, operating a computer for offices and law firms. Pick something you like to do because you may be doing it for a while until your name and talents as an actor are established. You might be much luckier than most and have success happen right away, but it generally takes actors ten years to become an overnight success.

Most employers in L.A. are used to hiring actors and will be sympathetic to your needs if you are sympathetic to theirs. Always let them know ahead of time that you are an actor and will be going on auditions. Sell them on yourself. Get them on your side so they will want to support you in reaching your goals. You should be reliable, conscientious and hard working. That way, should you have to take time off for an audition, your employer will tend to be supportive and you'll feel secure knowing you have an income. If you go the extra mile for an employer, your employer will do the same for you.

## Entertainment Industry Jobs

There are many opportunities in the entertainment offices around town for people with good clerical skills. There's a saying that is true in all facets of entertainment: "This week's secretary, next week's boss." One very bright, hard-working young lady I know went to work in the production office of a national variety show. Within two weeks, she was offered a producer's position. Any thing's possible. You can start out working in the office for a small film company as a production assistant and find yourself getting your first acting job on one of their projects.

Also, think about finding a job as an assistant or a receptionist for a talent agent or manager. This is an ideal job to have because the people you'd be working for understand the industry and will, often times, let you take time off for auditions. Who knows? You might even get taken on as a client. Meanwhile, you're getting to know casting people and producers and familiarizing yourself with the inner workings of the entertainment industry while simultaneously getting paid.

Another source for entertainment industry jobs appears in both of the entertainment industry's major trade papers: the *Daily Variety* and *The Hollywood Reporter.* Look for industry jobs in these papers on Fridays. New job listings come out each Thursday in the *Recycler* and Sundays in the *Los Angeles Times. Backstage West/Dramalogue,* a weekly theatrical publication highlighting the inside world of the actor, comes out every Thursday and also has job listings in it as well.

## Mystery and Kids Parties

Like to play dress up? With these companies you dress up as children's favorite animation character and entertain at kids parties. You must be very energetic and patient. It's a plus if you know how to face paint, tie balloon animals or tell kids jokes.

How about this one? A job that seems to be "a hoot" for Actors is murder mystery parties. actors are hired to play the characters in a scripted murder plot and to perform in front of small parties or gatherings. They are staged at private homes, restaurants, fund raisers, etc. If you're interested in hooking up with some of these acting troupes, look in the back of the *Los Angeles Magazine.* Also, check The *Los Angeles Times* **"Calendar Section."** Or probably the best way is word-of-mouth; i.e., asking other actors whom you know or meet. I can recommend one group to you check the list in the phone book under Jobs–Childrens.

## Temp Jobs

Because of the nature of the business, lots of actors find it more workable to take temporary jobs, both from within or without the entertainment industry. Temp job opportunities within the industry are listed in the **Working Actors Guide—** "Employment Opportunities Section." If you're leaning in the direction of temporary jobs, I highly recommend that you sign up with some of the temporary agencies geared exclusively for the entertainment industry. Two people that used those types of services ended up with full time permanent positions, one at a top talent agency and the other at a television network.

## Telemarketing

Telemarketing, although having a very high "burnout" rate, is a great job for an actor to practice his or her art of selling oneself while getting paid. This is a survival job, however; so, if you wind up doing telemarketing, make sure it's a product you believe in.

## Jobs at the Studios

At Universal, Paramount & NBC Studios there are opportunities to become pages. Pages are studio employees who conduct tours, usher audiences into studios for taping of shows, etc. From there, it's possible to move up to stand-in or "Regular Extra" on a motion picture or television show since you have access to all the TV shows on the lot and can smooze the staff.

A stand-in is the individual who stays on the set, in place of the "star" so that the crew can adjust the light-ing for a shot. A regular extra is a person who is assigned each week to the same television show to perform as a background actor in all the weekly episodes. Of course, like anything, there are upsides and downsides to these opportunities. For instance, I read in *Emmy* magazine that the current executive producer of *THE TONIGHT SHOW STARRING JAY LENO* started out as a page at NBC fifteen years earlier. On the other hand, one gal in my acting class became a Stand-in on *FULL HOUSE.* Unfortunately, five years later when I landed a Guest Starring role on that show, she was still employed there as a stand-in. Her work is very steady but her career is going nowhere. It's a long road ... perhaps for nothing. Then again ... who knows?

There is a great possibility of working at a major studio if you have dancing, singing, stunt, horseback, or weapons skills. Having gymnastic abilities or simply being in excellent physical condition can open up avenues for you.

You can become part of the team of actors who put on shows at area theme parks like the Waterworld Live Action Show at Universal Studios Hollywood. Actors are paid on a per-show basis, and you can easily get a fellow team actor to cover for you if you've got an audition. To apply, send your picture, resume and a short note to the people listed in the directory under Jobs - Studio.

## Street Performer

If you are a street performer (mime, puppeteer, juggler, singer, dancer or poet, etc.) and want to pick up extra money on weekends, consider Universal Citiwalk at Universal Studios. You receive no salary but are free to panhandle. Permission must be obtained from the Entertainment Departments listed in the section above. The same opportunities exist at The Third Street Promenade in Santa Monica and at Venice Beach in Venice. Check with other performers at these locations to see if any permits are required. In the *Working Actors Guide* under the "Agencies—Specialty" section, you will find listings of agents who specialize in variety acts, comedians, specialty acts, mimes, clowns, etc., for parties and industrial convention work.

## Free Movie Passes & Focus Groups

A fun job for extroverted personalities is canvassing for movie screenings or test marketing products. As a canvasser, you stand outside busy malls or grocery stores and, on behalf of the company employing you, offer people free passes to movies or to test new products. You are paid on a per-person basis, based on the number of people who accept and attend these events. Which is great for you because you can work as long or as little as your audition schedule permits. A list of these companies is in the *Working Actors Guide* under "Employment Opportunities".

Are you opinionated? There are people who are always looking for participants for product testing focus groups would love to hear from you. You are paid to giving them your two cents' worth of opinions and testing new products. Look up my picks in our phone book under Jobs - Assorted.

## Singing & Catering

Some of the other fun jobs you might find listed in the **Working Actors Guide** under the "Employment Opportunities" section are for singing telegram and catering jobs. Singing lets you use your musical talents in your day job and the catering enables you to attend Hollywood's best parties while being paid. The catering companies my actor friends like to work for are listed in the Hollywood Here I Come phone directory under Jobs-Assorted.

## Look-Alikes & Cabaret Acts

This one's really a kick: if you resemble or can make yourself up to resemble any famous person, contact Universal Studio's Entertainment Department for opportunities to make personal appearances as that character. Also, contact the companies listed in my phone directory under Jobs-Assorted. They can assist in personal appearance bookings as well as film and TV work.

Have you ever thought about showcasing your talents? If you're a singer with a polished act, contact you can be considered for various showcases. Ladies clubs and other organizations who see you perform might book performers in the future from booking showcases. Although there is a fee for your photo and your act to be printed in publicity books, it's well worth it. One such showcase is listed under Jobs - Assorted.

## Cruise Lines

Is your act suitable for cruise ships? This includes singers, dancers, musical groups, magicians and comics. Be prepared to travel up to six months at a time. Make sure a cabin is included in addition to your salary. It's a steady paycheck and a great way to see the world while getting paid. The course usually focus on one area of the globe and rotates ports in that part of the world. So pick a ship that cruises to ports that you will enjoy seeing over and over again. You'll be visiting them for six months. There is a list of the cruise ship lines in the phone directory under Jobs-Cruise Ships.

## Working in Las Vegas

If you have an act that would be suitable in Las Vegas or are a dancer seeking work, you can check with these hotels to see when they audition new talent. The shows are lots of fun and get attended by agents, producers and stars from Hollywood all the time. They also shoot many films in Las Vegas and the new series **Investigation CSI.** Plenty of opportunities to be noticed just doing what you love. There is a list of all the hotels in Vegas listed in my little black book in the back of this one under Jobs-Vegas.

## Dinner Theater & Traffic School

In addition to working cruise ships and Las Vegas, singers, dancers and actors should look into showcasing their work at local dinner theaters. **The Elizabeth Howard Curtain Call Dinner Theater**, located just outside of Los Angeles in a city called Tustin, offers a paying opportunity.

Another great venue for showcasing your comedic abilities is by teaching at traffic school. Believe it or not, if you're a stand-up comic or just a plain funny actor you can earn $100 per day in this wacky environment. Many producers end up in this class because they are always zipping around town and sometimes break the local speed limits. It is like having a whole day to strut your talent. (Check the **Yellow Pages** - "Traffic Schools.")

## Game Shows

Now, here's a great way to make thousands of dollars a half an hour at a time. The upside is that it's nothing but fun, you don't have to be smart, plus you get nationwide exposure. The downside is that it's a short-lived gig and there are no guarantees. So, what am I talking about? Game Shows!!! Yeah, go ahead! Try out for some! I made $8,000 in cash on **SUPER PASSWORD** and I only lasted through one show. But, as an actor, there are certain facts you need to know: Once you are in the Screen Actors Guild, you're allowed to go on only three game shows in your lifetime. However, if you are not yet a member of SAG, you can appear on as many game shows as possible. A list of game shows and where to apply appears in the **Working Actors Guide** under the "Game Shows" section. When you single out the shows you want to try out for, be sure to watch the show and know how to play the game well. They look for energetic personalities. When you go to fill out the applications, list either your current job or the most interesting job you've ever had; don't mention that you are an actor. And if you're lucky enough to win some big cash and prizes, you will be responsible for paying the taxes on all of you're winnings. Go for it!

## Apartment Management

Here's another income-producing idea for your consideration: After you start getting work as an actor, you might consider getting a job managing an apartment building. Taking on a job like this will enable you to cut your overhead because, as part of the terms of agreement between landlord and apartment manager, the apartment manager usually will get to live in an on-site apartment for free (or, at least, for nominal rent). In some cases, the landlord may even pick up utility expenses. If you can find a setup like that, a few acting jobs a year can pay the rest of your expenses. If you think this might work for you, get some experience now in the town where you currently live, even if it's assisting in a building or managing for a relative. If you pick a building of over 25 units, it can become more than just hectic to manage the building and have a career as well. Trust me. I know what I'm talking about. I have often managed apartment buildings while, simultaneously, having to run all over Hollywood for auditions, interviews and shows. To resolve the conflict between job and career, I got creative: I found some friends who are also actors and who, also, earn an income by managing apartment buildings. So, whenever the occasion arises, we cover each other's buildings when Hollywood calls. Note: If you decided to go this route, I strongly recommend that you only take a building in the areas listed in Chapter 16, "Moving to LA Home Sweet Home."

## Massage Therapist

Another service job that offers contact with directors, producers and famous actors is massage therapist. I'm talking about physical massage therapy here, not erotic massage. Although it requires training and a California license, job opportunities and, by extension, professional contacts are plentiful. All the nice hotels where producers and directors stay have a masseuse on call 24 hours a day. Or, you can start your own business and make on-site visits to clients. An actress I know has gotten most of her acting auditions and career breaks this way, not to mention making a darn good living.

## Nightclubs and Bars

A word to the wise about jobs in bars and nightclubs. If you stay and hang out at these places after you're done working, the only thing that will happen is . . . you get to be very popular in bars, if you know what I mean. (I've seen lots of promising careers lost to late-night drinking and drugging.) On the other hand, sometimes the clientele you meet while you're working can be in a position to give you "a break." Pay close attention to who your regulars are and what they do. Most importantly, make sure they are people whose names you recognize or, at least, that they genuinely do what they say they do. If they're for real . . . be bold! Introduce yourself and let them know you're an actor. After all, this is Hollywood. People love to see and be seen. So why not work it.

## Steer Clear of Here

One job that doesn't seem to work out for actors is with messenger/delivery services. You are required to use your own car and purchase your own gas and car insurance; in exchange, you are paid very little. And, while we're on the subject of things to avoid, I would strongly discourage you from living off of credit cards. One actor who worked a great deal in Texas was so sure he would get acting jobs in L.A. right away, that he decided to live off of his many Visa and Mastercard credit cards. Seven months later, he still hadn't worked and was in debt to the tune of $15,000.

## Survival Job Ideas

Speaking of survival jobs. Deborah Jacobson has written a wonderful book entitled *Survival Jobs—Over 117 Flexible Ways to Make Money*. Not only does Deborah offer great, creative ideas but she also instructs you step-by-step on how to make each one happen. Plus she has an entire section on jobs in the entertainment industry filled with names and phone numbers. Also, she has very creative ideas for home businesses that do not take up all of your time. Additionally, she provides you with resource information to access the components you will need: info on obtaining a license, where to find needed materials— stuff like that. You can purchase the book on our website. So, all right. Sounds pretty good so far, right? You've found a place to live and discovered a way to support yourself financially and still keep moving toward your dream. So, what's all this talk about struggling actors you keep hearing about? Staying financially solvent would probably be easy if you knew where all the low-cost or no-cost services could be found. A full list of everything needed is in the next chapter.

# Survival Job Check List

☐    Referral letters from home

☐    Job application info complied

☐    Ideas to start a home based business

☐    Get job experience or training

☐    Always realizing that my primary
job and goal is an acting career

# Chapter 18

# Be Your Own Best Friend

*The Hero's journey always begins with the call.
One way or another a guide must come to say,
"Look, you're in sleepy land. Wake. Come on a
trip. There is a whole aspect of your consciousness, your being, that's not been touched. So
you're at home here? Well, there's
not enough of you there."
And so it starts.
The call is to leave a certain social situation, move
into your own loneliness and find the jewel, the
center that's impossible to find when you're socially engaged. You are thrown off center, and when
you feel off center it's time to go. This is the
departure when the hero feels something has been
lost and goes to find it. You are to cross the thresh-
old into new life. It's a dangerous adventure,
because you are moving out of the sphere of the
knowledge of you and your community.*

**Joseph Campbell**

**M**any actors have an impoverished mind-set of self-denial which easily bleeds into a lack of self-care. If you start—from the very beginning of your career—to make room in your budget for health, auto and home owner's insurance and other services, not only will you put your mind at ease but your work as an artist will benefit as a result. Furthermore, making sure that you have adequately provided for your needs will leave you confident to handle the world around you. And, I guarantee you, one of the things that attracts fame fast is putting a confident foot forward.

This chapter is chock full of information on services to help you get the most bang for your buck. Unless you're arriving in Hollywood with a truckload of money, it will be important for you to be financially frugal during the process of setting yourself up here—no matter how much the glitz and glamour may seduce you. For example, I would rather see you select an apartment that may be small and more affordable than to spend more than you can realistically afford on an expensive place just so that you can look good. Living modestly for a while will enable you to have money available for basic human services and needs.

## Registering Your Vehicle

Within 20 days of your arrival, you are required by the State of California to register your car and acquire a driver's license. If you have a driver's license from another state, you will not have to take a driving test, just a written test and an eye exam. The cost of the license is $12. The Department of Motor Vehicles (DMV) locations are listed at the end of this book under Dept. of Motor Vehicles.

Before you can register your car, it has to pass a California Smog Test. I advise getting an inspection from a location that has a "Don't Pass—Don't Pay" policy. What this means is that if your car doesn't pass the smog test, you don't have to pay for the inspection. Most ARCO Gas Stations with "Smog Pros Inspection" signs displayed on the premises have such a policy. If your car fails the inspection, they will give you a list of repairs to do before retesting. If you find that your car needs fixing, shop around and get the best price on car repair. If the repairs are numerous and very costly, you can call DMV to have a "referee" decide what is fair. Once you have the smog certificate, which should cost about $27, make an appointment with the DMV to register your car. Bring a bill of sale, current registration, the title to the car, your current driver's license, proof of car insurance and an additional form of ID, such as a passport or Social Security card. If you don't have the bill of sale, the DMV will decide the value of your car. In order to assess the proper value of your car, DMV will split the difference between whole-sale and retail value of the vehicle as listed in the ***Kelly Blue Book.*** Your vehicle registration will cost 2% of the vehicle value. Each year thereafter, your registration can be completed by mail or with the Automobile Association of America (AAA) should you become a

member. If you don't make an appointment for these registrations and licensing, the wait in line is approximately five hours. If you phone ahead, you can walk right in and get waited on immediately. Confirm all documents needed.

# Car Insurance

Just imagine what it will cost to replace your car if it is stolen or wrecked, not to mention if you are sued. If you're involved in a car accident and cannot provide proof of insurance, the State of California will revoke your driver's license and take your car. Depending on where you live now, your monthly rates are probably going to take a jump once you get here, up to several hundred dollars a month. Get a copy of your driving record from your home state to supply to the insurance companies. If you have a good driving record (no tickets or accidents during the previous three years), make sure you mention this to the insurance company. That way, you'll receive an additional good driver discount in your auto insurance rates.

There is a list of companies with the lowest rates and Preferred Driver Discounts, according to the State of California, Department of Insurance in the back of the book under Insurance-Cars & Homes.

# Renter Insurance

If you own anything of value (e.g., VCR, TV, computer, jewelry, etc.), I highly recommend this very inexpensive piece of mind. Get earthquake insurance as well. Friends of mine with minimal damage during the 7.9 Northridge earthquake ended up paying $3,000-$4,000 to replace their ruined items. There is the list from the Department of Insurance of the companies with the best rates in the same place as the car Insurance.

# Telephone

Pacific Bell wants everyone to have a telephone, regardless of income. PacBel has designed a service called **Universal Lifeline** for lower income households. If you qualify, they will install a phone line and provide you with the same monthly service as their regular customers but at a discounted rate. There are income restrictions to qualify for Universal Lifeline. To order the service, look up the number in our directory under Housing - Settling In.

# Rock the Vote

Any resident of the State of California is entitled to vote in city, county and national elections. The Department of Motor Vehicles has been authorized by the State of California to publish a booklet of instructions on how to register. Call them to have a packet mailed to you or pick one up at the one of the DMV locations listed in the previous section. Or look for a kit at county election offices, local post offices or your next trip to the public library.

Once you receive your packet, follow the instructions provided. A voter ID card will then be mailed to you. And, just so you know, once you have registered to vote, your name is placed in a pool for jury duty in court cases. If you are subsequently contacted by the courts, you have to serve unless to do so would create a financial hardship. Because you are an actor and, therefore, self-employed, you can easily make a case to be excused due to financial hardship. Check out their number in Housing-Settling In.

## Stage Name-Bank Accounts

If you have a professional stage name that is different than your legal name and you want to add it to your bank accounts so that you can cash your acting paychecks, the process is simple.

Take a copy of your union documents or union card with your new name to your bank. The bank will then add that name to your signature card and have you sign your new name. That name can then be listed on your checks under your legal name by putting the letters "AKA" in front of your stage name. AKA stands for "Also Known As." Here is an example of how it will look on checks:

Marion Michael Morrison
AKA John Wayne
1300 Main Street
Hollywood, CA 90028

## Legal Name Change

Actors often change their names when they begin their professional career. Sometimes it is a necessity, especially if your given name is already being used by another actor registered as a member of one of the theatrical unions. It is not necessary to legally change your name for admission to the union or to cash your checks at your bank. It is necessary, however, to change your name legally if you want to

get credit cards and to set up a Living Revocable Trust in your new stage name to protect your earnings and assets.

So, if you've decided that you want to legally change your name, you will need some important information sheets and the necessary forms. To determine which sheets and forms you will need, call this recorded message delineating all the steps that must be taken in order for you to legally change your name. Then, on your next trip to downtown L.A., stop by the Newspaper Office at the Los Angeles County Courthouse, 111 N. Hill Street, Room 114 or Room 113, and pick up the proper information sheets and necessary forms.

1. Identification documents with your old name (e.g., drivers license or passport);
2. Documents with new stage name (e.g., an application to join a theatrical union or union contract containing your new name); and
3. A completed Form SS5 obtained from Social Security.

To find the Social Security Administration government office closest to you, check the "U.S. Government Listings" section at the front of your telephone director or call the number listed in our phone book under Legal Stuff.

## Passport

If you have changed your name or simply wish to procure a passport to travel for acting jobs out of the country, the process takes up to three weeks. If you have a passport and just wish to renew it, the renewal can be

done by mail. To hear a pre-recorded message detailing all the options available to you or to get a passport application mailed to you, call the **Los Angeles Passport Agency** at the number listed under Legal Stuff. The passport offices are located in the **Federal Courthouse** at Wilshire Boulevard and the 405 Freeway. If you do not wish to make a phone call and would just as soon stop by but hate waiting in long lines, I suggest the Passport Office at the Barrington Post Office. Both addresses are in our phone book.

### You need quite a few documents to obtain a passport. They include:

1. Proof of citizenship in the form of a birth certificate with the original county recorder's seal from the city where you were born. (Hospital and religious birth certificates are not acceptable.)
2. Two identical passport photos.
3. Evidence of identity. (This can be either a driver's license, a military ID or a Department of Motor Vehicle-issued ID.)
4. The proper fee. (The cost is $65 for a new passport, $55 to renew and $40 if the applicant is under the age of 18.)
5. The proper form. (To apply for a new passport, submit Form DSP-11; to renew, use Form DSP-82.)

The subject of lost or stolen passports is also covered on the pre-recorded message. Often, last minute, out-of-the county casting for film and commercials comes down to a question of who has a current passport.

## Legal Advice

This is a nationwide service offered by **Legal Assess Plans, Inc.** to make legal advice affordable. Legal Assess has a list of participating qualified lawyers who discount their fees to large groups such as theatrical unions. Although this service is available to anyone, you can receive a 15% discount rate

off attorney's hourly rates if you are a member of the SAG/AFTRA Credit Union. Just look up the number in our Legal Stuff section of our phone directory and, when the operator answers, tell her that you were referred by the SAG/AFTRA Credit Union. When she asks you about the nature of your legal matter, don't go into all the details of your case. Keep it simple. In fact, it is sufficient if you just tell the operator the general legal category into which your case falls, so that you can be referred to a participating plan lawyer in such areas as:

| | |
|---|---|
| Contractual Problems | Trusts |
| Estate Planning | Divorce |
| Real Estate Transactions | Custody |
| Drunk Driving | Small Claims |
| Juvenile Offenses | Wills |
| Criminal Defense | Pers. Injury |

## Unemployment

As you probably already know, many a working actor often finds himself not working, or "between projects" as some of us say. So, while you are between projects, you may be eligible for unemployment benefits. Your benefits will be based on money earned from the same time period during the previous year.

To find the **Office of Employment Development** closest to you, look in the telephone directory. If, on the other hand, you don't mind doing a little traveling, make your claim at the office in Santa Monica at 914 Broadway (9th and Broadway), phone number under Legal Stuff in our phone directory. Probably because this particular office handles a majority of unemployment claims made by actors, they are very familiar with the nature of the entertainment industry; therefore, the amount of time you'll have to wait in line is substantially less than those offices in other parts of the city. They also understand the concept that we don't seek employment in the conventional fashion but rather have to wait for auditions.

## Health Insurance

Very few actors actually make enough money through performing in union jobs to qualify for health insurance. So I am going to run a few options past you so you are not caught without in the case of catastrophic illness or accident. Although I will log on to ehealthinsurance.com to shop for rates and health plans When it comes to signing up and laying down the cash I prefer to have a live person.

Mr. Bruce Baichman has been providing a variety of health care programs to guild members for 20 years. One such program which is designed for people under 30, offers coverage as a "just in case" situation for Outpatient and Hospital stays with a $2,000 deductible. The only drawback to this plan is that you give up the ability to see a doctor for colds, flu and yearly check-ups. Mr. Baichman offers another program, however, that will cover doctor visits as well as hospital stays (with a $250 deductible) for a cost to you of $100 a month. If you're real low on dough, don't blow off health insurance; you can still have it no matter what your financial situation is.

For example, he can set you up with a Blue Cross Plan that covers Hospitalization, Emergency Room care and has a once-a-year provision for a physical examination at a cost of $20 co-pay and 20% of the entire bill. This same plan includes an annual gynecological exam in which the cost to a woman is only 20% of the entire bill. Call Bruce Baichman for a price quote per month on this one. His number is in our phone directory.

Bruce's office also offers **Smile Savers and Vision Savers.** The Smile Saver plan covers a yearly dental check-up, a low-cost cleaning, and X-rays. They also offer a 50-60% discount on any other services. Smile Savers splits these low payments over 12 months as well for about what it costs for a burger and fries. Vision Savers provides a free yearly eye exam and discounts on glasses for for these same low fees. I can't recommend health insurance enough. Without it, one brief stay in the hospital and you're wiped out financially.

## Motion Picture & TV Fund

This fund operates the Bob Hope Health Care Center. The center offers a wide array of services exclusively to all motion picture and television industry members who have insurance. Call for an appointment and they will take good care of you.

## Free Clinics

There are three clinics in L.A. that provide health services free to anyone who cannot afford to pay. Appointments are given out daily from 9:00 AM to 11:00 AM on a first call basis. It's tough to get through on the phone lines so you must be persistent. The locations are all listed in our directory under Health Issues. All three clinics also offer free pregnancy, HIV testing and give out no cost or low cost medication.

# Gynecology

When women run low on money, it is easy to forego the annual check -up. But, there's no need to. The wonderful nurse practitioners of the **Women's Clinic**, supported by state funding, make that necessary check-up affordable on a sliding scale based on income. Minimum fees start at $40. The Clinic also makes birth control and mental health counseling available. Other services include pregnancy testing, sexually transmitted disease testing, iron count testing and cholesterol level testing. Contact the Womens Clinic in our phone directory in the back.

# Low Cost Cancer Screenings

Once a year **The American Cancer Society** offers coupons at L.A. area hospitals and medical centers for low-cost mammograms. If you miss the screenings, do not panic. The **Cancer Screening Center at Queen of An-geles/Hollywood Presbyterian Medical Center** offers low-cost mammograms all year long. For women over 50 who have no insurance, the mammogram is free. The Cancer Screening Center, also, offers other low-cost health services,

including pap smears for women and prostate cancer screening for men.

Cancer Exam for Men
> Includes exam for Prostate, Testicular, Rectal, Skin, Oral Cancer; ColoCare Fecal Analysis, Hemoglobin, Urine Dipstick, Prostate Specific Antigen, Personal Risk Analysis.

Cancer Exam for Women
> Includes exam for Breast, Pelvic, Rectal, Skin, Oral Cancer; ColoCare Fecal Analysis, Hemoglobin, Urine Dipstick, Pap Smear, Personal Risk Analysis.

Screening Mammogram
> Includes Clinical Breast Exam and Personal Risk Analysis, (X-ray limited to four views). Additional fees required for clients with breast implants or suspicious findings.

Pap Smear Screen Only
> Includes Clinical Breast Exam, Pelvic Exam, and Personal Risk Analysis.

Prostate Cancer Screen Only
> Includes DRE and PSA, and Personal Risk Analysis.

20 Minute Check-Up Exam
> Includes Height, Weight, Blood Pressure, Blood Sugar, Blood Cholesterol, Hemoglobin, Audiometry, Vision Screen, Personal Health Risk Analysis and Choice of: Tetanus Booster, Mantoux for TB Screen or Influenza Vaccine.

Lab Panel Screen
> Includes complete Blood Count, Chemistry Panel 14, Urinalysis, Thyroid Study and Sed Rate (or any combination).

Chest X-Ray Screen
> Includes 2 views.

# Free Hiv Testing

**Jeffrey Goodman Special Care Clinic** offers optional pay HIV testing. The process is completely anonymous and the test results take one week to get back. This clinic is the primary care provider for 80% of the AIDS infected people in Los Angeles who have no insurance. The Jeffrey Goodman Special Care Clinic is located on the Third Floor of **The Gay and Lesbian Center** in Hollywood. If you go to get tested at this clinic, they will hand you an envelope for donations. If you can swing it, $20 would go a long way to help out these angels of mercy.

## Therapy

Given the chaotic times we live in (dysfunctional relationships, a hostile economy, unpredictable and explosive behaviors), it's not uncommon for most of us humans to struggle with unresolved personal issues, especially when these issues leave our lives in an unmanageable state. Actors are no different. If you find that you are overwhelmed by certain problems that inhibit you from clear thinking or a certain emotional state that smothers your drive and motivation, please . . . reach out for help. Nobody can succeed in this world by his or her own efforts all of the time. There are qualified people out here with an authentic desire to assist you in getting past the barriers that keep you from your dreams. The two following clinics offer expert support in exchange for fees based on a sliding scale commensurate with your income:

## Twelve Step Programs

If you decide that individual counseling is either limiting or that you need a different kind of support to change your behavior, you should consider a 12-Step Program. I have seen people come out of these programs with an experience of ongoing recovery and their lives undeniably transformed from very

debilitating addictions to liberation and productivity. So, the power to change within a group support system is not only possible, it's real and it's available. It's no accident that there are 2,500 Alcoholics Anonymous meetings a week in Southern California. Every one of the following programs is anonymous; so, not only will your personal identity remain confidential, but your professional identity and your career will be protected as well.

For more detailed information and a listing of times, locations and the meetings nearest you, phone the offices listed in our phone directory under Anonymous Programs. All of the other twelve step programs are listed there as well.

Los Angeles is a mecca of excess. If you come here with an addiction that you have not dealt with, don't be surprised if your climb up the ladder is thwarted by years of denial and pretense. Inevitably, it will separate you from your dreams. So don't be proud, be human and ask for help.

## Stop Smoking

The State of California provides a program to help you quit smoking. This regimen requires that you are taught by a coach on the use of techniques to help you cope with smoking withdrawal. After this initial instruction your coach will check in with you by telephone every day for two weeks. The service is free.

## Hot Springs

There is only one earth-fed hot springs in the city limits, the **Beverly Hot Springs** located near the corner of Beverly Boulevard and Western Avenue. They are open every day from 9:00 AM to 9:00 PM. The rates Monday through Thursday are lower and Friday to Sunday and holidays it goes up. The facility is gorgeous and offers a wide array of scrubs and wraps for an additional charge.

## Massage

There is a wonderful place called **Toluca Lake Tennis Club** where you can get a good massage from an angel named Seppo. The massage can be half-hour or one hour. Included in either rate is the use of the eucalyptus sauna, showers and your own private locker room for changing and napping. Call the club at  and ask for Seppo.

## HOUSEHOLD ITEMS

There are four chains of stores that provide bulk groceries and drugs to the retail buyer. Each offers something slightly different to the consumer.

## Trader Joe's

Trader Joe's is a chain of non-membership, specialized grocery stores open to the public. In addition to the normal foodstuffs you'd find at any grocery store, Trader Joes has a wide variety of gourmet foods, wine, their own line of vitamins and herbal remedies including sleeping aids, an extensive inventory of prepared appetizer, and fresh and frozen meals., all at below retail prices. With over 100 locations in the Los Angeles area, you can find the store closest to you by calling their (800) number in our directory under Groceries.

## Smart and Final

Smart and Final originally went into business to supply perishables and equipment to the restaurant and cleaning service industry, you the consumer can now purchase bulk quantities of food, liquor, frozen foods, soft drinks, paper products, tobacco and any kind of cooking and serving apparatus imaginable. They even have party supplies, including kegs of beer. There are about 25 Los Angeles Smart and Final locations; you will find them listed in the telephone book. Membership is not required to shop there.

## Price/Costco

Unlike Trader Joe's and Smart and Final, membership of approximately $30 per year is required to patronize Price Club/Costco. To qualify, you must either be a corporation or an employee. So, actors who incorporate meet the criteria. Price/Costco has warehouses full of merchandise. The full array of goods includes the usual bulk foods but extends to electronic equipment (video cameras, VCR's, televisions, computers, etc.), clothing, automotive accessories (tires, batteries, etc.), even lawn furniture. Almost everything is below retail. Want to know why? One of the reasons is because they don't hire employees to pack your purchases in bags; instead, they have boxes available for you to use in packing your own purchases.

## Sam's Club

The membership to this store is a low fee per year but unlike Price/Costco, membership is open to anyone who wishes to shop there. They have pretty much the same goods and services as Price Club/Costco so, the only real difference between the two is the membership requirements. They are listed in our directory under Groceries.

## 99 Cent Stores

Ever wonder where the goods inside a cargo truck end up after its been in a wreck? The undamaged goods are sold at salvage stores. The most popular one in Los Angeles is called the **99 Cent Store.** They are scattered all over the city and sell food, toiletries, pet supplies, baby products, toys and household items for 99 cents each, hence the name. You can get your designer bottled water, six-packs of soda, razor blades, shampoo and batteries all for less than a buck. A hard deal to beat. Look around your neighborhood or in our phone directory for the store nearest you.

## Dry Cleaning

Some of your first acting jobs may involve the use of your own wardrobe, especially for industrial films. Any spot on your clothing

will show up on camera. Not to worry: In every area of L.A., there are very reasonable cleaners and launders. Most charge less than a buck for laundry and a couple of dollars for dry cleaning. Any garment!! To get you started I have enclosed the names of two such cleaners in my phone directory.

# TELECOMMUNICATIONS

## Business Cards

Although there are plenty of unique and specialized merchants in this area, the best deal I have found for printing business cards is at OnTime Printing. They will print black ink on a white card for $10. Color on white is $20 for 500 and colored ink on colored card goes for $32. OnTime is listed in the phone directory under Office Supplies.

## Home Electronics

As a performer you are going to be forced into the world of 21st century technology. At some point in your career, you're going to need as much electronic equipment as you can handle to support you in forwarding your career. If you can't buy everything at once, I recommend you prioritize your purchases this way: (1) Assuming you already have a telephone, you will need an answering machine right away. The reasons, I hope, are obvious. (2) When you can afford to, purchase a television and VCR. These two pieces of equipment are particularly important for actors. If you anticipate auditioning for a spe-

cific television show or feature film, you will want to prepare yourself by studying program format, writing and directing styles, character and casting types, etc. (3) Having a video camera might come in handy if you want to view your own work in acting classes, plays, showcases, etc. Or, you might decide to create your own demo tape. (4) Finally, if you're going to get involved in voice-over work, think about getting a high-quality audio tape recorder.

If you are electronically savvy, you might find your best deals in the want ads of the local papers for this equipment. If you'd rather go retail to ensure quality and maintenance guarantees, two of the better chains of electronic stores that I recommend are Frey's and Best Buys. They are in our directory.

Getting nervous? Well, fear not; all of the expenses for your business cards and electronic equipment are tax deductible as are the following items. So, save those receipts.

## Mail and Messages

You may think you need a box right away, but the truth is until you travel a great deal, your home address will suffice. When you get to the point that you need a box, the ones offered through the Post offices in L.A. are the cheapest, coming in at $22.00 for six months. There may be a waiting period for a box, so contact your nearest post office before you actually need it.

You absolutely must have an answering machine or a voice mail to catch calls from agents when you are either out of town or simply away from your home phone. Of the two, the most cost effective is the answering machine, which should have a feature that allows you to pick up the calls by remote control. Your outgoing message should be brief, no matter how cute or creative it is. Busy agents won't hang on the line through a long one, especially if it features part of your favorite song.

If you prefer to have voice mail so you can keep your home number private, I recommend **Voice Mail Depot** who has the best deal at $6.95 per month for voice mailboxes, with no setup fees. You must, however, pay three months ($28.05) in advance. When you call up to place your order, they will set up your voice mail system over the phone and give you five days to mail in your check.

Your answering machine or voice mail is a critical part of your acting package so be professional in the way you handle this medium. Make sure it is always hooked up and working each time you leave home. It is very common for casting people to put out a rush call. Whoever responds the quickest gets the work. Check in frequently.

## Cell Phones

The best time to get a cellular phone is during the Christmas season. Every company is discounting rates trying to out-compete one another for the lion's share of the market. Sometimes they really go nuts and give away the farm. For example, there are certain times throughout the year where you can get a free phone, free installation, free weekend calling and even get the first month's service charge for free. Check every company's average monthly plan which offers 200 or more minutes of free calls for $29-$35. Since these phones have pager/voice mail capability and can be an effective system to keep in touch with your agents.

## Computers and Fax Machines

As you get busier, you will want to acquire a fax machine so that pages from audition scripts can be faxed to you instead of having to drive all over town to get them. If you are computer savvy you can just buy a program and have your computer pick up the fax line.

I consider a computer a necessity for any actor. You can update your own resumes, keep up with correspondence, track industry contacts, generate your own mailing labels and even access important industry information through an on-line service. And who knows, there may be a budding writer inside of you, dying to get out. Every couple of months many of the Southland computer manufacturers gather at the **Computer Marketplace Show**, and sell their brand new IBM compatible computers and accessories at very close to wholesale prices or better, if you know how to bargain. Call their 800 line for the next date and location. Most of the manufacturers will drop ship the equipment anywhere in California, although you may have to set it up yourself. I prefer Macintosh for acting. You can layout postcards and graphics so easily on that system. They are advertised in the *Recycler* newspaper which comes out every Thursday and is delivered to 7-11 Convenience Stores. You can often find computers new in the box for half the price it originally cost.

For printers, you can find great sales either at the Marketplace or in the newspapers. Every printer needs inkjet cartridges from time to time. When you start seeing your printed pages beginning to fade, you can

either buy a brand new inkjet cartridge or get the old ones refilled. The latter process is cheaper and environmentally friendly. The #1 refill system is called Universal Inkjet Refill Kit. It is very simple to use. You just put a syringe type instrument into the ink bottle and pull back the plunger. Each cartridge has a hole in it where it was originally filled with ink. You can refill an average cartridge six to eight times with this system and save tons of money. And who does like that. You can order the Universal Inkjet System at (800) 4 DREAMs. Color & Black Kits are $50 and Black Only are $25.

## Outlet Stores

**The Citadel Outlet Collection,** is an outdoor mall that contains 120 factory outlet clothes stores ranging from casual wear at **The Gap** to dress wear at **Ann Taylor.** The prices are way below retail. In my opinion, this is the perfect place to find the clothes to reflect your "image." The Citadel can be seen from the Interstate 5 Freeway as you go south past the Interstate 10 Freeway. It's easy to spot, it  looks like the wall of a castle.

## Swimwear

If you have the body to go on swimsuit auditions, it is nice to have one good suit that you use only for auditions and never swim in. **The Catalina/Speedo Outlet Store,** is just a few miles further down south from The Citadel on Interstate 5 Freeway. The prices are wholesale, sometimes even less. The Catalina/Speedo Outlet Store also has an entire line of workout clothing, tennis wear, skiing wear and swim accessories. It's great to make a day of shopping at these two outlets but I recommend going during the week to avoid massive crowds.

## Resale Shops

In the city of Burbank, there is a store that resells wardrobe originally worn by actors on hit televisions shows. **It's A Wrap,** stocks clothing that has generally been worn only once and, therefore is heavily discounted. It's a great store to get beautiful clothing at a fraction of the original cost.

## Props

Across the street from It's A Wrap is one of the largest thrift stores in the L.A. area. All profits derived from sales at **The American Way,** benefit The **California Council for the Blind.** In this warehouse/store, I have found almost every kind of unusual prop or costume I have ever needed for an audition, class or play. The clothing is extremely inexpensive and, on several days of the week, you will find additional discounts. The American Way is also a great place to find household items to furnish your apartment.

I think I have furnished you with plenty of ideas for you to take care of yourself, both personally and professionally. If you don't treat yourself well, no one else will. That's where the old adage "Charity begins at home" came from. I've noticed a funny thing happens to all my friends when they take conscious actions to care for themselves—prosperity and joy come along for the ride.

# Chapter 19
## The Future

Silent Pictures by Katie Maratta

Establishing a successful career as an actor and model is a monumental challenge; maintaining that success is still another. To be competitive in Hollywood today you need to possess unique skills to add to your repertoire of performing talents. The more diverse skills an actor or model has, the better the chances of continued success. In this chapter, we will look at ideas for acquiring some of the unique skills that are often called upon by Hollywood's filmmakers and television executives. Further, we will look at some of the training facilities and resources available to help you to develop and expand those capabilities. Also, we'll branch in another direction and explore some creative ways to get a script which you have either written or control produced as a way of forwarding your career.

To increase the percentages in your favor for sustaining a successful career, we will also look at ways for you to develop networking support in order to meet people you would like to work and, maybe, even get to know.

## Martial Arts

**Heei...yah.** It is a well-know fact that many stars have broken into the movies by demonstrating their mastery of the martial arts—Jean Claude Van Damme and Jackie Chan to name two. Since action films and television shows seem to be a staple of today's entertainment market, proficiency in the martial arts can be a plus on your resume when you are being considered for physically demanding roles. It is also a way for an actor or model to keep the connection between mind, body and soul which enhances one's ability to focus while performing.

One of the more popular dojos (the martial arts title for the studio where classes are held) is **Kung Fu San Soo**. If you have an impulse to develop a

skill in the martial arts, you can take all the classes you want here a month for a flat fee.

## ADR and Looping

Here's another valued skill which is always in demand. You know those busy restaurant scenes in movies and television? Do you ever wonder how they capture the atmosphere of the restaurant noise as well as the voices of all those people? Well, it isn't done on the set; it is added in post production by people called "loopers," people who are adept in the specialized talent of **ADR (Automated Dialogue Replacement).** The number of people who work in looping groups around town is very small because it is such an easy, fun job which pays scale wages for a short day's work. To break into these groups you must either speak an obscure foreign language, be a well-known actor, or be a voice artist.

Since creating dialogue on the spot is an integral part of ADR work, improvisational skills are a must. It also helps to know technical terms used in certain professions; such as: the language used by doctors for diagnoses and prescribed drugs; or, police codes and prescient jargon; or, a lawyer's vernacular in discussing legal terms. Sometimes you've got to seek out regional idioms such as the use of the term "pop" spoken in the midwest as opposed to the term "soda" spoken in the rest of the country. In other applications of ADR work, you may be selected to record your voice in a specialized way, such as in a hospital or airport scene where a page over an intercom system needs to be heard.

It's also important to know the names of streets in major metropolitan cities. Also make a list general conversation subject matter for scene filler such as vacation, raises, births, lunch spots. Keep them general. For example, you might say: "I'm going to the cabin" as opposed to "I'm going to the Catskills" which is only appropriate if the show/film is based in New York state.

ADR work is a rapid-pace occupation and requires an ability to think quickly on your feet. Typically, you will only have one quick look at a piece of film before you have to decide things like: the time of day in which the scene occurs, where the characters are, how crowded is the place, what the socio-economic class of the location is, what characters are doing, and what is appropriate jargon for that action. You might even be asked to match the mouth movements of a particular on-screen character.

## ADR Research & Classes

There is a lot to know. If you are already somewhat skilled at voice-over work but feel that you need some additional experience in honing your looping skills, you can take an evening class from **Sounds Great** . There, you will receive hands-on looping practice of an actual film inside a sound stage for two evenings. When the course is complete, you will have the experience and knowledge to walk on any looping stage and offer your ADR skills with confidence.

The gals at Sounds Great also recommend cutting out the "L.A. Speak" pages of the *Los Angeles Times Magazine* in the Sunday *Times*. This weekly article teaches you buzz words and jargon for a different profession each week. It is pretty hilarious but very valuable for expanding your ADR skills.

**Sandy Holt,** co-owner of **The Loopys,** teaches a class at UCLA Extension that lasts ten weeks. You are schooled in microphone techniques, tips for responding creatively on a moment's notice, how to create characters using only your voice and how to improvise scenes. When you complete this course, you will have mastered the art of looping.

Each year Lou Hunt and **Word of Mouth Productions** host a three-week extravaganza know as **The Voice-Over Special Events.** These popular events are facilitated by some of the most successful professionals in the area of looping and voice-over work. This is a fine opportunity to expose

yourself to various areas of voice-over with well-known veterans of the business. Lou pulls in the big guns and important casting directors each year to teach. Classes average about $80. If you want a brochure, call Lou. She is in our phone book under Looping.

## Looping List

*The Working Actors Guide* has a current list of looping groups under "ADR Groups" in the index. We have printed SAG lists of looping groups in our directory under Looping.

## Stand-up Comedy

It seems like every sitcom today is centered around a stand-up comic. It's certainly a way to skyrocket to fame. But do not think it won't require endless hours of hard work, cross-country touring and unappreciative audiences, because it will. Stand-up comedy is one of the hardest ways to make a living. However, if you are persistent and fortunate enough, this rough road can lead to a big payoff on a sitcom or sketch comedy show.

## Comedy Classes and Material

Naturally, the first thing you'll need to perform comedy is . . . material. Comedy coach **Judy Brown** takes the ideas, situations, and characters you already have in your head, adds them to the performing skill you currently possess and shows you how to turn yourself into an act that showcases your comedic skills. One of the skills you will learn in the course is writing a comedy monologue that can be used on auditions. Casting Directors are always impressed when they find out you can write as well as act. Each week of her eight-week class, you will be given an opportunity to work on joke writing and performance which, then, culminates with an on-stage performance at the **Comedy Store.**

Many students have used the taping of this performance on their demo reel. Mary Downey, Talent Coordinator for *EVENING AT THE IMPROV* and *STAR SEARCH* said "Judy Brown has an eye for discovering and developing upcoming comedy talent."

Stand-up comedienne **Judy Carter** also teaches a workshop that lasts for seven weeks . Based on her book *"Stand Up Comedy: The Book"* (required reading), Judy will teach you how to write and perform your own material. Classes are small. Each week you will work on a five-minute act which you will, eventually perform at a prominent comedy club in Los Angeles as your graduation.

If you are unable to make up your mind about whether or not this particular course is for you, come and audit the first class for free. If you cannot afford to take the class, Judy has made a Home Tape Workshop that includes four tapes, her book, a getting started workbook and flash cards. Additionally, Judy has a great newsletter that includes updates on stand-up comedy booking lines all across the country. You can receive it for free by calling her number in our phone directory under Comedy and Improv.

# Open Mikes

Once you've gotten enough practice and acquired the right skills via your participation in one of these courses, the next step is going out on your own and doing open mike nights at various comedy clubs. There is a list each week in *Backstage West, L.A. Weekly* and *The Reader.* Call the comedy clubs you think you'd like to perform at and find out when they begin to sign up talent. Tape record your performance so you know which jokes worked and which ones bombed. It takes

a lot of trial and error to build an act.

Comics are divided into three categories: openers, middlers and main acts. Opening acts should have five minutes of material, middlers about twenty and the main show forty-five minutes to one hour. A list of the major clubs in Los Angeles with open mike nights are in the back of the book under Comedy and Improv.

Once you are consistently getting laughs at open mikes catch your live performance (complete with audience laughter) on videotape. Then, you can use the tape to make demo reels to find an agent or a manager who can book your act throughout the country. And, from there, maybe the career you've been working so hard to have.

Until you get an agent or a manager of your own, read the appendix of Judy Carter's book; it has a list of comedy clubs and agents across the country you can use as reference to do your own bookings. Additionally, or, alternately, you can contact the folks at **The Creative Talent Network** for cross-country bookings. Lastly And, finally, contact the **National Association of Campus Activities** Once a year, NACA gathers to book talent for colleges across America. NACA is a great convention at which a stand-up comics can can be booked for dates. If you go to one of these conventions, be sure to bring plenty of video demos, headshots and business cards.

Finally, when your career has reached the level of an HBO Comedy Special level, you should attend the **Aspen Comedy Festival** to be considered for the following year's programs. All the details are available at the phone number in the back of the book under Comedy and Improv.

# Improvisational Comedy

If you're having trouble with spontaneity, especially on commercial auditions, an improv group is the answer. It's also a great way to stay loose and have a lot of laughs while building the give-and-take that make for successful ensemble casts. Furthermore, improvisational comedy is great training to learn how to trust your first impulse and develop your innovative skills as a great way to discover the characters who live in your head and realize them in the world. Properly encouraged they'll bloom into hilarious, outrageous eccentrics you can call on at a moment's notice. Improv spawned shows like *SECOND CITY TV, SATURDAY NIGHT LIVE* and *KIDS IN THE HALL.* Many members of improv groups are now familiar faces on network sitcoms.

Probably the finest improvisational comedy training ground in Los Angeles can be found at **The Groundlings School.** This highly reputable school offers a 12-week class that meets once a week. The only drawback is the fact that it will take two years before you can perform in the Friday & Saturday night troupe. The work, however, is consistently excellent. Many former students went on to become regulars on *SATURDAY NIGHT LIVE.* You can get more detailed information by contacting The Groundlings at their listing under Coaches.

If you feel you have enough training and want to audition for a group, I recommend the improvisational comedy troupe **"Off The Wall,"** performing at **The Improv** on Melrose Avenue every Monday night. Buy a ticket and catch the show to see if you're at their level of talent. If you think you are equal to the performance task of this group, call and

attend Andy Goldberg's class listed in our directory under Coaches. He is one of the founders of this group, which spawned the likes of Robin Williams and John Ritter. One of the opportunities available through these classes is "guesting" for any Off the Wall member who is unable to perform on a given night. It happens often and, if you fill a need, Andy will use you. For additional information and references about any number of performing improv groups in town, read the listing and take Dee Marcus's class, listed under Coaches.

# Singing and Cabaret

Los Angeles is a major center for the recording industry. And because the industry is in our own backyard, it is an excellent opportunity to broaden your talents. Just take a look at some of the successful Actors who have taken this path: David Hasselhoff, Rick Springfield, John Stamos and Donny & Marie all have dual careers singing and acting.

So, if you're inclined to see what you can do as a singer, a great coach is a sound start. (Ooops! No pun intended.) Some great ones are listed in our directory under Singing and Cabaret.

When you've gotten the training you need, the next step is a place to perform. If you sing rock, rap, R&B, anything but cabaret, check out the area clubs, which are great places to invite A&R people (Artists & Repertoire which act like agents for musical bands.)

For a complete list look under Singing and Cabaret in our phone directory. Don't forget to invite all your agents, so that they can see the talented client they are representing.

In addition to club dates, you might consider trying variations of performance singing to help pay the bills. Performance singing work ranges from singing telegram to cruise ship performers. You can find a listing for this assorted array of talent under the **"Variety Work"** in the ***Working Actors Guide*** and in Chapter 17 - "Survival Jobs."

# Dance

If you can sing, dance and act you are what is called "a triple threat." Many jobs in commercials and movies are only available to performers who are skilled at all three. If you wish to expand your talent and get into better shape at the same time. Some top-drawer coaches are listed in our telephone directory under Dancing Classes.

# Star Search

I don't need to tell you how many careers have been launched on this show. Although it is no longer on the air, shows like it have cropped up at the local level all across the country and national shows like **Showtime at the Apollo**. Their address is in our phone directory under Talent Shows. Check out our website for a televised world wide talent competition called The World Championships of Performing Arts.

Often called the official "Olympics" of the performing arts. It is the only official international competition for seasoned and up and coming performers and entertainers. A competition that is heavily industry attended and endorsed by Steven Spielberg and Ron Howard. Thirty countries send delegates to compete at Universal Studios Hollywood. Check out www.hollywoodhereicome.com for success stories, details, how to qualify and registration forms. The categories are: Acting, Modeling, Dance, Vocal, Comedy, Bands, Instrumentalists and Variety Acts. Covers ages 3-50.

# Screenwriting

Maybe you don't have the slightest interest or inclination for singing, dancing, stand-up comedy, or the martial arts. But . . . you can write. "Yeah, I can write," you think to yourself. "But, I'm an actor and I want a successful career as an actor. Besides, I've never even written a screenplay before." Do you have any idea how many writers are also successful actors? The ticket to stardom for Sylvester Stallone was writing **ROCKY,** then refusing to let the script be sold without him playing the lead. He turned down hundreds of offers to make the movie without him at a time when he desperately needed money. But it launching his long career.

Being able to write a good script is a much needed commodity in this town. This section has some of the tools you will need to develop this skill. The first step is to figure out how to write a script. Before you spend any money for classes, here a list of books that can give you a basic knowledge of the writers craft and then you can decide if you need any more help or the type of classes you would like to take. The key to becoming a writer is the daily discipline.

***How to Write a Movie in 21 Days*** by Viki King

***Making a Good Script Great*** by Linda Seger (A top script doctor)

***Hero of 1,000 Faces*** by Joseph Campbell

If you cannot afford to buy them, check the books out from the library. After reading them, you will have a good working knowledge of scripts and script writing. Pick a genre (i.e., horror, comedy, drama, thriller, mystery etc.) and lay pen to paper or hands to keyboard. It is a discipline and, like any other art form, requires daily practice. Every good writer writes everyday no matter what.

HOLLYWOOD

## Screenwriting Classes

If none of the books I've recommend are sufficient for you and you feel that you need a more hands-on kind of coaching approach, there are many people who are quite good at teaching the visual art of story-telling. A screenwriting seminar is taught by **David Freeman**. David lectures at the American Film Institute and UCLA Extension. He has sold scripts to Castle Rock (Rob Reiner), Buena Vista Television (Disney), and Columbia. Allison Lyon, Vice President of The Mark Gordon Company, producers of **SPEED** says: "David Freeman has a talent for creating compelling premises and plots." Mr. Freeman's class also includes "Pitching with Bob Kosberg, the King of Pitch." He is known as one of the strongest idea men in Hollywood.

**John Truby's** weekend class will give you all the structural tools to write a professional script by breaking writing down to "the 22 building blocks of every great script." John has been teaching for 11 years and has 15,000 students all over the world. The writers of **SLEEPLESS IN SEATTLE, BEETLEJUICE, OUTBREAK** and almost every TV series writer have all been his students. John Truby is also one of Hollywood's premier script doctors. If you can't take his weekend class or just want something to take home with you to remind you of all the important points of this class, the course is available on both audio and video cassette.

## Screenwriting Classes at Teaching Schools

Every January and June **The Sundance Institute,** holds screenwriting labs. The deadline for the January lab is June 15th of the preceding year. The following December ten projects are selected for the January lab. Novem-

ber 15th is the deadline for the June filmmaker/screenwriter lab. Each lab lasts one week. Sixteen projects are selected for hands-on rehearsing, shooting and editing scenes on videotape. You work with a team of creative advisors which, in the past, has included: Jeremy Kagan, John Landis, Sally Field, Morgan Freeman, Joan Darling, Alan Pakula and, of course, Robert Redford. This experience lasts one month. If you mail a self-addressed stamped envelope to: Sundance Institute, P.O. Box 16450, Salt Lake City, UT 84116, they will send you a packet, including rules for submitting projects and an application. All labs are on a scholarship basis at no cost to the participants.

**The American Film Institute** offers a variety of screenwriting classes. Geoffrey Grode, Ph.D., with 20th Century Fox,. teaches **Introduction to Screenwriting** for seven weeks. Tuition: $300. Carole Kirschner, former Director of Comedy Development at CBS, brought **DESIGNING WOMEN** and **MURPHY BROWN** to the air. Now, she teaches **Introduction to the Sitcom Spec Script.** Tuition: $150 for two days. AFI also offers something that sounds really fun called **Movie Camp!** The brochure says this is a once-in-a-lifetime chance to learn the nuts & bolts of motion picture production—and produce a 10-minute, narrative video—in just three weeks! Tuition is $1,000 for three fun filled weeks. AFI has a 39-page brochure of all the courses they offer which can be sent to you to assist you with your career development. For further information, call the American Film Institute listed in the back of our book under Writers Classes.

Not to be outdone, **UCLA Extension** has a 96-page brochure, which includes an abundance of classes offered in their "Entertainment Studies" section of the UCLA Extension catalogue. If you are interested in any aspect of film, television, video and theater, call for a catalogue. If you want the Writers Program, call the number listed in the back of our book. Just get a brochure and go nuts. Tuition ranges from $170-345. Additionally, UCLA sponsors a free program for writers twice a year. The name of the program is "The Writers' Program Open House."

Not to be outdone by their 'crosstown rivals, the **University of Southern California** sponsors a Summer Production Workshop each year through their **School of Cinema and Television.** They offer a slew of unusual opportunities and exceptional courses, some of which include: "Screenwriting," "Marketing the Screenplay," and "The Producing and Directing Program at Universal Studios" and much, much more. The Universal Directing/Producing class is taught at the studio's backlot. Not only will you get an opportunity to shoot your own project but you will learn from some of the industry giants. (Steven Spielberg and George Lucas are both graduates and supporters of the USC Film School.) Every class is $250. For a brochure, look in the back under Writers.

# Writing Scholarships and Fellowships

Universal Studios has the **Chesterfield Writing Program.** A scholarship of $20,000 is awarded every July to two recipients. Winners screenplays are then shopped around to the industry on their behalf. Call Universal Studios at number in our phone book under Writing Scholarships for details.

If you are from Minnesota or have a script involving locations in this popular filming location, you can compete for **The Minnesota Independent Film Fund.** The Fund is looking for filmmakers with artistic vision and an ability to complete production. Essentially this award goes to mid-career artists (producers, writers, directors) with some production experience who demonstrate significant promise as filmmakers. Three awards of up to $25,000, substantial in-kind gifts from national vendors,. and the invaluable technical assistance from the Fund Steering Com-

mittee made up of national experts and advisers in the film industry is what The Minnesota Blockbuster McKnight Film Fund offers. The moneys are to be used for development purposes only and are to be repaid upon the first day of production. If this is the ticket for you, check out Writing Scholarships.

The best book on screenplay contests is *How to Enter Screenplay Contests and Win!* by Erik Joseph. It can be found under Writers contests.

# Screenwriting Research

Say you're writing a who dunnit mystery script and decide that the murder weapon was a poisonous plant but you aren't familiar with gardening at all. Where do you go to find details important to your story? Open your *Working Actors Guide* to the "Research Libraries" section and you will notice that the **Los Angeles County Arboretum** has a plant reference library. Listings in this section of the *Working Actors Guide* can be invaluable when writing a technical or period piece.

# Writers Agents

Everyone who has ever written a screenplay dreams of the getting an agent who will immediately cut them the *"Shane Black Deal."* Shane Black was the first screenwriter to get $1 million  for his first screenplay, *LETHAL WEAPON,* written when he was fresh out of USC Film School at the ripe old age of 21. This rarely happens. The reality is

that it will probably be very difficult to get an Agent to even look at your screenplay. But, keep the faith, there are other ways of bringing attention to your screenplay. I'll teach you how and where to get your script to actors and bring it to an agent with a star already attached to the project.

Meanwhile, don't exclude the possibility of landing a literary agent even if your central goal is a career in acting. For a list of writers agents visit the **Academy of Motion Pictures Arts and Sciences,** go to the fourth floor and pick up a free copy of the *Academy Players Directory Reference Supplement.* Inside is the most up-to-date list of writing agents.

## Pitching Your Screenplay

This is the industry term used in Hollywood for a short meeting to sell producers, financiers and studios on doing your script. It is an art all its own. To learn and understand more about the art of pitching, I would, first, recommend reading *Getting Your Script Through the Hollywood Maze, An Insider's Guide* by Linda Stuart and *How To Sell Your Idea to Hollywood* by Bob Kosberg. Both should be available at theatrical bookstores. If you want to hear some actual pitching, take a course called "How to Be a Successful Screenwriter or Director" with Shelly Wile through the **Learning Annex,**. If the course is no longer in the catalogue, contact the Annex and find out which director or writer is teaching it next.

## Writing Accessories

Having a computer is a definite asset to writing but not absolutely necessary. Borrow one from a friend, rent one at any **Kinko's** or hire someone to type it for you. **Brenda Marshall**, listed under Typesetting will type a screenplay for around $1.50 per page.

When you finally can afford a computer, Each week in the *Recycler* are listings of almost brand new IBM compatible and Macintosh computers. The Macintosh that spawned this book was bought for half-price in that publication. Take someone with you who knows

computers to help you figure out what brand of equipment best fits your needs.

## Great Minds Think Alike

**Filmmakers Alliance**  is an amazing opportunity for anyone interested in making films. This group includes professionals from every facet of film making. RAPA meets once a week to discuss new projects and shooting schedules. The extraordinary thing about this group is that if you have a desire to be a director, you just sign up for that job on the next project. Then you seek out the services of an existing RAPA film director to mentor you through your project. It's the only hands-on group I ever encountered that offers combined support to fulfill the goals *you* say you want to achieve. Their monthly dues are less than $100 and are used to finance future film projects. Call the Filmmakers Alliance Hotline, listed in our directory under Production Experience, for info about the next meeting.

Finally, USC, UCLA and AFI listed under Writing Programs in our phone directory all have killer production classes culminating with the actual production of a short 20-minute film.

## Who's Who of Hollywood

Another invaluable resource for writers and producers are the books available from the *Hollywood Creative Directory.* This directory has addresses and phone numbers of all the producers and executives at studios or networks with over 6,000 names. Each company is listed with selected credits and any studio deals. This company has expanded to offer many other directories including:

*Hollywood Financial Directory*
*Hollywood Agents & Managers*
*Hollywood Distributors Directory*
*The Hollywood Creative Directory*
is also available on-line with weekly updates. You can access any list you need. If you are not yet on-line they have all the directories on computer disks. They also offer a mailing label

service. To speak to a representative, call the listing under Writers.

# Playwriting

This is certainly a tougher road to hoe than screenwriting because there is usually no money in theater until your plays are popular enough to be published by Samuel French. However, if you're serious and passionate enough about pursuing this particular avenue, here are a list of excellent support institutions to encourage you in that direction:

**The Sundance Institute** offers a "Playwrights Lab" each year. In the 90's, they developed nine new plays. The course lasts one week. The deadline for applying to this program is December 15th. Use the application address listed in this chapter under "Screenwriting." Or, you can call for an application and other pertinent information at our listing under Writers.

A couple of theaters in town have programs to develop plays and raise the money necessary for the production. They are listed in our phone directory under Theaters. If you wish to rent a theater and stage your own event, a list of some well respected houses that will rent out space is also listed in the same place under Theaters.

# Producing Your Own Projects The Straight Ahead Approach

Now that you know how to get that script written, you're probably thinking: "How am I going to get anyone to produce it?" Well, there are two ways—the conventional way and the unconventional way.

First, the conventional way: Secure the services of a literary agent or an entertainment attorney and have them submit your script to a production company, a movie or television studio executive, or a producer. If everything goes your way, you will have your script sold and contract negotiations will be handled by your representative agent or attorney. That's the accepted and conventional

practice and way of doing business.

# The Back Door Approach

Now the unconventional way. If you have an adventurous spirit, this is for you. So, how do you begin? Well, you take your script and you *"package"* it yourself. Packaging refers to assembling as many key elements (talent, director, and possible financing) as you can gather so that you can submit as

much of a ready-to-go project to a production company/producer/movie studio as you possibly can. For example, you might decide that Meryl Streep and Kevin Costner would be perfect for the lead characters. At this point, you can send your script to their respective talent agents (by looking in the *Academy Players Directory* or by calling the guilds to find out who they are) and see if you can convince them to pass it on to their clients for reading.

The problem with going through an agent to get to an actor is twofold: (1) The agent is sure to read your script first and make a decision on behalf of their client; and (2) even if the actor gets to read it at the agent's recommendation, the agent will come back to you and ask you to verify that you already have the money to pay the actor if he or she agrees to do it. Or worse, the agent will ask you for an advance as a show of good faith that there are, in fact, production monies committed to the project. But, that's more of the conventional way of getting an actor to sign onto your project. The unconventional way would look something like this: After you decide on the lead actors for your movie, do whatever you can to find them and approach them yourself to request that they read your script. I mean do **everything** you can to find ways to approach them directly! Ask all your friends if anyone knows them. Read the trades and see if they are getting any awards or will be present at an opening of a film; then, go to that location. Stand in the crowd and, when you spot the stars, hand it to them. If that doesn't work, try and leave it with their limo drivers. Get creative: read interview magazines and scan for restaurants they frequent or places where they hang out. Check out the local charities to see if they are on the board. You get the picture?

It is a rocky road getting a star attached but it can mean the difference between getting a project financed or not. Although stars are not customarily approached this way, you never know that he or she may be looking for a new project with which to become involved. A word of caution, however: You may find that, when approaching a star with your request, they may or may not be receptive. So, be bold enough to intrude and, at the same time, be respectful of the star's response to you. Remember ... if you don't ask, you don't get.

If you're fortunate enough to get an actor to read your script and, then, agree to do your movie, ask the star if he or she would be willing to write you a "*Letter of Interest*" or a "*Letter of Intent*" so that you can verify to a studio/producer/production company so-and-so's interest in appearing in your film wasn't just made as passing conversation.

In addition to attaching actors (known as "*talent*" in packaging terms), you might also want to consider including a top-name director in your package. As with the talent, you can approach a director the conventional way or the unconventional way.

As the final element in packaging your script, you might be fortunate enough to meet someone who is willing to put up some or all of the money to get the film made. For example, someone might be willing to put up the "*below-the-line*" costs (technical crew and post-production costs). Or, perhaps they would be willing to finance the "*above-the-line*" costs (money for talent, producers and director). Or someone may be willing to put up money for "prints and advertising" costs. Actually, there is an array of financial situations through which additional monies could be included in your package. The point is that the more elements you can package your script with, the higher the probability of getting your project made. If nothing else, it will certainly get priority attention from whomever you submit your package to.

## Shooting Your Own Movie

Dov Simens is a genius at teaching you how to produce and director your own projects. His film school gives you the most information in the shortest period of time for the least amount of money. After hearing his audio course Quentin Tarantino went out and shot **Reservoir Dogs** his first film. Phillippa Braithwaite produced her first feature, box office hit, **Sliding Doors** one month after taking Dov's Hollywood Film Institutes weekend course. Many types of courses are available and within months you can have your finished film. He can also teach you how to distribute your new movie. In listing under Production.

# Networking

One of the most effective ways to sustain the life of your career is by knowing other people in the industry and having other people know you. This takes you into the world of "you don't know what you don't know." You'd be amazed what surprises await you by word-of-mouth relationships. Taking the opportunity to tell other people who you are, what you are up to, and what your goals are can open up doors you never even knew existed.

The rest of this chapter offers suggestions on where to go to meet people and how to broaden your social landscape within the entertainment industry as another way to increase the probability of achieving your dream. In the unlikely event that nothing ever comes out of these professional, social relationships, you'll have made some close, new friendships to enrich your personal life.

# Visiting Other Working Actors

When a friend is working on a show or movie that features an actor and/or director you have been thinking about working with, go visit your friend on the set. Ask your friend to introduce you to the people you want to get to know. But, remember, you're not there to be hired as an actor. That's for another time and another place. You're there to introduce yourself and, hopefully, befriend someone who might have useful information to assist you in taking the next right step of your career, might eventually talk to others about you, or might tell you who you need to talk to yourself. Stay focused on your goal and be appropriate to the moment.

# Schmoozing

In the book **Power Schmoozing** by Terri Mandel, there are four rules to mastering this social skill: (1.) Tell the truth; (2.) take risks; (3.) tell your whole story; and (4.) Break the rules. Schmoozing is an art that must be mastered because it can happen anywhere: at the gym, at lunch, at parties, at sporting events, concerts, etc. Preparation and personality are key factors. One prominent producer told me he wanted to make another film with a certain actor because he was just so much fun to hang out with.

Here are some ideas to help you to schmooze at a social gathering, or, as it is commonly referred to, in the industry as "*working a party*." Talk to as many people as possible. When in doubt, overdress. Wear the lightest color possible. Talk about non-industry events (e.g., sports, politics, charities, etc.) Always arrive early. Offer to help the host/hostess. Eavesdrop. Interrupt. Brag. Have an opinion. Tell family secrets. Accept food when offered. Always RSVP. Look at people as your equal. Become an unofficial greeter. "Hi! I'm so and so. Who are you? What is your story?" Find out other's interests. Ask for business cards. Send people articles they would be interested in. Invite them to other social events. Don't get stuck with one person; excuse yourself and say something like: "It was so nice chatting with you but I promised to greet everyone, so I hope to see you again." Remember names. Put up a sexual barrier around yourself; you are not there to find a relationship. Sexy would be to lean forward, look at them and speak in whispers; a barrier is created when you talk louder and face the room. Ask your host if there is anyone you should meet . Have them introduce you.  The bottom line is have fun and  everyone will want to know you.

# Charities

Because a lot of prominent industry people give their time to their favorite causes, charity functions can be another way to access actors, producers and directors. However, it is important to keep in mind that, in most cases, the known figures who appear at these functions are there to serve others, not to draw attention to themselves or forward their careers. So, again, be sensitive and appropriate to the environment you're in when you make your approach.

Should you decide, then, to seek out specific people by attending charity events, there are some excellent resources available for identifying and locating the charities they might attend. Call the **Los Angeles Master planner** listed under Charities in our phone book in the back for a directory. If you can't or don't want to shell out the money, go to the library where you can look up a special interest group for any cause in the *Encyclopedia of Associations.* In addition, Beverly Hills publishes two weekly local papers which cover the charity and society events: *The Beverly Hills Courier* and *Beverly Hills 213.* Likewise, there is a column in the *Los Angeles Times* called "Save the Date" that has charities listed as well. Finally, *The Hollywood Reporter* prints their charities list Monday.

Once you have selected a charity, call it's office and find out who is on the board and who will perform at the next function. If you cannot afford a ticket, volunteer to work at the event. Some of the entertainment industry's favorite charities are listed under same.

## Taking Stock

Most large entertainment companies like **Disney Corporation** have stockholders events. You need only buy a few shares to be invited to these events. Some of the company's executives attend these events.

## And the Winner Is . . .

At every awards show there are celebrities coming out your ears. This is a good way to meet them socially because you already have credibility as a guest at a shared event. With the exception of the Oscar and Emmy Awards, whose tickets are only given out to members of the Academy, these are some events that anyone can attend. Call the offices for ticket information. If you can't afford a ticket, ask again to volunteer. All of the Award Shows are listed in our phone directory under Film Festivals.

## Conventions

Each year a number of entertainment industry conventions are well attended and offer a variety of lectures put together with some of the industry's top talent in all areas. If you can possibly attend, the contacts are priceless. Get a brochure before you sign up and see if anyone is speaking that is on your hit list. There is a partial list of some of the more popular conventions in our directory under Conventions.

## Actors' Support Groups

If you just can't seem to get the momentum going, look into Linda Buzzell's **"How to Make It in Hollywood: All the Right Moves"** by looking her up in our phone directory under Support Groups. This is a four-week course that utilizes homework assignments to force you into the workplace. The four weeker is affordable for the course with an additional fee per week if you want to continue. If you can't afford this, get her book *How to Make It in Hollywood.*

Breck Costin's **"Lifeworks Seminar Series"** teaches you how to break through blocks and have the kind of career you always dreamed of. The course is three-months. To reserve a space, call their

business office. They also offer a free introductory night, to see if it's for you.

**The Actors Network** is a supportive group of actors who all network to share information on current casting information, likes, dislikes and hobbies of casting directors and other useful information. They also have many other services available. Their library contains 500 entertainment books, industry trade magazines, newspapers and 180 feature film scripts. Their fax machine is available to receive sides for any audition for you. Guest lecturers including managers and casting directors who come monthly. They have two studios available for use and lots of demo reels for ideas. The fee is about $40 per month. You can reach The Actors Network in our phone book under Support Groups.

Each day you have to follow the example of Chuck Yaeger, one of the first test pilots in the space program and push the envelope to see how far you can go without getting killed or burned up. Develop friendships with like thinkers and stay in touch as you soar toward your destiny.

# Chapter 20
# Professional Organizations and Societies

**Silent Pictures by Katie Maratta**

There are many organizations that exist to promote professional achievement, exchange ideas and network with people who are on the same career path as you. Some are easy to join and some may take many years to gain admittance. I highly recommend that you seek to associate with at least one of the following organizations. Here's what it takes to join each organization and the benefits available to each one of its members.

# Writers Guild of America West

This union is the west coast office of the main Writers Guild. WGA is probably the only guild with which an individual can associate without having to become a member. Anyone can register a treatment (an outline of a movie, TV show or book idea), script or manuscript with the WGA to protect the idea somewhat from being stolen. Call their information line and listen to the recorded message with instructions on how to register *"properties."* When you go to register your property, you will be expected to bring an unbound copy of the treatment, script or manuscript to the WGA Registration Office between 10 AM and 5 PM. Fill out the application and your property will be sealed in an envelope and assigned a WGA number. The cost is $20 for non-members, $10 for members. The Writers Guild Registration Office phone and FAX number are in our phone directory under Professional Organizations.

To further protect yourself, go to the post office and mail a copy of the same document to yourself, registered mail. The postmaster will date stamp the seal on the envelope. Once you receive the package, make sure that you **don't** open it. Keep it in a safe, fireproof place in case it you ever need it in a court of law.

If you have ever entertained the idea of becoming a writer to complement your acting career, you'll want to become a member of the Writers Guild of America. It provides stature which says that you are recognized throughout the entertainment industry as a professional writer. Admittance is based on a point system for work done with a company that is a signatory to the applicable Writers Guild of America Collective Bargaining Agreement. It is a complicated system and points are awarded depending on the length of the show or film and several other variables. The Writers Guild office can give you a handout that clarifies the point system so that you can start working toward membership. Initiation fee to this union is several thousand dollars.

# The Academy of Motion Picture Arts and Sciences

The Academy of Motion Picture Arts & Sciences has offices in Beverly Hills, CA. This is the group of people who vote for the **Oscars** each year. The charter states that membership shall be by invitation of the Board of Governors. This is slightly misleading. The Governors will never call you up on the phone and ask you to join. You decide when you have enough film work which you believe entitles you to be reviewed for admittance to the Academy.

However, you can vote on the entire list of nominations in all categories in the final ballot. Your Oscar vote is tallied along with your fellow members' and the outcome is televised all around the world. As a member of the Academy you are also invited to purchase tickets to the annual television broadcast of the *ACADEMY AWARDS SHOW* and the **Governor's Ball** that follows, but you probably will only get tickets every third year or so. An application can be obtained by calling the Academy Office listed in our directory.

Roughly the requirements are that you have appeared in a scripted role of three theatrical feature films that were released over the five years prior to application. Another way in is to be nominated for an Academy Award in an acting category or to be judged by the Actors Branch Executive Committee to have achieved unique distinction, special merit or made an outstanding contribution as a motion picture actor. Next, you must find two current members to sponsor your application. Ask all your friends and acquaintances until you find two who are willing to be your sponsor and ask them to sign your application. When you receive your two endorsements, submit your application. Reviews occur twice a year, from May to June and again from October to November. There is no fee for the application but their is a yearly membership fee.

After you've been inducted into the Academy, you will be invited at regular intervals to screen all films being considered by the Academy for Oscar contention. The way you make your selection is by viewing the films in the Academy Theater on its premises. If you are unable to attend, the studios will often send, a tape of the movie to your home by mail for viewing. You can nominate only those candidates who belong to the category or branch to which you belong. So, for example, if you are inducted into the Actors Branch, you can only nominate actors whose performances you feel are worthy of honors.

## The Academy of Television Arts and Sciences

Recently this Academy has built stunning new offices in the San Fernando Valley Theater Renovation District. This is the organization responsible for awarding the prestigious **Emmy**. ATAS is broken down into peer groups just like the Motion Picture Academy: acting, writing, directing, makeup, even animation, etc. No group is overlooked.

Requirements to join this organization are very similar to the Motion Picture Academy. Three sponsors, who are current members of ATAS and members of the peer group you wish to join, are required to sign your application. Additionally, you must have a minimum of eight television credits in a principal or featured role over the last four years.

Their brochure contains two other ways to qualify. If you wish to become an associate (non-voting) member of the Academy, the requirements are less stringent. You will need only two years of acting experience: or one part in a national commercial/film on television in the last two years. If you work in various areas of television your application will be placed in the peer group where you have the most hours of work.

Once you are accepted into ATAS, you will be invited to catered screenings of TV movies, shows and special events. All screenings are held at the Television Academy's gorgeous, state-of-the art theater in North Hollywood. Each screening event is usually attended by the executive producer, the writer and sometimes the director. This affords you another networking opportunity.

In addition to screening events, you will periodically be invited to special panels to participate in discussions on current industry topics. The panelists usually are top professionals in their respective field. You can ask them questions and meet with them afterward.

ATAS has different workshop groups, such as, Performing, Directing, Writing, or How To Develop a Project and Pitch it. All workshops are open to members to assist them in honing their skills. An outline of each group's purpose and fees required are available by calling the Academy office.

Once a year you will be able to nominate anyone in your peer group, who you feel is deserving of an Emmy for both Prime time and Daytime categories. Being a part of the Blue Ribbon Panels that vote for the awards is strictly voluntary. You must commit to one or two days of back-to-back screenings of the competitors in each respective category. It's a lot of fun. The Academy has thought of everything during this two-day marathon so, a beautiful lunch is served between morning and afternoon screenings. You find out the results along with millions of other television viewers during either *THE EMMY AWARDS* or *THE DAYTIME EMMY AWARDS*. The membership can purchase tickets to the shows and Governors Ball. An outline of qualifications for nomination can be obtained from the administrative office.

Six times a year you will receive *Emmy Magazine* packed with articles and features about the present and future state of television. Quarterly you receive *Debut Magazine* outlining scholarships and intern programs offered through ATAS. Anyone you know who is interested in a job in television can intern with some of the top television production companies in this program. Interested parties can contact the ATAS office for details.

The application to become a member of the Academy of Television Arts and Sciences costs nothing; but, once accepted, the dues are on a per year basis for active membership and associates.

## Independent Feature Projects /West

The IFP/West, as it is called, has headquarters in the west side of Los Angeles. To quote the brochure: "this non-profit membership organization is one of the largest and most dynamic groups supporting quality independent film making today." IFP offers a variety of seminars, among which "The Producer Series" is one of the hottest. This series equips independent film makers with top level contacts and practical knowledge to make their films. One lecture IN the series, entitled "Method To The Madness," was sponsored by AGFA. It was advertised like this: "Learn the business of independent film making, meet key players in the industry, network with colleagues who can help your career. Build your professional profile by working with industry insiders who can expand your network." The panelists for this seven-evening series included a top publicist, a heavy hitting entertainment attorney, the producer of *TERMINATOR* and *ALIENS*, a distinguished casting director, an agent from William Morris and the producer of *HOFFA.* All at a cost of $20 to members!

Another great series of panel discussions are events called "Evenings With...." which features noted film makers. Past guests have included Gail Ann Hurd, Robert Altman, Quentin Tarantino and Rob Reiner.

Another great opportunity available with the annual membership is the Screening

Series where 60 or more independent films are screened per year at various theaters around town. Recent showings included: *FARGO, THE ENGLISH PATIENT,* **SHINE** *and* **SLING BLADE**. Finally, you'll also be invited to member gatherings, spotlight luncheons and the Breakfast Series.

Each month you'll be sent a calendar of events and each quarter you'll receive a copy of *Filmmaker: The Magazine of Independent Film* to inform you of upcoming events. IFP/West offers varied opportunities for you to learn and participate in every aspect of motion picture production. My recommendation is to take the initiative to join this organization and volunteer to take classes.

IFP/West takes into consideration that not everyone can afford all the events offered; so, they have organized a barter system where you can volunteer your time and exchange accumulated man-hours for admission to events. Call the office for details. A membership application and info packet will be mailed to.

Once a year this organization hosts the **Spirit Awards** for excellence in independent film making. Tickets to this event are highly coveted. Members vote for the best independent films. Many consider this the kick-off event to the Oscars since they are only days apart.

# Women in Film

This girl power group is located in the heart of Hollywood. This is yet another group that requires sponsorship by two current members for acceptance. The organization is open to both men and women despite the title. WIF makes it easy to find your sponsors: a directory of current members is kept in the office for you to browse through. Check to see if you know any members that you can call upon them to sponsor you. If

you don't know anyone, offer to volunteer at WIF's next event and start schmoozing. The application is free and yearly membership fees are very affordable.

WIF also has a slew of events and seminars to help advance industry professionals. These include:

**WIF Industry Mixers**—a business networking reception with 300 industry colleagues.

**WOW** (Work Opportunity Workshops)— These are classes offered throughout the month taught my respected industry professionals on a wide variety of topics.

**Networking Breakfasts**—Five different breakfasts, each in a separate part of town, some on studio lots, where members meet and brainstorm on how to help one another.

**Workshops** - Includes casting director/talent workshops where member casting directors, directors and member actors work together on showcases.

**Committees**—Public Service Announcements, Mothers in Film, WIF Foundation, Membership Gala, Stunt women and Issues & Advocacy.

**Crystal Awards Luncheon**—WIF's biggest fund-raiser. An inspirational industry event with 1,200 studio and independent film makers honoring accomplished female role models in film and television who have broken career barriers. Always attended by industry heavy hitters. A BIG ticket.

*Women in Film Newsletter*— is packed with information on upcoming industry events, film festivals, articles on women pioneers in the entertainment industry, grants and scholarships, a list of new members and available job listings.

HOLLYWOOD

# The Filmmakers Foundation

This foundation is a non-profit organization dedicated to providing emerging and established film making talent with the environment, information, opportunity, relationships and experience required to launch, further and sustain meaningful careers in the motion picture and television industries. This unique group of professionals offer many seminars, each designed to aid your growth in this industry.

The Story Development Training Program is a 12-week intensive course using a unique set of powerful tools for understanding and strengthening narrative screenplays being developed at the Foundation. This program is usually attended by development executives but is invaluable to anyone considering a writing career in the industry.

The New Film makers Program is an innovative production arm of the Foundation that creates three to four art-house films per year as well as public service announcements and corporate videos for other nonprofit organizations. This unique program guides the entire film making team through every phase of the process from development, finance, production, post-production, and distribution to marketing. The team includes the Actors Group, comprised of emerging players and seasoned veterans.

The Professional Screenwriting Workshop builds writers' craft by taking them through the entire writing process from story concept to a completed spec script, allowing them to work with each other in a structured, development-style relationships. The scripts are then shopped in the marketplace.

The Career Management Course is a 12-week in-depth training to launch future agents, managers and those seeking to understand career-building strategies.

The In-School is a wonderful community outreach program that brings specially trained, volunteer instructors to inner city high schools and gives students hands-on experience. The students write and produce 30-second public service announcements on current social issues. This program is partially funded by the City of Los Angeles Cultural Affairs Department.

The Film makers Foundation offers many other clinics and workshops in networking, career strategies and pitching your project and yourself. This non-profit organization offers a unique opportunity to any entertainment professional to decide which area of

your life you want to pursue and go after it. All are welcome regardless of background, level of experience or income. You can visit their web site at: www.FilmFound.org or e-mail at: NewFilmkrs@aol.com but if you are not cyberspace savvy their phone number is listed in the back of our book.. Visit their offices or call for an application:

# Performers Alliance

The slogan for this organization is "Working Performers for a union that works." In recent years many of the working members of SAG have become disgruntled with the way their interests have been sold out to producers by hired employees of the union without even a vote by the membership. When the Guild suggests its members ratify a contract that has been negotiated, we usually do. Often times contrary opinion about a contract will

not be aired in the Guild newletters. These newsletters are controlled by the employees, not the members, of SAG and by Board members who have become complacent with their jobs. Two glaring misuses of power by employees of the Guild resulted in a location move costing members over $2 million and huge giveaways in our latest Commercial Contract Negotiations. In these negotiations, union-hired employees agreed to pennies on the dollar for cable residuals saying it was the best deal they could get for us.

Instead of getting angry the Performers Alliance got busy. This group of working actors banded together and announced its own slate of candidates running for powerful positions on SAG's Board and National Offices. They contacted every voting member that could be reached and started a grass roots effort to change the status quo. Their mission is "To revitalize the leadership of the Screen Actors Guild and to restore its effectiveness through the active participation and influence of its working members."

Membership is free and you are encouraged to get involved. There are regularly scheduled meetings and you can attend the next one by calling the performers hotline, listed in our book  or getting in touch on the Web at www.actor.org

Before you decide which association is right for you, try attending a few events for each of the groups you are considering. This will give you a feel for the membership, letting you see if they are the group with which you would like to be associated.

Societies have always been a great way to advance one's career. Common bonds are easily and frequently formed through shared activities, such as: attending lectures and workshops; exchanging scripts; seeking career advice; etc. And since no member is better than any other member, it is easy to meet on equal footing with your idols. Someday when you are successful, you'll be able to come back to these same groups and be a guest lecturer and have the gratifying opportunity to give back some of what you got.

# IFP/West Membership Application

**I am a:** ___ New Member
___ Renewing Member, No._____

Name(s) _____
Title _____
Company _____
Address _____
City/State/Zip _____
Home Phone (___)_____
Fax (___) _____
Work Phone (___) _____

**Membership Type:**
___ $50 Student (Proof reqd.)
___ $85 Individual
___$150 2-Year Individual
___$135 Household
     (2 People, one Address)
___$150 Bi-coastal (IFP/West
     IFP in New York both)

**Method of Payment:**
___ Check Enclosed #_____
Charge my: ___Visa ____ MC
Visa/MC # _____
Expiration Date ____/___
Signature _____

## Please indicate your professional designation (check all that apply)

__Acquisitions       __ Cinematographer    __ Distribution       __Production Mgmt.
__Actor              __ Composer           __ Editor             __Script Supervisor
__Agent              __ Costume Design     __ Marketing          __Technical
__Attorney           __ Development        __ Producer           __Writer
__Business Affairs   __ Director           __ Production Design
                          __ Other _____

## Personal Information (For statistical purposes - confidential)

Age:                  Ethnic Origin        Material Status      Annual Income
__ under 18           __African American   __ Single            Less than $20,000
__ 18-24              __Asian/Pacific      __ Married           $20,001 - $30,000
__ 25-34              __Caucasian          __ Divorced          $30,001 - $50,000
__ 35-44              __Native American    __Widowed            $50,001 - $75,000
__ 45-54              __Latino/Chicano                          $75,001 - $100,000
__ 55-64              __Other _____   Gender:              __ Female __ Male

## Optional:

__ Do Not want to receive Industry-related mailings
__ Do Not want to receive update phone calls
__ Want to Volunteer

**Mail or fax application to:**      **Allow two weeks for processing**
        **IFP/West Membership Services**
   **1964 Westwood Blvd, #205, Los Angeles, CA 90025**
          **Phone 310/475-4379   Fax 310/441-5676**
   **Make checks/money orders payable to IFP/West.**

# Chapter 21
# Uncle Sam - Your Taxes

**Ah** ...Taxes! Or, the "T-word" as many of us refer to it. Distasteful to everyone. Especially to those performing artists who must make an investment in their own career yet who, initially, may get little in return.

In this chapter, you—the performing artist as taxpayer—will learn: (1) two options under which you might file your tax returns based on your income; and, (2) how you can use most of your expenses as legal deductions on your income tax. I will show you how to set up a simple system that will make it very easy for you to organize and maintain good records so that, come income tax time, processing your tax returns will be a worry-free and painless well, maybe I should say less painful effort. But, if after foraging through the next few pages, you are still bewildered about how to organize and pay your taxes as a performing artist ... fear not! There is help available. I will recommend excellent tax preparers to you.

Above and beyond everything else we will have talked about in this chapter, the most important thing for your to remember about your taxes is that in the final analysis, you are solely responsible for the tax return you file, whether you prepared the tax return by yourself or received professional assistance. Keep this in mind, especially if you just happen to "forget" to report some of your cash or non-documented income.

The average actor spends a minimum of $4,000-$5,000 every year on his or her career alone. If you can't spend this much, it is hard to be competitive. The good news is that almost every acting expense is deductible, whether you make a dime in your new career or not. Since you will get into the habit of keeping good records, it will save you thousands of dollars over the course of your career. This is the part of the career that many actors have a hard time organizing. But, if you can follow the easy system I am about to lay out, you're going to have Uncle Sam absorbing some of your cost for doing business in the form of tax savings. So, let's begin with this aspect of organizing your records.

## The First Step

Go to one of the **Staples Office Superstores** in your new neighborhood and buy a box of file folders. Call (800) 333-3319 for the location nearest you.

Beach cities: On Lincoln Boulevard in Venice Boulevard

Los Angeles: On Wilshire Boulevard just west of La Brea

San Fernando Valley: On Sherman Way between Coldwater Canyon and Whitsett Avenue.

## Step Two

Make a photo copy of every expense category from this chapter. Starting with the photo copy titled File #1—Income, cut the file number and category and paste it onto the identification tab of your first file folder. Then, paste the list of allowable deductions designated under File #—Income on the front of the file folder. Now, repeat this process for each category listed.

## Step Three

Ask for and keep receipts. When you get a receipt, file it in the appropriate file. If you write a check for a particular product, include the check number on the receipt so that you can match the check with your receipt when totaling at the end of the year.

Every merchant receipt must have the following information stamped on it: a company name, a date and a dollar amount. If it is not clear what the receipt is for, you must write some identification on the receipt (e.g., "Resumes," "Props," etc.). If you are audited by the I.R.S. and are unable to produce receipts, you will lose the deduction.

Proving a valid deduction is, sometimes, a judgment call usually determined by the I.R.S. But, you can hedge your bets by making entries into a daily calendar. For example, let's say you write a check to get your hair cut for a specific job. Writing down the service rendered, in this case, your haircut, along with related information (i.e. Name of job on such and such date) in your daily calendar will, at least, substantiate your declared expense and will probably be deemed as a valid deduction by the I.R.S. On the other hand, there are some declared expenses that could be judged as not valid. Here is an example: You buy clothes specifically for auditions and never wear them for anything else. You would think they can be written off, but because you can wear the clothes in your private life, they can't be written off (e.g., dancer's' leotards and tights). Haircuts and manicures can only be written off for a specific acting job.

## End of the Year Totals

At the end of each year, copy the pages from this chapter titled:

"Performing Arts Expenses"
"Pre-Appointment Checklist"
"Other Expenses" & "Vehicle Expenses"

Enter your totals for the year on the appropriate form and give it to your tax preparer. Also, double check to make sure that your paycheck stubs total up to the figure on the W-2's sent to you by your employer(s), whether it is a production company, a studio, a survival job employer, a temp agency, etc. (A W-2 is a form sent by an employer outlining your total income and taxes withheld by that employer).

## Tax Help Tips:

If you work for someone else there are basically three ways of getting paid for your work:

1.) As an employee for a company or individual who receive a W-2. This is how most of us receive reimbursement for our labors. Taxes are taken out of our paychecks, and the W-2 is a form used to tell the I.R.S. and ourselves how much these totals over the year. The employer pays half of our total Social Security and Medicare taxes as well as several other additional amounts. The additional cost to an employer to pay this way can sometimes exceed 20% of the salary we gross, before taxes each year. This is why some employers prefer to pay with a 1099-MISC.

2.) By check or cash and requiring a 1099-MISC. Your employer may or may not take out any taxes for you (usually not) and considers you an Independent Contractor or Self-Employed. In general, any time you work for a person or business and earn more than $600.00 they MUST report that payment to the IRS in the form of a 1099-MISC. You also receive a copy. The government is therefore aware that you have earned this money. In some cases individuals receive a 1099-MISC for an amount less than $600.00. It doesn't matter to the I.R.S.. Their ruling stipulates that they be informed if the amount is greater than $600.00, but they appreciate hearing you made money no matter how much you earned.

3.) Straight cash or "under the table." Your employer takes no taxes out for you and does not report this income to the government. In the eyes of the I.R.S., however, this is still taxable income and you are supposed to report it.

**WARNING:**

Be certain that you have received ALL of the W-2's and 1099's for ALL of the companies you worked for last year. If you do not receive them and do not declare the income you WILL be hearing from the I.R.S. Keep and compare your check stubs to (1.) Know how many and from who to expect W-2's, and (2.) Know how much the W-2's should be for. This is your responsibility, NOT your employer(s).

## Filing Status

Up to this point, I have introduced you to a system by which you, as a performing artist, can organize your records in preparation for filing your tax returns. Now, let's look at the way you, as a taxpayer, will be filing your returns.

There are two taxpayer roles under which you can file your tax returns based on income derived from wage earnings: employee or independent contractor.

As an "employee," your employer will give you a W-4 form to fill out when you begin working. (A W-4 form is the document you filled out upon being hired, where you designated your number of dependents.) On the basis of that information, they will pay you weekly or monthly or after principal photography or whatever. Your check will reflect the net amount of wages you are receiving after the employer has deducted all the required taxes. At the end of the year, your employer will send you a multi-copied W-2 form itemizing your gross wages, and all the taxes (federal, state, Social Security, etc.) taken out for that period of your employment. During tax filing time, you are then responsible for filing your tax return along with the W-2 and other itemized deduction forms.

As an "independent contractor," you will be paid by your employer without having any taxes deducted from your paycheck. The forms you will need to fill out are designated by the prefix "1099." And, similarly, you will have to be responsible for filing all the appropriate 1099 forms at income tax time. As an independent contractor, there are items you have to pay attention to, such as: Self-employment taxes to be paid on the profit you show from your acting business; acting expenses which can be written off against the income; interest on savings (Form 1099 INT) and a host of others (see *File #2—Income* for a detailed breakdown). The profit (income minus expenses) is taxable for both federal tax (the lowest bracket is 15%) and your self-employment tax (Social Security) of 15.3%. You must, therefore, put aside 30% of your gross salary to cover your tax liability.

If you have a non-industry survival job that includes tips (e.g., waiter, bellman, sky cap), there is a specific pamphlet from the I.R.S. that covers the reporting of tips. It is **Form 531—Reporting Income from Tips.** The restaurant business is very familiar with tips and reports your total food sales for the year to the I.R.S., so that they can estimate the dollar amount of your tips.

So, how will you know which way to file? Well, let's say that you book your first film and it's a non-union gig. And, let's say the production company doesn't have a sophisticated accounting system set up. When it comes time to get paid, the production company gives you a check. The production company may or may not have taken out taxes. If they did not, you are then considered to be an independent contractor. At tax time gather up and organizing your 1099 forms. Whether they send you a 1099-MISC at the end of the year or not, you are responsible for any federal and state taxes. So make copies of all checks before you cash them so that you can add up your total income.

## Tax Office Locations

The local I.R.S. and California state offices where you can get the pamphlet mentioned above and other information booklets can be found at the following locations:

California Franchise Tax Board
300 S. Spring Street
Los Angeles, CA
(800) 852-5711

333 N. Glen Oaks Boulevard
Burbank, CA
(800) 852-5711

United States Internal Revenue Service
300 N. Los Angeles Street
Los Angeles, CA
(800) 829-3676

6230 Van Nuys Boulevard
Van Nuys, CA
(800) 829-4477

The following pages contain all the expense categories and their respective allowable deductions I referred to earlier in this chapter. Photocopy these pages and follow the process outlined in Steps 1-3 to create you own personal I.R.S. file folder system:

# Taxable Income

## File #1: INCOME includes:

- W-2 Forms—Theatrical & Non-theatrical (Remember: this income includes the 10-25% commission paid to agents and managers, which is tax-deductible under File 16)
- Strike Benefits

## File #2: 1099 INCOME includes:

- 1099 Forms—Theatrical and Non-Theatrical
- 1099 INT—Statements of Interest from Bank Accounts
- 1099 DIV—Statements of Dividends from Stock Accounts
- 1099 G—Unemployment Compensation
- SSA 1099—Social Security Benefits
- 1099 R—Pension Benefits
- 1099 B—Stock Sales
- 1099 G —State Refund from Previous Year
- Prize Winnings from Game Shows & Lottery

# Expenses Other Than Professional

## File #3: MEDICAL (not reimbursed by insurance) including:

- Doctors
- Dentists
- Insurance Premiums
- Prescription Drugs
- Eyeglasses
- Special Equipment
- Transportation Costs for Visits
- Chiropractor
- Therapists

## File #4: CHARITY

(Any one-time contribution in excess of $250 or more requires a receipt from a charitable organization. Clothing and furniture donated must be priced at garage sale value, not original retail value.)

## File #5: INTEREST CHARGES PAID including:

- Loans for the Business of Acting
- Credit Cards (For acting only, if the credit card is used for even one non-acting expense, all interest will be disallowed.)
- Mortgage Interest on Home/Condo

## File #6: PROPERTY TAXES ON HOME

## File #7: CHILD CARE EXPENSES

(Only when working or looking for work. Cannot be a family member. Must be over age 19. If more than $600, record Social Security number and issue a 1099 at the end of the year.)

## File #8: IRA AND KEOGH CONTRIBUTIONS

## File #9: ALIMONY

(If you're paying, it is a write-off. If you are receiving, it is considered income.)

## File #10: DMV REGISTRATION COSTS

## File #11: LEGAL FEES (Acting only)

## File #12: INCOME TAX RETURN PREPARATION

(including books & software)

## File #13: EDUCATIONAL EXPENSES

(Only for a job you are currently employed in, not one you intend to begin.)

# Performing Arts Business Expenses on Form 2106

Only if you earn less than $12,000

## File #14: ACCOMPANIST & AUDITION EXPENSE

**File #15: ADVERTISING & PUBLICITY**
including but not limited to:
- Headshots
- Resumes
- Photographer Expenses
- Retoucher Expenses
- Ads in the Trades
- Fan Club Photos
- *Academy Players Directory*
- Business Cards
- Postcards

**File #16: AGENTS COMMISSION & MAN-AGERS FEES**
(10-25% included in W-2 income)

**File #17: ANSWERING SERVICE**
- Beepers
- Calling Services

**File #18: AUDITION TAPE** including:
- Video Resume
- Voice-Over
- Demo Tape
- Raw Tape Stock for Air Checks

**File #19: COACHING LESSONS** including:
- Coaching for Audition or Job
- Voice Coach
- Speech/Diction Coach
- Vocal Coach
- Dance Coach
- Acting Classes
- Dance Classes
- Casting Director Workshops

**File #20: COSTUMES**
For Professional Use Only NOT general streetwear, such as rehearsal hall clothing, ballet shoes, etc.

**File #21: ENTERTAINMENT** including:
- Business Lunches
- Drinks, Plays, Movies with Agent
- Business Dinners (Use "Entertainment Form" at the end of this chapter.)

**File #22: EQUIPMENT** including purchase:
- Audio/Visual Equipment
- Telephone
- Answering, FAX & Xerox Machines
- VCR and Television
- Musical Equipment and Tape Recorders (See "Equipment Form" at end of chapter. You must file Federal Form 4562 and CA State Form FTB 3885A for any item over $100 that is expected to have a life of more than one year.)

**File #23: GIFTS FOR BUSINESS**
A limit of $25. per recipient, per year including opening nights, birthdays etc.

**File #24: MAINTENANCE OF PROFESSIONAL COSTUMES** including:
- Cleaning
- Alterations
(Do not include general streetwear)

**File #25: MAKEUP, NAIL & HAIR CARE**
Professional only, for a specific booking. (Photo sessions, stage makeup)

**File #26: MISCELLANEOUS** including:
A personal trainer for specific diet or weight gain for a specific role. Must be able to prove it is needed for a role.

**File #27: OFFICE AT HOME** including:
- Secretarial & Clerical Services
- Portion of Rent or Mortgage
(Be careful here, it is a "red flag" to be audited, as the I.R.S. considers legitimate studios or locations our place of business.)

**File #28: OFFICE SUPPLIES / STATIONARY / POSTAGE / MAILERS** including:
- Fan Mail Submissions, Postcards

**File #29: REPAIRS AND MAINTENANCE FOR EQUIPMENT** including:
- VCR & Television Repair
- Music Equipment Repair
- FAX Repair
- Answering Machine Repair

## File #30: STUDIO RENTAL / RENT ON OTHER BUSINESS PROPERTY
including::
- Cable TV
- Equipment Rental
- Photocopier Rental

## File #31: SUPPLIES FOR RESEARCH
including:
- Sheet Music
- Records & Tapes
- Books
- Scripts
- Props

## File #32: TELEPHONE including:
- Business Long Distance & Toll Calls
- Call Waiting
- Pay Phone Expenses
- Mobile Phones
- Second Line/Fax Line
- Credit Card Calls for Business
(Basic phone service is not deductible.)

## File #33: TICKETS FOR RESEARCH
including:
(Personal costs not spouses or partners)
- Theater
- Film
- Film Societies
- Video Rentals

## File #34: TIPS & GRATUITIES BACKSTAGE

## File #35: TRADE PUBLICATIONS
including:
- *Variety*
- *Hollywood Reporter*
- *Backstage/Backstage West*
- *Ross Reports & Showbiz* etc.

## File #36: UNION DUES & INITIATION FEES including:
2% Actors Equity working fee

## File #37: VEHICLE EXPENSES
(See Vehicle Expense form for breakdowns)

## File #38: WARDROBE EXPENSES PAID BY EMPLOYER
This is listed on your W-2 form.

## File #39: CALENDARS AND APPOINTMENT BOOKS

# Travel Expenses

**-Tax Help:**

Travel expenses are those that you pay while traveling away from home. In general an overnight stay is required. Deductible expenses are those that you incur in the course of all *business-related* trips. Be careful to deduct only those expenses directly related to business, i.e., a trip to Chicago to visit your relatives doesn't count as business no matter how many auditions you may receive as a coincidence of your stay unless you went to Chicago primarily to audition and your family visit constituted a small part of the stay. Any costs incurred specifically during the family visit are not deductible.

The standard meal allowance is $26.00 for most areas of the country ($34.00-38.00 in major cities). This figure includes costs for laundry, cleaning and tips and you can use the appropriate amount in lieu of receipts. Commercial travel and lodging are not reflected in the allowance and for those individual amounts greater than $75.00 you must have a receipt.

The I.R.S. requires appropriate documentation (receipts, check stubs, etc.) and even if you use the standard meal allowance, you must keep a log to prove the time, place and business purpose of your travel.

# For File #37 - How To Figure Out Vehicle Expenses
### Business Mileage:

Defining and proving your business mileage is the biggest headache any of us have. If you are using mileage as a deduction you are asked to define and prove three things: (1) Your total mileage throughout the year; (2) miles you drove specifically for business; (3) miles you drove while commuting to work. Most people have trouble with number one, let alone two and three.

Obviously, if you write down your mileage on January 1st and then again on the following January 1st you know exactly how much you drove that year. Simply putting this figure down in your mileage log counts as proof (or repair bills with odometer readings on them substantiate the log.) Any miles you drive for business-related reasons, auditions, photography sessions, rehearsals, classes, movies, printers, entertaining agents, buying scripts, etc.; constitute business mileage, but only if you have written down the trip and the mileage in your log to prove it.

In additions, you have to define commuting mileage, and that figure is becoming more difficult to include. Commuting is defined by the I.R.S. as mileage to and from your place of employment. Unfortunately, most actors work only a few days a year and therefore we have a new ruling to contend with. The I.R.S. considers the first trip out in the morning and the last trip back to home as constituting commuting mileage for those days when we are not working. We can make as many trips as we want in between and those count as business mileage, but the first and last trip of the day are commuting (unless you can define otherwise).

This ruling may seem unfair to us but the IRS believes this makes our commuting mileage and the commuting of "normal" employees more equitable. Any actor who has been audited is a big believer in writing down mileage. "Winging it" only works until the audit. Consider this fair warning.

**Actual Expenses:**

For some people actual car expenses can far exceed their business mileage (multiplied by .30 cents per mile). In this case your gasoline, repair, car washes, insurance, or almost any expense for your car, can be included. If you have a large number of repairs or you are leasing the car you may consider this alternative. (Unfortunately depreciation is outside the scope of this book, please contact a paid preparer if this is a consideration.)

But, even if you plan to use actual automobile expenses you must define the percentage of your expenses that are deductible by the percentage of your total miles driven for business.

## Help Is On The Way

A little overwhelming? Maybe a little scary? Well, don't worry. You don't have to figure this out alone. I would like to introduce you to two tax preparers accustomed to dealing with entertainers' tax returns. Chuck Sloan is an actor himself and put together the forms I have included in this chapter. Because he is so skilled and experienced in the specialized area of a performing artist's tax preparation, I can't recommend him strongly enough.

Susan Levine up until last year was employed by the Internal Revenue Service. She has left government service and is a consultant to one of the largest talent payment companies in Los Angeles. She also prepares taxes for clients and of course knows exactly what the IRS will allow. Both people are listed in our phone directory.

## Free Tax Help

If you cannot afford a tax preparer and plan to fill out your own tax returns, there is free assistance available through the **Volunteer Income Tax Assistance Program (V.I.T.A.).** V.I.T.A. is offered by the Screen Actors Guild, A.F.T.R.A. and Equity unions as a service to those members who qualify. Although the unions sponsor this program jointly, the office is housed at the **Screen Actors Guild** at 5757 Wilshire Boulevard. During the first week in February, you can either drop by to pick up a packet and make an appointment or call (213) 549-6605 to have a packet delivered to you and make an appointment over the phone. When you arrive for your scheduled appointment, the

I.R.S.-trained volunteers will then guide you and a group of approximately ten other performers through your respective tax return preparations. The process takes about four hours. During that time, you fill out all the necessary forms under the volunteers' guidance and, by the end of the session, your returns will be ready to mail. The service is free to paid-up members of these three guilds.

Here are the guidelines for V.I.T.A. Please read all the stipulations for qualification. This program of free income tax help is provided by the Internal Revenue Service with the cooperation and support of AEA, A.F.T.R.A. and SAG. The unpaid volunteers who will help you are fellow union members who have been trained by the IRS to assist in the preparation of basic tax returns. However, since neither the volunteers nor the sponsoring unions receive remuneration for the service rendered, they are not legally liable for the return in any way. Responsibility for the accuracy and completeness of the tax return rests solely with the person(s) filing the return. Should the return be audited by the I.R.S., there is no guarantee that the V.I.T.A. Volunteer who assisted in its preparation will be available for help.

Some final tips. You can use acting expenses as deductions whether you are hired for union or non-union jobs. Your expenses above and beyond per diem, while you are on location, are tax deductible. (Per diem is living expense money, paid in cash, to you, each week you are on location.) If you have made any money as an actor in your current town, the relocation costs to Los Angeles are deductible.

So, there you have it! A simple, effective system for organizing your taxes. The great thing about setting up this file folder system is that you only have to do it one time; thereafter, you can use the same file folders year after year to collect your receipts. At the end of the year, after you've filed your returns, gather that year's receipts and bind them together. Put them in a big manila envelope with the tax year marked on them. Store them in a safe place for seven years. After that seven-year period, you can't be audited.

All the big actors in Hollywood know that the way to cash in on the "Treasure Chest" of your sweet Uncle Sam lies in good record keeping. I was on location recently, having lunch away from the set with some fellow cast members. There was an Academy Award winner among us. We all practically fell over each other getting separate receipts from our waiter. You see, no matter who you are, you still have to pay your taxes.

**Please remember, I am not a tax preparer or a CPA. I am an actor/writer. The ideas contained in this chapter are my recommendations based on my research and personal experience. You should consult with a qualified tax specialist before making any final decisions.**

For individual assistance, your total income for the year cannot exceed $50,000 gross.

V.I.T.A. is not designed to prepare returns which include any of the following:

> Out-of-state returns
> Out-of-country returns
> Schedules D, E,. or F
> 1099 Income exceeding $2,500.00
> Sale of stocks and bonds
> Sale of house or real estate
> Vehicle or equipment depreciation

Note: If you are going to participate in the self-help program, none of the above applies.

The following pages contain the forms that will help you to organize your tax information and figures every year. I suggest that, annually, you copy and use: (1.) The Pre-Appointment Checklist; (2.) Other Expenses - Schedule A Deductions; (3.) Performing Arts Expenses; (4.) Vehicle Expenses Worksheet. Then, at the end of the year, take one of the files you've made up and total all the receipts in that file. When you have the final figure, enter it in the appropriate slot on these forms. Do the same for all the files you've made. Make a complete copy for yourself and take one to your tax preparer, if you have one. Go down the checklist before your appointment and make sure you have everything need for your tax preparation. Although the forms in this book may refer to another tax year, they can be photocopied and used every year.

Pre-Appointment Check List for tax preparer:

Do you have the following:

| | YES | NO |
|---|---|---|
| W-2 Forms | o | o |
| 1099's and/or records of Income | o | o |
| Statements of Interest Earned | o | o |
| Statements of Dividends Earned | o | o |
| Unemployment Compensation | o | o |
| State Tax Refund | o | o |
| Strike Benefits | o | o |
| Welfare Aid | o | o |
| Social Security Benefits | o | o |
| Prior Year's Tax Return | o | o |
| Other Income Records (Cash or otherwise Not Reported) | o | o |
| Completed Tax Information Packet | o | o |

# OTHER EXPENSES

SCHEDULE A Deductions

| | |
|---|---|
| **MEDICAL** - Expenses NOT reimbursed by insurance. These can include Doctor, Dentist, Insurance Premiums, Therapists, Chiropractor, Eyeglasses, Prescription Drugs, etc. | |
| **DMV REGISTRATION** - Enter TOTAL amount paid to register your car(s) | |
| **CHARITABLE CONTRIBUTIONS:** CASH Contributions | |
| GOODS: (Other than Cash, i.c, Goodwill, Salvation Army) | |
| **MORTGAGE INTEREST CHARGES:** _(Don't Forget Points)_ | |
| **PROPERTY TAX PAID:** | |
| **INCOME TAX PREPARATION:** | |
| **LEGAL FEES: (For Business Purposes Only)** | |

Do NOT Total

| ADJUSTMENTS TO INCOME (1040) | |
|---|---|
| ALIMONY PAID: Amount:               Ex-Spouse's Soc. Sec. # | |
| MOVING EXPENSES: Shipping/Truck Rental, Lodging, Misc. Expenses | |

# PERFORMING ARTS EXPENSES

| DESCRIPTION | TOTAL |
|---|---|
| ADVERTISING & PUBLICITY (Photos, Resumes, Post Cards, Players Directory, Ads, Etc. | |
| AUDITION TAPE (Video Resume, Voice-Over, Demo Tape, Etc. | |
| GIFTS FOR BUSINESS (Limit $25 per person per year) | |
| AGENTS COMMISSION & MANAGERS' FEES | |
| THEATER COMPANY DUES | |
| EQUIPMENT (Restrictions may apply, enter total, amount from form) | |
| OFFICE SUPPLIES/STATIONARY/POSTAGE | |
| STUDIO RENTAL/RENTAL OF BUSINESS PROPERTY (Cable TV, Equip. Rental) | |
| MAINTENANCE OF PROFESSIONAL COSTUMES (Do not include general streetwear) | |
| REPAIRS AND MAINTENANCE ON EQUIPMENT | |
| WARDROBE/AUTO EXPENSES PAID BY EMPLOYER (From W-2) | |
| COSTUMES FOR PROFESSIONAL USE (Not general streetwear) | |
| MAKE-UP, HAIR CARE & NAILS (Performance Supplies, Photo Sessions, Specific Job Requirements, i.e. Hand Model-Not general street use) | |
| SUPPLIES FOR RESEARCH (Sheet Music, Books, Tapes, Scripts, Props, Etc.) | |
| ANSWERING SERVICE/BEEPER/CALLING SERVICE | |
| TELEPHONE (Business Toll Calls & Long Distance, Call Waiting, Pay Phones, Mobile Phones, Second Line, Fax Line, Credit Card Business Calls, Etc.) | |
| COACHING LESSONS FOR PERFORMANCE (Acting & Dance Classes, Casting Director Workshops, Etc.) | |
| TICKETS FOR RESEARCH (Theater, Movies, Video Rentals, Film Societies) | |
| TRADE PUBLICATIONS (Variety, Backstage, Dramalogue, Hollywood Reporter, Ross Reports, etc.) | |
| ACCOMPANIST & AUDITION EXPENSE | |
| UNION DUES & INITIATION FEES (Include 2% AEA Working Dues) | |
| TOTAL | |

## DO NOT WRITE IN THIS BOOK. PERMISSION GRANTED TO PHOTOCOPY

# EXAMPLES OF DEDUCTIBLE BUSINESS MILEAGE

| Miles per Round Trip | x | Total Trips | = | Total Mileage | x | $ Per Mile | = | Total $ Deductible | Purpose of Trips |
|---|---|---|---|---|---|---|---|---|---|
| 25 | x | 40 | = | 1000 | x | $.275 | = | $275 | Agent Visits |
| 26 | x | 36 | = | 936 | x | $.275 | = | 257 | Interviews |
| 26 | x | 12 | = | 312 | x | $.275 | = | 86 | Making Rounds |
| 40 | x | 22 | = | 880 | x | $.275 | = | 242 | Classes |
| 40 | x | 18 | = | 720 | x | $.275 | = | 198 | Workshop |
| 20 | x | 18 | = | 360 | x | $.275 | = | 99 | Non-Paid Rehearsal |
| 110 | x | 2 | = | 110 | x | $.275 | = | 30 | Return to LA from out of town |
| 15 | x | 1 | = | 30 | x | $.275 | = | 8 | Trip(s) from 1st to 2nd Job |
| 2 | x | 2 | = | 20 | x | $.275 | = | 5 | Trip(s) to photographer |
| | | | | 4368 | | $.275 | = | $1,201 | |

## AVERAGE ROUND TRIP COMMUTING TO A PAID JOB (NOT DEDUCTIBLE)

| Miles per Round Trip | x | # of Total Days | = | Total Mileage | Job | Describe |
|---|---|---|---|---|---|---|
| 40 | x | 3 | = | 120 | MGM | Movie - "All is Found" |
| 26 | x | 4 | = | 104 | Paramount | TV - "Somebody Spoke" |
| 14 | x | 10 | = | 140 | Universal | TV - "Apple Mountain" |
| 10 | x | 40 | = | 400 | Mom's Diner | Singing Waiter |
| 18 | x | 20 | = | 360 | Hudson | Play - The Tea Party |
| | | | = | 1124 | | |

Assume you drove your car a total of 10,000 miles during the year.

| | |
|---|---|
| 10,000 | Total Miles |
| 4,368 | Deductible Business Miles |
| 1,124 | Non-deductible Business Miles |
| 4,508 | Personal Miles |
| _____ | |

HOLLYWOOD

# VEHICLE EXPENSE FORM

**DO NOT WRITE IN THIS BOOK. PERMISSION GRANTED TO PHOTOCOPY**

| | Car # 1 | Car # 2 |
|---|---|---|
| YEAR, MAKE & MODEL | | |
| DATE VEHICLE PLACED IN SERVICE (When you started using the car) | | |
| TOTAL MILES DRIVEN THIS YEAR (Interview, Agents, Photography, Printers, etc.) | | |
| COMMUTING MILES DRIVEN THIS YEAR (Work: To and From) | | |
| MILES FOR MEDICAL PURPOSES (Doctors, Dentists, Therapists, Rx, etc.) | | |
| MILES FOR CHARITABLE PURPOSES | | |
| CAB, BUS FARE, etc. | | |
| PARKING FEES (include Meters, Garages, etc. for Business Purposes) | | |
| **ACTUAL VEHICLE EXPENSES** | | |
| GAS, OIL REPAIRS, INSURANCE, etc. | | |
| VEHICLE RENTALS (Total of all Rentals) | | |
| LEASE AGREEMENT (Total of all Payments) | | |
| PRICE OF CAR (if purchased this year) | | |
| DATE OF PURCHASE: | | |

HOLLYWOOD

# EQUIPMENT EXPENSE FORM
## (TV, VCR, FAX MACHINE, PHONE, TAPE RECORDERS, ETC.)

Employ specifically for business. The same is true for any equipment purchased that can have applications in your life outside your Equipment purchased for business use is a deduction up to the limit you use that equipment SPE-CIALLY for business. Some items, like a Phone Answering Machine, you must have in the acting profession but since most people have an answering machine, the IRS wants you to determine what percentage of use of that machine you performing profession, i.e,. Camcorders, Televisions, etc.

| Item Description | Date | Amount | % Business Use | Net Write-Off |
|---|---|---|---|---|
| | | | (times) | = |
| | | | (times) | = |
| | | | (times) | = |
| | | | (times) | = |
| | | | (times) | = |
| | | | (times) | = |

# ENTERTAINMENT FOR BUSINESS FORM

## (EVENTS, BUSINESS LUNCHES & DINNERS, ETC.)

Although we do not expect you to write the information down for every entertainment event you are deducting here, you must be able to offer the following information to substantiate your expenses. This information should be kept in your expenses log or diary accompanied by proper records or receipts. You MUST have the following information for every event. If there is insufficient room on this form just place the total expense figure here.

| NAME (Person Entertained) | Date | Business Purpose | Location | Amount |
|---|---|---|---|---|
| | | | | |
| | | | | |
| | | | | |
| | | | | |
| | | | | |
| | | | | |
| | | | TOTAL AMOUNT | |

# OUT OF TOWN - INTERVIEW & JOBS - EXPENSES FORM

(These are the forms you use when shooting on location.)

| Trip No. | Employer & Address | Inclusive Dates | No. of Days |
|---|---|---|---|
| 1. | | | |
| 2. | | | |
| 3. | | | |
| 4. | | | |
| 5. | | | |
| 6. | | | |
| | | TOTAL No. of Days | |

| EXPENSES | # 1 | # 2 | # 3 | # 4 | # 5 | # 6 |
|---|---|---|---|---|---|---|
| Commercial Expenses | | | | | | |
| Lodging Expenses | | | | | | |
| Local Transportation | | | | | | |
| Auto Rental | | | | | | |
| Gasoline / Oil / Repairs | | | | | | |
| Telephone | | | | | | |
| Parking | | | | | | |
| Tips / Laundry / Other | | | | | | |
| Sub Total | | | | | | |
| Per Diem Paid (Subtract) | - | - | - | - | - | - |
| Total Above Expenses | | | | | | |
| Meals / Food | | | | | | |

TOTAL MEALS (Only) [ ]

Total Expenses (except meals) [ ]

HOLLYWOOD

# Appendix

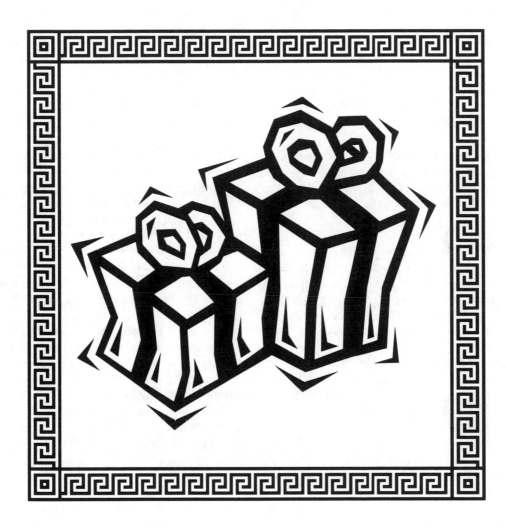

# GLAM SCAM
## WHAT'S WRONG WITH THIS PICTURE?
### By Erik Joseph

**"Since the dawn of motion pictures as an industry, glam scams have been a perpetual blight for legitimate producers and a variety of victims."**

The whole town is talking about the exciting upcoming major film project. Paramount Film's sequel to The Long Rider, starring Keith Carradine. The city has extended the red carpet to the production company's location manager. He asked for a complimentary rental car for scouting, and got it. He asked for a complimentary cellular phone, and got it. He asked for complimentary hotel accommodations, and got them. He needed a production office for casting the female lead and he got it!

Cut!

What's wrong with this picture? Let's take a moment to analyze the scene. First of all, what is "Paramount Films?" Is it affiliated with Paramount Pictures or simply an intentional sound-a-like? Second, United Artists made The Long Riders, not Paramount! Third, Is Keith Carradine really attached to the project? A call to his agent would verify (or discount) such a claim. And the kicker: Why is a location manager conducting a casting call— for the female lead? Upon scrutiny, this project and the location manager seem a sham.

Fraudulent individuals who pass themselves off as legitimate producers can leave a damaging impression of the entire industry ruining reputations of legitimate production companies, plus complicating the life of a film commissioner. Local businesses can get "taken" of goods and services, not to mention the possible perils the local talent may face. Entertainment industry frauds can be a public safety issue—sometimes a matter of life and death. Extreme cases have revealed incidents of kidnappers pretending to be photographers, rapists pretending to be producers, and murderers pretending to be agents.

May 11, 1987; South Lake Tahoe, California: Herbert J. Coddington, aka "Mark Clayton," poses as a producer and kidnaps two teenage models and their adult escorts. Coddington strangles the adults, then proceeds with his twisted plan to murder the young girls in full view of news cameras. The FBI makes a last second rescue.

Glamour industry scams, or "glam scams," are not uncommon. Since the dawn of motion pictures as an industry, glam scams have been a perpetual blight for legitimate producers and for a variety of victims. From Portland to Corpus Christi, from Toronto to Boise, Memphis, San Diego, Oklahoma City—glam scams have even crossed the country and back.

For nine months in 1992, glam scammers calling themselves "Patrick Swayze Productions," defrauded actors in numerous cities. Also known as "Rob Lowe Productions" this bogus set-up promised parts in non-existent movies. All actors had to do was send $250-$450 through the mail for "union dues."

What can be done? Studios need to be open with information that will expose the perpetrator. In the case of sound-a-like situations, Joan Hansen, 20th Century Fox's legal counsel advises film commissions to "contact the head of production at the studio. They will know the names of all projects in production and in preparation." Another option is to call the studio's Legal Affairs Office directly. Studios and production companies are extremely sensitive to unauthorized use of their names, properties and copyrights and will act promptly and aggressively to stop such malpractices.

For concerned producers, film commissioners or talent, business license checks are a fundamental defense against glam scams. A general rule of thumb to remember is that any individual or business involved in the exchange of money for goods or services must possess a business license. Nearly all forms of commerce are regulated through licensing.

Have difficulty getting through to Business Licensing, Secretary of State or

Department of Labor? Data Resources Unlimited (P.O. Box 26119, Las Vegas, NV (702) 792-1332), is an organization that is working to provide extensive licensing and consumer information via a new on-line computer network. Although currently completing its Nevada database, Data Resources' spokesperson Paula Young says the company's goal is to provide national coverage in six to nine months.

The system operates by modem and is updated every twenty-four hours. With a few simple keystrokes comprehensive business license data is provided. There are other protective steps to take, more easily handled by commissioners.

Let your city, county and state laws work for you. If a county regulation holds that model agencies can not advertise using phrases such as:

"Someone to enjoy"
"Group discounts"
"Call anytime"
"Nude models"

then your local newspaper should not print such advertising. Establish a positive working relationship with your area newspaper advertising managers. Help them and they will help you.

Ask your daily newspapers, entertainment weeklies and campus newspapers to publish a periodic public notice, like the one the "Oregonian" runs for Oregon Film Office Director David Woolson:

**If you have questions regarding advertising for actors and/or production companies, you may call the State of Oregon Film Office at (503) 373-1232.** The notice serves a two-fold purpose, says Woolson. "First, it sensitizes people. It allows them to pause. It also helps to dissuade scam artists thinking of placing and ad."

Meet with your city and county licensing investigators, Labor Division, Consumer Affairs, Better Business Bureau, Chamber of Commerce, Metro Police (Fraud, Bunco, Vice), FBI branch office, Attorney General, District Attorneys, Secretary of State and local television consumer affairs reporter. Let them know of your goal to help keep the entertainment industry a safe industry in your state.

Another way to check out a company's or individual's legitimacy is by analyzing their business card. Though you won't always be able to tell the good guys from the bad guys simply by looking at a business card, it is tangible evidence—a starting point. For instance, note any union, guild or professional association logo. Is the individual in good standing? What is their reputation within the organization? The information provided by the business card reflects the professionalism and credibility of the person who offers it. Business cards without addresses and/or phone numbers, misspellings or pretentious phrases, like "Feature Entertainment Specialist," should be dubiously regarded.

*While shopping in a mall, a former beauty queen and model was approached by a man who claimed to be the producer of "Wheel of Fortune." His business card include his name, the word "Producer" and a phone number scratched out and replaced with his home number on the back of the card. "Call me," he told her, and he would make her the new Vanna White. The model called her state film office to check the man's validity. One phone call to the producers of "Wheel of Fortune" proved the man was a fake.*

The short term effect of unrestricted glam scam activity is a matter of risk. If an area is perceived as unsafe, production companies may re-think their location choices. Long-term effects involve permanent relocation and economic development. Businesses do not relocate to dangerous places, they move out of them!

Last year, Sue Wagner, Nevada's Lieutenant Governor and Chair of the Commission on Economic Development sponsored statewide anti-scam workshops through her State's Motion Picture Division.

"The state has a responsibility to create awareness of the potential problems brought on by unscrupulous talent agents, producers and photographers," says Wagner. She says the workshops were a successful public service effort.

Nevada Motion Picture Division Director Bob Hirsch believes a pro-active, anti-scam effort promotes the industry in-state and out-of-state. "Above all, we feel we have a definite duty to our communities. After all, we brought the business in, it's our responsibility to warm against the bad elements," says Hirsch. "The entire industry sighs with relief when an industry con is caught."

**July 22, 1993; Detroit, Michigan:** Marc Hendley, the "Transvestite Scam Artist," is charged with multiple counts of fraud. Alias "Angela Barnett," Hendley claimed to be a temperamental soap-opera actress and conned Lear Jet flights, limousines, expensive champagne, bouquets of flowers, cellular phone service and more.

Hendley was extradited to Las Vegas where a District Judge sentenced him/her to six years in prison.

A recent breakthrough report compiled by the Nevada Film Office, at the request of that state's Labor Commission, summarizes regulations which govern "Entertainment Agencies" (i.e., talent, model, theatrical, booking agencies) nationwide. *Entertainment Agencies: Laws & Regulations Nationwide* contains information on states that have specific talent agency laws and those that do not. Laws are different from state-to-state, so it is not surprising that the most convenient plea by glam scammers is ignorance of the law. Conversely, this can be used to the state's advantage since ignorance of the law is no excuse. The issue is black and white: if the law says you need a license, get one-or move on.

States handle problems differently. Some do not have problems with glam scams. AFCI President Leigh von der Esch says safety procedures start with providing a production directory. Generally, production and support service companies are only listed in production manuals if they show proof of a business license. Individuals are usually asked to provide verifiable references and/or resumes. Von der Esch also suggests that film commissioners have information available on talent agency laws. She adds that the AFCI is in the process of establishing policies in the area of scam abatement.

Some states already offer printed materials cautioning talent and models about unscrupulous agents, producers, photographers, etc.

Recent glam scams have been reported by reality-based and investigative TV shows, trade publications and general interest magazines. The media likes consumer protection stories. Film commissioners can use this to their advantage by involving the media in public service announcements; and public anti-scam workshops. The recommended public message from the industry should be:

*The mechanisms of the star-making machinery do not include people who hang out at malls, health clubs, beaches, high schools, video stores or ice cream shops looking for undiscovered talent. The days of "I can make you a star" are gone. The entertainment industry is no longer that simple.*

---

*Erik Joseph is Assistant Director of the Nevada Film Office. He conducts entertainment industry anti-scam seminars and is the author of The Glam Scam, from Lone Eagle Publishers.*

## U.S. Department of Justice
Immigration and Naturalization Service

OMB No. 1115-0136
Employment Eligibility Verification

Please read instructions carefully before completing this form. The instructions must be available during completion of this form. ANTI-DISCRIMINATION NOTICE. It is illegal to discriminate against work eligible individuals. Employers CANNOT specify which document(s) they will accept from an employee. The refusal to hire an individual because of a future expiration date may also constitute illegal discrimination.

**Section 1. Employee Information and Verification.** To be completed and signed by employee at the time employment begins

| Print Name | Last | First | Middle Initial | Maiden Name |
|---|---|---|---|---|

Address (Street Name and Number | Apt. # | Date of Birth(month/day/year)

City | State | Zip Code | Social Security #

I am aware that federal law provides for imprisonment and/or fines for false statement use of false documents in connection with the completion of this form

I attest, under penalty of perjury, that I am
___ A citizen or national of the U.S.
___ A Lawful Permanent Resident (Alien # A _____
___ An alien authorized to work until ___/___/___
(Alien # or Admission # _____

Employee's Signature | Date (month/day/year)

**Preparer and/or Translator Certification.** (To be completed and signed if Section 1 is prepared by a person other than the employee.) I attest under penalty of perjury, that I has assisted in the completion of this form and that to the best of my knowledge the information is true and correct.

Preparer's/Translator's Signature | Print Name

Address (Street Name and Number, City, State, Zip Code) | Date(month/day/year)

**Section 2. Employer Review and Verification.** To be completed and signed by employer. Examine one document from List A OR examine one document from List B and one from List C as listed on the reverse of this form and record the title, number and expiration date, if any, of the document(s)

| | List A | OR | List B | AND | List C |
|---|---|---|---|---|---|
| Document title | _____ | | _____ | | _____ |
| Issuing Authority | _____ | | _____ | | _____ |
| Document # | _____ | | _____ | | _____ |
| Expiration Date (if any) | _/_/_ | | _/_/_ | | _/_/_ |
| Document # | _____ | | | | |
| Expiration Date (if any) | _/_/_ | | | | |

**CERTIFICATION** I attest under penalty of perjury, that I have examined the document(s) presented by the above-named employee, that the above-listed document(s) appear to be genuine and to relate to the employee named, that the employee began employment on (month/day/year) _/_/_ and that to the best of my knowledge the employee is eligible to work in the United States. (State employment agencies may omit the date the employee began employment).

Signature of Employer or Authorized Representative | Print Name | Title

Business or Organization Name | Address(Street Name and Name,, City, State, Zip) | Date (mo/day/yr.

**Section 3. Updating and Reverification.** To be completed and signed by employer

A. New Name (if applicable) | B. Date of rehire (mo/date/yr) (if applicable).

C. If employee's previous grant of work authorization has expired, provide the information below for the document that establishes current employment eligibility.

Document Title: _____ Document #:_____ Exp. Date (if any)_/_/_

I attest, under penalty of perjury, that to the best of my knowledge, this employee is eligible to work in the United States, and if the employee presented document(s), the document(s) I have examined appear to be genuine and to relate to the individual.

Signature of Employer or Authorized Representative | Date(month/day/year)

Form I-9 (Rev 11-21-91) N    **ACTUAL FORM AVAILABLE FROM DEPT. OF JUSTICE**

# I-9 LIST OF ACCEPTABLE DOCUMENTS

| LIST A | LIST B | LIST C |
|---|---|---|
| **Documents that Establish Identity and Employment Eligibility** | **Documents that Establish Identity** | **Documents that Establish Employment Eligibility** |
| | OR | AND |

**LIST A — Documents that Establish Identity and Employment Eligibility**

1. U.S. Passport (unexpired or expired)

2. Certificate of U.S. Citizenship (INS Form N-560 or N-561)

3. Certificate of Naturalization (INS Form N-550 or N-570)

4. Unexpired foreign passport, with I-551 stamp or attached INS Form I-94 indicating unexpired employment authorization

5. Alien Registration Receipt Card with photograph (INS Form I-551 or I-551)

6. Unexpired Temporary Resident Card (INS Form I-688)

7. Unexpired Employment Authorization Card (INS Form 668A)

8. Unexpired Reentry Permit (INS Form I-327)

9. Unexpired Refugee Travel Document (INS Form I-571)

10. Unexpired Employment Authorization Document issued by the INS which contains a photograph (INS Form I-688B)

**LIST B — Documents that Establish Identity**

1. Driver's license or ID card issued by a state or outlying possession of the United States provided it contains a photograph or information such as name, date of birth, sex, height, eye color, and address

2. ID card issued by federal, state, or local government agencies or entities provided it contains a photograph or information such as name, date of birth, sex, height, eye color, and address

3. School ID card with a photograph

4. Voter's registration card

5. U.S. Military card or draft record

6. Military dependent's ID card

7. U.S. Coast Guard Merchant Mariner Card

8. Native American tribal document

9. Driver's license issued by a Canadian government authority

**For persons under age 18 who are unable to present a document listed above:**

10. School record or report card

11. Clinic, doctor, or hospital record

12. Day-care or nursery school record

**LIST C — Documents that Establish Employment Eligibility**

1. U.S. social security card issued by the Social Security Administration (other than a card stating it is not valid for employment)

2. Certification of Birth Abroad issued by the Department of State (Form FS-545 or Form DS-1350)

3. Original or certified copy of a birth certificate issued by a state, county, municipal authority or outlying possession of the United States bearing an official seal

4. Native American tribal document

5. U.S. Citizen ID Card (INS Form I-197)

6. ID Card for use of Resident Citizen in the United States (INS Form I-179)

7. Unexpired employment authorization document issued by the INS (other than those listed under List A)

**DOCUMENT HAS BEEN ALTERED TO FIT THE PAGES OF THIS BOOK**

## AFTRA PRIME TIME DRAMATIC TELEVISION (EXHIBIT A)
## EMPLOYMENT OF <u>DAY</u> ACTOR

Company _____ Date _____

<u>Date Employment Starts</u> _____ Name _____

<u>Part</u> _____ Address _____

<u>Production Title</u> _____ Telephone No. _____

<u>Production Number</u> _____ Social Security No. _____

<u>Daily Rate</u> _____ Weekly Conversion Rate _____

THIS AGREEMENT covers the employment of the above-named performer by_____ _____ in the production and at the rate of compensation set forth above and is subject to and shall include, for the benefit of the performer and the Producer, all of the applicable provisions and conditions contained or provided for in the AFTRA 1991-1994 National Code of Fair Practice for Network Television Broadcasting (herein called the "Code"). Performer's employment shall include performance in non-commercial openings, closing, bridges, etc., and no added compensation shall be payable to performer so long as such are used in the role and episode covered hereunder in which performer appears; for other use, performer shall be paid the added minimum compensation, if any, required under the provisions of AFTRA;s agreements with Producer.

Producer shall have all the rights in and to the results and proceeds of the performer's services rendered hereunder, as are provided with respect to programs in Exhibit A of the Code and the right to Supplemental Market use as defined in Exhibit D of the Code.

Producer shall the unlimited right throughout the world to telecast the program and exhibit the program theatrically and in Supplemental Markets in accordance with the terms and conditions of Exhibits A and D of the Code.

If the program is rerun on television in the United States or Canada and contains any of the results and proceeds of the performer's services, the performer will be paid for each day of employment hereunder the additional compensation prescribed therefor by Exhibit A of the Code, unless there is an agreement to pay an amount in excess thereof as follows:

_____
_____
_____
_____
_____

If there is foreign telecasting of the program as defined in Exhibit A of the Code, and such program contains any of the results and proceeds of the performer's services, the performer will be paid the amount in the blank space below for each day of employment hereunder, of if such blank space is not filled in, then the performer will be paid the minimum additional compensation prescribed therefor by Exhibit A of the Code.

If the program is exhibited theatrically anywhere in the world and contains any of the results and proceeds of the performer's services, the performer will be paid for each day of employment hereunder $_____, or if this blank is not filled in, then the performer will be paid the minimum additional compensation prescribed therefor by Exhibit A of the Code.

If the program is exhibited in Supplemental Markets anywhere in the world and contains any of the results and proceeds of the performer's services, the performer will be paid the Supplemental Market fees prescribed by the applicable provisions of Exhibit D of the Code.

Initial

If the performer places his initials in the box he thereby authorizes Producer to use portions of said television program as a trailer to promote another episode or the series as a whole, upon payment to the performer of the additional compensation prescribed by the applicable provisions of Exhibit A of the Code.

By_____

_____

NOTICE TO PERFORMER: IT IS IMPORTANT THAT YOU RETAIN A COPY OF THIS CONTRACT FOR YOUR PERMANENT RECORDS.

Production time reports are available on the set at the end of each day, which reports should be signed or initialed by performer.

**CONTRACT HAS BEEN RESIZED TO FIT CONSTRAINTS OF THIS BOOK.**

# UNIFORM MODEL RELEASE

| Invoice To |
| --- |
| Address |
| City & State |
| Attn. Of |

| Studio/Client | Dept/Product |
| --- | --- |

| P.O. No./Release No/Catalog |
| --- |

| Model | | |
| --- | --- | --- |
| Date | | |
| Rate | Time<br>Fr    To | Amount |
| Overtime | Time<br>Fr    To | Amount |
| Fitting<br>Date | Time<br>Fr    To | Amount |
| **Total subject to<br>service charge** | | |

In consideration of receipt of the fee (inclusive of service fee) negotiated with

my manager, I hereby sell, assign and grant to _____

(Ad Agency or Publication)

_____ The right and permission to copyright

Client or Advertiser

and/or publish one photograph or likeness of me in which I may be in whole or

in part of composite or reproduction thereof in color or otherwise, in United

States and _____ For _____

Other Territories                    Usage, for example print, packaging

for _____ for _____ months to begin no later

Product

than four(4) months from this date.

Accordingly, I release and discharge the companies and persons named above and
persons acting for or on behalf of them from any liability by virtue of any blur-
ring, distortion, alteration, optical illusion, or use in composite form that may
occur or be produced in the taking of said picture or in any processing thereof
through completion of the finished product.

Usage rights apply only to the above mentioned. All other usage to be renegotiated.

_____        _____
Client's Representative                            Model's Signature

**OFFICE COPY - WHITE        MODEL'S COPY - YELLOW        CLIENT'S COPY - PINK**

HOLLYWOOD

# Glossary

**Airbrushing**—A photographic process whereby certain flaws in a picture are gently blown off of a master print.

**Air checks**—A recording made of a televised show on 3/4" tape to be used for demo reels.

**Apple Boxes**—Wooden crates that elevate either an actor, a camera or furniture on a set.

**Billing**—The size of an actor's role such as starring or guest starring. Also, where the actor's name will be placed in the credits and if the name will be shown on the screen alone or with others.

**Book Out**—A call to all of your agents to let them know you are working, traveling or are unavailable for auditions or a job.

**Borderless** —A photograph that takes up the full space of the paper with no white edges.

**Boom Mike**—A microphone on the end of a pole, held above actor's heads to record dialogue.

**Bump Up**—An upgrade in pay and billing when an Extra says a few words.

**Buyout**—A one-time payment for shooting and airing a commercial.

**Callback**—A second audition where an actor is either presented to the producer and director or, in the case of commercials, is filmed on tape again for final consideration.

**Circle Takes**—A director's favorite or most usable filming of a particular scene. Used to expedite the editing process.

**Class A Network Spot**—Commercial airing at prime time on a major network.

**Concept Meeting**—A gathering of the producer, director & casting director to reach an agreement about the look and quality of each character in a script.

**Continuity**—Matching action in each take of a scene with the same wardrobe and make up.

**Control Booth**—A glass-enclosed area full of equipment where an engineer and director sit during looping and dubbing sessions.

**Copy**—A slang term for dialogue in a commercial.

**Dark Night**—An evening on which a theater is not scheduled to have a public performance.

**Day Shot**—A specific scene in the script to be filmed or taped while the sun is out.

**Drive To**—Monies paid to an Actor by a production company for driving to location other than a studio lot.

**Earprompter**—A small tape recorder system which the entire script is recorded and is transmitted to an earpiece through a loop around the neck. It is activated by a foot or hand control. Known in the industry as "the ear."

**Exterior Shot**—A scene filmed or taped out of doors.

**Generation**—The process whereby each time you copy a piece of film or tape it losses some clarity.

**Headshot**—A term used to designate an 8" x 10" photograph of an actor used for securing television, film and theatrical work.

**Hiatus**—Time of year when the cast and crew of a TV series is on vacation.

**Hold Over**—When a director decides to use an actor for an extra day not originally scheduled.

**Honey Wagon**—A bank of dressing rooms attached together and pulled by a tractor trailer to a shooting location.

**Image**—The casting type or quality you wish to convey and portray to the theatrical community.

**Interior Shot**—A scene shot inside a sound stage or inside a set on location.

**J-Card**—The artwork on an audio cassette box named for the shape it makes when folded to fit in the box.

**Lithography**—A printing process as opposed to a photographic process used to inexpensively reproduce a large quantity of headshots.

**Local**—A commercial airing in only one city, generally close to where it is cast.

**Looping**—The art of matching lip movements and vitality of action in a scene. Dialogue that is added in post-production on a sound stage.

**Mark**—An "X" taped to the floor on commercial auditions where the camera is pre-focused.

**Meal Penalty**—Additional monies paid if a working cast or crew member has not been fed after the six hours allotted by union contracts.

**Mike**—Attaching a wireless transmitter to an actors body or clothes to record dialogue.

**Model Zed Card**—A series of photographs, usually in color, printed on a two- or four-sided card used for securing modeling work.

**Must Join**—A situation in which an actor has used up the 30-day grace period to join a union and upon hiring for the next job must join that union.

**National**—A commercial airing everywhere in the United States.

**Night Shot**—A scene specified in the script to be filmed when it is dark out.

**Non-Linear Editing**—Putting scenes together in a computer with the ability to move them around out of order for ease in building a demo tape, or a scene in a movie or commercial.

**On Hold**—A situation that occurs when an actor is contracted to be available for the next day's shoot but will not have to report to the set until called.

**Out Takes**—Parts of an original filming or taping that will not be used in editing the finished product.

**Parent Union**—The first professional union you join; subsequent unions are sister unions.

**Pay-per-airing**—Monies paid to an actor each time a television commercial is shown.
**Photo Double**—An actor who physically resembles a star and replaces the star during dangerous or nude scenes.

**Pilot Presentation**—A one-day shoot to give a network an idea of the look and feel of a proposed program available to be produced into a new series.

**Playbill**—A theatrical program in which an actors' biography appears.

**Pre-reads**—An advance reading by a casting director who is unfamiliar with an actor's work prior to taking the actor to meet a producer or director.

**Press Kit**—A presentation including: newspaper clippings, review of movie and theater productions, a biography, headshot and resume given to the media and interested industry professionals. Also called a press *package*.

**Queued Up**—Previewing a tape and having it set to start playing at the beginning of a scene.

**Reader**—Another actor who is paid or volunteers to help the casting office by playing all the other characters during an audition so the casting director can concentrate on the actor being screened.

**Recall**—When at the end of a work day, a production company decides to use your services for an additional day.

**Regional**—A commercial airing in a part of the United States.

**Retouching**—A photographic process whereby certain flaws in a picture are covered up or removed.

**Rider to Contract**—An addition to a performer's union contract that outlines a special circumstance for pay and airing privileges given to the production company by a union.

**Run Throughs**—Rehearsals before the actual filming of a scene.

**Rush Calls**—A last minute call by an agency to an actor for an audition or a job.

**Second Take**—Being taped or filmed an additional time in a scene or audition allowing an actor to change his or her performance.

**Second Team**—A group of stand-ins who take the primary actors' places allowing them to rest during lighting changes and camera rehearsals.

**Set Call Time**—The moment the actor is expected to be in front of the camera in full make up and wardrobe, ready to begin working.

**Shoot Around You**—Shooting other scenes in a script until a particular actor is available.

**Showcase**—An evening of scenes either prepared and rehearsed ahead of time or done as a cold reading for industry professionals who may cast the actors in roles.

**Sides**—Several important scenes pulled out of an entire script to be used for auditions.

**Sign-in Sheet**—Exhibit E SAG/AFTRA Audition Report which an actor fills out and initials upon arrival at a casting office.

**Signing Out**—The act of entering the time you exit an audition on the Exhibit E Sign-in Sheet.

**Sister Union—One or more a**dditional unions you join after the first one. The first union you join is your parent union.

**Size Card**—A form filled out at commercial casting sessions to inform wardrobe people of your clothing sizes.

**Slate**—The act of stating your name on a commercial audition while being videotaped.

**Sloppy Border**—A type of border surrounding a photograph that looks as though it were painted on with a paint brush and has an uneven quality.

**Spots**—An industry term for commercials.

**Squibs**—Radio-controlled explosive packets of fake blood attached to an actor's body.

**Storyboard**—A series of hand-drawn pictures depicting the sequence in which a commercial will appear in its final form to tell the story.

**Stunt**—A dangerous scene; alternately, a publicity event designed to call attention to a project or a particular actor.

**Stunt Pay**—Additional hazard money paid to an actor or stuntperson to perform dangerous scenes.

**Tear Sheets**—An actual copy of a print ad torn out of a newspaper or magazine and put in a model's portfolio.

**Teleprompter**—A machine placed in front of the lens of a camera on which an actor's dialogue is projected. The dialogue scrolls by and is read when at eye level.

**Test Photographers**—Photographers willing to barter their services at a reduced rate to help themselves and a new model build their respective portfolios.

**The Trades**—Industry newspapers and magazines read by all professionals to keep up with trends and news in the entertainment business.

**Trailer**—A mobile dressing room for an Actor sometimes in a camper. See *Honey Wagon*.

**Usage Fee**—The practice of assigning each city in the U.S. points based on population. An actors residuals on television commercials are calculated based on the accumulation of these points in 13-week cycles.

**Video Toaster**—A popular computer editing system for actor's demo tapes.

**Wild Spot**—A commercial airing randomly in any given market.

**Work Vouchers**—A paper given to an Extra at the time of check-in. It must be filled out and turned in at the end of the day of shooting to receive wages.

# Bibliography

**The Agencies—**
**What An Actor Needs to Know**
Hollywood, Acting World Books, 2001

**Back to One—A Movie Extra's Guidebook:**
**How to Make Good Money as a Background**
**Actor in Film**
Chambers, Cullen
Los Angeles, Cullen Chambers, 2000

**casting by...A directory of the Casting Society of America, its members and**
**their credits**
Casting Society of America
Los Angeles, Breakdown Services, 2001

**The CD Directory**
Breakdown Services
Los Angeles, Breakdown Services, 2001

**Getting Your Script Through the**
**Hollywood Maze-An Insiders Guide**
Stuart, Linda

**Hero of 1,000 Faces**
Campbell, Joseph
Doubleday, 1988

**How to Enter Screenplay Contests**
**and Win!**
Joseph, Eric
Lone Eagle Publishing, 1998

**How to Make It In Hollywood—**
**All the Right Moves**
Buzzell, Linda
New York, Harper Perennial, 1996

**How to Star in Your Own TV Show**
**for $50 or Less**
Darby, Glenn
Big Red Barn Productions, 1999

**How to Write a Movie in 21 Days**
King, Vicki

**How to Sell Your Idea to Hollywood**
Kosberg, Bob

**It's A Freeway Out There**
Belshe, Judy
Los Angeles, Judy Belshe, 2000

**The Long Schmooze**
Belshe, Judy
Los Angeles, Judy Belshe 2001

**Making a Good Screenplay Great**
Seger, Linda

**Power Schmoozing—The New Etiquette for**
**Social and Business Success**
Mandell, Terri
New York, McGraw-Hill, 1996

**Show Biz Kids Quest for Success: An**
**Enlightened Guide for Succeeding and Sur-**
**viving in Hollywood,**
**(Ages Infant - 18)**
Grant, Ruthie O.
Los Angeles, E.T.C. Publishing House, 1994

**Survival Jobs; 118 Ways to Make Money**
**While Pursuing Your Dreams.**
Jacobson, Deborah
Los Angeles, Windtree Publishing, 1998

**The Thomas Brothers Guide**
Thomas Brothers Maps
Los Angeles, Thomas Brothers Maps, 2001

**The Working Actor's Guide, L.A.**
Aaron Blake Publications
Los Angeles, Aaron Blake Productions, 2001

**MAGAZINE ARTICLES & REFERENCES**

*Details*
**Heidi Fleiss—Hollywood Madam**
Finke, Nikki
New York, Conde Nast Publications,
October 1993

**Glam Scam - What's Wrong With**
**This Picture?**
Joseph, Erik
Las Vegas, *Locations Magazine*
Expo '94 Issue. p46-52

# Index

HOLLYWOOD

## The Working Actors Guide $40

A resource book with everything to survive as a person and every service for a performing artist. This extensive guide is approximately 600 page. A must for actors and entertainers heading to L.A.

## The Secrets of Modeling A-Z $40

Produced by Elite Modeling Agency to give beginners all the tolls they will ever need to launch a career. Hosted by legendary career builder and former head of Elite, Valerie Trott. Five - 90 minute tapes.

## European Agency List $25

A newly published guide with all of the European Modeling agency addresses, phone and fax numbers to secure representation.

## Back to One - Background Extra Guide $20

How to make good money as a background actor in film. Includes a list of all extra casting offices and calling services. Each are rated from 1-4 stars for service to actors.

## New York Models Black Book $20

All the agencies in New York broken down by Fashion, Commercial, Children's and Specialty. Features a list of test photographers and places to garner showroom work.

## Mailing Labels $20

Looking for an agent or during a casting director to let them know your in town or working? The most up0 to date labels anywhere. 260 Agents or 325 Casting Directors

## Survival Jobs-Making Money While Pursuing Your Dreams $16

Hundreds of fun and stable survival jobs for artists everywhere. Outlines qualifications, pay scale, licenses and materials needed to carry out a successful sideline business.

**www.hollywoodhereicome.com**

## The National Casting Notices $99

Every week we will e-mail or fax you listings so you can submit your headshot and resume. In the U.S. we cover: films in development, films in preparation, films in pre-production, union films, non-union films, music video's, open casting calls, game shows, theater auditions, graduate films, student films and special type talent searches. Take charge of your career & let us point you toward the work. For those serious about their career.

## The Thomas Guide $25

The premier Los Angeles street guide and directory to help you locate audition offices and studios. It has an easy to index and is a necessity for people locating to L.A.

## Models Boot Camp Video - The Right Way to the Runway $25

The hottest new how-to-break into modeling video featuring the agents from L.A. Models & Talent, sexy TV stars Steve Wilder, Days of Our Lives; Ed Wasser, Babylon 5 and Cerina Vincent of Power Rangers.

## The Right Manager or Agent $15

Detailed lists of acting or modeling agents in the Los Angeles market. Each has a write up on the types of clients they handle. Also a hot sheet on types currently seeking.

## The Modeling Handbook $16

Offers advice from top models, agents & photographers covering the U.S. and European markets.

## The CD Directory $12.

This is a through listing of all the casting directors in Los Angeles along with their office addresses. Also has listing of casting offices in studios and locations of all commercial casting houses in L. A.

## Major Cities Help List $10

A list of agents, casting directors, photographers, theaters and film commission offices available for most major cities. Gets you going. Complete list on the web site.

HOLLYWOOD

# Hollywood
# Little Black Book

## Acting and Modeling Coaches
## Cartoons
    **Delores Diehl** (323) 384-9251

    **Susan Blu** (818) 783-9130

    **Louise Chamis** (818) 985-0130

## Children's Coaches
    **Academy Childrens Workshop** (818) 763-4431
      Everything from theater to dance.

    **Belinda Balaski** (323) 650-KIDS

    **Center Stage LA** (310) 837-4536
      Kevin McDermott handles kids 6-18 years old.

    **Divisek Casting** (323) 876-1554
      Karen is a childrens coach and a well known casting director.

    **Sarah Wood** - one of the best (818) 769-6424

    **Weist, Barron-Hill** - Andrea Hill for Television (818) 846-5595

    **David Wells** - for Teens (818) 753-5393

    **Young Actors Space** - Diane Hill Hardin (818) 785-7979

## Cold Reading
    **Brian Reise** (323) 274-5593

    **Stuart Fratkin** (818) 704-7701

    **Marjorie Haber** (310) 854-0870

## Commercials
    **Michael Cutt**- Adults and Children (310) 625-0397

    **Carolyne Barry** (323) 654-2212

    **Stuart Robinson** (310) 558-4961

## Improv
    **Acme Comedy Theater** (323) 525-0233

    **The Groundlings** (323) 934-4747

    **Harvey Lembeck** (3100 271-2831

    **Dee Marcus** (310) 395-1830

    **Avery Schreiber** (818) 989-4775

## Scene Study
    **Julie Ariola** (310) 535-6530

    **Janet Alhanti** (323) 465-2348

    **Joel Asher** (818) 785-1551

    **June Chandler** (800) 992-4948

    **Howard Fine** (323) 951-1221

    **Darryl Hickman** (323) 462-6565

    **Gordon Hunt**-Craig (818) 506-5566

    **David Kagen** (818) 901-8879

    **Harry Mastrogeorge** (323) 343-9102

    **Larry Moss** (310) 393-3801

## Voice-Over
    **Cindy Ackers/Voicetrax West** (323) 850-1112

    **Kalmenson & Kalmenson** (818) 342-6499

## Stand-Up Comedy
    **Judy Brown** (310) 396-8425

    **Judy Carter** (310) 915-0555

## Actors Equity Association Casting Hotlines

| | |
|---|---|
| **Atlanta** | (404) 257-2575 |
| **Boston** | (617) 720-6048 |
| **Chicago** | (312) 641-0418 |
| **Cleveland** | (216) 779-2001 |
| **Dallas/Ft. Worth** | (214) 922-7843 |
| **Florida** | (407) 345-9322 |
| **Los Angeles** | (323) 634-1776 |
| **Milwaukee/Madison** | (414) 963-4023 |
| **New York City** | (212) 869-1242 |
| **Philadelphia** | (215) 785-2232 |
| **Phoenix** | (602) 265-7117 |
| **St. Louis** | (314) 851-0906 |

## Actors Equity Association Regional Offices

**Los Angeles** (323) 634-1750
5757 Wilshire Blvd, Suite 1, Los Angeles, CA 90036
**New York** (212) 869-8530
165 West 46th Street, New York, NY 10036
**Chicago** (312) 641-0393
203 N. Wabash Avenue, Chicago, IL 60601
**San Francisco** (415) 391-3838
235 Pine Street, Suite 1100, San Francisco, CA 94104
**Orlando** (407) 345-8600
10369 Orangewood Blvd, Orlando, FL 32821

## AFTRA - Regional Offices (*Denotes SAG Office as Well)

**National Office**, 5757 Wilshire Blvd. 9th Floor, LA, CA 90036-3689    (323) 634-8100
     Main Fax Number    (323) 634-8246
**\*Atlanta**, 455 East Paces Ferry Road, NE, Suite 334, Atlanta, GA 30305    (404) 239-0131
**\*Boston**, 11 Beacon Street, Suite 512, Boston, MA 02108    (617) 742-2688
**Buffalo**, 2077 Elmwood Avenue, Buffalo, NY 14207    (716) 874-4410
**\*Chicago**, One East Erie, Ste 650, Chicago, Il 60611    (312) 573-8081
**\*Cleveland**, 1030 Euclid Avenue, Suite 429, Cleveland, OH 44115-1504    (216) 781-2255
**\*Dallas/Ft. Worth,** 6060 N. Central Expressway    (214) 363-8300
     Suite 302, L.B. 604, Dallas, TX 75206
**\*Denver**, 950 South Cherry Street, Suite 502, Denver, CO 80222    (303) 757-6226
**\*Detroit**, 27770 Franklin Road, Southfield, MI 48034    (248) 355-3105
**\*Fresno**, 4831 East Shields Avenue, Suite 32, Fresno, CA 93724    (209) 252-1655
**\*Hawaii**, 949 Kapiolani Boulevard, Suite 105, Honolulu, HI 96814    (808) 596-0388
**\*Houston**, 2650 Fountainview, Suite 326, Houston, TX 77057    (713) 972-1806
**Kansas City,** 4000 Baltimore, 2nd Flr, Kansas City, MO 64111    (816) 753-4557
**Miami**, 20401 N.W. 2nd Avenue, Suite 102, Miami, FL 33169    (305) 652-4824
**Milwaukee**, 301 N. Water Street, Milwaukee, WI 53202    (414) 291-9041
**\*Nashville**, 1591 Country Haven Trails, Mt. Juliet, TN 37122    (615) 327-2944
**New Orleans,** 2475 Canal Street, Suite 108, New Orleans, LA 70119    (504) 822-6568
**New York,** 260 Madison Avenue, 7th Floor, New York, NY 10016    (212) 532-0800
**Omaha**, 3000 Farnham Street, Suite 3 East, Omaha, NE 68131    (402) 346-8384
**Orlando**, 5728 Major Boulevard, Suite 264, Orlando, FL 32819    (407) 334-2230
**Peoria**, Garry Moore, c/o Station Week-TV, 2907 Springield Road    (309) 698-3737

East Peoria, IL 61611

| | |
|---|---|
| **\*Philadelphia**, 230 South Broad Street, Suite 500<br>    Philadelphia, PA 19102 | (215) 732-0507 |
| **\*Phoenix**, 1616 E. Indian School Road, Suite 330, Phoenix, AZ 85016 | (602) 265-2712 |
| **Pittsburgh**, 625 Stanwix Street, The Penthouse, Pittsburgh, PA 15222 | (412) 281-6767 |
| **Portland,** 3030 SW Moody, Ste 104, Portland, OR 97201 | (503) 238-6914 |
| **Rochester**, 87 Fairlea Drive, Rochester, NY 14622 | (716) 467-7982 |
| **Sacramento/Stockton,** 836 Garnet Street, Sacramento, CA 95691 | (916) 372-1966 |
| **\*San Diego,** 7827 Convoy Court, Suite 400, San Diego, CA 92111 | (619) 278-7695 |
| **\*San Francisco,** 235 Pine Street, 11th Floor, San Francisco, CA 94104 | (415) 391-7510 |
| **Schenectady/Albany,** 170 Ray Avenue, Schenectady, NY 12304 | (518) 381-4836 |
| **\*Seattle**, P.O. Box 9688, 601 Valley Street, Suite 100, Seattle, WA 98109 | (206) 282-2506 |
| **\*St. Louis,** 1310 Papin, Ste 103, St. Louis, MO 63103 | (314) 231-8410 |
| **Tri-State (Ohio, Indiana, Kentucky)**<br>    128 East 6th Street, Suite 802, Cincinnati, OH 45202 | (513) 579-8668 |
| **\*Twin Cities (Minneapolis, St. Paul)**<br>    708 N. First Street, Itasca Bldg., Suite 343A, Minneapolis, MN 55401 | (612) 371-9120 |
| **\*Wash/Baltimore,** 4340 E. West Highway, Bethesda, MD 20814 | (301) 657-2560 |

## AFTRA National Committees

| | |
|---|---|
| **Dancers' Committee** | Lee Linderman |
| **Equal Employment Opportunity** | Sumi Haru |
| **Events & Seminars** | Marvin Kaplan |
| **Newsperson' Committee** | Mike Laurence |
| **Orientation Committee** | Frances Reid |
| **Performers with Disability** | Bill Supernaw, Barbara Adside |
| **Rap Session Committee** | Jay Gerber |
| **Seniors' Committee** | Alice Backes |
| **Singers Committee** | Darlene Koldenhoven, Rick Logan |
| **Stunt Committee** | Roger Richmond |
| **Womens' Committee** | Jackie Joseph, Peggy McCay |
| **Young AFTRAns Committee** | Carol Lombard |

## AFTRA Telephone Directory - National Office

AFTRA's Los Angeles Office automated phone system operates 24 hours a day. Their offices are open from 9:00 AM to 5:30 PM, Monday through Friday.

| | |
|---|---|
| **Main Switchboard** | (323) 634-8100 |
| **Accounting** | (323) 634-8218 |
|     Fax | (323) 634-8220 |
| **Administration** | (323) 634-8103 |
|     Fax | (323) 634-8107 |
| **Agency** | (323) 634-8186 |
|     Fax | (323) 634-8190 |
| **Board of Directors** | (323) 634-8131 |
|     Fax | (323) 634-8246 |
| **Broadcast (Call Staff Directly)** | |
|     Fax | (323) 634-8120 |
|     Gerry Daley, Director | (323) 634-8115 |
|     Jay Barnett, Exec. Asst. | (323) 634-8116 |
|     Leslie Simon, Bus. Rep | (323) 634-8118 |
|     Kristen Harper, Field | (323) 634-8117 |
| **Cast Clearance** | (323) 634-8231 |
|     Fax | (323) 634-8228 |
| **Casting/Info Line** | (323) 634-8263 |
| **Check Department** | (323) 634-8248 |

| | |
|---|---|
| Fax | (323) 634-8213 |
| **Communications/Member Services** | (323) 634-8123 |
| Fax | (323) 634-8126 |
| **Commercials**  Eva Deal, Ext. 165   Maria Wilson, Ext. 167 | (323) 634-8160 |
| Fax | (323) 634-8196 |
| **Dues (Membership)** | (323) 634-8200 |
| Fax | (323) 634-8213 |
| **Executive Director** | (323) 634-8132 |
| Fax | (323) 634-8137 |
| **Frank Nelson Memorial Sick & Benefit Fund** | **(323)** 634-8154 |
| Fax | (323) 634-8107 |
| **Health and Retirement Department** | (800) 367-7966 |
| **Membership** | (323) 634-8200 |
| Fax | (323) 634-8213 |
| **National Office** | (323) 634-8192 |
| Fax | (323) 634-8194 |
| **New Technologies/Information Systems**, | (323) 634-8243 |
| Fax | (323) 634-8220 |
| **President's Office** | (323) 634-8130 |
| Fax | (323) 634-8246 |
| **Residuals** | (323) 634-8227 |
| Fax | (323) 634-8228 |
| **Sound Recordings**, Stan Farber at Ext. 150. | (323) 634-8141 |
| Fax | (323) 634-8147 |
| **Sexual Harassment/Discrimination** | (323) 634-8124. |
| **Television** | (323) 634-8173 |
| Fax | (323) 634-8177 |
| Lauren Bailey | (323) 634-8180 |
| Jay Barnett | (323) 634-8197 |
| Kathleen Ewers | (323) 634-8179 |
| Jean Frost | (323) 634-8181 |
| Chris Hagstrom | (323) 634-8182 |
| Frank Messineo | (323) 634-8183 |
| Billy Murphy | (323) 634-8178 |
| Joan Halpern Weise | (323) 634-8174 |

## AFTRA Digest of Rates

**Dramas and Sitcoms (ABC, CBS and NBC)**
Day Player          $544
3 Days     $1,367 (for 24 cumulative hours over 3 days)
5 Days     $1,876 (for (3) 8 hour or (2) 10 hour days)
**Fox Television Network**
Day Player          $516
(10 hours over 2 days with 4 hr min.)
**Syndicated Shows**
Day Player          $596
(10 1/2 hours of the performers time)
**Commercials**     $478.70 on camera   $359.95 off camera
**Stand Ins**          $115
**Extras**               $95 Prime Time  $285 Commercials

## AFTRA - SAG Federal Credit Union Offices

| | |
|---|---|
| **Los Angeles - Main Office** | (323) 461-3041 |
| 6922 Hollywood, Suite 304, Hollywood, CA  90028 | (800) 826-6946 |

**Los Angeles - Valley Office**          (818) 509-3690
12711 Ventura Boulevard, Suite 180, Studio City, CA 91604
**Los Angeles - ATM Only**    SAG National Headquarters
5757 Wilshire Boulevard, Los Angeles, CA 90036
**Miami Office**          (305) 770-9206
20401 NW 2nd Avenue, Suite 103, Miami, FL 33169
**Chicago Office**          (312) 553-1924
75 E. Wacker Drive, Suite 900, Chicago, IL 60601

## Anonymous Programs

**Alcoholics Anonymous**  Central Office      (323) 936-4343
SAG AA Meeting Friday 8:30PM in the James Cagney Room
**Cocaine Anonymous**        (310) 216-4444
**Marijuana Anonymous**        (323) 964-2370
**Overeaters Anonymous** (Eating Disorders)    (323) 653-7499
**Nicotine Anonymous**        (800) 642-0666
**Gamblers Anonymous**        (213) 386-8789
**Debtors Anonymous**        (310) 855-8752
**Narcotics Anonymous**        (213) 850-1624
**Non-Anon** (Family and Friends of Addicts)    (310) 547-5800
**Alanon** (Family and Friends of Alcoholics)    (818) 760-7122
**CODA** (Co-Dependents Anonymous)      (310) 840-2262
**ACA** (Adult Children of Alcoholics)      (310) 534-1815
**Battered Women**        (310) 392-8381
**Suicide Prevention**        (310) 391-1253

## American Guild of Variety Artists - Regional Offices

**National Headquarters**        (212) 675-1003
     184 Fifth Avenue, New York, NY 10010-5908
**West Coast**        (818) 508-9984
     4741 Laurel Canyon Boulevard, Suite 208, North Hollywood, CA 91607

## American Guild of Variety Artists - Sick & Relief Fund

**AGVA Sick & Relief Fund - East**      (212) 675-1003
184 Fifth Avenue, 6th Floor, New York, NY 10010
Michiko Terajima, Administrator
**AGVA Sick & Relief Fund-West**      (818) 508-9984
4741 Laurel Canyon Boulevard, Suite 208, No. Hollywood, CA 91607
Ron Huber, Administrator

## Animation Houses

**DIC Enterprises,** Casts animated series      (818) 995-5400
303 N. Glen Oaks, Burbank, CA 91502 Attn: Marsha Goodman
**Duck Soup Productions,** Casts animated series
2205 Stoner Avenue, W. Los Angeles, Ca 90064 Attn: Roger Chouinard
**Film Roman,** Casts Garfield specials      (818) 761-2544
12020 Chandler Blvd., Suite 200, No. Hollywood, CA 91607 Attn: Phil Roman
**Warner Brothers Animation,**  Casts animated series    (818) 977-7500
15303 Ventura Boulevard, Sherman Oaks, CA 91403 Attn: Collette Sunderman

**Intersound,** dubbing foreign cartoons to English (310) 652-3741
8764 Sunset Boulevard, Los Angeles, CA 90069 Attn: Edwardo Torres
**Saban Entertainment,** casts animated series (310) 235-5100
10960 Wilshire Boulevard, Westwood, CA 90024 Attn: Jamie Simone

## Car Rental Agencies
**Dollar** $139/week for a compact (800) 800-4000
**Thrifty** $116/week for a compact (800) 367-2277

## Charities
**AIDS Project Los Angeles** (818) 993-1600
**Childhelp U.S.A.** (800) 4 A CHILD
**Masterplanner Media** - Lists of all charity events (310) 888-8566
**People for the American Way** (310) 478-6657
**Project Angel Food** (323) 845-1800
**Starlight Foundation** (332) 634-0080

## Checking People Out
**The Casting Society of America** - casting by (213) 463-1925
606 N. Larchmont Boulevard, Suite 4B,
**Directors Guild of America (DGA)** (323) 289-2000
7920 Sunset Boulevard
**The Hollywood Creative Directory** (800) 815-0503 (310) 315-4815
**National Conference of Personal Managers (NCPM)** (818) 762-NCP
**Samuel French Bookstores**
Hollywood - 7623 Sunset Boulevard (323) 876-0570
Studio City - 11963 Ventura Boulevard (818) 762-0535

## Child Labor Laws- State of California  Roberta O'Can (818) 901-5484

### 15 days to 5 Months
2 hrs. max at location
20 minutes of work time
Maximum 100 ft. candle light
30 seconds exposure

### 6 Months to 2 Years
4 hrs. max at location
2 hrs. max of work time
0 hrs. education
2 hrs. rest & relaxation

### 2 Years to 5 Years
6 hrs. max at location
3 hrs. max of work time
3 hrs. of rest & relaxation

### 6 Years to 8 Years
School Days
8 hrs. max at location
4 hrs. max of work time
3 hrs. education
1 hr. R & R
1/2 hr. for meal

Non-School Days
8 hrs. max at location
6 hrs. max of work time
0 hrs. education
1 hr. R & R
1/2 hr. for meal

## 9 Years to 16 Years

| School Days | Non-School Days |
|---|---|
| 9 hrs. max at location | 9 hrs. max at location |
| 5 hrs. max of work time | 7 hrs. max of work time |
| 3 hrs. education | 0 hrs. education |
| 1 hr. R & R | 1 hr. R & R |
| 1/2 hr. for meal | 1/2 hr. for meal |

## 16 Years to 18 Years

| School Days | Non-School Days |
|---|---|
| 10 hrs. max at location | 10 hrs max location |
| 6 hrs. max of work time | 8 hrs. max of work time |
| 3 hrs. education | 0 hrs. education |
| 1 hr. R & R | 1 hr. R & R |
| 1/2 hr. for meal | 1/2 hr. for meal |

## Children's Agents

| | |
|---|---|
| **Abrams, Rubaloff & Lawrence,** Holly O-Brien | (323) 935-1700 |
| **Acme Talent & Literary Agency,** Steve Simon | (323) 954-ACME |
| **Amatruda/Benson & Associates,** Kimberly Gola | (310) 276-1851 |
| **Amsel, Eisenstadt & Frazier,** Carolyn Thompson-Goldstein | (323) 939-1188 |
| **Bobby Ball,** Kim Door, Keri Whitehead—Commercials | (818) 506-8188 |
| **Barbara Cameron & Assoc.,** Barbara Cameron | (818) 888-6107 |
| **Iris Burton,** Iris Burton - No one under 6 | (310) 288-0121 |
| **Coleen Cler Modeling,** Craig Schulze-Largest kids print agency | (818) 841-7943 |
| **Coast to Coast**, Meredith S. Fine—Coast Kids | (323) 845-9200 |
| **Cunningham, Escott & Dipene,** Bob Preston | (310) 475-2111 |
| **Dale Garrick Int. Talent**, James Wycoff | (310) 657-2661 |
| **Beverly Hecht Agency,** Teresa Valente, Laurie Zeiden | (818) 505-1192 |
| **Hervey/Grimes Talent,** Marsha Hervey | (818) 981-0891 |
| **Kazarian/Spencer & Assoc.,** Jody Alexander, Bonnie Venits<br>Victoria Morris—Children's Dance | (818) 755-7516 |
| **L.A. Talent/L.A.Models,** Tracy Dwyer | (323) 436-7777 |
| **Osbrink Agency** - Cindy Osbrink | (818) 760-2488 |
| **Herb Tannen,** Stephanie Tessmer—Commercials<br>Joy Stevenson—Film and TV | (310) 446-5802 |

## Children's Managers

| | |
|---|---|
| **Academy Kids Management** | (818) 769-8091 |
| **Hardin-Eckstein Management** | (323) 851-2337 |
| **Deborah McLeod** | (323) 960-4356 |

## Children's School & Theater

| | |
|---|---|
| **North Hills Prep**, 9433 Sepulveda Boulevard, North Hills, CA 91343 | (818) 894-8388 |
| **My Art Musical Youth  Repertory Theater,** Dana Hanstein | (800)  400-2985 |

## Children's Work Permit

| | |
|---|---|
| **LA/Hollywood/Whittier** | (818) 901-5484 |
| | (213) 897-4037 |

HOLLYWOOD

| | |
|---|---|
| **Bakersfield** | (661) 395-2710 |
| **Inglewood/Van Nuys** | (818) 901-5312 |
| **Long Beach** | (310) 590-5044 |
| **San Diego** | (619) 237-7334 |
| **Santa Ana** | (714) 558-4111 |
| **Santa Barbara** | (805) 963-1438 |
| **Stockton** | (209) 948-7770 |

## Clothing - Outlet Stores

| | |
|---|---|
| **Catalina/Speedo Outlet Store**, 6040 Bandini Boulevard | (323) 724-4693 |
| **The Citadel Outlet Collection**,  5675 Telegraph Road, | (323) 888-1220 |
| **It's A Wrap**, 3315 W. Magnolia,- Famous Clothing Resale | (818) 567-7366 |
| **The American Way**, 3226 W. Magnolia, | (818) 841-6013 |

## Comedy and Improv

| | |
|---|---|
| **Aspen Comedy Festival** | (970) 925-1940 |
| **The Comedy Zone**  - books comics across the country | (800) 489-6331 |
| **Judy Brown's Comedy Course** | (310) 396-8425 |
| **Judy Carter's Comedy Course** | (310) 915-0555 |
| **National Association of Campus Activities** | (800) 845-2338 |

## Conventions

| | |
|---|---|
| **Digital World,** Interactive and Virtual Reality Convention | (800) 488-2883 |
| **NATPE**-National Association of Television Producing Executives | (310) 453-4440 |
| **Showbiz Expo,**  Lot of well-known industry speakers. | (800) 331-5706 |
| **SIGGRAPH** - International Conference on Computer Graphics | (312) 321-6830 |

and Interactive Techniques http://www.siggraph.org

## Dance Classes

**Katnap Dance Center,**                                        (310) 306-7069
Run by choreographer Kathleen Knapp, has African and street dancing classes
in addition to the traditional fare of jazz, tap and ballet. There are 5-20 students
per class. Both adults and children are welcome. Discounts for union members are
available and series of classes are offered at a reduced rate.

**Studio of Performing Arts,** 8558  West Third Street in West Hollywood(323) 275-4683
Home of the dance troupe L.A. Dance Force, offers all styles of jazz, ballet
and tap. They have over 40 instructors and a Junior Program for dancers 8-13.
Full scholarships or discounts are for students in a trade union.

**Morro-Landis Studio,** 10960 Ventura Boulevard in Studio City        (818) 753-5081
A schedule that includes movement for actors, jazz, ballet, tap and funk.
Call to schedule a class.

**Debbie Reynolds Dance Studio,** 6514 Lankershim, No. Hollywood        (818) 985-3193
Offers ballet, tap and ballet.

## Demo Reel - Air Checks & Transfers
**Jan's Video**                                            (213) 462-5511
    1800 N. Argyle, Suite 300, Hollywood
    $15 but you must edit your demo tape at their facility or pay $80 hour to edit
**Phase-L Productions**                                        (818) 764-3094
    7451 Lankershim Blvd., North Hollywood
    (A very popular air check place. Done on first come/first serve basis)

## Demo Reel - Blank Tapes

**Ametron,** Hollywood, CA 90028       (323) 462-1200

**Edgewise,** 1215 North Highland, Hollywood, CA 90038       (323) 769-0900

## Demo Reel - Dubbing Voice-Over

**Armadillo Digital Audio**       (818) 754-1253

**Audio Cassette Duplicator Co.,**       (818) 762-2232

**Abbey Tape Duplicators,**       (818) 882-5210

**Dynamite Dubs,** (at Voice Traxx West)       (323) 851-3850

## Demo Reel - Editing

**Phase-L Productions** - Editing using Video Toaster $60 per hour.       (818) 764-3094

**Gosch Productions** - Busy editing facility, call for an appointment       (818) 509-3530

**Video Resources Group,** Bob Telford a great editor at $40 per hour       (213) 655-8022

**Video Tech,** will dub the tape, label, hard cover case for $1.72       (818) 765-1778

**Ross-Hunt,** provides the tape and label for $2.80. Hard case add $0.79 (818) 763-6045

## Demo Reel - Shooting

**Nu Print Stationery, John** - Movie Scripts $20       (818) 509-0003

**Allen Fawcett Demo Production Lab**       (818) 763-8252
> Alan teaches a 12-week lab for actors where you study script analysis, camera and acting technique. After completion of the lab you leave with a demo reel.

**EZ TV,** 6522 Hollywood Boulevard       (323) 462-3678
> Shoots demo tapes at their facility. Titles and special effects are included when you edit there.

**Phase-L Productions, Rick Fazel**       (818) 764-3094
> Tape a demo scene in his studio. They use broadcast quality beta-cam cameras. The prices are rated by the hour according to how many cameras you want to use: 1 camera—$60, 2 cameras—$80, 3 cameras—$90. Same rates for outdoors.

**Rich and Famous Productions,** Joan Biles       (323) 654-6550
> Joan builds reels for actors from existing on new material you will shoot with her. This Public Relations Society of America award winner is very good with newcomers.

## Demo Reel - Voice Over

**Voice Traxx West,**       (323) 850-1112
> Book a session and Cindy will create your demo. Susan will engineer the session and make the cassette dubs.

**Tele-Talent,** whose motto "I make you sound like God,"       (323) 466-7371
> Mike is honest and direct with people. If he feels that you need to brush up before recording or if you need extensive training to be competitive, he will tell you.

**Pip Printing**       (818) 845-2474
> You bring in a black and white photo of yourself. They design a J-card and print it on 76 pound velum bristol stock and "score" the paper for easy folding. The cost of 100 J-cards is $65. They can also typeset 100 labels for about $31.

## Department of Motor Vehicles
**Santa Monica DMV-**2235 Colorado Avenue
M-F 8:00 AM - 5:00 PM
Thurs 8:00 AM - 6:30 PM
**Hollywood DMV-**Drivers Licenses Only

803 North Cole
M-F 8:00 AM - 5:00 PM
Thurs 8:00 AM - 6:30 PM
**Hollywood DMV**-Vehicle Registration Only
1600 N. Vine (TBG 593 F-4)
M-F 8:00 AM - 5:00 PM
Thurs 8:00 AM - 6:30 PM
**San Fern. Valley DMV** -14920 Vanowen Street
M-F 8:00 AM - 5:00 PM
Thurs 8:00 AM - 6:30 PM
**Phone Numbers for All Locations**
(213) 736-3101 Appointment Line
(213) 744-2000 Information Line

## Dry Cleaners

| | |
|---|---|
| **Marquis Cleaners,** 1246 N. Vine Street $1.25 per garment | (323) 465-5564 |
| **Venice Cleaners,** 11277 Venice Boulevard $1.25 per garment | (310) 390-2165 |

## Extra Work

| | |
|---|---|
| **Bill Dance** | (323) 878-1131 |
| **Central Casting**, 1700 Burbank Boulevard, Burbank, CA 91506<br>Interviews: Mon. & Wed. 10 AM-12 Noon.<br>Bring proof of American citizenship. They take photo. Fee of $5. | (818) 562-2700 |
| **Cenex Casting,** Most widely used non-union | (818) 562-2799 |
| **Hollywood Casting Inc.** | (323) 856-9070 |
| **Idell James Casting** | (310) 394-3919 |
| **Messenger & Associates,** Charlie or Trish Messenger | (818) 760-3696 |
| **Producer's Casting,** Gabrielle or Virginia | (310) 454-5233 |

## Extra Work - Children

| | |
|---|---|
| **Casting Kids & Studio Kids** | (562) 902-9838 |
| **Hollywood Kids** | (818) 766-4441 |
| **Kids BG Talent** | (818) 872-2171 |
| **Screen Children** | (818) 846-4300 |

## Film Festivals and Award Shows

| | |
|---|---|
| **Hollywood Legacy Awards** | (323) 469-9151 |
| **IFP West Spirit Awards** | (310) 475-4379 |
| **L.A. Independent Film Festival** | (213) 937-9137 |
| **NAACP Image Awards** | (213) 622-2796 |
| **Palm Springs Film Festival** | (619) 778-8979 |
| **Santa Barbara Film Festival** | (805) 963-0023 |
| **Sundance Film Festival** | (801) 328-3456 |
| **Washington D.C. Intl. Film Festival** | (202) 274-6810 |
| **Women in Film Crystal Awards** | (323) 463-6040 |
| **Worldfest Film Festival** | (713) 965-9955 |

## Government Agencies

| | |
|---|---|
| **Federal Trade Commission** | (310) 825-4300 |

1100 Wilshire Boulevard, Los Angeles, CA 90024

**Los Angeles City Offices,** 200 N. Main Street, Los Angeles, CA 90012     (213) 485-4495
**Los Angeles County Department of Consumer Affairs**     (213) 974-1452
    500 W. Temple Street, Room B-96. Los Angeles, CA 90012
**Los Angeles County Human Resources Commission**     (213) 974-7611
    320 W. Temple Street, Room 1184, Los Angeles, CA 90012
**Los Angeles Judicial District Small Claims Court**     (213) 974-6131
    110 N. Grand, Room 429, Los Angeles, CA 90012
**Los Angeles Police Department, Bunco (Frauds) Division**     (213) 485-3795
**State of California Department of Consumer Affairs**     (800) 344-9940
    400 "R" Street, Room 1080, Sacramento, CA 95814
**State of California -Industrial Relations Dept.,**     (213) 620-6330
    **Labor Standards Enforcement**
**State of California - Office of the Attorney General**     (916) 322-3360
    Sacramento, CA 95814
**United States Postal Service - Office of the Postal Inspector**     (626) 405-1200
    281 E. Colorado Avenue, Pasadena, CA 91102, Attn: Mail Fraud

## Groceries - Discount
**99 Cent Stores**     (323) 466-1075
**Price Club/Costco**
    **Burbank:** 10950 Sherman Way and Vineland     (818) 840-8115
**Sams Club**
    **Hawthorne:** 5175 W. Marine at Inglewood Avenue     (310) 643-7338
    **Torrance:** 2601 Skypark Drive at Crenshaw Boulevard,     (310) 534-0134
**Trader Joes -** over 100 locations     (800) SHOPTJS

## Hair Salons
**Supercuts** - Diedra, $10, 7064 B Sunset Blvd.     (323) 463-8023
**Vidal Sassoon Academy,** $15, 321 Santa Monica Boulevard     (310) 393-1461
**Shawn's Haircutting** - Shawn, $25, 4455 Van Nuys Boulevard     (818) 981-1500
**Figaro Unisex Salon** - Diana, $25, 9731 Wilshire Blvd.     (310) 276-6279

## Health Clubs & Martial Arts
**Beverly Hot Springs**     (323) 734-7000
**Billy Blank's Tae-Bo Classes**     (818) 906-8528
**Crunch,** 8000 W. Sunset Blvd.     (323) 654-4550
**Gold's Gym - Hollywood,** 1016 N. Cole Avenue     (323) 462-7012
**Kung Fu San Soo** - Martial Arts     (310) 398-5200
**Power Yoga with Brian Kyest** - 4th & Santa Monica Blvd. 10:45 AM M-F, 6PM MWF
**Toluca Lake Tennis Club** - Massage     (323) 851-6000

## Health Issues
**Bob Hope Health Care Center**     (323) 634-3850
**Bruce Baichman Health Insurance**     (800) 794-9401
**Hollywood-Sunset Free Clinic,** 3324 W. Sunset Boulevard     (323) 660-2400
**Individual and Family Counseling Center**     (818) 761-2227
**Jeffrey Goodman Special Care Clinic** - HIV Testing     (323) 993-7500
**Los Angeles Free Clinic,** 8403 Beverly Boulevard     (323) 653-1990

| | |
|---|---|
| **Stop Smoking Clinic** | (800) 7NOBUTTS |
| **Valley Free Clinic**, 5648 Vineland Avenue | (818) 763-8836 |
| **Womens Clinic** | (310) 203-8899 |

## Help I Have Been Scammed

If your complaint is with a franchised Agent:

**Association of Talent Agents (ATA)**            (310) 274-0628
9255 Sunset Boulevard, Suite 318, Los Angeles, CA 90069

**Screen Actors Guild (SAG)**            (323) 954-1600
5757 Wilshire Boulevard, L.A., CA 90036-360
They will take action including revocation of the agent's franchise. If you are sexually harassed on the set or at an audition, contact the guild immediately. On the automated answering system they have a sexual harassment selection for your protection If you willingly have sex with someone and are of consenting age, no crime has been committed in the eyes of the law.

**American Federation of Television and Radio Artists (A.F.T.R.A.)** (323) 634-8100
5757 Wilshire Boulevard, 9th Floor, Los Angeles, CA 90036

**Actors Equity Association (AEA)**            (323) 634-1750
5757 Wilshire Boulevard, Los Angeles, CA 90036

**American Guild of Variety Artists (AGVA)**            (818) 508-9984
4741 Laurel Canyon Boulevard, #208 North Hollywood, CA 91607

**Better Business Bureau**            (213) 251-9696
3400 W. 6th Street, Suite 403, Los Angeles, CA 90020

**California Lawyers for the Arts**            (310) 998-5590
1641 18th Street, Santa Monica, CA 90404

**National Conference of Stage Directors**   New York Office            (212) 421-2670
10231 Riverside Drive, Suite 303, Toluca Lake, CA 91602

**Office of Private Post Secondary Education**
721 Capitol Mall, Sacramento, CA 95814.

**Society of Stage Directors & Choreographers-(SSDC)**            (800) 541-5204
P.O. Box 93847, Hollywood, CA 90093

## Home Electronics

| | |
|---|---|
| **Best Buys,** 11301 W. Pico Boulevard at 405 Freeway | (310) 268-9190 |
| **Fry's Electronics** | |
| Burbank:  2311 N. Hollywood Way | (818) 526-8100 |
| Woodland Hills:  6100 Canoga Avenue | (818) 227-1000 |
| Manhattan Beach:  3600 Sepulveda Boulevard | (310) 364-3700 |

## Housing - Furnishings

| | |
|---|---|
| **IKEA Burbank,** 600 N. San Fernando Boulevard | (818) 842-4532 |
| **IKEA Carson,** 20700 S. Avalon Boulevard | (310) 527-4532 |
| **Universal Lifeline** - Low Income Telephone Service | (800) 310-BELL. |

## Housing - Temporary & Permanent

| | |
|---|---|
| **Department of Housing** | (213) 847-7368, (800) 994-4444 |
| **Home Hunters - Apartment Finders** | (323) 848-3490 |
| 1038 Fairfax Avenue, Fee: $69 for three months | |
| **Heritage Motel,** $640 shower only, $720 Month w/kitchen & full bath | (818) 981-0500 |

15485 Ventura Boulevard, Encino, CA 91403

All rooms have in-room, coffee service, cable TV, air conditioning, direct dial phones with $20 deposit, free parking and pool. Some rooms have a full kitchen with stove and refrigerator. Great location at 405 and 101 freeways.

**Jolly Roger Hotel-Beach Area** $320 per week        (800) 822-2904

2904 Washington Boulevard, Marina del Rey, CA 90291

Ask for a motel room that faces the street; these are a little noisier but much cheaper. Rooms feature: Room phones, color TV, cable, heated pools, complimentary coffee, ample free parking, shower tub, queen size or double beds.

**Oakwood Apartments**        (323) 878-2100

The monthly rates for a furnished studio apartment is $983 which includes utilities, local telephone service, voice-mail, cable television, pool and spa. There is a one-time credit check and administration cost of $50.

**Stars Inn** $350/Week or $55/Night        (310) 556-3076

10269 Santa Monica Boulevard, Century City, CA 90067

Rustic and centrally located next to Beverly Hills and across from Century City Shopping Center featuring Steven Spielberg's restaurant Dive! Features: Room phones with a $20.00 deposit, color TV with cable, free parking and each room has a refrigerator. Remodeled rooms cost $5 more per day.

**Wellman Realty,** helps find residences by the beach for a fee        (310) 829-2593

1415 Stanford Avenue, Santa Monica

**Westside Rentals-Apartment Finders**        (310) 395-7368

630 Santa Monica Boulevard Fee: $49 for three months

## Industrial Agents

**Bobby Ball Talent Agency**        (323) 964-7300

**Brand-Clarke**        (714) 850-1158

**Marion Berzon**        (714) 631-5936

## Industry Newspapers

**Backstage/Backstage West** - Sunbelt Fulfillment        (800) 458-7541

8:30 AM-5:00 PM Central Time

1 Year $75, 2 Years $125, 1 Year 1st Class $199

1 Year Canada $135, 1 Year Canada 1st Class $245

**Backstage West** Attn:Theater Openings - Send Announcements for Play Review

5055 Wilshire Boulevard, 6th Floor, Los Angeles, CA 90036        (323) 525-2356

Backstage West's FAX        (323) 965-1340

**The Hollywood Reporter**        (213) 525-2150

1 Year Daily $189 (+$15.59 tax in CA)

2 Years Daily $350 (+$28.87 tax in CA)

1 Year NYC Air Express $298, 1 Year Weekly Int'l Edition $110

Publicity:  let them know about your next

opening,air date or screening by faxing the information to        (323) 525-2377

Paid Ads in Special Issues        (323) 525-2011

Currently cost: 1/16 page—$280, 1/8 page—$495

1/4 page—$700, 1/2 page—$1,215, Full page—$2,000

**Variety,** 5700 Wilshire Boulevard, Suite 120, Los Angeles, CA 90036        (323) 857-6600

Subscription:    1 Year Daily $197 (+$16.25 tax in CA)        (800) 552-3632

Paid Ads - Current rates are:
1/7 page—$600 (either 4" x 5" up and down or 6" x 3 1/3" up and down)
1/4 page—$850, 1/3 page—$1,105, 1/2 page—$1,475
Full page—$2,380
There is a $60 charge for design, picture and typesetting.

## Insurance - Car & Home
**Automobile**
20th Century Car Insurance, (Seniors, 35+ Females)      (818) 704-3000
Geico Insurance      (800) 841-3000
Farmers Insurance (Preferred Drivers)      (213) 872-3826
Mercury Insurance      (800) 4MERCURY
Safeco Insurance (Male/Female—no violations)      (800) 553-1861
**Home and Apartment Insurance**
Allstate Insurance (Alliance Group)      (877) 463-4217
State Farm General Insurance      (818) 841-5935
United Services Auto Association (USAA)      (800) 531-8080

## Jobs - Assorted
Hettie, focus groups      (818) 366-1126
Cheers Catering, catering      (310) 273-9002
California Celebrations, caters events at TV Academy      (310) 305-8849
Angel City Talent, look-a-likes      (323) 463-1680
Mulligan Management, look-a-likes      (323) 660-4142
All Showtime Entertainment, look-a-likes      (800) 994-9951
Aimee Entertainment, cabaret showcase      (818) 783-9115
15000 Ventura Boulevard, Suite 340, Sherman Oaks, CA 91403

## Jobs - Children & Mystery Parties
All Showtime Entertainment, kids parties      (800) 994-9951
Characters Kids Love, kids parties      (323) 931-0606
Entertainment 4 All Kids, kids parties      (800) 321-5867
Happy Parties, kids parties      (310) 282-0818
Keith & Margo's Murder Mystery Weekend. Send a picture and resume to
Keith and Margo at: 15130 Gault Street, Van Nuys, CA 91405.

## Jobs - Cruise Ships
Carnival Cruise Lines, Attn.: Roger Blum      (305) 559-2600
     3655 NW 87th Avenue, Miami, FL 33178
Casino Productions, Attn.: Don & Candi Casino      (305) 935-0137
     19511 NE Court, No. Miami, FL 33179
Crystal Cruises,      (310) 785-9300
     2049 Century Park East, Suite 1400, Los Angeles, CA 90067
Cunard Lines, 555 Fifth Avenue, New York, NY 10017      (212) 880-7500
Holland American, 300 Elliot Avenue West, Seattle, WA 98119      (206) 281-3535
Jeanne Ann Ryan Productions, Attn.: Sara Falconer      (305) 523-6414
     Cunard & Royal Norwegian, 308 Southeast 14th Street, Ft. Lauderdale, FL 33316
Musical Inc., Attn.: Jene Chandler      (305) 525-2540

916 N. Federal Highway, Ft. Lauderdale, FL 33304

**Princess Cruises,** Attn.: Rai Caluori (310) 553-1770
10100 Santa Monica Boulevard, Los Angeles, CA 90067

**RCCI/Royal Viking,** Attn.: Morag Veljkovic (305) 460-4793
95 Merrick Way, Coral Gables, FL 33134

**Royal Caribbean,** Attn.: Mary Ann Delany (305) 379-2601
1050 Caribbean Way, Miami, FL 33132

**Sun Line Cruises,** Attn.: Tina Smith (212) 397-6400
One Rockefeller Plaza, Suite 315, New York, NY 10020

## Jobs - Las Vegas (Ask for Entertainment Director)

| | |
|---|---|
| **Aladdin Hotel,** 3367 Las Vegas Boulevard, Las Vegas, NV 89109 | (702) 736-0111 |
| **Bally's,** 3645 Las Vegas Boulevard South, Las Vegas, NV 89109 | (702) 739-4111 |
| **Bellagio** | (702) 693-7111 |
| **Caesars Palace,** 3570 Las Vegas Boulevard, Las Vegas, NV 89109 | (702) 731-7110 |
| **Excalibur,** 3850 Las Vegas Boulevard, Las Vegas, NV 89119 | (702) 597-7777 |
| **Flamingo Hilton,** 3555 Las Vegas Blvd., Las Vegas, NV 89109 | (702) 733-3111 |
| **Golden Nuggett,** 129 E. Fremont, Las Vegas, NV 89101 | (702) 385-7111 |
| **Hacienda,** 2535 Las Vegas Boulevard, Las Vegas, NV 89109 | (702) 739-8911 |
| **Hard Rock Hotel** | (702) 693-5000 |
| **Harrah's,** 3475 Las Vegas Boulevard, Las Vegas, NV 89109 | (702) 369-5000 |
| **Hollywood Hotel,** 305 Convention Center, Las Vegas, NV 89109 | (702) 734-0711 |
| **Imperial Palace,** 3535 Las Vegas Boulevard, Las Vegas, NV 89109 | (702) 731-3311 |
| **Las Vegas Hilton,** 3000 Paradise Road, Las Vegas, NV 89109 | (702) 732-5111 |
| **Luxor,** 3900 Las Vegas Boulevard South, Las Vegas, NV 89109 | (702) 262-4000 |
| **Maxim,** 160 East Flamingo, Las Vegas, NV 89109 | (702) 731-4300 |
| **MGM Grand,** 3799 Las Vegas Blvd. South, Las Vegas, NV 89109 | (702) 891-1111 |
| **Mirage,** 3400 Las Vegas Boulevard, Las Vegas, NV 89109 | (702) 791-7111 |
| **New York/New York** | (702) 740-6969 |
| **Paris Las Vegas** | (702) 946-7000 |
| **Rio,** 3700 West Flamingo, Las Vegas, NV 89109 | (702) 252-7777 |
| **Rivera,** 2901 Las Vegas Boulevard, Las Vegas, NV 89109 | (702) 734-5110 |
| **Sahara,** 2535 Las Vegas Boulevard, Las Vegas, NV 89109 | (702) 737-2111 |
| **Sheraton Desert Inn,** 3145 Las Vegas Blvd, Las Vegas, NV 89109 | (702) 733-4444 |
| **Stardust,** 3000 Las Vegas Boulevard, Las Vegas, NV 89109 | (702) 732-6111 |
| **Treasure Island,** 3300 Las Vegas Blvd, Las Vegas, NV 89109 | (702) 894-7111 |
| **Tropicana,** 3801 Las Vegas Boulevard, Las Vegas, NV 89109 | (702) 739-2222 |
| **Vegas World,** 2000 Las Vegas Boulevard, Las Vegas, NV 89109 | (702) 382-2000 |
| **Ventian** | (702) 414-1000 |

## Jobs - Studio

**Knotts Berry Farm,** Entertainment Office (714) 220-5394
8039 Beach Boulevard, Buena Park, CA 90620

**Six Flags Magic Mountain,** Entertainment Office (661) 255-4100
Production Coordinator, P.O. Box 5500, Valencia, CA 91385

**Universal Studios,** Director of Entertainment, (818) 622-3851
Entertainment Dept. SC-41, 100 Universal City Plaza, Universal City, CA 91608

## Legal Stuff

**Barrington Post Office (Passports)**                     (800) 275-8777
> 200 S. Barrington Boulevard at Sunset Blvd.
> Monday-Friday 8:00 AM - 5:00 PM

**Federal Courthouse (Passports)** , 11000 Wilshire Boulevard at the
> 405 Freeway, 13th Floor, Room 13100, West L.A., CA 90024-3615
> Monday-Friday 8:00 AM - 3:00 PM

**Legal Hotline**                                         (800) 562-2929
**Name Change - recorded info**                           (213) 974-5299
**Register to Vote**                                      (800) 345-8683
**Los Angeles Passport Agency**                           (900) 225-5674
**Social Security Administration**                        (800) 772-1213
**Unemployment - Office of Employment Development**       (310) 546-6430

## Libraries

**Beverly Hills Library,** 444 Rexford Drive              (310) 288-2200
**Los Angeles Public Library Regional Branches**
> Exposition Park: 3665 S. Vermont Avenue             (213) 732-0169
> North Hollywood: 5211 Tujunga Avenue                (818) 766-7185
> Hollywood: 1632 N. Ivar                             (323) 467-1821
> Arroyo Seco: 6145 N. Figueroa Street                (213) 237-1181
> San Pedro: 931 S. Gaffey Street                     (310) 548-7779
> West Valley: 19036 Vanowen Street                   (818) 345-4393
> West Los Angeles: 11360 Santa Monica Boulevard      (310) 575-8323

## Lithographers

**Anderson Graphics,** 6037 Woodman Avenue, Van Nuys      (818) 909-9100
Takes the usual four to six days. The postcards cost $52.50 for 300.

**Cinema Prints,** 7515 Sunset Boulevard in Hollywood     (323) 876-3830
Postcards 500 for $85 and 1,000 for $110. Printing takes 4-6 days.

**CK Designs,** 9455 Little Santa Monica Blvd., Beverly Hills, CA   (310) 246-0118
120 Models Zed Cards for $120 with up to 7 images. 2-3 day turnaround

**Digital Playground,** 1321 Westwood Blvd., Suite A Westwood   (310) 312-3003
300 lithos for $59.95 The cheapest place in town to get headshots.
They use a digital scanning processing and a great quality thin paper like photos.

**Final Print,** 1958 N. Van Ness, L.A. 90068             (323) 466-0566
6305 Yucca, Suite 401, Hollywood 90028                    (323) 466-5404
6308 Woodman Avenue, Suite 113, Van Nuys 91401            (818) 780-6467
4560 Admiralty Way, Bldg. 110 #7, Marina del Rey  90292   (310) 306-1154
250 lithos are $77.50 but their best bargain is photo postcards at
500 cards - $65. Offers 24-hour drop-off capability and can offer
rush service for a fee of $35. Processing will take 7 to 10 days.

**Genesis,** 5872 W. Pico Boulevard                       (323) 965-7935
1,000 5" x 7" B&W Zed cards. Headshot with four photos on the back
for $190 or 500 for $140. Headshots are 300 - $69. The best ZED card
printers in Los Angeles. Experts at layouts with lots of free extras.

**Grand Prints,** 6143 Laurelgrove, Avenue, No. Hollywood    (818) 763-5743
250 lithos for $75; but the real bargain is 500 prints for $105.
Newcomers get special care. They offer worldwide mail-order.
Prints are shipped directly to your home. You can get 1,000 postcards
printed for $110. Since most actors only use about 500 postcards per mailing,
they have provided you with two options: (1) You can divide the order—with
half being a postcard with a printed message and the other half for future use
and having only a picture and a blank area for a personal message; or, (2) you
can split your 1,000 postcard order with another actor for $10 more. If you only
wish to order 500, it will cost $70. In either case, it will take about 10-14 days to
be printed. Grand Prints does not charge for typesetting, negative or UPS delivery.

**Imagestarter**    (323) 848-3663
100 headshots are $65 and 300 for $79. Imagestarter offers digitized
printing making the prints look like photo quality. Takes three to five days.

**Modern Postcard**    **www.modernpostcard.com**    (800) 959-8365
They have the cheapest color postcard in town. 500 color for $95.

**NKS Printing,** 11688 Ventura Boulevard, Stuido City    (818) 761-6475
100 lithos for $59 and 300 at $64.95. If you mention this book, you
will receive a 10% discount. These prices include the savings. Lithos
printed in four working days, the quickest turn around time in town.

**Paper Chase,** 7176 Sunset Boulevard, Hollywood    (323) 874-2300
Zed cards start at $155 for B&W and $425 for color. 300 headshots
for $69. A full-service printer for headshots and Zed cards.

**Prints Charmin',** 1657 Sawtelle, West L.A. or    (310) 312-0904
11020 Ventura Boulevard    (818) 753-9005
The quickest turn around time available anywhere. Normal service
taking 4 to 6 days cost $80 for 500 postcards. A two-day rush is $25 extra
and for same day service add $35.

**Supershots**    (323) 724-4809
$125 for 500 copies specializing in printing two-sided photos,
one head shot on one side and another on the flip side. Worldwide
mail-order service. Lots of experience with first time models ZED cards.

## Lithography - Adding Typesetting to Existing Postcards
**Top of the Line Printing**    (818) 842-5167

## Looping Groups
**ADR Voice Services,** 15527 Hart Street, Van Nuys, CA 91406
Requirements: Native foreign language speakers or true fluency in a foreign
language. Pictures/resumes/voice tapes accepted.

**Barbara Harris Casting,** P.O. Box 846, Burbank, CA 91503. Pictures/resumes accepted.
Do not send audio/video tapes unless a written request is made.

**Cosmopoloop International,** 664 Kingman Avenue, Santa Monica, CA 90402
Requirements: Superior improvisational skills, true fluency in foreign language,

or specialized character voices. Resumes/voice tapes accepted.

**Joyce's Voices,** P.O. Box 6061-136, Sherman Oaks, CA 91413.
Requirements: Excellent improv skills, fluent foreign language and dialect
skills a plus. Pictures/resumes accepted—no tapes.

**L.A. Loopsters,** 10757 Hortense Street, Suite 209, Toluca Lake, CA 91602
Requirements: Walla (wall to wall dialogue)/ADR experience.
Resume/voice tapes accepted.

**Super Loopers**, P.O. Box 3458, Santa Monica, CA 90408-3458
Requirements: Expert improv skills, authentic dialects, multi-lingual facility
with Asian, Middle Eastern, Scandinavian or Slavic languages. Pictures/resumes
and voice tapes accepted.

| | |
|---|---|
| **Sounds Great** - Looping Classes Toby or Joan (818) 760-0588 or | (818) 766-2808 |
| **Word of Mouth Productions** - Looping Classes | (818) 763-4260 |

## Low Budget Film Makers

| | |
|---|---|
| **Crown International** | (310) 657-6700 |
| 8701 Wilshire Blvd., Beverly Hills, CA 90211 | |
| **Concorde/New Horizons** | (310) 820-6733 |
| 11600 San Vicente Blvd., L.A., CA 90049 | |
| **Cinetel Films** | (323) 654-4000 |
| 8255 Sunset Blvd., L.A., CA 90046 | |
| **Promark Entertainment** | (323) 878-0404 |
| 3599 Cahuenga Blvd. West, 3rd Floor, L.A., CA 90068 | |
| **Harmony Gold** | (323) 851-4900 |
| 7655 Sunset Blvd., L.A., CA 90046 | |
| **Propaganda Films** | (323) 462-6400 |
| 940 N. Mansfield Avenue, L.A., CA 90038 | |
| **PM Entertainment** | (818) 504-6332 |
| 9545 Wentworth Avenue, Sunland, CA 91040 | |

## Make-Up Artists & Supply Stores

| | |
|---|---|
| **Samantha Brooke** $50 | (323) 858-0165 |
| **Samantha Weaver** $100 | (310) 420-9584 |
| **MAC Cosmetics** - 133 N. Robertson Boulevard | (310) 854-0860 |
| 40% Discount to SAG/AFTRA Members | |
| **Frends Beauty Supply** - 5270 Laurel Canyon Boulevard | (818) 769-3834 |
| 10% Discount to Professionals | |
| **Joe Blasco Make-Up Center** | (323) 467-4949 |
| **Mary Kay Cosmetics,** Rosalie Maretsky | (310) 551-3153 |

## Nail Salons

| | |
|---|---|
| **All Star Nails & Waxing,** 7312 Santa Monica Blvd, West Hollywood | (323) 845-0962 |
| **Creations Nails & Waxing,** 1955 Westwood Boulevard, West LA | (310) 470-7454 |

## Office Equipment

| | |
|---|---|
| **On Time Printing,** Business Cards | (323) 466-2333 |
| Voicemail Depot, Voice Mail Boxes | (800) 309-8888 |

## Personal Trainers

| | |
|---|---|
| **Craig, Chris and Buffy Price** | (818) 728-1106 |

## Photographers

**Mark Attebarry** (310) 226-7110
> 3 rolls for $275.  Will go on location and does an amazing job.
> Make-up available for an extra charge. 8x10's are $17  Negs are negotiable.

**Dan Chapman** (323) 463-5995
> 2 rolls for $200.  A full 1/3 of his business is children's headshots.
> Does 4x6 prints for easier selection of your headshot. Near Paramount Studios.

**Heather Dobson** (213) 444-0116
> 2 rolls for $150.  Easy style that has made her one of the most popular commercial
> photogs in town. $10 for 8x10's make-up available by quote.  You get negatives.

**Melinda Kelley** (818) 353-8008
> 2 rolls for $200 and 3 rolls at $250. Her photos capture the fun side of people.
> Also does commercial print shots. You keep the negatives here too.

**Tom Lascher** (310) 581-1980
> Charges $250 flat rate for shooting plus $15 per rolls includes developing
> and a proof sheet. No make-up or 8x10's included.  One of the best in town.

**Trent Studios** (213) 891-9345
> 3 rolls for $165 or 7 rolls for $375 and you keep the negatives.
> This is great for models building books as they will shoot on location.

## Photo Reprinters

**DPI,** 1522 N. Highland, L.A., CA  90028 (323) 466-7544
> 25  for $27, 100 for $62,  Name strip - $14 & negative costs $8.50.

**Iris Photo Lab,** 6767 Sunset Boulevard (323) 463-2233

**Isgo Lepejian,**  1145 N.LaBrea Avenue,Hollywood, CA 90038 (323) 876-8085
> M-F 9 AM-6 PM and Sat 11 AM-4 PM

**Isgo Lepejian Burbank,** 3108 W. Burbank Blvd, Burbank, CA 91505 (818) 848-9001
> M-F 9 AM-8 PM, $25 for 25 prints,, $70 for 100, $157 for 250,
> negative-$11, name strip at $1.

**Photo Farm,** 903 N. Fairfax Avenue,W. Hollywood, CA  90046, (213) 650-5446
> M-10AM - 5:30 PM, $25 for 25 prints, 100 for $70,
> negative- $15, name strip is $6.

**Quality Custom Lab** (323) 938-0174
> 142 N. LaBrea Avenue, L.A., CA  90036.  25 for $25, 50 for $40 and
> 100 for $70.  Name strip is $10 and the negative costs $20.

## Photo Retouchers

**Elliott Photography,** 1151 N. LaBrea Avenue, LA, CA  90038 (323) 876-8821
**Nichan Photo Services,** 5851 Melrose Avenue, LA, CA 90038 (323) 467-5638

## Production Experience

**Filmmakers Alliance Hotline** (310) 281-6093
**Dov S-S Simens - Produce or Direct Your Own Movie** (323) 933-1464

## Professional Organizations

**Academy of Motion Picture Arts & Sciences**   www.oscar.org (310) 247-3000
> 8949 Wilshire Boulevard,Bev. Hills  90211

**Academy of Television Arts and Sciences** www.emmys.org (818) 754-2800
> 5220 Lankershim Boulevard, North Hollywood, CA 91601-3109

**Academy Players Directory**  - players@oscar.org (310) 247-3058
> 8949 Wilshire Boulevard, Fourth Floor, Beverly Hills, CA 90211

**Filmmakers Foundation** - www.FilmFound.org      (323) 937-5595
     5858 Wilshire Boulevard, Suite 205, Los Angeles, CA 90036
**IFP/West,** 1964 Westwood Boulevard, Suite 205, Los Angeles, CA 90025 (310) 475-4379
**Performers Alliance** - www.actor.org      (323) 878-0560
**Theater Authority West**      (323) 462-5761
**Women In Film** - www.wif.org      (323) 463-6040
     6464 Sunset Boulevard, Suite 550, Hollywood, CA 90028
**Writers Guild,** 7000 W. Third Street, Los Angeles, CA 90048-4329      (310) 550-1000
     Registration Office      (323) 782-4540
     Registration Recorded Information Line      (323) 782-4500
     **www.wga.org**      FAX      (323) 782-4803

## Pubic Access Shows

**Adelphia,** 15055 Oxnard Street, Van Nuys, CA - Larry Jones      (818) 781-1900
**Buenavision,** Channel 6 & 56, 912 N. Eastern Ave., L.A., CA 90063      (323) 269-8266
**Century Cable,** 3037 Roswell St., LA, CA 90065-David Yerena      (323) 255-9881
**Century Comm.** Channel 77, 2939 Nebraska Ave. Santa Monica      (310) 315-4444
**Cox Cable,** Channel 33, 33 Peninsula Center, Rolling Hills Estate      (310) 377-7207
**Media One,** 900 N. Cahuenga Blvd., Hollywood, CA 90038      (323) 993-8000
**Media One,** 4223 Glencoe Avenue, C-125, Marina Del Rey, CA 90292      (310) 822-1575
**Media One,** 6314 Arizona Place, LA, CA 90045      (310) 216-3525
**Media One,** 1855 W. Manchester Ave., L.A., CA 90047      (323) 565-2807
**Media One,** 10625 Plainview Ave., #10, Tujunga, CA 91042      (818) 353-9304
**Media One,** Channel 41, 605 East "G" Street, WIlmington, CA 90744      (310) 513-1534
**Time Warner,** 9260 Topanga Cyn. Blvd., Chatsworth, CA 91311 (818) 998-2266

## Pubic Transportation - Bus & Cabs

**Metro Rapid Transit District** (L.A. area bus company)      (213) 626-4455 has
Info line to help you. between 5:30 AM and midnight, 7 days a week

## Publicity - Press Clubs

**Los Angeles Press Club** at **Hollywood Roosevelt Hotel**      (323) 469-8180
     7008 Hollywood Boulevard, Hollywood, CA 90028
**Hollywood Press Club**      (323) 466-1212

## Publicity - Public Relations Firms

**Baker, Winokur, Ryder**—David Pollick      (310) 277-6200
     Wesley Snipes
**Frank Brown Group**      (310) 841-2010
     Assists actors with public relations, self-promotion, bios and cover letters.
**Levine Communications.**—Michael Levine      (310) 659-6400
     Janet Jackson, Charleton Heston with five offices worldwide
**Parker Public Relations**—Joel Parker      (310) 312-4562
     Arnold Schwarzenegger, Delta Burke, Dyan Cannon
**PMK Public Relations/Susan Culley & Associates**—Susan Culley      (310) 288-0077
     Christian Slater, Liam Neeson, Jimmy Smits, Barbara Hershey, Carrie Fisher.

## Publicity - Flyers & Newspapers

**L.A. Times,** Lynne Heffley, Theater Listings.      (213) 237-7748
     Calendar Section, Los Angeles Times, Times Mirror Square, Los Angeles, CA 90053
**Breakdown Services** - Flyers to Publicize Plays      (310) 276-9166

## Resume Paper and Xeroxing

| | | |
|---|---|---|
| **Kelly Paper** | Wilshire District - 844 N. La Brea | (323) 957-1176 |
| | Santa Monica - 1601 Olympic Boulevard | (310) 452-7590 |
| | LAX/Marina - 5752 Mesmer Avenues | (310) 390-1666 |
| | North Hollywood - 12651 Saticoy Street | (818) 764-0850 |
| **Office Depot,** for the location nearest you | | (800) 685-8800 |
| **Staples Office Superstores,** for location nearest you | | (800) 333-3330 |

## Scripts for Auditions

**Cast Net** (323) 964-4900

Their sides are available on the internet by membership only at a cost of $99 year. which also includes plenty of other great services for actors.

**Showfax** (310) 385-6920

Faxing is $1 per page for 1-5 pages, & 50 cents thereafter. By internet at $69 per year unless you have a listing in the Academy Players Directory, then it is $49.

## Screen Actors Guild Offices (Regional Offices Listed Under AFTRA)

**National Headquarters** (323) 954-1600
5757 Wilshire Boulevard, Los Angeles, CA 90036-3600

**Florida Regional Office** (305) 670-7677
7300 North Kendall Drive, Suite 620, Miami, FL 33156-7840
(Office covers Florida, Alabama, Arkansas, Louisiana, Mississippi, North Carolina, South Carolina, West Virginia, U.S. Virgin Islands, Puerto Rico and the Caribbean)

**New York Office** (212) 944-1030
1515 Broadway, 44th Floor, New York, NY 10036

## Screen Actors Guild Department Telephone Directory www.sag.org

| | |
|---|---|
| **Main Switchboard** | (323) 954-1600 |
| **Accidents on the Set** | (323) 549-6404 |
| **Actor Locator Service** | **(323)** 549-6737 |
| **Address Changes** | **(323)** 549-6776 |
| **Affirmative Action** | **(323)** 549-6644 |
| **Agency Department** | **(323)** 549-6745 |
| **Agent's List (recorded info)** | (323) 549-6733 |
| **Call Sheet & Screen Actor Magazine** | **(323)** 549-6805 |
| **Casting Seminars & Showcases** | (323) 549-6540 |
| **Casting Hotline (recording)** | (323) 937-3441 |
| **Child Actor Hotline (recording)** | (323) 549-6030 |
| **Child Actors Coogan Law (recording)** | (323) 549-6639 |
| **Commercial/Music Video** | (323) 549-6858 |
| **Committee Office** | (323) 549-6418 |
| **Communications & Publications Dept**. | (323) 549-6654 |
| **Credit Union** | **(323)** 461-3041 |
| **Dues Information** | (323) 549-6755 |
| **Emergency Fund** | (323) 549-6773 |
| **Events Hotline (recording)** | (323) 549-6650 |
| **Executive Offices** | |
| Ken Orsatti, Natl. Exec. Director | (323) 549-6610 |

| | |
|---|---|
| Len Chassman, Hollywood Exec. Director | (323) 549-6613 |
| **Film Society Office** | (323) 549-6658 |
| **Industrial/Education Interactive Media** | (323) 549-6850 |
| **Info on How to Join SAG (recording)** | (323) 549-6772 |
| **Legal Affairs** | **(323)** 549-6627 |
| **Membership Assistance/Leniency Committee** | (323) 549-6773 |
| **Membership Services, Station 12**   (Work Clearance) | (323) 549-6778 |
| **New Membership** | **(323)** 549-6769 |
| **Office Services** | **(323)** 549-6478 |
| **Pension & Health** | (818) 954-9400 |
| **President's Office** | (323) 549-6676 |
| **Production Services** | **(323)** 549-6811 |
| **Residuals/Residual Claims Department** | (323) 549-6505 |
| **SAG Conservatory at A.F.I.** | (323) 856-7736 |
| **SAG Foundation & Book Pals** | **(323)** 549-6709 |
| **Screening Schedule (recording)** | (323) 549-6657 |
| **Signatory Records** | (323) 549-6869 |
| **Singers Rep.** | (323) 549-6864 |
| **TDD Line Hearing Impaired** | (323) 549-6648 |
| **Television** | (323) 549-6835 |
| **Theatrical** | **(323)** 549-6828 |

| | Daily | 3 Day | Week |
|---|---|---|---|
| **Commercials Rates** | $443. | | |
| **Industrials** Rates | $407. | 1,023 | 1,428 |
| **Television Rates** | $596 | 1,957 | 2,000 |
| **Theatrical Rates** | $504 | 1,957 | |
| **Low-Budget Theatrical** | $448 | 1,558 | |

## Showcases

| | |
|---|---|
| **A.F.T.R.A.** Sponsored Showcases | (323)  634-8262 |
| **Screen Actors Guild Showcase Hotline** | (323) 549-6540 |
| **In the Act** | (818) 783-9160 |
| **In the Act - West in Santa Monica** | (310) 581-1955 |
| $25 each or $115 for a series of six | |
| **Primetime** | (323) 874-4131 |
| $25 each and special intensives with industry leaders | |
| **Casting Network** | (818) 788-4792 |
| $25 each or $125 for a series of five | |
| **One on One** | (818) 789-3399 |
| $35  each workshop and 4 week intensives with industry giants | |
| **Reel Pros** | (818) 788-4133 |
| $35  each workshop | |

## Singing and Cabaret Coaches

**Shelly Markham,** (213) 852-9655, arranges and conducts for cabaret-style singers.
**Bill and Irene Chapman,** (818) 787-7192, have coached singers for 25 years.
**Bob Corff,** (213) 851-9042 (star of three Broadway shows), can work on your musical theater performance.  www.mnusa.com/corff

## Singing and Cabaret Venuses

| | |
|---|---|
| **Cinegrill at the Hollywood Roosevelt Hotel** - Cabaret | (323) 466-7000 |
| **Club Lingerie** - Rock Bands | (323) 466-8557 |
| **The Gardenia** - Cabaret | (323) 467-7444 |
| **The Gig** - Rock Bands | (323) 936-4440 |
| **The Jazz Bakery** - Cabaret | (310) 271-9039 |
| **Luna Park** - Cabaret, Comedy and Rock | (310) 652-0611 |
| **The Roxy** - Rock Bands | (310) 276-2222 |
| **Troubadour** - Rock Bands | (310) 276-1158 |
| **The Viper Room** - Rock Bands | (310) 652-7869 |
| **The Whiskey** - Rock Bands | (310) 652-4202 |

## Student Films

**University of Southern California**  Student Production Office    (213) 740-2895
Off the Santa Monica Freeway, exit at Hoover Street and head south. Turn right on Jefferson Blvd to Gate 5. Tell the guard you're auditioning and expect to be no more than 20 minutes. You can park at meters in front of the film school. Ask for a map so you can find the Television & Cinema building. They accept photos and resume.

**University of California—Los Angeles**   Student Production Office (310) 825-5761
Located off Wilshire Boulevard in Westwood. Information kiosks are located by turning north on Hilgard and a few blocks to the guard house. Ask for a map to the Film School Building. There is plenty of metered parking, bring quarters.

**American Film Institute**                                    (323) 520-2000
AFI is located on Western Avenue, just north of Franklin Avenue. .Roomy campus wit free parking. Join the **Screen Actors Guild Conservatory at AFI** (info in Chapt. 11) your headshots will  be included in  casting books for student projects.

## Studios                            Thomas Brothers Guide Coordinates

| | |
|---|---|
| **ABC**, 2040 Avenue of the Stars, Century City, CA 90067 | TBG 632 E-3 |
| **ABC Television Center** | TBG 594 B-4 |
| 4151 Prospect Avenue, Los Angeles, CA 90027 | |
| **Castle Rock Entertainment** | TBG 632 G-1 |
| 345 N. Maple Drive, Beverly Hills, CA 90210 | |
| **CBS Studio Center** | TBG 562 G-5 |
| 4024 Radford Avenue, Studio City, CA 91604 | |
| **CBS Television City** | TBG 633 B-1 |
| 7800 Beverly Boulevard, Los Angeles, CA 90036 | |
| **Columbia Pictures Television** | TBG 563 E-3 |
| 3400 Riverside Drive, Studio Plaza, Burbank, CA 91505 | |
| **Concorde/New Horizons** | TBG 631 H-4 |
| 11600 San Vicente Boulevard, Brentwood, CA 90049 | |
| **Culver Studios** | TBG 672 G-1 |
| 9336 W. Washington Boulevard, Culver City, CA 90232 | |
| **Disney/Hollywood Pic/Touchstone** | TBG 563 F-3 |
| 500 S. Buena Vista, Burbank, CA 91521 | |
| **DeLaurentis Entertainment** | TBG 632 H-2 |
| 8670 Wilshire Boulevard, 2nd Floor, Beverly Hills, CA 90211 | |
| **Dreamworks** | TBG 563 B-5 |
| 10 Universal City Plaza, Universal City, CA 91608 | |

| | |
|---|---|
| **Fox Television** | TBG 593 G-4 |
| 5746 Sunset Boulevard, Hollywood, CA 90028 | |
| **HBO (Home Box Office)** | TBG 632 E-3 |
| 2049 Century Park East, 41st Floor, Century City, CA 90067 | |
| **Los Angeles Theater Center,** 514 S. Spring Street, L.A. CA 90012 | TBG 634 F-4 |
| **Mark Taper Forum,** 601 W. Temple Street, L.A., CA 90012 | TBG 634 F-3 |
| **MGM,** 2425 Colorado Avenue, Santa Monica, CA 90404 | TBG 631 G-7 |
| **Miramax Film Corp.** | TBG 593 B-5 |
| 7920 W. Sunset Boulevard, Los Angeles, CA 90046 | |
| **NBC Productions** | TBG 563 E-3 |
| 330 Bob Hope Drive, Burbank, CA 91523 | |
| **NBC Studios** | TBG 563 E-3 |
| 3000 W. Alameda, Burbank, CA 91523 | |
| **New Line Cinema** | TBG 632 H-1 |
| 116 N. Robertson Boulevard, Los Angeles, CA 90048 | |
| **Paramount Pictures** | TBG 593 G-6 |
| 5555 Melrose Avenue, Los Angeles, CA 90038 | |
| **Raleigh Studios** | TBG 593 G-7 |
| 650 N. Bronson Avenue, Los Angeles, CA 90004 | |
| **Spelling Television, Inc.** | TBG 633 B-2 |
| 5700 Wilshire Boulevard, #575, Los Angeles, CA 90036 | |
| **Sony Pictures Entertainment** | TBG 672 G-2 |
| 10202 W. Washington Boulevard, Culver City, CA 90232 | |
| **Sunset/Gower Studios** | TBG 593 F-5 |
| 1438 N. Gower Street, Los Angeles, CA 90028 | |
| **Television Center** | TBG 593 F-5 |
| 6311 Romaine Street, Los Angeles, Ca 90038 | |
| **20th Century Fox Studios** | TBG 632 E-4 |
| 10201 W. Pico Boulevard, Los Angeles, CA 90035 | |
| **Universal Studios** | TBG 563 B-5 |
| 100 Universal City Plaza, Universal City, CA 91608 | |
| **Warner Brothers** | TBG 563 E-4 |
| 4000 Warner Boulevard, Burbank, CA 91522 | |
| **Warner Hollywood** | TBG 593 D-6 |
| 1041 N. Formosa Avenue, Los Angeles, CA 90046 | |

## COMMERCIAL CASTING HOUSES

| | |
|---|---|
| **Baker/Nesbit** | TBG 592 J-7 |
| 451 N. LaCienega Boulevard, Los Angeles, CA 90048 | |
| **Castaway Studios** | |
| 8899 Beverly Boulevard, Los Angeles, CA 90048 | |
| **The Casting Studios** | TBG 633 B-1 |
| 5724 W. Third Street, Hollywood, CA 90036 | |
| **Chelsea Studios** | TBG 562 A-4 |
| Ventura Boulevard, No. Hollywood, CA 91602 | |
| **Cole Ave. Studios** | TBG 593 F-5 |
| 1006 N. Cole Avenue, Los Angeles, CA 90028 | |
| **Divisek Casting** | TBG 593 B-5 |
| 7715 Sunset Boulevard, #100, Los Angeles, CA 90046 | |
| **Fifth Street Studios,** 1216 5th Street, Santa Monica, CA 90401 | |
| **HKM/Casting Underground,** | |

1641 North Ivar Street, Hollywood, CA 90028
**Sessions West Studios,** 1418 Abbott Kinney, Venice, CA 90291          TBG 672 A-5
**Sheila Manning**          TBG 632 J-2
508 S. San Vicente, Los Angeles, CA 90048
**Village Studio,** 519 Broadway, Santa Monica, CA 90401
**Westside Casting,** 2050 S. Bundy, LA, CA 90064          TBG 631 J-6
**Zydeco Studios,** 11317 Ventura Blvd., Studio City, CA 91604

## Support Groups
**The Actors Network**          (818) 509-1010
**Breck Costin's - Lifeworks Seminar**          (323) 848-9665
**How to Make It in Hollywood: All the Right Moves**          (310) 553-9660

## Talent Shows
**Showtime at the Apollo,** 3 Park Avenue, New York, NY 10016
**World Championships of Performing Arts,**          www.hollywoodhereicome.com

## Tax Preparation
**Susan Lewis**          (818) 505-9637
**Chuck Sloan**          (818) 769-2291

## Theaters
**The Coast Playhouse**          (323) 650-8507
**The Court**          (310) 652-4035
**LAT—Los Angeles Theater Center - development program**          (213) 627-6500
**Mark Taper Forum** - development program          (213) 972-0700
**The Met**- development program          (323) 957-1152
**The Odyssey**          (310) 477-2055
**The Tiffany**          (310) 854-3684
**The Zephyr**          (323) 951-9545

## Theater Groups
**The Actors Gang,** 6201 Santa Monica Boulevard, Hollywood, CA 90038(323) 465-0566
Founded by Tim Robbins and John Cusack. It's a tough group to get into but not impossible.
Cutting edge political presentations and a heavy-hitting industry Board of Directors insure
great attendance.
**The Actors Co-op,** 1760 N. Gower Street, Hollywood, CA 90028          (323) 462-8460
They enjoy the utmost respect in this town. Auditions are held twice a year and entail a
lengthy process. Worth the work as there are no initiation fees and a minimal monthly fee.
**The Company of Angeles,** 2106 Hyperion Avenue, L.A., CA 90027          (213) 666-6789
One of the most respected companies in town with a long tradition of excellence. Once a
year they open their doors to new members. Initiation fee and monthly dues.
**Theater West,** 3333 Cahuenga Boulevard West, L.A, CA 90068          (323)851-4839
Auditions are held in the fall to join this group that offers many diverse classes to its mem-
bers. Only membership is permitted to appear in productions. Initiation and monthly dues.
**West Coast Ensemble,** 522 N. LaBrea Avenue, Hollywood, CA 90036.          (323) 876-9337
A wonderfully supportive group of professionals with many productions going all at the
same time. An initiation fee and varying monthly dues contingent upon your work contribution to the company. Always well-attended, wonderful shows. Auditions are held twice a year.

## Theatrical Bookstores

**Bodhi Tree Used Bookstore,** 8585 Melrose Avenue — (310) 659-1733
**Larry Edmonds Bookstore,** 6644 Hollywood Boulevard — (323) 463-3273
**Samuel French Theatrical Bookstores,** 7623 Sunset Boulevard — (323) 876-0570
11963 Ventura Boulevard — (818) 762-0535

## Typesetters

**Actors Resume Service,** entmktgco@aol.com — (818) 769-7574
**Imagestarter,** mbesq@ix.netcom.com — (323) 848-3663

## Typist

**Brenda Marshall —Typist!** — (818) 766-8735
She will computerize your mailing lists, type cover letters, help you write biographies, newsletters, you name it.

## Vitamin Stores

**Great Earth Vitamins** Beverly Hills - 258 N. Beverly Drive — (310) 278-1180
W. Hollywood - 8365 Santa Monica Blvd — (323) 650-0181
Hollywood - 1653 N. LaBrea Avenue — (323) 851- 9437
**Power Food** www.greatglobalproducts.com
**Trader Joe's** - has 100 LA Locations — (800) SHOPTJS

## Writers Classes

**American Film Institute** — (323) 856-7690
**David Freeman** — (310) 478-6552
**Learning Annex- Writers Classes** — (310) 478-6677
**The Sundance Institute** — (801) 328-3456
**John Truby** — (800) 33-TRUBY
**UCLA Extension - Catalogue** — (310) 825-9064
Writers Program — (310) 825-9415
**University of Southern California** — (213) 740-1742

## Writers Scholarships

**Chesterfield Award at Universal Studios** — (818) 777-1000
*How to Enter Screenplay Contests and Win!* — (800) FILMBKS
**Minnesota Independent Film Fund.** — (612) 338-0871

NOTES

This is the end of our adventures together and the beginning of yours. I have offered pieces of knowledge, experience, background information, every suggestion and all the advice I could think of to help you along the way. I am passing the baton off to you. Now it's your turn to run with it. Take charge of your career. You have my every good thought and wish for your future. If a successful career in acting or modeling is your dream, never give up on it, no matter how many people say no. "No" only means no today. If in your travels your come across someone this information would benefit, share this book with them.

Success is a journey not a destination,    Cynthia Hunter

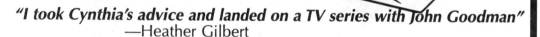

# Hollywood, Here I Come! Order Form

 **By Telephone:**
(800) 4DREAMS
Credit Card Orders

 **By Web site:**
www.holllywoodhereicome.com

 **By Mail:**
Yellow Deer Press
P.O. Box 93335
Hollywood, CA  90093

**Please Circle One:**

MASTER CARD      VISA

AMERICAN EXPRESS      DISCOVER

## Please ship materials to:

Name _____ Telephone (_____) _____

Address _____ EMail _____

City _____ State _____ Zip _____-_____

Card Number _____--_____--_____--_____

Name on Card _____ Exp. Date: _____/_____

Signature of Cardholder _____ Billing Zip Code _____

| | |
|---|---|
| ___Hollywood, Here I Come! | $19.95 |
| ___One on One Career Consulting with Author 90 minutes $70 or 1 1/2 hrs. | $125.00 |
| ___National Casting Notices | $99.00 |
| ___Star Power Seminar | $59.00 |
| ___Say Hello to Hollywood-Personal Industry Introduction | $1,500. |
| ___The Working Actor Guide | $39.95 |
| ___Secrets of Modeling from A-Z Five - 90 minute Video's from Elite Pres. | $39.95 |
| ___European Agency List - Modeling and Talent Agencies | $24.95 |
| ___Models Boot Camp Video a 90 minute Video | $24.95 |
| ___Thomas Brothers Guide | $24.95 |
| ___Back to One-Background Extra Guide | $19.95 |
| ___New York Models Black Book | $19.95 |
| ___Mailing Labels | $20.00 |
| ___      L.A. Casting Directors | |
| ___      L.A. Talent and Models Agencies | |
| ___      New York Casting Directors | |
| ___      New York Talent and Models Agencies | |
| ___The Modeling Handbook | $15.95 |
| ___Survival Job-118 Ways to Make Money | $15.95 |
| ___The Right Agent - Guide to Los Angeles Agents | $15.00 |
| ___The Right Manager-Guide to L.A.'s Managers | $15.00 |
| ___How to Star in Your Own TV Show for $50 or Less | $14.95 |
| ___CD Directory - List of Casting Directors Addresses | $11.95 |
| ___Major Cities Help Lists - complete cities list on web site | $ 9.95 |
| ___The Blue Book for Child Actors | $ 9.95 |

**(California add 8% Sales Tax.** Allow 2-4 weeks for delivery)

## DO NOT WRITE IN THIS BOOK - PERMISSION GRANTED TO PHOTOCOPY

# Books Available through our Bookshelf

### The Working Actors Guide $40
A resource book with everything to survive as a person and every service for a performing artist. This extensive guide is approximately 600 page. A must for actors and entertainers heading to L.A.

### The Secrets of Modeling A-Z $40
Produced by Elite Modeling Agency to give beginners all the tolls they will ever need to launch a career. Hosted by legendary career builder and former head of Elite, Valerie Trott. Five - 90 minute tapes.

### European Agency List $25
A newly published guide with all of the European Modeling agency addresses, phone and fax numbers to secure representation.

### Back to One - Background Extra Guide $20
How to make good money as a background actor in film. Includes a list of all extra casting offices and calling services. Each are rated from 1-4 stars for service to actors.

### New York Models Black Book $20
All the agencies in New York broken down by Fashion, Commercial, Children's and Specialty. Features a list of test photographers and places to garner showroom work.

### Mailing Labels $20
Looking for an agent or during a casting director to let them know your in town or working? The most up0 to date labels anywhere. 260 Agents or 325 Casting Directors

### Survival Jobs-Making Money While Pursuing Your Dreams $16
Hundreds of fun and stable survival jobs for artists everywhere. Outlines qualifications, pay scale, licenses and materials needed to carry out a successful sideline business.

**www.hollywoodhereicome.com**

### The National Casting Notices $99
Every week we will e-mail or fax you listings so you can submit your headshot and resume. In the U.S. we cover: films in development, films in preparation, films in pre-production, union films, non-union films, music video's, open casting calls, game shows, theater auditions, graduate films, student films and special type talent searches. Take charge of your career & let us point you toward the work. For those serious about their career.

### The Thomas Guide $25
The premier Los Angeles street guide and directory to help you locate audition offices and studios. It has an easy to index and is a necessity for people locating to L.A.

### Models Boot Camp Video - The Right Way to the Runway $25
The hottest new how-to-break into modeling video featuring the agents from L.A. Models & Talent, sexy TV stars Steve Wilder, Days of Our Lives; Ed Wasser, Babylon 5 and Cerina Vincent of Power Rangers.

### The Right Manager or Agent $15
Detailed lists of acting or modeling agents in the Los Angeles market. Each has a write up on the types of clients they handle. Also a hot sheet on types currently seeking.

### The Modeling Handbook $16
Offers advice from top models, agents & photographers covering the U.S. and European markets.

### The CD Directory $12.
This is a through listing of all the casting directors in Los Angeles along with their office addresses. Also has listing of casting offices in studios and locations of all commercial casting houses in L. A.

### Major Cities Help List $10
A list of agents, casting directors, photographers, theaters and film commission offices available for most major cities. Gets you going. Complete city list on the web site

# Hollywood, Here I Come! Order Form

 **By Telephone:**
(800) 4DREAMS
Credit Card orders

 **By Web site:**
www.holllywoodhereicome.com

 **By Mail:**
Yellow Deer Press
P.O. Box 93335
Hollywood, CA 90093

**Please Circle One:**

| MASTER CARD | VISA |
|---|---|
| AMERICAN EXPRESS | DISCOVER |

## Please ship materials to:

Name _____ Telephone (_____) _____

Address _____ Email _____

City _____ State _____ Zip _____-_____

Card Number _____--_____--_____--_____

Name on Card _____ Exp. Date _____/_____

Signature of Cardholder _____ Billing Zip Code _____

| | |
|---|---|
| ___Hollywood, Here I Come! | $19.95 |
| ___One on One Career Consulting with Author 90 minutes $70 or 1 1/2 hrs. | $125.00 |
| ___National Casting Notices | $99.00 |
| ___Star Power Seminar | $59.00 |
| ___Say Hello to Hollywood-Personal Industry Introduction | $1,500. |
| ___The Working Actor Guide | $39.95 |
| ___Secrets of Modeling from A-Z Five - 90 minute Video's from Elite's Pres. | $39.95 |
| ___European Agency List - Modeling and Talent Agencies | $24.95 |
| ___Models Boot Camp Video One - 90 minute Video | $24.95 |
| ___Thomas Brothers Guide | $24.95 |
| ___Back to One-Background Extra Guide | $19.95 |
| ___New York Models Black Book | $19.95 |
| ___Mailing Labels | $20.00 |
| ___     L.A. Casting Directors | |
| ___     L.A. Talent and Models Agencies | |
| ___     New York Casting Directors | |
| ___     New York Talent and Models Agencies | |
| ___The Modeling Handbook | $15.95 |
| ___Survival Job-118 Ways to Make Money | $15.95 |
| ___The Right Agent - Guide to Los Angeles Agents | $15.00 |
| ___The Right Manager-Guide to L.A.'s Managers | $15.00 |
| ___How to Star in Your Own TV Show for $50 or Less | $14.95 |
| ___CD Directory - List of Casting Directors Addresses | $11.95 |
| ___Major Cities Help Lists - complete cities list on web site | $ 9.95 |
| ___The Blue Book for Child Actors | $ 9.95 |

**(California add 8% Sales Tax.** Allow 2-4 weeks for delivery)
## DO NOT WRITE IN THIS BOOK - PERMISSION GRANTED TO PHOTOCOPY